# Fishers and Scientists in Modern Turkey

# Studies in Environmental Anthropology and Ethnobiology

General Editor: **Roy Ellen**, FBA
*Professor of Anthropology, University of Kent at Canterbury*

Interest in environmental anthropology has grown steadily in recent years, reflecting national and international concern about the environment and developing research priorities. This major new international series, which continues a series first published by Harwood and Routledge, is a vehicle for publishing up-to-date monographs and edited works on particular issues, themes, places or peoples which focus on the interrelationship between society, culture and environment. Relevant areas include human ecology, the perception and representation of the environment, ethno-ecological knowledge, the human dimension of biodiversity conservation and the ethnography of environmental problems. While the underlying ethos of the series will be anthropological, the approach is interdisciplinary.

# Fishers and Scientists in Modern Turkey

The Management of Natural Resources, Knowledge
and Identity on the Eastern Black Sea Coast

*Ståle Knudsen*

**Berghahn Books**
New York • Oxford

First published in 2009 by

*Berghahn Books*
www.berghahnbooks.com

©2009, 2011 Ståle Knudsen
First paperback edition published in 2011

**Library of Congress Cataloging-in-Publication Data**

Knudsen, Ståle, 1963-
Fishers and scientists in modern Turkey : the management of natural resources, knowledge, and identity on the eastern Black Sea coast / Ståle Knudsen.
    p. cm. -- (Environmental anthropology and ethnobiology)
    ISBN 978-1-84545-440-1 (hbk) -- ISBN 978-1-84545-375-6 (pbk)
    1. Fisheries--Turkey--Black Sea Coast. 2. Fishery management--Turkey--Black Sea Coast. 3. Fishers--Turkey--Black Sea Coast. 4. Black Sea Coast (Turkey)--Social life and customs. I. Title.

    SH291.K56 2008
    333.95'609561--dc22

                                                    2008026636

**British Library Cataloguing in Publication Data**

A catalogue record for this book is available from the British Library

Printed in the United States on acid-free paper.

ISBN: 978-1-84545-440-1 (hardback)
ISBN: 978-1-84545-375-6 (paperback)

# Contents

# List of Figures

All photographs are reproduced with permission of Ståle Knudsen.

# List of Tables

# Preface and Acknowledgements

This book has been long in the making. I have been engaged in Turkish Black Sea fisheries since I started my first fieldwork in 1990. From the very beginning I had an interest in studying how fishers managed the fishery resources. During that first winter in 1990–91 the Turkish Black Sea fisheries experienced the most dramatic crisis it has ever seen. That brought home to me, as it did to the fishers, how vulnerable both this enclosed sea and the fishers are. Those initial experiences also told me that knowledge was contested, and that the social distance between fishers on the one hand, and marine scientists and managers on the other, was huge. I subsequently set out to get a better understanding of the relationships between fishers, marine scientists and bureaucrats, and increasingly positioned the study of the fisheries within the Turkish modernization process. This brought me to survey the history of fisheries and fishery policies and to explore issues such as identity negotiations through seafood consumption, claims about fishers being ignorant and scientists being corrupt.

While this expansion in space, time and thematic certainly is called for to understand complex issues such as the management of modern sea fisheries embedded within a large developing nation state, it becomes a challenge to integrate the diverse topics and materials into one coherent text. This is not a study of a village, of one fishery, not even of fishers and scientists in one region of Turkey. It is about fisheries and fishery management in modernizing Turkey. It is my hope that the analytical focus on knowledge should give some coherence to the discussions through the chapters in the book.

Because of the wide scope of the study, data gathering has been composite. Participant observation has formed the groundwork, with longer ethnographic fieldworks in 1990–91 and 1997–98 and frequent briefer visits in between 1991 and 1997 and after 2002. In all I have conducted approximately one and a half years of ethnographic fieldwork among fishers and, to a lesser extent, marine scientists. During these years I have studied closely events in one particular fieldwork site, the small town Çarşıbaşı near the city of Trabzon in the eastern Black Sea region. I have also spent considerable time studying fishers in Samsun and Sinop, and have frequently visited and sometimes stayed for longer spells in Ankara and Istanbul. For the historical narrative I draw upon a range of sources, most of it in the original Turkish, ranging from ministerial reports, laws and marine science textbooks to travel accounts, newspaper articles, encyclopaedic entries and a few published books. Public statistics, my own questionnaire surveys, interviews, cookbooks, and a range of other public expressions of culture and ideology contribute to the mix of data and methodologies applied.

No work like this is possible without a lot of people being forthcoming and many actively assisting or encouraging the effort. The fishers in Çarşıbaşı, too many to name, showed an impressive willingness to share their lives with me, and – once they understood I could endure life at sea – brought me fishing with mutual pleasure. A few individuals in Çarşıbaşı should be mentioned: Osman Keleş for providing me with places to stay, Cemil Kurt for help and assistance, and Şaban Çağlar for unbiased introductions into the social landscape of the township and enthusiastic introduction into marine life of the Black Sea. I also want to thank the following individuals in Turkey for their generousness, hospitality and help: Ahmet Mutlu – the head of the eastern Black Sea association of fishery cooperatives; researcher Dr Mustafa Zengin at the Trabzon Fishery research Institute; Professor Ertüğ Düzgüneş at the Sürmene Faculty of Marine Sciences, Karadeniz University, Emin Özdamar – previously researcher at Sinop Faculty of Marine Sciences, later local expert with Japan International Cooperation Agency. Over the years I have come to know a range of individuals responsible for fisheries within the Ministry for Agriculture and Rural Affairs. Their willingness to attend to me in between their manifold tasks has been impressive. Last, but not least, Hakan Koçak in Istanbul has through two short periods as assistant become a close personal friend who shares his knowledge and ideas about Turkish society as well as love for Turkish food with me. Thanks to Hakan also for providing me with relevant articles that he has come across during his owns survey of 1920s to 1960s newspapers and other archival material.

I thank Jenny White for repeatedly encouraging me to write this book and for providing very helpful advice. Other readers of larger or smaller parts of the material include Edvard Hviding, Kjetil Fosshagen, Kari Telle, Olaf Smedal, Tim Bayliss-Smith, Maria Mangahas, Yael Navaro-Yashin and Bruce Kapferer. They have all provided helpful advice, if not to the final book manuscript, then to earlier versions of the text. Thanks also to series editor Roy Ellen for perceptive advice, especially as concerns the introduction to the book. Thanks to Graziella Van Den Bergh and Vemund Årbakke for helping me in interpreting French and Greek texts, and to Kjell Helge Sjøstrøm for production of many of the figures in this book.

Some of the material contained in this book has, in different form and partly addressing other agendas, been published before as journal articles: Chapter 2 in *International Journal of Middle East Studies*, Chapter 3 in *Middle East Studies*, Chapter 5 in *Human Ecology*, and Chapter 8 in *Perspectives on Global Development and Technology*.

I have used pseudonyms for the names of most fishers. Scientists are more public figures and their identities are more difficult to disguise. In a few cases I have extracted permissions from individuals to write about them under their full name, and a couple of scientists have read and commented upon text about them. Except for obviously public figures or when explicitly mentioned, all names are pseudonyms.

During the 1980s and 1990s and well into the 2000s inflation was very high in Turkey. In 2004 the Turkish Lira was substituted by the New Turkish Lira, in one stroke slating six zeros. Since the material in this book spans so many years and since local currency in different years is difficult to compare, I have chosen to present monetary figures in U.S. dollars, at current rates calculated on the basis of Central Bank of Turkey exchange rates.

Fieldwork and writing for this book has primarily been financed by the Research Council of Norway. University of Bergen, Black Sea Environmental Programme and EU FP6 (through the project European Lifestyles and Marine Ecosystems) have funded some research activities resulting in material used in this book. Production of this book has been supported by the Research Council of Norway.

# List of Abbreviations

| | |
|---|---|
| AKP | Adalet ve Kalkınma Partisi (Justice and Development Party) |
| EBK | Et ve Balık Kurumu (Meat and Fish Foundation) |
| GDEP | General Directorate of Environmental Protection, Turkish Republic Ministry of Environment |
| GDPC | General Directorate for Protection and Control, Turkish Republic Ministry for Agriculture and Rural Affairs |
| GDWP | General Directorate for Water Produce, Turkish Republic Ministry for Food, Agriculture and Stockbreeding |
| GNAT | Grand National Assembly of Turkey |
| ICC | Istanbul Chamber of Commerce |
| IK | Indigenous knowledge |
| MARA | Turkish Republic Ministry for Agriculture and Rural Affairs |
| MOF | Turkish Republic Ministry of Forestry |
| MSY | Maximum sustainable yield |
| NIE | New institutional economics |
| STS | Science and technology studies |
| SSK | Sociology of scientific knowledge |
| TEK | Traditional ecological knowledge |
| TFRI | Trabzon Fishery Research Institute |

CHAPTER 1

# Introduction

This book tells the story of fish and fishing in Turkey. Through the ethnography and history of fish production, seafood consumption, state modernizing policies and marine science *Fishers and Scientists in Modern Turkey* narrates and analyses the role of knowledges in the management of marine resources on the eastern Black Sea coast of Turkey. Why does there seem to be such a long distance between fishers' and scientists' knowledge, and what are the implications for management of the marine resources? What are the characteristics of the knowledges? Whose knowledge counts and why? Which theoretical tools are best fitted to analyse these knowledges? Knowledges are not regarded here as separate systems or beliefs. Knowledges are discussed as diverging or converging practices and models within a specific historical context: the modernizing secular Turkish state as it developed out of the passage from the Ottoman Empire to the Republic.

After fisheries had for several decades been on the development agenda of the Turkish State, the 1970s and 1980s saw the advance and expansion of technologically advanced industrial fishing. In the Black Sea, Turkish fisheries surpassed in catch volume neighbouring nations' fisheries and emerged as one of the largest in the Middle East. The successful increase in production was, however, followed in the early 1990s by a severe resource crisis. This brought attention to the challenge of sustainable management of marine resources, access to which had come to be regarded widely as free and largely unrestricted. The challenge was compounded by the fact that fishers, scientists, bureaucrats and others involved in the sector had very different opinions as to the reasons for the disappearance of fish and the solutions that should be sought. There was conflict over who was knowledgeable and what knowledge counted in fishery management.

This project started out as a fairly classical human ecology or ecological anthropology study of fishing in a small Black Sea township. As work progressed, I found it difficult to understand what I was observing and get answers to my questions without including new dimensions and expanding the scope in both time and space. I came to realize that there was no single body of authoritative theory which could guide analysis of my increasingly complex material, and I have sought inspiration in diverse quarters. In this chapter I introduce some of the substantive issues as well as theoretical positions to which this book relates. I first briefly survey conventional ecological anthropology, especially how knowledge has been studied. This leads into a discussion of the expanded agenda advanced by environmental anthropology and political ecology, touching on issues such as common pool resources, the role of states and science, fisheries studies, consumption and indigenous/traditional ecological knowledge. This is followed by an exploration of epistemological concerns before I introduce the ethnography. More extensive theoretical discussions are embedded within the chapters, especially in Chapter 4.

## From Ecological Anthropology to the Anthropology of Environment

The old concerns of ecological anthropology[1] – evolutionism, to what extent culture is an adaptive tool, how to develop a grand theory for 'nature with humans' (or 'humans in nature') – became to a large extent marginalized with the interpretive, reflexive and critical turns in anthropology during the 1980s and 1990s. The categories, assumptions and practices of the field itself were questioned. It became, for example, difficult to sustain the idea of 'culture as an adaptive tool'. Building on and incorporating these new criticisms, and with anthropologists increasingly confronting pressing environmental concerns during ethnographic practice, ecological anthropology was gradually reborn as engaged ethnography trying to understand environmental issues. Thus, the agenda of environmental anthropology differs from classical ecological anthropology. Environmental anthropology is, to put it simply, anthropology that focuses on environmental issues (Ellen 2002; McCay 2001). New tools and concerns developed. And new theoretical programs manifested themselves, most notably the interdisciplinary approach of political ecology. Environmental anthropology now intersects with many other 'anthropologies' and some interdisciplinary approaches to environment, resource management and knowledge. While Biersack (1999) identifies three new ecologies (symbolic ecology, historical ecology and political ecology) in the wake of Rappaport, Tsing (2001) finds four currents in contemporary environmental anthropology (environmental history, science studies, political ecology and cultural anthropology).

Aletta Biersack, in her introductory essay in *Reimagining Political Ecology* (2006), moves this field of inquiry from the structuralism of neo-marxist dependency/world systems-inspired political ecology, to a political ecology sensitive to the challenges of constructivism and moderated by practice theory, giving more space for agency. In my understanding, political ecology does not constitute a grand theory. Rather, it designates an agenda or a field of study. It is a broad, comparative and interdisciplinary effort to study the complex interrelationships between ecological processes, natural resource management, environmental problems, socioeconomic marginalization and politics. The agenda is closely related to the emergence of politically potent environmental issues, and studies primarily aim at unravelling dynamics in individual cases while attending to larger cultural, social and economic contexts.

In his article 'Anthropology in the Middle', Bruce M. Knauft argues that anthropologists are increasingly 'braiding together different approaches or perspectives' and cultural anthropology 'augurs to be post-paradigmatic'. '[T]opics, analytical frameworks and epistemological perspectives are cross-mapped in creative new ways' (Knauft 2006: 408, 410). Observing that anthropologists are less concerned to develop and contest master narratives and theory, Knauft explicitly draws on Herzfeld's concept 'militant middle ground' (2001) to explain such middle positions. It is not an 'anything goes' approach, but a discipline where theory, field experience and practice are more closely interwoven so that 'anthropologists increasingly connect historical specifics, political economic analysis, and insights from lived experience' (Knauft 2006: 421). This book can be read as an attempt to make such connections in an environmental anthropological study of fishers' and scientists' knowledges in modern Turkey.

The political ecology and anthropological research agendas as articulated by Biersack, Herzfeld and Knauft give legitimacy to integrating different approaches, theory and observation in new and creative ways. Environmental ecology, political ecology, as well as cultural anthropology absorb new impulses and expand into new fields of inquiry. This is exemplified in this study by the attention given to, for instance, history, state, power, discourse analysis, science studies, practice studies as well as theorization related to substantive fields such as common property studies, fisheries, technology and consumption. Therefore, the kind of inquiry that this book exemplifies incorporates a multitude of data material spanning many years and different locations, themes and social situations.

## Issues

### Common Pool Resources

Many of the major environmental issues facing us today can be characterized as comprising a common action dilemma: the environment may be ruined if we do not cooperate, but in the short term individuals may profit by maximizing profit instead of cooperating and restraining resource use. This is known as the Tragedy of the Commons thesis (Hardin 1968) or as a CC-PP (commonized costs – privatized profits) game (Hardin 1985). Hardin famously suggested that, with population increasing faster than resources, only private property or strict state control could ensure the necessary restraint and avoid the 'tragedy' of resource depletion. Ocean fisheries, tropical forests and the atmosphere's capacity to absorb greenhouse gases are typical examples of common-pool resources (CPR). In the case of climate and fishing, privatization through the use of quotas has emerged as one of the major management tools.

Pointing to examples of local, communal management of natural resources, anthropologists early questioned the validity of Hardin's thesis and the comprehensiveness of the solutions he proposed (see, e.g., McCay and Acheson 1987). Further theorizing of the finding that local communities could manage natural resources wisely has to a large extent been left for other disciplines to develop, especially to political science. Through the effort of Ostrom (1990) and others New Institutionalism has come to have considerable influence on the theoretical agenda of CPR studies (see, e.g., Dolšak and Ostrom 2003). New Institutional Economics' agenda focuses on the collective action dilemma and, using a methodological individualist approach, elaborates how individuals work out voluntary institutions for the management of common-pool resources. In 'New Institutionalism' parlance 'institution' is roughly synonymous with rules (and not organizations), either formal or informal, that can be enforced. This approach can help focus attention on informal rules and has proved to be a powerful comparative tool.

The NIE approach to studies of CPR has, however, been criticised for disregarding history and subject positions (Agrawal 2003) and issues of power and poverty (the 'entitlement school', see C. Johnson 2004). Brox (1990) questioned whether Hardin's thesis could properly be regarded as a theory. He 'downgraded' it to a model of certain aspects of the reality, and emphasized that only a historically informed political economy of fishing in Norway could explain the development of the Norwegian fishery management regime. In the same vein, Agrawal points out that scholars of common property 'place only a limited emphasis on questions of allocation and distributive politics', and 'consider politics and knowledge only in their relationship to institutions' (2006: 207, 214). These comments together point in the direction of the need for a political ecology of CPRs. We need to ask questions such as: What are the politics of greenhouse gas quotas? Who make the decisions about the quotas, and what are the effects on the environment and in society? Who benefit and who lose in the quota management system of greenhouse gases? In Turkey there is today a hegemonic discourse stating that the sea is free for all. Is this based on age-old conceptions, and if not, how did it come about? Who profits from it, and what are the consequences for fishery management?

An additional concern is that NIE has difficulties accounting for how rules emerge and how they are embedded in society (Acheson 2003: 208). It is difficult to precipitate out traditional institutions and norms without specifying cultural depth and context. Although accepting the importance of informal rules, approaches to resource management inspired by NIE tend to limit their view to cost–benefit considerations directly related to the resource in question. These approaches risk ignoring how rules and knowledges are embedded in persons and in society and may therefore also fail to appreciate the complex interplay of natural environment, technology, skills and ethical know-how. In experiential reality rules and norms involved in a resource management regime are often difficult to isolate from a wider set of norms, social relations and local culture.

## Fisheries Studies

Management advice to fisheries has been dominated by bio-economic perspectives, focusing on maximum sustainable yield (MSY), stock advice, total allowable catch (TAC) and fishing quotas, sometimes in the quasi-privatized form of individual transferable quotas (ITQs). Science has thus been trusted a central role in fishery management. The failure of many fisheries managed according to this model, such as the Grand Banks cod fisheries as well as many fisheries managed by the European Union, has stimulated the formulation – if not implementation – of alternative or complementary approaches. One reorientation centres on the concept of ecosystem management, while key words such as comanagement, participatory governance, stakeholder involvement, customary marine tenure, fishers ecological knowledge and social sustainability inform a new social science of fishing. This discourse is to a large extent motivated by governments' and institutions' needs for more comprehensive management advice and a realization that institutional reform away from the 'command and control' mode of decisionmaking can be beneficial (Symes 2007). All in all, as the objective for fishery development has moved from the simple goal of economic development to a multiplicity of goals and strategies, fishery management has generally become much more complex (Hersoug 2004). In this process anthropology has sometimes been given a more important role in social impact assessments (McCay 2001).

Anthropology's interest in fisheries has typically focused on the fishing community and fishing activities. Through what Bonnie McCay (2001) has termed 'sea tenure' studies, anthropologists have demonstrated that there exist in fisheries around the world complex and sometimes resource-conserving management forms that are not informed by Western science and controlled by states (e.g., Hviding 1996; Hviding and Jul-Larsen 1993; Acheson 1988, 2003). As such, this research tradition has made important contributions to the CPR debate. Sea-tenure studies have particularly had a focus on 'nonwestern', 'traditional' tropical and sub-tropical island communities in the western Pacific. The North Atlantic has been another regional focus in anthropological studies of fishing. Here management issues were initially of less relevance than questions concerning rural development, social structure, and culture (McCay 2001: 257). With the collapse in important fisheries in the region, attention turned to environmental issues and the role of fishers' ecological knowledge.

Comprehensive understanding of the 'sector' cannot be gained unless fisheries managers, science, the state, and history are included in the analysis. Hersoug (2004), for instance, has stressed that fisheries development in the Third World must be understood within a larger context of the global economy, the developmental state and aid. Often, fisheries have been part of modernization and developmental efforts. While some historical and sociological studies of fishery science have been undertaken (most notably Finlayson 1994), there is a lack of studies that situates fishery science within a wider examination of fisheries development (but see Holm 2003; Pálsson 1998a).

## Indigenous Knowledge and Traditional Ecological Knowledge

The notion of 'fishers' ecological knowledge' is related to the more inclusive concepts indigenous knowledge (IK) and traditional ecological knowledge (TEK). Studies of TEK and IK are epistemologically grounded in anthropology, but the use of these concepts now stretches far beyond anthropology and they have become key ideas in 'environmental management' (see, e.g., Berkes and Folke 1998). Fikret Berkes, one of the major contributors to the research agenda focusing on TEK, has defined TEK as 'indigenous knowledge in ecology' (F. Berkes 1999). Like the NIE approach to studies of common pool resources, scholars of IK and TEK tend to emphasize how groups of resource users are able to manage natural resources wisely. However, IK and TEK approaches seem to be more sensitive than NIE to local collective culture, the embeddedness of rules, and how knowledges are intertwined with place, practice and ethics.

Within these approaches natural resources and knowledge are usually perceived to be closely connected to lifestyle and identity – typically of culturally distinct groups of marginal and peripheral people such as native populations. It is common to essentialize and romanticize such knowledge and either implicitly or explicitly contrast it with science. Paralleling this contrast is an academic partitioning of tasks that in effect means that different bodies of theory and scholarly work focus on IK/TEK and science respectively. As I will discuss in more detail below, this compartmentalization of studies of knowledge is problematic.

The vision of knowledge supported by the Turkish state is a version of the model that differentiates between indigenous or traditional knowledge on the one hand, and scientific knowledge on the other. Taking the modernistic yet rigid framing of knowledges and practices inherent in the idealism of Turkish modernization as a point of departure, I discuss the conspicuous absence of academic attention to customary resource management, 'indigenous knowledge', and 'traditional ecological knowledge' with regard to Turkey and the Middle East. This neglect is partly explained by the marginal position that the field of natural resource management, especially locality-based rules and practices of common pool resources, has in recent scholarship on the Middle East. No book-length English-language study exists of marine fisheries in the Middle East and there is in general a remarkable lack of published research of natural resource management, CPR and human/political ecology in the Middle East (Knudsen 2007). While Europe and America has been well covered by ecological and environmental anthropological studies and many important works have focused particularly on South East Asian societies (e.g., Vayda, Ellen, Brosius, Dove, Lansing) during the last two decades, there have been almost no such studies in the Middle East. There is an intriguing parallel in the regional focus of studies of IK/TEK, CPR and environmental issues.

## Widening the Scope

A common thread through the preceding discussion has been the need, as noted by Knauft, to combine 'historical specifics, political economic analysis, and insights from lived experience' (Knauft 2006: 421). Chapter 2 and Chapter 3 in this book outline the histories of seafood consumption and fishery policies. However, these chapters should not be read as introductory 'context' or 'backdrop' chapters: they are a proper part of the field of investigation and analysis. They are part of the explanatory framework. A contextualized understanding of what makes possible, or obstructs, different kinds of knowledges and discourses about knowledges requires us to historicize traditions of knowledge. Foucault's historical analyses and Scott's discussion of 'high modernity' ideals, and states' strategies to standardize (Scott 1998), stimulate us to look for aspects of knowledge often ignored in the research traditions of IK/TEK and CPR and can contribute to an expansion of the view of environmental anthropology and political economy (see, e.g.. Brosius 1999; Agrawal 2006).

In his book *Seeing Like a State*, James Scott (1998) convincingly argues that many states have articulated ambitious development plans which grossly ignore local cultures, practices and knowledges. What characterizes these schemes is a willingness to shape the natural and social landscape according to some great, scientifically informed master plan. Scott has termed this ideal 'high modernism', a 'strong version of belief in scientific and technical progress' (Scott 1998: 89). Ideals of high modernism have been articulated in many modernizing states and have sometimes been authoritatively implemented by totalitarian states, often with dire environmental consequences. Unacknowledged by Scott, Foucault has presented a historical analysis of the transformation from a rule of 'sovereignty' to 'governmentality' in Europe during the sixteenth to eighteenth centuries. The concept of governmentality embodies an assemblage of notions, of which I will in my analysis primarily focus on the shift in the goal and tactics of the state. '[W]hat characterizes the end of sovereignty', Foucault writes, 'is in sum nothing other than submission to sovereignty' (Foucault 1991: 95). On the other hand, what characterizes governmentality is that 'the finality of government resides in the thing it manages ... [T]he instruments of government, instead of being laws, now come to be a range of multiform tactics' (ibid.) With such a shift, which can also be seen during the late Ottoman and early Republican period in Turkey, the state attains a much more active and penetrating tactic relative to the 'governed' population. The notion of governmentality may also include instruments that work on and through desires, lifestyles – how the government of people is moulded through transformations of mentalities and selves.

While the fisheries sector in Turkey clearly cannot be understood without a historical survey of the changing role of the state, it is similarly clear that interaction between fishers and scientists is not shaped within a state guided framework alone. Fishers, traders, scientists and bureaucrats relate to each other in a multitude of ways that entails a politics of identities and negotiation of lifestyles related to issues such as language style, seafood consumption, refinement, cleanliness and so forth.

In cultural ecology (e.g., White 1943) and the ecological anthropology of Rappaport and others (Rappaport 1968; Little and Morren 1977) consumption was important in terms of humans' material relation to their environment. For Rappaport, measurements of calories and protein intake, in particular, were used to identify carrying capacity, stress levels, etc. At a more general level these issues were central also in Marvin Harris's (1977) cultural materialism that sought to explain culture, taboos, etc., as human adaptation to the limits and stress exerted by the environment. An emerging interest in consumption relative to humans' place in nature in political ecology and environmental anthropology is more related to the fact that consumption can often be seen to be a major driver of environmental problems (Heyman 2005; Wilk 2006). Wilk has claimed that 'no form of anthropological ecology…can be a comprehensive tool for understanding change at either local or global levels until it incorporates consumption' (Wilk 2006: 150). He is concerned to demonstrate how new forms of consumer culture contribute to increase demand and cause environmental problems. It is clear that overfishing in the Black Sea could never have occurred without there being demand for the catch. I try to show why and how demand has increased, but in my analysis, consumption has one additional meaning: consumption is one primary field of experience through which identities and lifestyles are shaped and articulated. Styles of seafood consumption, for example, are important signposts in the articulation of relative identities of scientists, managers and fishers in Turkey.

## Symmetry

The militant middle ground approach may, of course, result in non-rigorous theoretical bricolage and theoretical laziness. I believe that this can be met by two strategies: (1) by clearly stating epistemological challenges and position(s) and (2) by trying hard to set ethnography and theory in dialogue with each other. Therefore, theoretical discussions are embedded within historical and ethnographic expositions throughout the book, while I make an effort below to clarify my epistemological position.

However many labels there are for different 'knowledges', there are basically two main approaches to social studies of knowledge currently in favour within academia: studies of indigenous knowledge (IK), traditional ecological knowledge (TEK) and so forth, on the one hand, and studies of technology and science (STS) on the other. These approaches in essence focus on different sociocultural settings and different 'kinds' of knowledge largely without relating to one another. Rather than this carving up of the field of study I want to confront the challenge of crafting a 'symmetrical' approach. I agree with the handful of scholars who have called on students of STS and IK/TEK/anthropology to 'talk to each other' (Gonzales et al. 1995; Nader 1996; Leach and Fairhead 2002; Philip 2002).

It is necessary to explain my epistemological baseline in order to clarify my scepticism of approaches that: address knowledges head on as separate 'systems' or 'traditions'; often assume apriori that different characteristics distinguish the various 'systems'; define 'other' knowledges in simple contrast to science, and are insensitive to how knowledges are coconstructed or constructed in opposition to other knowledges. I strongly support the claim that anthropology is a universal science with an ambition to describe, understand and give informed explanations of various ways of living. This universalism should also imply that no preconceived distinctions between peoples, places or times are made. Furthermore, I would ask how one can make symmetrical studies of traditions of knowledge, including science, without falling into the excesses of an extreme relativist/constructivist position that I feel contradicts my intuition that some kind of reality exists and that good or relevant knowledge of the world, if not accurate and objective knowledge, is possible. Thus, a study of environmental knowledges raises two sets of epistemological challenges: how to study all knowledges within the same analytical framework, and how to reconcile realism and constructivism?

Addressing these challenges I find Latour's (1993) symmetry postulate intriguing and, to a certain extent, useful. He criticizes the symmetry postulate of the Strong Programme of the Edinburgh school (Bloor 1976; Barnes and Bloor 1982), the 'foundational' program for sociological studies of scientific knowledge (SSK), maintaining that this lets society bear all the burden of explanation. In the framing of the Strong Programme, nature is only present as a social construct. The equivalence postulate of the Strong Programme is based on the presupposition, inspired by 'late' Wittgenstein (Grimen 1997), that language is detached from reality. In their quest to place truth and falsehood within all traditions of knowledge on the same footing, they erase the possibility of humans having access to 'external reality'. Latour claims that this position, and in effect most critical studies of science, is locked into the nature-society dualism of what he labels the 'modern constitution' (Latour 1993).

Central to the modern constitution is the double separation, first between nature and culture, the 'work of purification', and secondly between this work of purification and the 'work of translation' (or mediation). On the one hand, we try to sort all phenomena into the domains of 'humans' and 'non-humans' (purification, the creation of the Cartesian division). On the other hand we continuously, in practice, engage in the work of translation and create 'hybrids' on a larger scale than ever before. We practice both, Latour claims convincingly, but we only see and acknowledge the work of purification. That is why we continually switch between nature and society as sources of explanations, between realism and idealism. Thus, in addition to the equivalence postulate of the Strong Program – (1) truth and falsehood must both be explained – Latour (1993: 103) includes two other requirements: (2) generalized symmetry, and (3) no a priori Great Divide between 'us' and 'them'.

Requirement number (2) maintains that we should study and compare what Latour terms 'natures-cultures', without trying to stipulate the relative weight of nature and culture. Descriptions should start from the centre, with the phenomenon. Furthermore, the nature-culture dichotomy has also sustained a sharp distinction between 'us' and 'them' since it has been assumed that 'we' (who have science) are the only ones who are able to make the 'correct' separation between nature and society and therefore know nature 'as it is'. Our idea of a pure, transcendent nature which only science can represent without bias has propped up our distinction between 'us' and 'them'. In 'their' world the social and natural were blended while 'we' had pure access to nature. And when 'we' (here: western social science) finally addressed science we (i.e., STS/SSK studies) used the same coin, just turning it around and declaring that science has no access to nature, that it is solely a social construct. To avoid this mutual reinforcement of these two dichotomies, it must therefore be an important requirement for symmetrical anthropology to avoid (3) 'Great Divide' distinctions between the West and the rest, or between science and the common people.

## Great Divide

A programme that critically examines the instruments of border construction between 'us' and 'them' has been widely endorsed and articulated in anthropology since the 1980s (to name but a few: Fabian 1983; Herzfeld 1987; Said 1978; Marcus and Fisher 1986; Gupta 1992). Radical and critical approaches deconstruct the earlier boundaries of enquiry and open up new social fields to cultural critique. This has also stimulated studies of scientific knowledge, also by the anthropological camp, which has worked to undermine the objectivist claims of science. Following the radical critiques in anthropology during the last twenty to thirty years, the 'native', the scientist and the anthropologist have thus come to be situated in the same world. If I am to take heed of these new insights it becomes a central challenge for me to approach fishers', bureaucrats' and scientists' knowledges in a symmetrical manner. I make a point of situating the various knowledges in the same world and not treating them as homogenous, monolithic and separate 'systems'. Knowledge is carried by individuals, and individuals meet and may also be meeting points of knowledges. For ethnography of knowledge it is, as Nader (1996) has argued, profitable to focus on the borders. It has been my ambition to take heed of the fact that although fishers and scientists for the most part live separate lives, they do take part in the same society and the same social system. The analysis demonstrates a large degree of overlap, interdependency and convergence in knowledges held by those people that relate to sea and fish.

The STS–IK/TEK distinction implies a partitioning within the field of social studies of knowledge that works against symmetry. If we focus too much on IK/TEK as the contrast to modern science we risk ignoring, suppressing or failing to acknowledge many kinds of practical knowledge 'between' IK/TEK and science. I find that conventional understandings of indigenous knowledge and traditional ecological knowledge are unable to account for the character and complexity of the knowledge of fishers on the eastern Black Sea coast of Turkey. The sharp distinction between

IK/TEK and scientific knowledge leaves us with poor tools for understanding knowledges of people who are not easily put into these categories. I argue that there is no absolute difference between science and other knowledges – it is rather a question of degrees of difference.

Not only should new perspectives be brought into each tradition ('social constructivism', historical analysis to IK/TEK, 'cognitive content' to STS), but, more importantly, we should study all the knowledges that are situated between these extremes. IK and TEK are constructions that contribute to the reproduction of these distinctions. Furthermore, I argue that not only the 'content' of the various traditions of knowledge, but the contexts within which conceptualizations such as IK or 'science' work and that make possible their existence should be examined.

## Generalized Symmetry

The second epistemological challenge relates to the requirement for generalized symmetry – to try not to stipulate the relative weight of nature and society. Like Knauft, Aletta Biersack draws on Herzfeld's formulation of a 'militant middle ground', but less to posit anthropology at the creative interface between practice and theory than to argue for a middle ground between materialism and idealism (Biersack 2006: 28). Her concern is that while the linguistic and postmodern turns in anthropology and political ecology have demonstrated that all nature is 'constructed', we cannot completely do away with nature. She has argued for a 'new materialism' based on a 'reformed semiotics' and anthropological approaches to the body inspired by phenomenology (Biersack 1999). Drawing on Stephen Lansing's (1991) analysis of the importance of water temples in Balinese irrigation, she employs the Marxian concept 'second nature' (or 'humanized nature') about 'nature as it has been transformed through human activity: 'a nature that is *humanely* produced (through conceptualization as well as activity)' (Biersack 2006: 14).

I am sympathetic to the idea of a new materialism, but have difficulties in seeing how 'second nature' can be used as an analytical concept. It may seem like she tries to recapture this as an analytical concept by drawing on Escobar's 'After Nature' article (1999) where he suggests that we focus on 'nature regimes' (i.e., 'second natures'), of which he identifies three: capitalist nature, organic nature and technonature. These categories are also informed by Latour's idea about 'collectives' (assemblages of nature-cultures). While this is a commendable attempt at not only deconstructing earlier approaches, but also (re)constructing new tools for political ecology, I find that the categories coined by Escobar reintroduce essentialisms. Moreover, his suggestion (ibid.: 6) that the three different nature regimes can each most fruitfully be studied by different approaches reproduces classical divides in the social sciences and fails to satisfy the 'great divide' criteria for symmetry. He accords 'the anthropology of local knowledge' a role only in the study of 'organic nature'. I find no reason why we should assume, at the outset, that fishers' and scientists' knowledges can most fruitfully be studied using different analytical and methodological tools.

Biersack is concerned to retain a measure of realism in political ecology, but does not clarify the epistemological foundation of this realism. What kind of realism? Tempered by the constructivist critiques, this is certainly not positivist realism. George Lakoff (1987) argues against the 'mind as machine' model and what he calls 'the correspondence theory of meaning' (and the associated 'scientific realism with objectivist metaphysics'). He maintains that language finds its meaning in Idealized Cognitive Models (ICM) that are organized on the basis of bodily experiences. Basic level concepts and kinaesthetic image schemes (the latter are preconceptual) constitute the roots of imagination, and therefore language. Language is embedded in physical reality and language and culture are therefore not constructed independently of biophysical reality. It may be claimed that people actually perceive differences because differences and structures exist in the world, and that concepts are not entirely arbitrary or 'cultural', without assuming that our categories correspond one-to-one with those structures. Thus, I take a basic realist (or 'internal realist', Putnam 1981) position in which I assume that the world exists, that it has certain structures, and that it has an impact upon our actions and knowledges, but in which claims about the existence of an absolute yardstick or a God's eye view are unfounded.

## Experience

I am not entirely satisfied with the metaphor of social construction (or only 'construction' in Latour's approach) on which STS approaches capitalize. The focus on the object of attention, in place of the attention itself, brings the concerns of 'explanation' and 'ontological truth', and hence metropolitan technoscience, to the forefront of the research agenda. Hence, the STS approach has stimulated almost no research on the various uses of technology, peripheral technoscience, the experience of truth, and the lived world of researchers and experts. I consider Latour's tool kit extremely useful in charting the 'social life of knowledge' through, among other things, his attention to inscription. But since he focuses on the knowledges (facts, collectives, the socially existing knowledges) and not the knowing itself, he is better equipped to describe how knowledge is organized outside of or in between humans – 'what they know' – rather than to study 'the way humans know'.

This book explores how knowledges are constituted as experience and to what degree and in what manner experience, also among scientists, becomes articulated, externalized, inscribed and objectified. For insights into 'ways of knowing', I explore a perspective on knowledge based in phenomenology and related theories of embodied cognition (e.g., Lakoff 1987; Shore 1996) and situated knowledge (Ingold 1992). In particular, I draw on the insights of Merleau-Ponty (1962) to resituate language and knowledge in material reality. I seek to demonstrate that this approach can better account for the experienced aspects of knowledge and provide an alternative to the discredited distinction between practice and language/theory. Thus, another strength of the embodied cognition/language perspective is to retain the basic realist position without presupposing correspondence between the world and our categories.

The phenomenological approach is here also employed to emphasize the social embeddedness of knowledges and rules (in fishing), as argued by Varela (1999) when he distinguishes between ethical know-how and ethical know-that. This groundedness of rules and institutions tends to be ignored, for instance, in NIE approaches to CPR studies. The phenomenological impulse may be employed in order to counteract analytical reductionism (a danger of cognitive approaches for example). However, as should be apparent from what I have written above, I do not want the analysis to remain on the level of phenomenology of personal experience. Phenomenology may best be viewed not as a theory, but as an approach that gives authority to the world(s) that one encounters. Therefore, fishing, science and other ways of knowing and relating to fish and the sea are analysed as particular ways of life conditioned by history, ideology, and daily practice as articulated in lifestyles and consumption preferences.

## Introducing the Ethnography

Although this book focuses on fishers and marine scientists, at a more general level it aims to illuminate how different forces come together in the changing relationships among state, peoples, substances and discourses in modernizing Turkey. It is also a book about how people in modernizing Turkey manage identities, be it though moralistic discourse about fishers being ignorant, the elite being corrupt, or the articulation of different identities and lifestyles through the consumption of seafood.

There are demonstrably alternative styles and moralities of seafood consumption in Turkey, particularly the refined Istanbul-style seafood consumption and the more conservative Anatolian and Black Sea approaches to seafood associated with the 'common man' (Chapter 2).

Alcohol plays a major role in the images of the Istanbul-style seafood culture, while the popular Black Sea anchovy is a core symbol in the Trabzon fish culture which is more sensitive to Islamic morality. Recent developments indicate considerable change and creativity, resulting in an increasingly porous boundary between these cultures and the emergence of a new nationwide middle-class culture of seafood consumption. Through their impact on demand, in particular a high demand for fresh fish, styles of seafood consumption contribute to shaping the fishery management regime. Moreover, lifestyles and identity politics, as articulated by seafood consumption, affect the context of rules and institutions in fishery management since such consumption practices constitute a symbolic framework for the interaction between different 'stakeholders' in the management of fishery resources.

My historical survey depicts changes in styles and identities related to seafood since Ottoman times. Processing, trade and consumption of fish and seafood remained largely beyond the influence of the Republican state despite initial attempts at control. The importance of seafood consumption in the negotiation of identities therefore went unnoticed in official presentations of culture and consumption in Turkey. The nineteenth and twentieth centuries saw a general shift in emphasis in state policy from taxation to economic development (Chapter 3). Fisheries became a focus of economic policy and knowledge. Increasing production and maximizing proteins, rather than taste, became the main concern and challenge. 'High modernism' ideals (Scott 1998) became embedded in development plans, laws, bureaucratic structure, as well as in policy initiatives.

The growth of Turkish marine sciences was thus intimately intertwined with developmental ideals that instilled in scientists and other state elites, such as bureaucrats and managers, the idea of a decisive break between past traditions and new developments. Science became part of a moral project related to the Turkish nationalism and the civilization effort. This book examines how developmental ideals together with ideals of cultivation are ingrained in bureaucratic texts and initiatives as well as in the scientific work and lifestyles of marine scientists in the city of Trabzon on the eastern Black Sea coast of Turkey (Chapter 7). I discuss the lives and careers of these marine scientists as well as the politics of knowledge they are involved in. For scientists, as well as managers, being a state employee is an important fact of life. Scientists regard higher education as a training or cultivation that ideally transforms the self of the person and distinguishes her from uncultivated people such as fishers. However, when dealing with fishers during the practice of concrete projects it is not all that easy to stick to the elite ideals of cultivation and disinterest.

As late as at the close of the Ottoman Empire, detailed state sanctioned rules of privileged access to fishing grounds were common, especially in and around Istanbul. These rules are all but forgotten today. This indicates that not only current institutions and rules in CPR management, but also the larger historical and ideological context of production, as manifest in state modernization policies, marine sciences and seafood consumption, should be accounted for to explain the current management regime in Turkish Black Sea fisheries. The nature of the resources, the ascendance of a mobile and capital-intensive fishing fleet that preferred an 'open access' regime, and the idealistic bent of Turkish modernization ideology have worked together to establish the idea that access to the fish commons is free and open (Chapter 3). The state cocreated this regime, partly through its ignorance of traditions of restriction on access, partly through deliberate policy.

In what respect are fishers' knowledges of the marine environment and fishing practice 'traditional'? Fishing on the eastern Black Sea coast of Turkey is a dynamic tradition with continuities in ethical standards and social relations underlying observable changes in fishing practices and regulation patterns. The book demonstrates how fishers' knowledges are embedded in practice and social organization by discussing themes such as: fish classification; informal regulations in small boat fishing; the development of fishing careers; and the increasing importance of politics in capital-intensive and technologically advanced fishing. Starting out from a detailed description of a fishing trip, I discuss the character of the models fishers engage when they relate to bottom topography, classification, and fish behaviour (Chapter 4). The ethnography of these everyday practices and fishers' models is set in dialogue with several sections discussing theoretical positions and challenges. I discuss what is the character of fishers' knowledges, and by paying attention to processes of externalization, inscription and objectification I argue that fishers' knowledges are not only 'embodied' or 'situated', but organized in multiple ways. I also explore 'knowledge' as perceived by marine scientists (Chapter 7). There is some overlap between fishers' models and scientists' models. Yet scientists increasingly employ models that find no correspondence among fishers' knowledges. New data-processing technology, a new management focus on sustainability, together with increased interaction with international fisheries science have, since 1990, resulted in the increasing importance of bio-economic models.

The long time span between my first and last field visits provides me a unique opportunity to discuss to what degree and in what respects a 'tradition of knowledge' exists in fishing (Chapter 5). I document living traditions for informal types of local-level management in small boat fishing on the eastern Black Sea coast and detail the ways in which technical know-how and ethical know-how, both 'embodied', are tightly connected at the level of everyday fishing activities. What happens to this knowledge and the rules when the fishery in question is discontinued and replaced by a new fishery? I argue that 'tradition' is reproduced at the level of informal, embodied and situated features of rules, institutions and knowledges – features often ignored in the somewhat instrumentalist approach of most CPR scholars.

The social dimensions of fishing knowledge are further elaborated in a survey of fishery development in the district of Çarşıbaşı since approximately 1950 (Chapter 6). An ethnographic account informed by oral history focuses on individual careers of the owners of big fishing boats and on overall development of the fishing fleet to identify different epochs in the development of big-boat fishing. As technological development and capitalization in the fisheries have become more and more important, success has become increasingly dependent upon skilful manoeuvring relative to circles of powerful men. Yet the basic organizing principles remain family relations and local interpersonal relations and social networks. These relations are to a large extent couched in an idiom of sharing, friendship and Islamic sociability.

The last chapters describe and analyse how different actors, practices and discourses meet and impact upon each other. The lives and knowledges of fisher and scientist meet in the case of the conflict over the use of the fish-finder device sonar, in the politics related to fishery cooperatives, and during scientists' surveys of fishing. Most fishers claim that sonars scare away or kill fish while local marine scientists and some fishers contend that sonars have no such effect (Chapter 8). I explore scientists' understanding of the sonar by focusing primarily on an experiment they set up to test its effect on fish. I address the fishers' understanding by paying attention to their use of the sonars. Additionally, I survey the two sides' narratives about the experiment and the use of sonars. Both scienctists and fishers are implicated in the politics of the sonar and the fishers' and scientists' different understandings of the sonar are not totally independent of one another.

State modernizing policies directed at fisheries are reengaged in a discussion of the discrepancy between social organization in the fisheries and the bureaucratic ideal of fishery cooperatives (Chapter 9). State-initiated reforms in the fisheries only began to have an effect in the 1950s, after the main rush of reforms in Turkey. Technologically and economically the fisheries have been greatly transformed, especially after the late 1970s. Thus, it may seem that state development policies have been a success. The state also took a range of initiatives to organize fishers into cooperatives. The idealism inherent in the state developmental effort meant that the focus was on what was to be achieved, while traditional and contemporary social structures in the fishing communities were ignored. Thus, the state has not infiltrated the social organization of the fisheries to the depth intended in the ideals and plans for fishery development. Yet in practice the state accepts and involves itself in social and political arrangements that diverge from the ideal. This indicates that there may not have been a complete change from one kind of state to another. State representatives try to negotiate this ambivalence by blaming the failure of cooperative organization on fishers; fishers are perceived as ignorant and selfish. The fishers have allegedly not cultivated the right kinds of selves. This view of fishers and their customs helps legitimize a hegemonic discourse concerning rights to access in the fisheries.

In the final chapter I return to discourses about identities and, by implication, about knowledgeable and moral persons. The elite's concerns about ignorance are coupled to a pervasive idealism and concern about 'civilization'. The fishers twist the terms of discourse. They reformulate their perceived ignorance to a confession of 'unaware or irresponsible' behaviour, and commonly criticize, partly from within an Islamic moral universe, state representatives and other elites for having immoral consumption patterns and being 'eaters' (corrupt). This interpretation is set within a wider and very pervasive morally impregnated discourse on a national scale concerning 'hunger' and 'eaters'- politics and corruption – as articulated, for instance, in imageries of seafood consumption and lifestyles. The story of the transformation of a local sea festival into a state-sponsored cultural festival serves to bring more nuance to the complex relationships between tradition, modernity, education/ignorance, Islam and Turkishness in modern Turkey.

CHAPTER 2

# Seafood Consumption and Turkish Identities

The small town of Çarşıbaşı near Trabzon in the eastern Black Sea region of Turkey is one of the area's major fishing centres. The sizeable harbour is filled with boats large and small, there are fishmeal and sea-snail processing plants, and fishing constitutes the primary livelihood for a significant portion of the population. Local people love to eat fish. Yet, surprisingly, in the 1990s it was impossible to buy a plate of seafood in the fifteen eating establishments in this town of ten thousand inhabitants. Nor was there a seafood restaurant in Çarşıbaşı. On the other hand, almost half of the top-class restaurants in Istanbul were listed as seafood restaurants. This chapter sets out to explain this discrepancy by exploring the contemporary practices and public imageries of two distinct cultures of seafood consumption in Turkey: the elite Istanbul-style seafood culture and the regional Trabzon fish-food culture. These seafood cultures can be interpreted as expressions of contrasting ways to design modern Turkish lives or lifestyles, particularly at the interface between the elite and the common people.[2]

While Istanbul and Trabzon have been and continues to be natural centres of fishing and seafood consumption, fish has not been a popular food in the 'Anatolian peasant' villages of the interior. Per capita consumption of 'water produce' in Turkey has averaged 7–8 kg during the last decade (SIS 2002), varying from 25 kg in the Black Sea region to 16 kg in the larger cities (Istanbul, Izmir and Ankara) to only 0.5 kg in east and southeast Anatolia.[3] The Anatolian attitude has seemingly come to define the role of fish and fishing in 'Turkish culture', as indicated by the fact that most marine animal names are Greek (Oğuz 1976: 573) and a general image of the Turk having his back turned to the sea. While per capita consumption of red meat, which is commonly referred to as a measure of welfare, is much greater among high-income groups than low-income groups ('Yoksula ayda 100 gram et'. *Yeni Şafak*, 11 March 2003), per capita consumption of seafood is much more evenly distributed among income groups[4] and therefore seemingly not an important measure of relative status. There is, however, more to seafood consumption than volume. Surveys of seafood consumption in specific villages or urban neighbourhoods[5] indicate that roughly seventy per cent of the population does not like to eat non-fish seafood, and about ten per cent do not eat fish and seafood at all. Nevertheless, embedded as they are within a hegemonic scientific-bureaucratic discourse on seafood in Turkey that focuses on production, nutrition and protein (to be elaborated in Chapter 3), none of these surveys are able to identify the reasons for, nor outline different styles and histories of, seafood consumption.

In this chapter I argue that different styles of seafood consumption articulate powerful symbols of identity and that most Turks have vivid imageries of what it means to eat fish. Alcohol plays a major role in these images. To begin with I sketch typical practices and images in the Trabzon and Istanbul styles of seafood consumption during the 1990s and discuss how they relate to each other. While people along the eastern Black Sea coast love to eat fish, they share with the population of the Anatolian interior a cautious approach to certain ways of seafood consumption. I consider whether this can be explained within the context of Islamic seafood taboos. This is followed by a historical survey of seafood consumption that amounts to a critical examination of the ostensible continuity of the referents for identity claims. The different approaches to seafood and its consumption can be interpreted as being expressions of starkly contrasting ways of shaping contemporary Turkish lives or lifestyles. However, recent developments, in particular the rapid spread of new non-alcoholic 'Meat and Fish' restaurants along the eastern Black Sea coast, indicate considerable change and creativity, resulting in an increasingly porous boundary between cultures of consumption.

## Istanbul Style Seafood Culture

In Turkey the *lokanta* is the most common kind of eating establishment, typically serving quick meals at lunchtime but no alcohol. While one fills one's stomach at lokantas, one dines at *restorant*s and drinks at *meyhane*s, the traditional-style drinking establishment. In the more refined and expensive of these evening eating establishments seafood occupies a very important position. Although the annual consumption of fish in Turkish restaurants may only amount to about ten thousand tonnes (Elliott and partners 1996: 156) out of a total seafood consumption of 400–500,000 tonnes, the economic and symbolic significance of the fish restaurants far exceeds this. Expensive seafood restaurants are found in large cities across

Turkey, including Trabzon, but Istanbul is clearly the symbolic centre of this consumption. In a 1998 list of top class Istanbul restaurants, 44 out of 105 were classified as fish restaurants.[6]

A visit to a seafood restaurant in Istanbul, and elsewhere in Turkey, is generally a (late) evening social outing with family or good friends, preferably in a seaside location. The food – a first course of *meze* followed by a few warm dishes before the main meal of fresh fish, usually an entire fresh fish each – is invariably accompanied by wine or the stronger anise-flavoured *rakı*. The variety of marine products that are served far exceeds the common person's tastes and/or purchasing power; in addition to *lüfer* (bluefish) – the most popular and archetypal restaurant fish – the menu includes fish such as turbot, swordfish, sea bass, red mullet, and angler fish. A wide variety of non-fish seafood is highly esteemed, including crab, lobster, octopus and squid, prawns, and molluscs.[7] Small, cheap fish such as *hamsi* (anchovy), horse mackerel and sardines are generally not among the preferred choices at the expensive restaurants.

Eating seafood out in Turkey is considered a luxury. While a filling meal at some lokanta may cost less than U.S.$2, a portion of fish/salad/drink and a small selection of meze at some meyhane or middle range restaurant will generally exceed U.S.$12 per person.[8] And a proper seafood meal at a good restaurant along the Bosporus will cost not less than U.S.$40 per person. To get to the restaurants most people will also have to travel by private car or by taxi. Thus, fish restaurants are generally frequented by the urban upper and upper-middle classes. In Istanbul, or elsewhere in Turkey, it is hard to find any regular lokanta that also serves fish. There are very few purely fish-lokantas.

Seafood is associated with luxury, but riches and luxury may also be associated with dining on seafood (see Figure 2.1). One seaside hotel in Çanakkale marketed itself to the Turkish upper class through an advert in the elite secularist daily newspaper *Cumhuriyet* (28 July 1998):

> ÇAĞIN MOTEL, fish for every meal, the sea like an aquarium, quiet holiday far from the crowds and the vulgarity (*kabalık*). 2 persons 1 week 98 Million TL [U.S.$375].

The cartoon (Figure 2.1) also demonstrates other important aspects of restaurant seafood consumption. First, the fish should be very fresh and preferably served whole, including the head, when possible. Even prawns are served with the head intact. Fish seems fresher if it is uncut, its identity is unobscured; a whole fish makes the best impression aesthetically. At the more refined restaurants, however, elaboration of dishes may take precedence over serving whole fish. The aesthetic aspect of fish and seafood is repeated in conspicuous cooler showcases, containing several prestigious fish and wine or rakı, placed in front of the restaurant to attract customers, as well as in the elaborate decorations and the orderly

## SEMİH BALCIOĞLU'NUN NOT DEFTERİNDEN

Lig şampiyonu     Kupa şampiyonu     Küme düşenler !

**Figure 2.1. Football champions: wine, women and fish.** During the latter half of the 1990s the enormous sums of money earned by the top players and clubs in Turkish football caught the attention of the public. In order to convey an idea of wealth and prestige, seafood is one of the primary means of illustration in this newspaper cartoon (1996). Note that the fish is presented whole. The text reads as (from left to right): 'League Champions', 'Cup Champions', 'Those Falling into [a lower] League'. Reprinted with Semih Balcıoğlu's permission.

arrangement of seafood and whole and uncut fish at well-stocked fishmongers. Secondly, seafood restaurants are regularly frequented by women, who are invariably 'secular' and uncovered (*açık*). Thirdly, there is a very strong and pervasive association of seafood with alcohol in the public imageries of contemporary Turkey. It is commonly believed that fish will die unhappy and be *mundar* (filthy, unclean) if not consumed together with rakı. Of greater significance is the symbolic importance of 'civilized' alcohol consumption as a signifier of a wealthy, secular lifestyle. Consuming seafood together with alcohol is seen by the elite as a hallmark of a wealthy, secular lifestyle, a refined and sophisticated way of creating moments of *muhabbet* – intimate, friendly conversation, companionship, joy and intimacy – within a context that is shielded from the crowds of vulgar, common people.

The sea and the *sahil* (seaside), especially along the Bosporus and in Aegean seaside resorts, are considered the ideal place for pleasure and recreation, for creating an atmosphere of the exceptional. The Istanbul-style seafood consumption carries all the hallmarks of civilized, yet relaxed, manners: the polite language, the napkins, the wiping of forks and knifes before eating, new plates and utensils for each new serving, and so forth. Although this seafood culture finds its main expression in the restaurant and tourist sectors, luxury seafood is also consumed at home. Fishmongers seldom sell turbot and red mullet for less than U.S.$10/kg,[9] which is considerably more expensive than red meat. Nonetheless even when fish is served in the home – often on weekends or when entertaining guests (Elliot 1996: 191, 208, 210) – or at some large workplace, it will certainly be commented upon and perceived to mark, or create, a special occasion.

## Trabzon 'Fish Food' Culture

When talking about eating fish in Trabzon, what comes to mind is the Black Sea anchovy, the hamsi. Turkish hamsi fisheries comprise one of the largest fisheries in the Middle East and provide approximately three quarters of all Turkish catches in the Black Sea. Hamsi is really cheap food; in the winter of 1998–9 a kilo sold for as little as U.S.$0.50 in Trabzon, which is much less expensive than other fish and meat. Some intermediately priced fish are also commonly consumed in the eastern Black Sea region, but other locally available species such as crab, black mussels, sole, flounder, eel, greater weaver, and scorpion fish are rarely consumed. They are, however, quite popular in the Istanbul seafood culture. In Trabzon the more expensive species tend to be consumed within a cultural framework of the upper-class Istanbul-style seafood culture among urban secular upper classes throughout Turkey. Seafood restaurants in Trabzon even import valued species not found in the Black Sea from Istanbul or the Aegean.

The people of Trabzon also prioritize freshness when serving fish, and fish is always bought whole. Yet the Trabzon fish culture differentiates itself in several respects from the Istanbul way of consuming seafood: fish stands are not 'decorated'; fish will invariably be prepared and served without the head; and the multitudes of ways of preparing hamsi are a source of both pride and ridicule. 'They even make hamsi sweets!' Of the fifty recipes (excluding sweets) included in an official publication on traditional meals from Trabzon, eleven recipes are with hamsi, while only two are with other kinds of fish and six with red meat (Canalioğlu et al. 1997). Hamsi is generally served in two contexts: (1) at everyday family meals at home; and (2) at open air locations where fresh hamsi is grilled over charcoal and eaten with bread – cheap, tasty and filling fast food. Hamsi is 'everyday' food for all classes of people and during the winter months the most important source of protein for the larger share of the eastern Black Sea population. In addition, it fills an important place in peoples' lives by providing a topical focus for shared experiences and desires, and by contributing to a feeling of abundance in otherwise poor families.

Songs are sung about hamsi, poems are written about it. No other fish in Turkey, and no other produce in the Black Sea region, is as exalted, as familiar, as beloved as the hamsi. There can be said to exist a hamsi 'cult'. Fish in general is believed to be nutritious, but the hamsi is praised for having life-giving power, for being *şifalı* (having healing, health-giving properties) and for enhancing sexual potency. Many interpreted the absence of hamsi around 1990 as the death of the Black Sea.

Unlike the semiotics of seafood in general, hamsi is used not to signify the difference between classes, but is rather a potent symbol of the identity of a region, for the *halk* (people) at large. Because hamsi pervades so much of the eastern Black Sea existence it simply cannot be overlooked by the elite classes and finds expression in literature and refined hamsi recipes. Even the cultivated approach to hamsi consumption partly defines itself in opposition to the Istanbul seafood culture. One writer praises the 'Trabzon' way of eating hamsi with one's fingers.[10]

There are, in sum (see Figure 2.2), many differences between the seafood cultures. In contrast to seafood in the Istanbul culture, there is not a single reference to alcohol in texts and poems about hamsi, and in people's talk and practice it is rare to combine hamsi and alcohol. Moreover – and contrary to some meze within the Istanbul seafood culture – hamsi is never eaten uncooked.

| Istanbul seafood culture | Trabzon fish culture |
|---|---|
| Restaurant/meyhane/sahil | Home/public open air space |
| Alcohol | No alcohol |
| Garlic, bay leaves etc | – – – |
| Cooked and uncooked | Cooked |
| Fish and non-fish | Fish |
| Few taboos | Many taboos |
| Lüfer (bluefish) | Hamsi (anchovy) |
| Exceptional occasions | Normal --> exceptional |
| Leisure | Life-giver |

**Figure 2.2. Characteristics of and contrasts between the Istanbul and Trabzon culinary cultures of seafood.**

## Contrasting Images: Cultivation and Morals

Thus far I have roughly sketched what the two seafood cultures mean to their practitioners. Below I look more closely at public images and stereotypes of seafood consumption (summarized in Figure 2.3). Both in local self-definition and in popular nationwide imagery, the hamsi is portrayed as a key symbol, a metonym, for the eastern Black Sea region and the people living there. Once when I was riding in a taxi in Istanbul, the radio was tuned in to a local (Istanbul) call-in radio programme. When one caller said that he had his roots in Trabzon, the programme leader immediately sang, 'Hamsi, hamsi, hamsi', mimicking the folk song style of Trabzon. Hamsi is said to embody many of the region's characteristics, primarily the energetic activity and vigour of its people. While the largely positive images concerning the hamsi are fairly uniformly shared, the cultivated elite tends to look upon the Anatolian and Trabzon approach to seafood as being steeped in traditionalist Islamic superstition, ignorant of modern, civilized food and dining. As is so common in Turkey, lack of education and cultivation is the perceived culprit.

The two seafood cultures clearly have contrasting approaches to alcohol, echoed, for instance, in diverging images of the Beyoğlu shopping and leisure quarter in Istanbul. Here many of the central elements of the Istanbul seafood culture come together: alcohol; Westernized living; uncovered women; meyhanes; fish markets and a cosmopolitan/foreign heritage. Beyoğlu holds some attractions for the common man: it's a place to demonstrate one's maleness, vigour and strength through occasional, but massive drinking, sexual conquests (prostitutes), and perhaps gambling – all mediated by good food, often seafood.[11] For the religiously observant, alcohol and female modesty are very sensitive issues and

| Istanbul seafood culture | | Trabzon fish culture | |
|---|---|---|---|
| Positive image | Negative image | Negative image | Positive image |
| refined/ sophisticated | morally corrupt | vulgar | decent |
| clean | dirty (alcohol etc.) | dirty | clean |
| (civilized) Istanbul | (decadent) Istanbul | Anatolia/Trabzon | Trabzon/Black Sea |
| civilization | infidel/Rum | rural, Anatolia | Turkish, Muslim |
| cultivated elite | economic elite | poor | the common man/halk |

Figure 2.3. Contrasting images of the seafood cultures.

Beyoğlu, with its meyhanes and brothels is, therefore, a symbol of all vices. For a man, drinking alcohol, gambling and illicit sex consume his money, erode his moral standing, and ruin his family. The meyhanes – and by extension, the fish restaurants – are places of moral corruption to be avoided.

When the Islamist Welfare Party (Refah Partisi) won the 1994 municipal elections in Istanbul, a restrictive policy on alcohol was one of the primary ways the new city administration tried to assert itself in Beyoğlu (Çınar 1997: 23–40). Underlying this policy seemed to be a general preoccupation with physically isolating the 'forbidden' activities to the private sphere in order to prevent temptation and contagion. This policy was shared with other municipalities governed by the Welfare Party such as Trabzon where the city administration campaigned for their view on large signboards along some main roads that declared that 'Alcohol is the source of all kinds of evil'.

People in and around Trabzon are popularly regarded as being, by Turkish standards, conservative and religiously devout. When, during the 1990s, parts of the city centre became the focal point for meetings between Turkish men and *Nataşa*s, women from the former Soviet Republics, the association between illicit sex and alcohol was strengthened. It became even more important for 'good Muslim' men to avoid places serving alcohol, for example the approximately ten seafood restaurants located just outside of town. These restaurants can only be reached by car and are unaffordable for many. An added reason for devout or traditional Muslims to avoid seafood restaurants and meyhane is that they, contrary to lokantas, have no separate room for *aile* (family) – men's legitimate female companions and children.

With its long history in trade and higher education and a high degree of involvement in national politics, the city of Trabzon hosts a substantial secular and culturally refined urban upper class. The people in and around the small coastal town of Çarşıbaşı are generally accepted as being among the more conservative in the province of Trabzon. When, in 1998, I asked why there were no lokanta or restaurants that served fish in Çarşıbaşı, it was difficult to get any clear cut answers, but one fisher tellingly said, with a smile: 'There is this: if there is fish there should be alcohol'. Being a very sensitive issue, there was no place in Çarşıbaşı that served alcohol, and the sale of alcohol for private consumption was surrounded by secrecy. Although eating fish in Çarşıbaşı and Trabzon is not generally associated with alcohol, the Istanbul seafood culture has such a dominant position in the national discourse on consumption of seafood and fish that it has prevented anyone from trying to open a fish restaurant in Çarşıbaşı. For the same reason, non-alcohol-related Trabzon style fish consumption was not represented in lokantas in Çarşıbaşı and was only very poorly represented in the lokantas in Trabzon's main square. The lack of drinking establishments and the lack of places that serve seafood in Trabzon are both Muslim reactions to the immorality of a non-Muslim (secular) life.

The Istanbul seafood culture is perceived by many Black Sea Muslims as expressing a non-Muslim, *Rum* (Greek)[12] and infidel lifestyle and identity. It is common among conservatives in Çarşıbaşı to state that ninety per cent of the people in Istanbul are Rum, implying that ninety per cent of the Istanbulites behave as if they were Rum. Two young fishers in Çarşıbaşı discussed the prospect of going to Izmir to sign on as crew on a fishing boat there. One of them said that they should go before the upcoming Ramadan. His friend was sceptical: 'That will be difficult. People there do no fast, you become very sinful'. People in Çarşıbaşı have a clear conception of themselves being religiously more observant and morally less lax than people in western Turkey. Scepticism towards the 'Istanbul way of life' is based on very strongly felt moral concerns.

While Beyoğlu for many is an alluring, but decadent place, it is for the self-declared civilized elite the symbol of (foregone) cosmopolitanism, civilization and elegance. The cultural divide between the Aegean areas/Istanbul- and Anatolia is further articulated in the special significance attributed to the Istanbul sahil (seaside) which is popularly perceived (e.g., in films, music videos, literature)[13] to be a zone of strong emotions, freedom, recreation, beauty and muhabbet. Popular texts on Istanbul and fishing invariably stress that the pursuit of lüfer has been an intensely social and cultivated practice since the classical Ottoman Age when men of the noble classes, including pashas, actively participated. Through the civilized sahil and the lüfer contemporary Istanbul seafood culture evokes a historical connection to classical civilization. It is even claimed that 'thanks to the lüfer, the Istanbul – even the Bosporus – culture came into being' (*www.netbul.com*, accessed 6 October 2003).

In Istanbul pockets of pleasant urban sahil can still be found that are accessible to the public, especially parks and small-boat fishing harbours. Thus, even though it may be a '*fantasi*' for the common man to visit a seafood restaurant, it is still possible to enter a sahil world of seafood, alcohol and muhabbet. Because of this the fisher's environment is often romanticized by the elite. Under the headline 'Oh, that fisher's shelter!' one journalist relates how he forgets his problems and worries when he dives into this world: 'In the fisher's shelter there is peace of mind and friendship. What are the pleasures of the 'liner' ... A little tea, a little imbibing, and, yes, plenty of conversation. Is there anything more beautiful in this life?' (Ünsal 1998). This non-elite sahil is surely a romanticized world, but it also carries the negative connotations of being dirty, bad-smelling, poor and pitiable and the 'inhabitants' of this world are easily stereotyped as pleasure seekers and drunkards. Fishers therefore have to tread very carefully not to be perceived as immoral: small-boat fishers in Trabzon seldom prepare fish meals in the harbour or at the seaside, but rather on the boat, and on the larger boats in Trabzon drinking (and card playing) is strictly 'forbidden', being regarded as a sin (*günah*). Many small-boat fishers in İstanbul have special *kahve* (coffeehouses), and small-boat fishers in Çarşıbaşı commonly change clothes on their boats.

The images discussed here may indicate considerable continuity in seafood consumption and associated images since the Ottoman era. The styles and ways of seafood consumption seem to articulate historicized ethnoreligious identities. However, the native images may blur important aspects of this seafood semiotics and create an incorrectly static and essentialized picture of such consumption. My strategy for exposing the dynamic relationships between identities and seafood consumption involves a survey of historical changes in seafood consumption, analysis of recent changes in seafood 'fashions', and a short discussion of the possible importance of Islamic food taboos for the Trabzon approach to seafood.

## Seafood Taboos in the Trabzon Fish Food Culture

One explanation for the differences between these two seafood cultures that easily offers itself relates to religious food taboos: are people in Anatolia and Trabzon more observant with regard to Islamic dietary laws? Islam does not have very clear-cut dietary rules for sea animals (Pellat et al. 1995: 306–307; Viré 1995: 1022). The Maliki school is in general the most liberal while the Hanefi school, which was the school the Ottoman emperors supported and is still the most influential in Turkey, is much stricter. Across the Muslim and Arab world approaches to seafood vary considerably. Most species – including prawns and crabs – are popular where seafood has traditionally been easily available. There is a tendency, however, to regard non-scaled fish (especially among Shiite) and shellfish as suspect (Bromberger 1994: 189; McGoodwin 1990; Iddison 1997). In Turkey some consider fish to be *haram* (forbidden) for good Muslims since it cannot be properly slaughtered – it is difficult to make the blood run and it is difficult to know whether one is using the knife in a religiously acceptable way. The 'Anatolian' approach to seafood is seemingly influenced by this concern. In the rural regions of Trabzon this concern has seemingly found its solution in a common rule that cutting live fish is haram – it will result in misfortune for the man who committed the sin, such as the birth in the family of a crippled child.

While some men in Çarşıbaşı referred to Islamic rules to explain specific taboos, many also declared, with reference to Maliki, that 'if my father comes out of the sea, even he is edible'. Thus, there is disagreement about what is haram, suggesting that people attempt to give local traditions a veneer of legitimacy by anchoring them in Islamic rules. Most people in

Çarşıbaşı are actually hard put to explain the taboos. If a particular fish or sea animal is regarded as forbidden, various criteria (from Islamic jurisprudence) other than rules pertaining directly to seafood are applied. Thus, seafood taboos articulate concerns related to the primary Islamic food taboos regarding blood, pork and alcohol (Tapper and Zubaida 1994: 14).

What connects and constitutes many of the seafood taboos is the association with meyhane culture, an indecent, secular lifestyle and, above all, alcohol. Fishers liberally consume high-value species such as turbot and red mullet on the boats. These species are also popular among the Black Sea populace during Ramadan. When asked why they do not consume a certain sea animal and fish, such as sole or crab, people in Çarşıbaşı often say simply that 'they eat it in Istanbul', 'it is possible to sell it to meyhane/restaurants', or 'that's the business of the rich men'. In the Muslim Middle East (Hafez 1994: 257–280), meyhane and alcohol are often associated with erotic and illicit sex. In Turkey, seafood, together with alcohol, are considered to draw one closer to tempting, yet immoral, erotic adventures. I suspect that this is why it is acceptable for young boys, but not adult males, in Çarşıbaşı to eat black mussels; alcohol and sex are not relevant temptations for young boys.

The way Muslim morality is articulated in approaches to seafood consumption in Turkey is clearly not predicated on a taxonomic system and related notions of purity and contagion alone. Food taboos are closely connected to the sociohistorical context of the consumption. Among Arab Muslims, where seafood occupies a less important place at the meze table and where the Rum context is lacking, prawns are very popular food.[14] Devout Black Sea Turks, on the other hand, do not eat prawns, precisely because of the association with the meyhane culture. The seafood taboos as expressed within the Trabzon fish food culture cannot be said to operate according to, or be reducible to, some cultural logic à la Douglas (1966) or Sahlins (1976). Albeit of possible importance, a structure of symbols cannot fully explain animal classifications (Goody 1998:148–160) and food taboos (Rouse and Hoskins 2004).

## History of Seafood Consumption

Popular imagery of identities expressed through seafood in Turkey during the 1990s tended to confine identity formation to two reified and essentialized sociocultural groupings: Turk/Anatolia versus Rum/Istanbul. A mapping of these identities onto the Istanbul of the Ottomans could imply surrendering the terms of academic inquiry to politicized identity discourses of the present. Indeed, the Rum were an integral part of the Ottoman empire. Moreover, combinations of several identities were common, especially during the early and middle phases of the Ottoman reign. Below I outline the general pattern of seafood consumption in Istanbul and Trabzon during Ottoman and early Republican times. Although sources on relations between seafood consumption and cultural patterns are scarce, especially when it comes to Trabzon, enough evidence exists to address adequately questions such as: how was seafood consumption configured within identity negotiations? Was Greek lifestyle appropriated by the new Turkish elite? In pursuing these questions, it is convenient to identify four different periods in the development of Istanbul-style seafood consumption.

## The Classical Ottoman Era

In Ottoman Istanbul seafood seemingly constituted one of the few culinary distinctions between the different ethnic-religious groups. A close association between Rum, seafood and alcohol was grounded in several conditions. First, the general interpretation of the Koran and the specific regulations enacted by the Sultan meant that production, distribution and sale of alcohol became primarily a task for Greeks and foreigners in Constantinople.[15] Secondly, seafood consumption outside the house was most likely concentrated in *taverna*s that were most often run by Greeks. Salted, dried and marinated fish were regarded as ideal meze in the tavernas.[16] Third, the Greek Orthodox and Armenians (as well as Catholic Levantines) seem to have had a special preference for non-fish sea animals during Lent (Gilles 1988: xliii; Pamukciyan 1988: 218), probably stimulating a rich 'Greek', non-fish sea animal cuisine (see, e.g., Yordanidu 1990). Its close association with religious life probably made seafood an important symbol in inter-religious border constructions, although there seems to have been a slackening of the Lent rules over the centuries to include fish (White 1845, Volume I: 75; Neave 1933: 205).

It is, however, too simplistic to claim that seafood was mostly a Rum business. Armenians were an integral part of the non-Muslim seafood culture and Armenian men were influential as cooks in Istanbul (White 1845, Volume III: 89–90). Furthermore, fish and seafood was regularly consumed by both the 'common and poorer sorts of Turks' (Bon 1996: 102) and by the noble and rich (Reyhanlı 1983: 68). Some Sultans did secure regular deliveries of seafood (Kömürciyan 1988: 5), and at times the menu included non-fish seafood such as oyster, lobster and prawns (Oğuz 1976: 593). Seafood even had its place at the tables of Muslim brotherhoods that drew together people from different classes (Artan 2000). In the tavernas, Muslims joined the Rum and other Christians, and all, even Muslims, joined in the consumption of alcohol (Pamukciyan 1988: 219; Zat 1993/4: 437).

Lent rules, Muslim concerns about alcohol, and the association of Rum with tavernas probably meant that Muslims and non-Muslims had a tendency to approach seafood from different viewpoints, with the Muslim's attitude being more ambivalent. But how did seafood develop from being important Lent food for the common Rum to being associated with upper-class Istanbul culture? There is little reason to believe that the Rum of Ottoman Constantinople considered seafood to be elite food. Early developments in consumer culture provide some answers. Already in the seventeenth century '[a] perception of [Constantinople] as a place of comfort, sophistication, culture and opportunity' (Murphey 1990: 116) began to take shape. The Constantinople way of life, a multicultural Ottoman or Levantine culture (Mansel 1995), came to be known for the joint pleasures of food, wine, music, *taverna* (nightclub) and, often, the sahil and recreational night fishing for lüfer (Oğuz 1976: 597). This culture further developed during the early-eighteenth-century Tulip Era – a time that also marks the onset of a culture of consumption (Quataert 2000: 130).

In Constantinople the expression of social hierarchy through consumption used to be demonstrated through the provision of food to followers (Artan 2000: 164–165). Prepared dishes differed little between the court and elsewhere. From the early eighteenth century sophistication, not largesse, became the tool of distinction. The rise of a cosmopolitan multicultural Mediterranean culture connected to trade (Artan 2000: 144, 151–152) brought with it a strong association of olive oil, vegetable dishes, the sea and the noble classes – bringing seafood within a new semiotics of distinction. A visitor to Constantinople was served almost identical food, including 'Constantinople style' seafood, in the homes of wealthy Greek and Turkish families (Pardoe 1837).

## Tanzimat to Republic – New Ottoman Lifestyles

Because of the 'capitulations' and Tanzimat[17] (1839–76) policies, the wealth and cultural liberties of Greeks and other non-Muslims increased during the nineteenth century. The classes connected to the Sultanic household and the state were no longer able to keep pace with changes in, let alone monopolize, instruments and symbols for the expression of a prestigious lifestyle and 'non-Muslims replaced Muslims as fashion leaders' (Quataert 2000: 146, 155). There evolved new elite lifestyles – expressed, for example, in architecture, consumption, rise of a restaurant culture, and 'cultural activities' – that by and large were perceived as 'Western'. It was from this point onwards that the Rum emerged as representatives of the West in the East (Millas 1993/94: 363–368).

Although the Rum may have led the way, cultural intermingling likely resulted in similar patterns of elite consumption across a range of 'nationalities' (Mansel 1995: 290–296). Lifestyles were probably more a matter of class or status than expressions of 'national' identity. The *Turkish Cookery Book* from the period (Turabi 1987) includes a range of 'Istanbul style' seafood recipes (also shellfish and molluscs). A shared upper-class elaboration of seafood as an articulation of refined manners and cultivation is thus probably a relatively recent phenomenon. There is little to indicate that specialized fish restaurants became common during this period (Arkan 1993/94: 220–223). While most restaurants, or lokanta as they were then named, served alcohol as an accompaniment to the food, meyhanes/tavernas were primarily considered places to drink and constituted a separate tradition. The meyhanes, for instance, remained exclusively male space.

The majority of the population did not take part in the development of refined consumption, and the extravagant consumption of the elite was widely criticized. While the Patrona Halil revolt in 1730 may have been an attempt to restore Constantinople's 'moral economy' (Salzman 2000), nineteenth century criticism increasingly focused on the adoption of a 'Western' lifestyle. Especially gender roles and alcohol remained sensitive issues (Sülker 1985: 160). Importantly, not only Muslims but conservative Orthodox Christians criticized the new lifestyles of the elite (Exertzoglu 2003).

## Early Republic – The Exclusion of Istanbul from Turkishness

The Young Turk and Republican elites increasingly located the core or home of the newly constructed national identity in Anatolia. Istanbul became suspect to the new nation and Republic since it symbolized both Islamic traditionalism and Western imperialism (Keyder 1999). Perhaps that is why Turkish scholars considering subjects such as Turkish culture, Turkish food, and the like hardly pay attention to the urban traditions and practices of Istanbul (and Izmir). In stark contrast to the emphasis on seafood in the pre-Republican *Turkish Cookery Book*, Oğuz (1976: 693), in his monumental work about the cultural roots of the Turks, sets aside only half a page for seafood (notably hamsi) in his fifty pages about 'Turkish' food. Oğuz's selection was made on the basis of what was, at the time, a hegemonic nationalist and essentialist construction of the 'Turk' that excluded cosmopolitan and urban experiences and lifestyles.

Yet, Istanbul culture, despite official efforts to discount it, remained the cultural source for elite articulation, be it in language, clothing or food. The elite even tried to re-create some of the Istanbul sahil atmosphere in Ankara where they could visit newly constructed *gazinos* and the like on the 'shores' of pools constructed in the shape of the Sea of Marmara and the Black Sea (Şenol 1998). Seafood remained elite food and a preferred object of hospitality (Orga 1958). Although alcohol remained a sensitive and heated issue during the first years of the Republic (Sülker 1985: 151–158; Arkan 1993/94: 222), the secular state and elite classes of the early Republic had a liberal attitude towards alcohol, and Istanbul and meyhanes figured prominently in the elite's idealized visions of drinking parties and muhabbet. During the Republican period all drinking poems have been about Istanbul, often praising its seaside, fishing boats and seafood (Sülker 1985: 168). The new rulers in Ankara probably had very ambivalent feelings about Istanbul. It was ideologically suspect, but at the same time the 'Istanbul lifestyle' was embodied and reproduced in everyday practice and images of cultivation.

While Istanbul-style seafood culture was reproduced in Ankara, in Istanbul the restaurant culture lost much of the late Ottoman splendour. Demand for seafood decreased, but since many kinds of fish were cheap (Tutel 1998) it must have been common food among the urban poor. With the loss of status to Ankara as the centre of government, economic recession, and the later exodus of the minorities during the 1950s and 1960s (Arkan 1993/94: 222), the city was becoming 'poor and provincial' (Mansel 1995: 424). Although the number of meyhanes also diminished during this period, they were probably instrumental in the preservation of the association of seafood with alcohol. About half of the approximately fifty mezes listed in a 1950s text on meyhanes are various kinds of seafood (Zat 1993/94).

## Urban Growth, Istanbul Nostalgia and the Birth of the Fish Restaurant

Although the Turkish state tried, especially after 1950, to stimulate seafood consumption, it was socioeconomic change and mass migration to the urban centres that would set in motion cultural forces that transformed styles, tastes and meanings of seafood consumption. Murat Belge, a prominent Turkish columnist, writer and intellectual, identifies the first seafood restaurant in Turkey as the Amatör Balıkçılar Kulübü that was established under the Galata bridge in the 1960s. In those days, he writes, when the fish-loving minorities had left the city, and the new inhabitants of the city had little relation with fish, the lokanta under the bridge 'served fish-loving Istanbulness' for the 'real' (*has*) Istanbulites (Belge 2001: 342–343).

Thus, the Istanbul-style seafood restaurant may have been 'invented' as a reaction to the recent phenomenon of mass migration to Istanbul from Anatolia that brought uneducated and 'vulgar' people to the city. The sahil, the lüfer, the traditional meyhane, the cosmopolitan Beyoğlu – all of these gradually emerged as important figures in an Istanbul nostalgia that during the 1990s were increasingly represented in popular books. Many would cite, for example, the early twentieth century saying: 'The one who does not have knowledge of fish, who does not know the *lüfer*, does not count as an Istanbulite' (Dursun 1999: 264).

The new seafood restaurants were rapidly appropriated by the upper classes who continued to look to Istanbul for inspiration concerning models and codes for cultivated and refined lifestyles. The new rich may care less about Istanbul nostalgia and simply patronize these restaurants because they are believed to confer prestige on the customers. The growth of seafood restaurants in Istanbul and elsewhere in Turkey was part of a general change and increase in consumption since the 1960s. Many of the new *restoran* (the luxury tag of lokanta had been eroded) were located out of town, especially along the Bosporus, requiring the guest to come by car (Arkan 1993/94). Although these new, expensive restaurants had increasingly complex codes of conduct, such as making table reservations, leaving one's car at the restaurant entrance to be parked and so on, the dining arrangements at the seafood restaurants closely followed traditional meyhane etiquette. Therefore, Belge argues (Belge 2001: 344), the seafood restaurants are derived from the meyhanes.

During the 1980s and 1990s the number of restaurants in general and seafood restaurants in particular rapidly increased. The situation of two different styles of seafood consumption described at the beginning of this chapter emerged. After this historical survey it is, however, apparent that the identity formations that were articulated through the Istanbul-style seafood culture in the 1990s answered to very different economic and cultural contexts than seafood consumption during the late Ottoman period. Perhaps seafood per se was not an important element in late Ottoman upper class work at distinguishing themselves from the poorer and vulgar classes because the 'others' that they distinguished themselves from were themselves Istanbulites frequenting meyhanes and eating seafood? Certain kinds of seafood were clearly associated with alcohol, but not necessarily with wealth.

## Notes on History of Seafood, Alcohol and Rum in Trabzon

Although sources are scarce, there is little reason to doubt that hamsi has been of continuous and stable nutritional and symbolic value for a majority of the people in the Black Sea region.[18] A (probably) late Ottoman poem praises the hamsi for being 'the life giving food of the poor, the cure for the very ill'.[19] An early Republican publication states: 'Nothing creates among the rich, the middle and the poor the same love and joy. And no foodstuff is as democratic and liberal as it'.[20] The Rum of Trabzon undoubtedly took part in the hamsi 'cult' alongside other groups in the region. Relations to Rum identity have, however, a more complex history.

Before 1916 there was a substantial rural Rum population in the eastern Black Sea region and thereby considerable Rum or Greek Orthodox influence on a partly shared culture and praxis among the populations of the region. In the city of Trabzon the Rum and the Armenian commercial bourgeoisie benefited most from the Trabzon trade boom during the middle of the nineteenth century. The ties of this Christian bourgeoisie with Greeks in Istanbul and elsewhere (Turgay 1982), the presence of many representatives of European powers, the widespread migration from Trabzon to Istanbul, as well as the local political elites' age-old close ties with Istanbul (Meeker 2002) meant that many in Trabzon probably were familiar with the latest fashions in Istanbul and that Levantine-Istanbul lifestyles were emulated in Trabzon. Thus, a lokanta culture not very different from the one in Istanbul was likely widespread in the city of Trabzon. In 1876 there were as many as ten gazinos and 51 meyhanes and 150 coffee houses in the city of Trabzon (*Trabzon Vilayeti Salnamesi 1876* 1995: 263).

Alcohol was clearly an important issue in the local articulation of Turkishness in the heated years around 1920. At the very first meeting of the *Meclis* (Parliament) in Ankara (1920), a Trabzon MP called for a very strict and sweeping law to restrict the sale and consumption of alcohol. He complained that '[a] handful of Pontos Greeks (*Pontoscu*) [in Trabzon] produce *rakı*, exploit the local people (*memleketi*), and smuggle the money to Greece' (Sülker 1985: 152). In 1933, after the ships and caravans had stopped visiting Trabzon and after the Greeks had left, there were together 102 coffee houses and gazinos in the city (Odabaşıoğlu n.d.: 171). Yet scepticism towards what was seen as the decadent, rich, drinking Rum was probably a response to the lifestyle of the emerging Greek bourgeoisie in the city of Trabzon (and similar experiences in Istanbul) and not an effect of inter-ethnic relations in rural communities (see Andreadis 1995).

War, emigration, assimilation and Turkification of Greek place names have worked to largely erase the Rum/Greek legacy on the Turkish Black Sea coast. There is today some uneasiness and ambivalence among people concerning a Rum past that may live on in their own practices. When Black Sea people today tend to denounce Istanbul-style seafood consumption by saying that it is Rum, one aspect of this discourse may be a need to distance oneself from the taint of 'Greekness'. In the eastern Black Sea region articulation of Turkishness seems to have become closely associated with Islamic morals.

## Recent Developments

New styles of seafood consumption have gradually emerged since the early 1990s. New twists have appeared in elite seafood consumption, partly in response to the erosion of classic Istanbul seafood culture as the new rich 'eat into' this consumption style. Cooks come up with creative (and expensive!) seafood dishes, and sushi bars are the recent rage in Istanbul. The change and expansion in non-alcohol-related seafood consumption is even more remarkable and of greater consequence. Places along the Istanbul seaside that serve very cheap 'fish in bread' multiplied during the 1990s – numbering approximately 150 – until abolished by the municipality from 2004 onwards (Dönmez 2004); small stands (*büfe*) serving fast seafood, including mussels, have appeared not only in Istanbul but also in Trabzon; fish is making inroads in regular lunch-time lokantas; and picnic-style outdoor establishments serving farmed trout have proliferated along rivers all over Turkey. Of particular interest is the sudden appearance and spread of 'meat and fish' eating establishments in Trabzon and elsewhere along the Black Sea coast since the late 1990s.

'Meat and fish', by 2005 numbering perhaps fifty around Trabzon, including two in Çarşıbaşı, are typically located fifteen to thirty minutes drive from Trabzon or other larger Black Sea cities. These often spacious establishments (see Figure 2.4) emphasize cleanliness and are conspicuously well lit. They avoid use of the terms restoran or lokanta in their names, but often include 'family' (*aile*) on the signboard. Most of them do not serve alcohol and some are even decorated with Koranic citations. Their menus do not incorporate mezes, and the choices of seafood are limited to a few 'acceptable' species of fish. These elements combine to create a profile that is an outright denial of most of the semiotics of the meyhanes and the luxury seafood restaurants. On the other hand, main business time is evening and weekends, there is no separation between a male section and the family section, and some Istanbul-style etiquette is followed. Although more expensive than an ordinary lokanta, prices are well below restaurant prices. Both covered women, secular professors and children feel at home here.

The inclusion of fish in eating establishments that do not serve alcohol indicates that the rigid distinction between the Istanbul-style seafood culture and the Trabzon fish food culture is diminishing. This is related to another trend: the development of a nationwide shared culture of fish consumption, especially at home or private consumption of a limited range

**Figure 2.4. 'Meat and fish' restaurant.** One of the nicer 'meat and fish' at the Akçaabat seaside near Trabzon (2004).

of increasingly well known, easily available, cheap or intermediately priced fresh fish such as hamsi, mackerel, sea bream and sea bass, as well as canned tuna. Fresh trout became a 'new' species during the 1990s and is especially popular among those who did not consume fish previously (Elliott and partners1996: 183, 186). More recently fresh salmon imported from Norway has entered the market and is sold by most well-stocked fishmongers.

Many contextual changes have helped stimulate or make possible changes in seafood consumption. First, seafood is increasingly coming within the orbit of the expanding sector of industrialized, big-capital production and distribution of food and other consumer goods in Turkey. While over fifty per cent of the overall retail market is still in the hands of small-scale shopkeepers (*bakkal*) and open air bazaars, the hyper- and supermarkets have rapidly been increasing their share since the mid 1990s (Nicely 2000; Sirtioğlu 2004; Tansaş 2003). Seafood retailing in Turkey was until recently completely in the hands of specialized fishmongers and itinerant vendors. Now some of the larger corporations in Turkey have included seafood in their attempt to create brands and to expand their share of the retail sector, and aesthetically arranged seafood and fresh fish, including expensive and imported produce, are incorporated as choice in large separate, refrigerated sections or rooms of supermarkets and hypermarkets.

Secondly, cage rearing of sea bream and sea bass in the Aegean, and freshwater trout in the Black Sea region and Anatolia, 'took off' during the 1990s. Since 1998 farmed fish has accounted for more than ten per cent of 'water produce' production in Turkey (Çeliker 2003. See also Figure 3.3), supplying increasingly cheap fish. Third, the price of fish and seafood relative to red meat has decreased as livestock production has been in crisis, primarily brought on by the unrest in the southeast. Thus, contrary to popular perceptions, Turks now generally consume more fish and seafood than red meat. Red meat consumption fell during the 1990s from 9.9 to 5.6 kg per capita (Oral 2002). Fourth, the EU-accession process implies that Turkey adopts many of the EU laws and regulations, including stricter hygiene measures requiring all seafood to be sold from 'clean' refrigerated steel counters.

Both well-established and more recent concerns shape the direction of the new developments. Age-old conceptions of the life-giving power of fish articulate easily with popularized scientific discourse about the health benefits of eating fish and seafood. Mention fish and many will respond, 'Medicine!' (*ilaç*). At the same time people are increasingly aware that seafood must be fresh and clean. In the supermarkets that sell seafood there is almost an obsessive concern about hygiene. Some of the retail chains emphasize that they control the quality of the product through their 'cold storage chain' or their integrated control 'from field to table' that Carrefour in Turkey first applied to farmed fish (Evran 2004). However, concerns about the permissibility of certain kinds of seafood persist. Most of the catches of sea snail, prawn and some other non-fish species are still exported. On the other hand, the previously strong association of all kinds of seafood served at eating establishments with alcohol has been weakened.

'Meat and fish' eating establishments seem to be a Black Sea trend while supermarkets that sell seafood are primarily found in larger cities. No supermarket in Trabzon, for instance, sells fish – not even processed seafood. Supermarkets selling seafood are often located within larger multipurpose shopping and entertainment centres, submerging shopping into an experience of leisure. Shopping centres are typically, but not exclusively, patronized by secular middle and upper-middle classes, who often reside in new kinds of suburban, residential areas. 'Meat and fish' eating establishments in the outskirts of Trabzon provide an arena where people from many walks of life, including a devout new middle class, can intermingle and take part in modern lifestyles that are not framed by the stilted classical stereotypes. It is part of modern consumer culture, and may look 'Western' at the surface, yet is sensitive to Muslim moral concerns. For an increasing number of people, irrespective of social background, the Black Sea seaside is perceived as a zone especially suited to new forms of recreation and leisure (Gülez 1996).

Although anchored in very different economies, both 'meat and fish' establishments and the incorporation of well stocked seafood counters within supermarkets articulate a desire for 'modern living'. Leisure has become, in time and space, an identifiable and important part of new lifestyle patterns that increasingly pull in the middle class, family and women in a culture of recreation and consumption. Use of private cars is often a requirement to take part in this. Despite severe economic crises in 1994 and 2001 the number of private cars in Turkey more than tripled between 1990 and 2004.[21] By 2005 there were in the Province of Trabzon, with a population of approximately one million, 38,500 private cars (SIS 2005b). In Trabzon, the upgrading of the coastal road has made travel to coastal locations outside of the city much more convenient.

## Conclusions

The meaning of seafood consumption in Ottoman and Turkish societies has been constructed primarily in local and national contexts. Shifts in seafood consumption patterns are primarily a result of negotiation of economic and demographic changes within Turkey. While these economic and demographic changes have increasingly been shaped by economic globalization, recent developments in seafood culture are not the result of exposure to global consumer patterns. Changes in the symbolic referents of seafood consumption also predate the 'new' phenomena characteristic of the post-1980 liberal era in Turkey. This is demonstrated, for instance, by the new search for 'Istanbulness' through the genesis of the Istanbul-style fish restaurants during the 1960s. The sharp distinction between Trabzon and Istanbul styles of seafood consumption that I observed during the 1990s was stimulated by changes in socioeconomic conditions, including mass urbanization since the 1960s and economic liberalization since 1980.

The ambivalence towards seafood, as a simultaneously prestigious and suspect food, has been negotiated in a multitude of ways through the centuries with different mappings onto class, regional, urban-rural, religious, and ethnic identities. Devout Muslims' concerns about alcohol as part of the seafood meal and the (late) Republican association of certain kinds of seafood with the secular upper class have had a formative influence on the semiotics and consumption of seafood. The widespread scepticism towards Istanbul-style seafood consumption illustrates the way in which mainstream Islamists do not criticize or oppose the class system directly; rather they attack the symbolic referents of a secular high-class lifestyle (Navaro-Yashin 2002, White 2002).

I agree with Rouse and Hoskins who, in a study of food consumption among African American Sunni Muslims, argue that 'food taboos are mired in a dialectical relationship between historical memory and identity versus social and ideological change. As a result, most food occupy more than one category allowing fluidity for constantly shifting subject positions' (Rouse and Hoskins 2004: 237). Thus, I do not consider the Trabzon (and Anatolian) style of seafood consumption, with its many taboos, to be the traditional background upon which creative modernizing change is taking place in the large urban centres of Turkey. The widespread concern among the Black Sea population about the kind of seafood they eat not only refers to different 'tastes' within a competitive game of prestige, but is grounded in a morally significant way of living. At the same time their consumption choices involve not only a rhetoric of difference or resistance. They creatively produce new consumption patterns and lifestyles. The new non-alcoholic eating establishments that incorporate seafood articulate syncretistic lifestyles responsive to Muslim moral sensibilities.

'Meat and fish' eating establishments attract customers across the secular-Muslim divide and demonstrate that there is widespread sharing of lifestyles across this ideological divide. Thus, the advent of 'meat and fish' cannot be seen, like 'Islamic chic' *tesettür* (Islamic female garb) (White 1999) as an expression of a refined taste in a new cultivated upper-class lifestyle appropriate for nouveau-rich believers (cf. Bora 1999; Göle 1997). Several other factors contribute to make the conventional dichotomous mapping (as in Figure 2.2) problematic. On the one hand, 'meat and fish' eating establishments, along with 'trout picnic', are patronized not only, not even preferably, by the economic elite, but also by a growing middle class. On the other hand, with the Justice and Development Party (AKP) elite preferring to eat kebab or Black Sea-style pizza (*pide*) and drink fruit juices when they visit restaurants (Mercan 2004), it is no longer as easy to stigmatize all elites as seculars indulging in seafood and alcohol. While through the larger part of the twentieth century it had been the 'secular' Istanbul lifestyle versus the rest, there is now an increasing complexity and multiplicity of foodways. The lines of stratification are less obvious. Increasingly it is the same choice for all, throughout the country.

There is an increasing desire to take part in consumer and leisure culture in Turkey, and municipal authorities design landscapes appropriate for new middle-class leisure acceptable to Muslim sensibilities. In Samsun and other Black Sea cities new large parks suited to family leisure are created along the seaside. To the extent that seafood is part of this new culture of leisure it is obviously a driver for increased demand for seafood, although much of the increased demand is met by farmed fish. Additionally, large multinational and national corporations, sometimes in joint ventures, now spearhead a radical transformation of seafood marketing and consumption in Turkey. Yet, however much change there is, in the public imaginary certain ways of consuming seafood with alcohol are still closely connected to a rich and secular lifestyle, and many poor people, including most fishers, are unable to take part in this new culture of leisure.

Some have claimed that consumption of food must be understood against the backdrop of attempts to create 'national' cuisines (Zubaida 1994; Mintz and Du Bois 2002). Yet, neither Trabzon nor Istanbul-style seafood culture fit the requirement to be 'national'. Both have been suspect in relation to an ideology of Turkish nationalism: the Istanbul style because of its association with Rum, Istanbul etc.; the Trabzon style because it is traditional (many taboos) and Islamic. Despite its attempts, the modernizing state never managed to impose a national seafood cuisine.

Many kinds of nationally important agricultural produce (e.g., sugar, tea) were appropriated by the Republican State and standardized into undifferentiated produce (see, e.g., Alexander 2002; Hann 1990). The next chapter describes how similar aims were formulated for the fisheries. Processing, trade and consumption of fish and seafood remained, however, largely beyond state influence despite initial attempts at control by the state. Although the state has tried to stimulate seafood consumption, for example by serving fish in military canteens, it has been less effective in influencing the culinary cultures of seafood. The official focus has been on the nutritional value of seafood. The importance of seafood consumption in the negotiation of identities therefore went unnoticed in official presentations of culture and consumption in Turkey. There came to be a large distance between idealized 'Turkish' culture and the actual practices and meanings related to seafood. In particular, the elite Istanbul-style seafood culture, together with Istanbul in general, was marginalized or ignored in state approaches to the fishery sector.

CHAPTER 3

# Fisheries and the State

Through a historical overview ranging from the Ottoman era until present, this chapter details the changing approach of the state to the fisheries. What interests did the Ottoman and Republican state have in the fisheries? To what degree and in what manner has the state influenced fishing practices? What has the role of science been? At a general level there has been a shift in emphasis in state policy from taxation to economic development, and, recently, to natural resource management. In parts of the Ottoman Empire, and especially in Istanbul, fishing was a very important industry. The Ottoman state heavily taxed these fisheries but also formally acknowledged local management forms. One might therefore envision that indigenous or traditional ecological knowledge together with comanagement could have constituted useful management tools in the Turkish fisheries. This chapter explores what happened to these management forms and surveys how and why the State policies that underpinned them discontinued.

## Fishing during the Ottoman Era

Turkish fisheries in the Black Sea and the Sea of Marmara are today among the largest fisheries in the Middle East. Istanbul and Trabzon on the eastern Black Sea coast constitute the two major centres of fishing in contemporary Turkey. There is fairly rich source material concerning prerepublican fishing in Istanbul, but almost nothing about fishing in Trabzon during the same period. The noted traveller and writer Evliya Çelebi, among others, describes an especially rich fishing tradition in  ·
Constantinople. Since ancient times a variety of different fishing technologies has been known and used there and elsewhere in the empire.[22] Certainly fishing in Constantinople had a special position in the empire and was considered throughout Europe to be very advanced. In

1723 The French Minister of the Marine commissioned twelve paintings of the Istanbul fishers' method of fishing as part of a program to revive French fishing (Mansel 1995).

Evliya Çelebi also visited Trabzon, of which he gives fish and fishing some mention. He limits his discussion of Trabzon's fish primarily to the *hapsi* (hamsi) (İhsan 1972: 14–15). Of the fishers we learn only that they are ranked lowest among the seven classes of people in Trabzon that Çelebi identifies (Çelebi 1991: 173). Although fishing in Trabzon probably shared much of the fishing technology and terminology of Istanbul, it appears that fishing in these two places developed to some extent into distinct traditions. Several factors combine to allow consideration of fishing in Trabzon as a partly independent tradition, including: a particular focus on hamsi (and the need for special technology, such as the *roşi* – fish schoop-net); a tradition of catching dolphins in the Black Sea region (a specialty of Sürmene); different ways of calculating the shares in the fisheries; and some region-specific fishery terminology. At the beginning of the twentieth century double or triple-walled trammel nets were called *molozma* in Trabzon (Kazmaz 1994: 273) and *dıfana* in Istanbul (Devedjian 1926).

While hamsi fisheries supplied an important food for people in the Black Sea region, dolphin oil was more important as an export commodity. Fish oil (in other words dolphin oil) is mentioned already in sixteenth century sources (Gökbilgin 1962) as well as in many later sources (Yıldırım 1990: 516). In 1940 twelve teams, comprised of forty to fifty persons each, were engaged in the dolphin fishery in Sürmene. Although some fishers went to catch dolphins in Russian waters before the First World War (Yıldırım 1990: 517), the fishing activities in Trabzon and other Black Sea towns were for the most part very local. There was probably little direct contact between Trabzon and Istanbul fishers. Moreover, there seems to have been little fishing outside of the urban centres in Ottoman times and during the early Republic. Except for the hamsi catches, which reached the general populace, poor and rich, urban and rural, the Trabzon market must have been considerably smaller than the Istanbul market. In the eastern Black Sea region fishing as a livelihood and an adaptation to a monetary economy was probably limited to the city of Trabzon and a few other towns. Trabzon was not a great exporter of fish (at times the town imported fish). During Ottoman times export of salt sturgeon and caviar from the northern shores of the Black Sea to Constantinople was much more important (Bryer 1980: 382–383). *Hamsi-Name* (İhsan 1972), first published in 1928, is in its entirety dedicated to the hamsi, but as in other sources one finds little information concerning the social organization of fishing in Trabzon and how it was treated by the state, and rather more about the culinary and poetic elaborations of this popular fish.

Although Constantinople may have had a special position in Ottoman fisheries thanks to a large urban market and very favourable natural conditions, I believe that a survey of sources about fishing in Constantinople would reveal some general information concerning the Ottoman administration's approach to fish and fisheries. In Constantinople fishing with the *dalyan*, a special 'Turkish' variant of fishing weir, was both an important and widespread technique. The dalyan is usually constructed by driving pieces of wood into the seabed to form a trap into which fish, in particular migratory fish, swim. Sometimes the entire trap is constructed of wood; more often nets are stretched between poles. One or more men keep watch from a tower located beside the dalyan and as soon as a shoal has entered the weir they signal to other crew to close the opening of the dalyan. In Constantinople the dalyans were set up every spring and autumn, with the opening directed southwards and northwards respectively to capture the fish that migrated through the strait.

Dalyans have been used in the Black Sea, Marmara and Aegean Seas (von Brandt 1984: 161–62; Çelebi 1984: 185–87; Kahane et al. 1958: 478–80; Marciniak and Jentoft 1992; Naval intelligence Division 1944: 96) since the pre-Byzantine era (Oğuz 1976: 592). In other maritime areas under some Ottoman influence, such as along the Arab peninsular, there have been seemingly different and independent traditions of fishing (see, e.g., Serjeant 1968: 486–514). Along the coast of what constitutes present day Turkey, the use of dalyans during the Ottoman era was especially important in Constantinople and in parts of the Sea of Marmara and the Aegean Sea (for dalyans and *voli* places along the Bosporus, see Figure 3.1). There are, however, few reports of dalyans in what is now the Turkish Black Sea region. There were several dalyans on the Black Sea coast near the mouth of the Bosporus, probably close enough to supply Istanbul with fresh fish. At Sinop there were eight dalyans in the beginning of the twentieth century (Devedjian 1926), and according to fishers in Sinop there were three or four dalyans in operation there until the mid 1970s. I have come across no reference to or mention of such weirs in Trabzon. However, further east, there were, and possibly still are, a few dalyans. One reason for the absence of dalyans in Trabzon may have been a lack of suitable sites for their use. The construction and operation of dalyans requires shallow and fairly protected waters on a fish migration route, conditions hard to satisfy in Trabzon.

The right to use dalyans was granted by the Sultan (or, if far from Constantinople, by local lords). By distributing such privileges, a strategy in no way restricted to fishing, the Sultan both secured followers (those granted the leases) and income from taxes. Charles White[23] gives an interesting description of one of the larger dalyans in the vicinity of Constantinople (White 1845, Vol. I: 88–90):

MER NOIRE

**VOLIS (Places for reserved fishing)**

| | | |
|---|---|---|
| 1 Büyük Liman | 35 Altınbaş | 69 Çengelköy |
| 2 Sazlıdere | 36 Dolmabahçe | 70 Karakol-önü |
| 3 Küçük Semerkaya | 37 Fındıklı Cami-önu | 71 Çöplük İskelesi |
| 4 Büyük Semerkaya | 38 Fındıklı Aralık İsk. | 72 Çöplük-Paşa Limanı |
| 5 Sarıkaya | 39 Han-önü | 73 Dereağzı |
| 6 Kumsal | 40 Kasımpaşa Dereağzı | 74 Mumhanı-önu |
| 7 Sarıtaş ve İskele | 41 Cibali Değirmen-önu | 75 Şemsipaşa |
| 8 Mutfak | 42 Cibali İskelesi | 76 Eskivoli (Kınalıada) |
| 9 Yenimahalle | 43 Ayakapı | 77 Aya Foti " |
| 10 Saray | 44 Fener | 78 Petrokilis " |
| 11 Çamur | 45 Fener İskelesi | 79 Piyasa (Burgazada) |
| 12 Sığ | 46 Balat kayakhanesi | 80 Manastır " |
| 13 Bülbül Sokak | 47 Hasköy Cami-altı | 81 Psitu " |
| 14 Maltız–Çarşı | 48 Soğan Adası | 82 Halik " |
| 15 [Surp Hiripsimyants] | 49 Poyraz | 83 Dam " |
| Ermeni Kilisesi | 50 Filburun | 84 Niriça " |
| 16 Kefeliköy | 51 Gökkaya | 85 Cami (Heybeliada) |
| 17 Çakaldere | 52 Kavak | 86 Baş " |
| 18 Ağaçaltı | 53 Macar | 87 Apidya " |
| 19 Kireçburnu | 54 İncirdibi | 88 Yalaki " |
| 20 Kalender | 55 Başvoli | 89 Değirmen " |
| 21 Tarabya | 56 Dip–Ocak | 90 Stra " |
| 22 Yeniköy Tabyası | 57 Kaplumbağa–Taş | 91 Kundo " |
| 23 İstiniye | 58 Sığ | 92 Çamliman' " |
| 24 Boyacıköy | 59 Serviburun | 93 Salhane (Büyükada) |
| 25 Baltalimanı | 60 Toptaş | 94 Man " |
| 26 Bebek | 61 Burunbahçe | 95 Yeni–voli " |
| 27 Bebek Feneri | 62 Kozaltı | 96 Petro–voli " |
| 28 Arnavutköy | 63 Çubuklu | 97 Mavro–vroho " |
| 29 Taşvoli | 64 Hamam İskelesi | 98 Hakiki " |
| 30 Kuruçeşme | 65 Göksu | 99 Kokordoviya " |
| 31 Defterdar Yeni–voli | 66 Kabaklı | 100 Yorguli " |
| 32 Ortaköy Cami–arkası | 67 Vaniköy | 101 Dalyan " |
| 33 Ortaköy Cami–önü | 68 Manyat | 102 Meyandros " |
| 34 Haraççıbaşı | | 103 Sedef " |

**MAP OF FISHERIES**
IN THE WATERS OF CONSTANTINOPLE

1. The placement and limits of Dalyans
2. The placement of Volis
3. The placement of oyster beds

D = Dalyan V = Voli ⬤ = Oyster beds

by

**KAREKIN DEVEDJIAN**

**DALYANS**

| | | |
|---|---|---|
| 1 Karaburun | 29 Kumkapı | |
| 2 Kilyos | 30 Yedikule | |
| 3 Uzunya | 31 Taşlıkçi and Katrehane | |
| 4 Mermercik | 32 Göçburun and Yolağzı | |
| 5 Öreke | 32* Kapanık and Yeni– | |
| 6 Bağlar–altı | Dalyan | |
| 7 Garibçe | 33 Soğan Adası | |
| 8 Büyükliman | 34 Anadolufeneri | |
| 9 Karataş | 35 Filburnu | |
| 10 Mavromolos | 36 Anadolukavağı | |
| 11 Sırataş | 37 Ümüryeri | |
| 12 Otuzbirsuyu | 38 Sivriburun | |
| 13 Tellitabya | 39 Saray (Beykoz Sarayı | |
| 14 Pazarbaşı | açığında) | |
| 15 Mesarburnu | 40 Beykoz | |
| 16 Bülbül Sokak | 41 Karacaburun | |
| 17 Barutçubaşı | 42 Toptaş | |
| 18 Büyükdere | 43 Kanlıca | |
| 19 Çay | 44 Vaniköy | |
| 20 Kefeliköy | 45 Çengelköy | |
| 21 Kireçburnu | 46 Üsküdar | |
| 22 Kalender | 47 Salıstra and Şapka | |
| 23 Yeniköy | 48 Kiri | |
| 24 İstiniye | 49 Soğanlık | |
| 25 Bebek | 50 Aya Nikola or Batmış | |
| 26 Küçük Bebek | 51 Karataş | |
| 27 Salıpazarı | 52 Dil | |
| 28 Ahırkapı | | |

ILES DES PRINCES

MER DE MARMARA

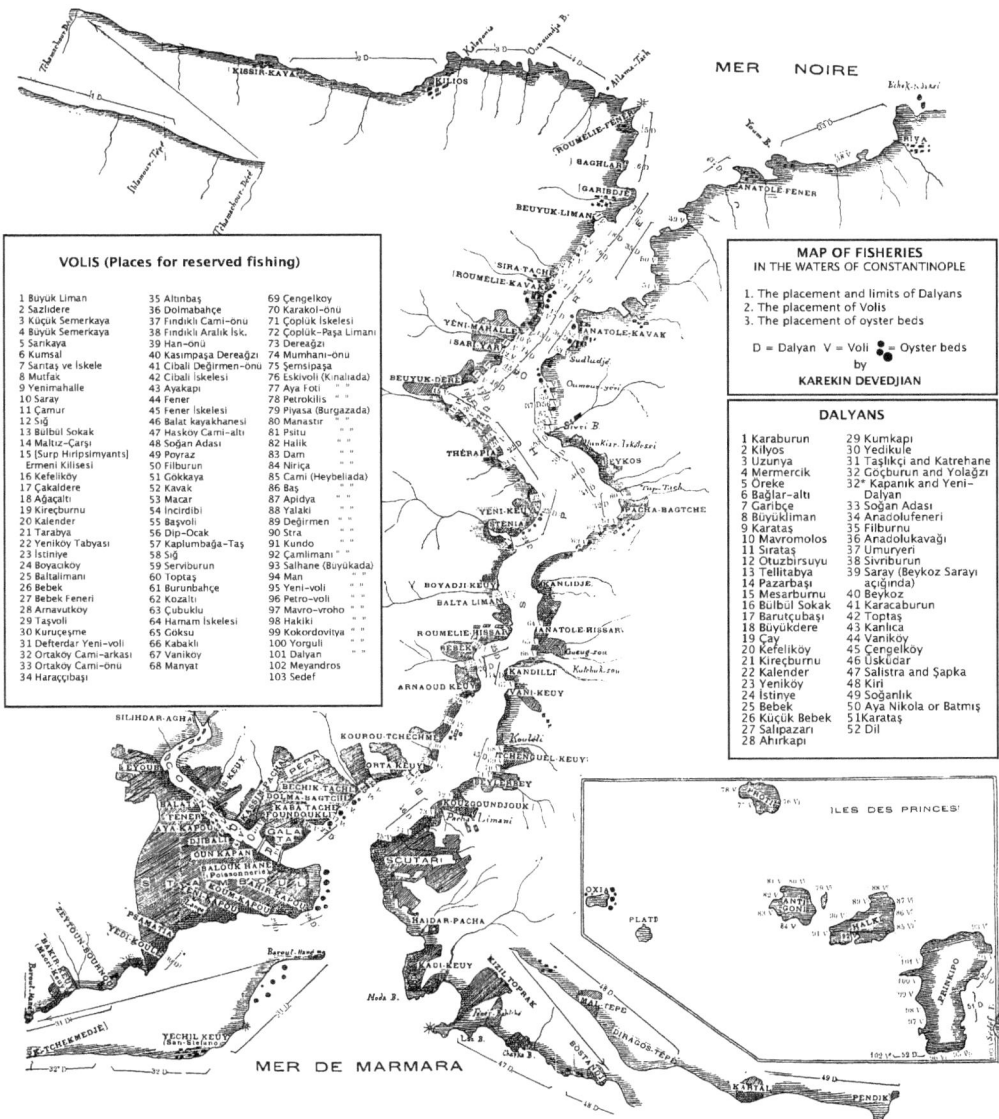

**Figure 3.1. Map of privileged fishing spots along the Bosporus.** Devedjian's map of fishing weirs (dalyan) and seine fishing locations (*voli*) in the Bosporus. Source: Devedjian 1926; Deveciyan 2006. Map reprinted with permission from Aras Yayıncılık. In boxes, text is adapted to English from the French 1926 original, while names are given in modern Turkish, as in Deveciyan 2006.

[The dalyan] at the small...island of Cromyon (onion) [on the Black Sea coast east of the mouth of the Bosporus] is of considerable magnitude, and occupies one hundred and fifteen men, with twelve or more large boats. A third of the latter, with proportionate crews, are employed in carrying fish to the market; the remainder are constantly engaged in working the nets. This fishery is rented by Achem Agha, a respectable Turk, from the grand marshal, Riza Pacha, who himself farms the fisheries on this coast from government. ... The organization of Achem Agha's dallyan differs only from those already described in its magnitude, and in the peculiarities arising from situation. As many as twenty thousand palamoud [bonito] and five hundred sword-fish are frequently trapped in the course of twenty-four hours.

The operation of the fixed dalyans implied clear and sanctioned rules for gear use and access to a specified sea space. Dalyans were usually erected on seascapes that were also suited for casting seines, primarily shallow waters close to shore, generally called *voli* places. The use of seines on voli places was likewise often restricted to a village or a person. As in the case of dalyans, the right to cast seines at volis was granted by the Sultan (Koçu 1960: 2014). Devedjian[24] (1926: 411–434) made an extensive and detailed list of volis in his comprehensive work on fish and fisheries in Istanbul and the Sea of Marmara at the beginning of the twentieth century. He pays special attention to volis in the Bosporus and the Sea of Marmara, but also mentions some outside of this region, for example five around Görele (ibid.: 434) on the eastern Black Sea coast. A wide variety of rules applied to the around five hundred volis that he lists. The use of some is described simply as *libre pour tous le pêcheurs* or *tous le monde, réservé au proprietare,* or reserved for inhabitants of a particular village. However, for many others he notes more specific and detailed customary rules (*us et coutumes*). The customary rules for use of the Sténia voli in the Bosporus are described this way (Devedjian 1926: 413):[25]

The fishing is reserved for seine boats from Sténia and their co-proprietors who live in Kanlidja and Indjir-keuy. It is exploited during winter and summer. Every boat from Sténia pays an annual rent to the proprietors [of the voli]. If the fishers from Sténia or the boats of the proprietors are not present, the boats with seines or beach seines from other places may fish without paying any rent. Fishing by seine boats is decided by drawing lots.

Devedjian's material is supported by other sources. According to Salamone, who recounts the memoirs of Greeks fishers who left the Marmara Islands in the early 1920s, there was (Salomone 1987: 77):

a system of territoriality which strictly defined the areas of the Sea of Marmaras within the vicinity of the Marmaras Islands which could be exploited by each village. The Sea of Marmaras was treated, in other words, as a landed territory within the Ottoman feudal bureaucratic system. Each village received a franchise from the Turkish authorities delineating which 'fishing spots'... could be exploited. ... [O]nly companies from that particular village could fish there.

He notes that ten *'voles'* (volis) were allotted to the village of Galmi on the Marmara Islands and that the fishers were not allowed to fish in other villages' volis. Further, Devedjian (1926: 439) writes of the customary right of possessors of volis to destroy any fishing equipment set on the voli. Thus, restrictions placed on access or use of gear were primarily intended to protect the rights of those entitled to exploit the resources rather than the resource itself. Nonetheless, there seems also to have been a general understanding that one should avoid catching undersized fish. In the Sea of Marmara the use of small-meshed hamsi nets was officially permitted all year, but only as long as hamsi were to be seen (Devedjian 1926: 50).[26] This must have been nearly impossible to police. Moreover, there were regulations that stipulated seasonal limits in certain fisheries. These were certainly marginal concerns in a fishery regime in which fish were perceived to be abundant and where taxing was a major state objective.

Thus, a very large share of the fishing activity in Turkey during the Ottoman era was highly regulated, with a wide variety of specific rules of access. The rules were to a large degree sanctioned by the state. A combination of the limited portability of much of the fishing gear and the state's interest in distributing privileges and securing taxes, facilitated a high degree of 'closure' (Pálsson 1991) in the fisheries, especially where levels of activity and profits were high.

## Tax … and Tax Again

Law, tax, war and the provision of the capital with food and other necessities were the main concerns of the Ottoman State. From the fifteenth century the Ottoman State depended on various forms of 'tax farming', short term contracts with local lords that gained the right to collect taxes on behalf of the Sultan, to fund the bureaucracy and the military as well as to supply the imperial family. Tax farming was a flexible administrative model widely used throughout the empire. All land belonged to the Sultan; local lords usually did not receive hereditary rights to land. Although the state tried several times to introduce direct taxation (to be collected by salaried bureaucrats), more than ninety-five per cent of the revenues collected until the end of the empire came by way of financial consortiums and local notables through tax farming (Quataert 1994: 855).

The state designed policies to ensure supplies of sugar, wheat and sheep for the general populace of the capital. Such policies were apparently not aimed at fisheries (there is no account of such in Devedjian and other sources). There is good reason to believe that the Ottoman administration's primary interest in fisheries was its potential for generating tax revenue, securing followers through allocation of privileges, and, to a lesser extent, providing seafood for the palace. Up until the Tanzimat a special corps of Muslim seine fishers were responsible for supplying the Sultan's household with seafood (Koçu 1960: 2013; Efendi 1968: 158). The catch from certain dalyans was probably reserved for the Sultan's household (Kömürciyan 1988: 5; Somçağ 1993/4: 17). Charles White writes: 'All sea and river fisheries are fiscal monopolies; they are farmed annually to the best bidder in each sanjiak (district), generally some wealthy pacha, by whom they are relet to various sub-tenants, under the supreme control of the balyk eminy (inspector of fisheries), who is responsible for the proceeds and police' (White 1845: 90). Salamone writes of the privileged fishing spots around the Marmara Islands that 'the Turkish government only farmed them out by imperial edict for the sake of taxation – and taxation on fishing catch was a steep 20 per cent' (Salomone 1987: 77).

The administration and taxation of fisheries were probably more complex than described above. The State most likely secured income from the fisheries by taxing it in two ways (Somçağ 1993/94). First, many dalyans and volis in the Bosporus were operated according to a tax farming arrangement whereby the renter paid an annual rent or commission (*mukataa*) in return for privileged usufruct (Devedjian 1926; Koçu 1960: 2013; Somçağ 1993/94: 17).[27] One such tax farming (*iltizam*) arrangement may have included the right not only to farm individual dalyan or voli, but all fishing within a certain coastal region. This tax farming system closely resembles the kind of tax farming applied in the much more important agricultural sector during (at least) the nineteenth century. However, rights to some dalyans, like the Beykoz dalyan, were given as reward (*ödül*) to high ranking military officials (*paşa*) and remained in effect private property through inheritance (Pasiner 1993/4: 545).

The second method of taxing the fisheries was a tax (*rüsum*) on sales in the fish market (Somçağ 1993/94: 117). Soon after occupation of Constantinople, the Ottoman rulers established the Balık Emaneti or Balık Eminliği (Fish 'Trustee' or Control). Its chief, the Balık Emin (Fish Chairman), was connected to the Başdefterdar (Ministry of Finances). The Balık Emaneti had the authority – in accordance with the law on trade – to supervise the taxation of all fish brought into Constantinople. Illegal fishing (and marketing) was regarded as a problem; it implied tax evasion and falling prices at the fish market. Such negative results for both the state (less tax) and the clients of the state who had been granted the right to exploit the fishing grounds were unacceptable.[28]

That the primary interest the fisheries held for the state throughout the Ottoman era was its potential as a source of tax revenue is evident from the following oral reminiscence of a refugee Greek who talks about the Marmaras Island at the beginning of the twentieth century: 'We were a village of three hundred families (Galimi), and we had only one Turk among us! The only Turks we saw in our village were the ones that the government sent – 'bureaucrats', they called them *memoudes*[29] in Turkish, that is 'government employees' … Whoever went fishing had to pay them the tax' (Salamone 1987: 77). However, it remains unclear whether the village had to pay both this sales tax and a tax for the franchise.

All in all, until the end of the Ottoman Empire, a complex regime of ownership, local usufruct rights to particular seaspaces, and different kinds and rates of taxation were in operation. Devedjian (1926) distinguished, for instance, between volis with privileged access by village(s) and private volis. There were, moreover, three types of privately operated volis: (1) commissioned volis where six to ten per cent of the gross income was paid to the proprietor, (2) rented volis where a set price was paid, and (3) private volis where only the proprietor had access. Furthermore, rather than applying a universal tax regime, the Ottomans designed special rules for each province. While one cannot easily generalize from Constantinople to the rest of the Ottoman Empire, we know that during the sixteenth century the regime for the Trabzon *livası* (province) included a tax (tithe) on the catch of all kinds of fish as well as a transit tax on fish brought into the town of Trabzon to be transported elsewhere (Gökbilgin 1962). During the sixteenth century, tax revenue from dalyans was entered as a separate category in the official registers of Sinop (Ünal 1988: 192). In addition, fishing in the empire's inland waters was often similarly regulated and taxed (*miri*, tax on state property, of 10–21 %, and 5 %) (Devedjian 1926: Appendix E). While the administration's ambition may have been to tax all 'commercial' fishing within the empire, the state may have had little interest in stimulating change, or 'development', in the fisheries. A 1577 *ferman* (Sultanic decree) orders that Muslim fishers without a permit to use *ığrıp* (seine) should be forbidden to do so: 'let them catch fish the way they have always been doing (*kadimdenberi*)' (Koçu 1960: 2013).

## Prelude to Reforms: Tanzimat and Public Dept Administration

Tanzimat reforms were already focused on education in the 1840s; agriculture and other sectors soon followed. During the latter half of the nineteenth century the state began to implement measures, such as supplying substantial credit, intended to develop the agricultural sector in keeping with ideas of economic progress (and not purely for taxation). A state bureaucracy for agricultural development was established and well-paid agricultural 'controllers' (*müfettişler*) were appointed to serve in the provincial (*vilayet*) centres. In 1888 the Agricultural Bank (Ziraat Bankası) was established in order to handle the credit afforded to farmers. The modernization project included investments in transport and educational infrastructure. Like most other regions of the empire, the eastern Black Sea region was also affected by these initiatives. Trabzon had schools for agriculture (*çiftlik*) and milk production. As early as 1871 there were country credit unions (Memleket Sandıkları) in the district of Vakfıkebir and other rural areas in the region (*Trabzon Vilayeti Salnamesi 1871* 1993: 227). In 1908 almost 30,000 people in the eastern Black Sea region had loans from the Agricultural Bank (Duran 1988).

Did the state take similar steps to develop the fisheries? One of the official Trabzon Yearbooks (Trabzon Vilayeti Salnamesi) from just before the turn of the century notes that 'we must do like the Europeans and try to profit from the hamsi by putting four or five of them in cans' (İhsan 1972: 16). Although the idea of developing the fisheries was clearly not alien to the Ottoman bureaucrats, in general this sector does not seem to have caught the attention of the reformers. Compared to reforms in military organization, education, law, science, or even agriculture, reform of fishery policies were a relative latecomer to the catalogue of reforms. After the middle of the nineteenth century the Ottoman State became increasingly indebted to foreign creditors, and by 1875 the empire was essentially bankrupt. In 1881 the Public Debt Administration (Düyûnu Umumiye İdaresi) was established to manage many of the empire's important sources of income, for the benefit of the foreign creditors and controlled by the major European powers (Zürcher 1993: 88; McCarty 1997: 310). Fisheries in Istanbul and the Marmara region came under the Administration's control.[30] The first coherent legal arrangement for fisheries was codified early in the regime of the Public Debt Administration (1882, or according to some sources 1879).[31] The new law concerned primarily taxation and the protection of usufruct rights to fishing grounds and was thus an 'inscribed' collection and record of existing formal and informal practices.

In the early 1890s the Public Debt Administration brought in the fishery expert de Bellesme to undertake studies with the intention of developing the fisheries (Kazgan 1983: 710). However, the recommendations of this expert were not put into practice. Devedjian was one of the directors of the Istanbul Fish Hall, and his study was commissioned, ratified and first published in Ottoman by the Public Debt Administration in 1915 (Koçu 1960: 2037). In his introduction to this first edition[32] Devedjian articulates objectives beyond taxation when he writes that 'if the Turkish fishers had been enlightened about the progress that had been realized other places, and if they had possessed modern equipment', they would easily have caught fish that they were at that time unable to catch. This, he stresses, would have secured for the country a considerable amount of food, objects of trade and income every year. He laments the lack of fish processing industries that could satisfy the European taste (very expensive canned tuna was imported to Constantinople from Europe) and provide the country with important income.

The extensive mapping of current practices in Devedjian's book, the fishery law, as well as the compilation of Trabzon Province yearbooks between 1869 and 1904, should probably be understood as attempts by the modernizing Ottoman state and semi-colonial foreign powers to codify practices in order to develop and modernize them. The interest of the Public Debt Administration in fisheries did not differ markedly from that of the Ottoman administration. Although the (unrealized) strategy of the Public Debt Administration may have included intervention in the practice and structure of the fisheries, such intervention was probably done with the view of increasing their own revenue. Fishery taxation was likely not very different from earlier arrangements,[33] the main distinctions being that the Public Debt Administration, not the Ottoman State, was at the end of the tax chain, and that they were possibly more effective in policing the tax regime.

## Republican Statism: Lofty Ideals

After the war of independence and the Lausanne treaty (1923) with the European powers, the fisheries administration set up in Istanbul by the Public Debt Administration was taken over by the Turkish Republic's Ministry of Finance (Koçu 1960: 2011).[34] The new Turkish leadership and administration showed a striking determination to intensify the reforms across Turkish society. But was there a new policy concerning the fisheries? Little information is published concerning developments in the fisheries from the establishment of the Republic through 1950. However, it is fairly clear that the new administration, at an ideal level at least, had a different approach to the fisheries than their Ottoman predecessors. In the mid 1930s there were plans for a new fishery law and the establishment of a Fishery Bank (*Tan Gazetesi* 1936; *Akşam Postası* 1938). An Austrian envoy to Turkey, who seems to have worked as an adviser of sorts to the Turkish government during the early 1930s, surveyed and evaluated the government's efforts in many sectors of the Turkish society, among them the fisheries (Ritter von Kral 1938: 81, italics omitted):

> A legal regulation of the Turkish fisheries is planned, which requires detailed preliminary studies. In the meantime provisional measures have been taken to mitigate old evils; for example, abolition of the fishing-tax which had long been felt as an imposition, reduction of duties on tackle and accessories, promotion of sales by increasing the manufacture of canned fish and the consumption in military barracks, public services, schools, etc. In the meantime a decree was drafted to reorganize the entire fisheries law. It contains modern regulations as to admission to the fishery trade, the manner of practicing it, the close-season, the prohibition of the use of explosives,

working conditions, union questions, etc. The material conditions of the fishermen are to be improved by the elimination of middlemen, by a revision of their relations to the lessees and wholesale traders and by the foundation of a Fishery Bank.

Ritter von Kral goes on to note that discussions were held in Ankara between government representatives and parties interested in fisheries, and concludes that '[i]t will thus be seen that the Turkish fishery trade, which procures work and livelihood for many thousands of men and is of the greatest significance for the nutrition of the people, is well on the way to being modernized' (Ritter von Kral 1938: 81).

One can conclude that the new administration's ambitions and plans for fisheries implied a radical break with the existing fishery regime. These ideals were probably greatly influenced by the radical 'statism' ideals of the nationalist-communist *Kadro* ('cadre') movement that led the ideological-political debate during the early 1930s. Yet, partly because of the indecisive and inconsistent approach of the bureaucracy, most of these lofty plans were never implemented (Karaömerlioğlu 1998). After a period of growth in the fisheries during the latter half of the nineteenth century, there seems to have been a general decline during the early Republic.[35] The state's neglect of fishery policy reforms during the early years of the Republic grew, most likely, from economic stagnation coupled with efforts to establish independent industrial production in more important sectors. There was, in effect, little change. Not even the commercial potential of the dolphin fishery in Sürmene was acknowledged by the state. Rather than abolishing the fish trade tax in the 1930s, as had been suggested by Ritter von Kral, the state more likely only reduced it. In 1928 the tax on fish sales was eleven per cent in Trabzon (İhsan 1972). In the years around the establishment of the Republic some fish sales taxes were even increased (Devedjian 1926: 441, 445).

We can blame the lack of effective state policies and economic stagnation in the fisheries from 1920 to 1950. However, the pervasive assertion is that the stagnation can be ascribed to the departure of the Greek population. In her study of *The Fisherman's Problem in the Marmara Sea*, Leyla Taner (1991: 83), who relies primarily on Günlük (1983), claims that '[a]fter the Independence War ... exchange of Greek and Turkish population between Greece and Turkey have swept away the fishing sector.' In public perception as well as in historical sources, the association between fish and Greeks keeps popping up. Many claim, even contemporary Turkish fishers themselves, that the Turks learned the art of fishing from the Greeks. It seems to have been a common conception among European travellers and commentators from the turn of the nineteenth century that fishing and seafaring was yet another occupation that the 'Turks' didn't have a liking for or competence in (see, e.g., Hamilton 1984: 284; Aflalo 1911). In contemporary writings by both Turks and Greeks the views of the

Europeans are reiterated (Günlük 1983; Kuban 1996: 306; Kulingas 1988; Salomone 1987; Terzis 1997).

I believe it would be far too simplistic to regard the fishing sector as purely 'Greek' before and during the Ottoman era, to be succeeded by 'Turks' only after the revolution and population exchanges. Muslims were clearly fishing long before the Greeks left. Although the degree of separation along lines of religious-ethnic background within the fishing sector appears to have varied over time and from place to place, fisheries have probably been the business of a mixed population during the Ottoman centuries. Undoubtedly, the Turks can be said to have learned fishing from the Greeks. The contemporary language of fishing contains to this day a fundament of Greek. But this applies to the entire eastern Mediterranean and northern Africa as well as the Black Sea region (Kahane et al. 1958: ix). Fish terminology, and especially fishing terminology – such as that presented in Devedjian's book – was, and still is, a mixture of Greek and Turkish.

All in all, it is difficult to get a clear picture of the Ottoman fishing population, even in Constantinople. There may have been considerable continuous flux and change throughout the centuries. Furthermore, the Greek presence in Istanbul fishing continued for some decades after the revolution and population exchanges since the Greek population of Istanbul was left out of the population exchange (*mübadele*) with Greece in the 1920s. In 1934 the total Greek population (both Turkish and Greek citizens) was still as high as 100,000, making up approximately one tenth of the population of Istanbul (Millas 1993/94: 365). This number remained stable until the mid 1950s (Mansel 1995: 424) and Greek fishers who were involved in small scale-fishing intermingled with Turkish fishers for decades after the population exchanges.[36]

In the Black Sea region, however, the Greek presence came to a more abrupt end with ethnic conflict and expulsion of the Christian populations in the years before the War for Independence. There is evidence of Muslim fishers in Trabzon at an early date (Lowry 1981: 84) and Muslims/Turks from the eastern Black Sea region have for centuries been deeply involved in fisheries and seafaring (Şen 1998: 235). The Black Sea Turks' competence in fishing is also attested to by the fact that it was primarily Black Sea Muslims who took over the fishing activities of the Greek fishers in the upper Bosporus. Muslims from the environs of Rize, in particular, fleeing from the Russian occupying forces in 1916,[37] settled in Rumelifener and Poyraz, both close to the northern mouth of the Bosporus.

Thus, I cannot agree with Taner's assertion that the fishing sector in Turkey was swept away with the population exchanges after the War of Independence. Although the republican revolution and the population exchanges temporarily reduced the population of experienced fishers and brought about a restructuring of the fisheries, there is insufficient evidence to suggest that it amounted to a complete break with the past. Quite the contrary. The purse-seine technique (*gırgır*) was first developed by fishers in the Greek-Armenian community in Kumkapı (in Istanbul) around 1885 (Devedjian 1926: 333). Yet, the knowledge of the gırgır clearly survived the War of Independence and Greek emigration since it soon afterwards came to be the preferred gear among (Muslim) fishers in Istanbul and the Black Sea.

Instead of regarding fishing and seafaring as something inherent to the 'Greek people', it may be wiser to consider the multicultural Istanbul and Marmara region as the centre of seafaring, fishing, and seafood cultures of the eastern Mediterranean region. The decline or lack of development in the fisheries prior to 1950 might equally be ascribed to a general stagnation in the population and the economy of Istanbul as to the emigration of the Greek fishing communities. The loss of its status as the centre of government to Ankara and a general economic decline meant that people left Istanbul. The upper classes were shrinking and Istanbul was becoming 'poor and provincial' (Mansel 1995: 424). There might simply not have been a market to allow for any substantial expansion in the fisheries during this period. Average per capita consumption of seafood in Istanbul was a mere 5.3 kg during 1939–1948 (currently at 16 kg per capita) and approximately half of fish catches landed in Istanbul were consumed outside of the city.[38] Bonito, important food for the poor during the difficult war years, made up approximately half of the seafood consumption in Istanbul. In the book *Boğaziçi Konuşuyor* ('The Bosporus Talks'), Câbir Vada[39] does not attribute the lack of development in the fisheries to the emigration of the Greeks. Although he laments the stagnation (*durgunluk*) in the Istanbul fisheries, he writes that it had been like that for at least sixty years. 1950 may, therefore, be regarded as a more important watershed in the history of the Turkish fisheries than the emigration of the Greeks in the early 1920s.

## Fisheries on the Development Agenda

After the Second World War important changes took place in the political and economic situation of Turkey. There was increasing international and domestic pressure for democratization and multi-party politics, which meant that parties started to compete for votes. The main contender for power, the Democrat Party, argued for a more liberal economic policy. At the same time, Turkey came within the scope of the Marshall Plan. Between the World Wars the government, aiming at self-sufficiency and economic independence, had given highest priority to the development of heavy industry and the construction of a network of railways. In 1947 the government, still in the hands of the 'Atatürkist' Republican People's

Party (CHP, Cumhuriyet Halk Partisi), drew up a new development plan that emphasized free enterprise, the development of agriculture and agriculture-based industry, and the construction of roads. With American Marshall Plan aid, important new roads were built – for example the Samsun-Trabzon road – and large investments were made in the agricultural sector – with tractors as the chief instrument and symbol (Zürcher 1993: 226).

The new development priorities with their emphasis on agriculture also encompassed fishing when, in 1947, the Ministry of Economy saw the economic potential of this sector. Between 1949 and 1961 the Marshall Plan contributed U.S.$47,000 to Turkish fisheries (Tören 2007). In 1950 probably in an effort to win votes a month before the parliamentary election, the state tax on fish catches was removed.[40] A number of other initiatives to develop the fisheries quickly followed one upon the other.[41] Social policies, on the other hand, did not change appreciably; unions remained illegal. Contrary to the Kadro ideals of eliminating the middleman, no serious attempt was made to check the power of the fish *kabzımal* (wholesale trade commission agents) over the fishers.

In 1952 the semi-autonomous Meat and Fish Foundation (Et ve Balık Kurumu, EBK) was founded within the Ministry of Economy. The goal of EBKs activities were to organize, plan, produce, distribute and research meat and fish resources. The institution received substantial economic assistance from the Marshall Plan and a few years later the EBK commanded a fleet of no fewer than twenty-one boats for various purposes (fishing, research and so on) as well as cold storage facilities in approximately twenty urban centres. The EBK established several fish processing plants, among which was a fish oil and meal factory in Trabzon (1952) that initially processed mostly dolphin oil (Yıldırım 1990: 518). During the 1950s EBK cooperated closely with the FAO and fisheries experts from USA. During the 1950s many studies were undertaken and reports written – often as cooperative projects between Turkish and foreign scientists (Bilecik 2003; Çelikkale et al. 1999). Authorities took initiatives also at regional levels. At a conference in Trabzon in 1952 where the issue of 'progress' in the province was discussed (Trabzon Vilayeti Kalkınma Kongresi 1952), fisheries was explicitly selected as a sector to be developed.

Credit for investments in fishing technology was made available from 1953–54 onward from the 'General Directorate for Agricultural Credit' along the same basic lines as for agriculture. In 1955 the first fisheries statistics were collected and from 1967 were produced annually on the basis of questionnaires (Acara et al. 2001: 124). The state also started to build several new large protected harbours along the exposed Black Sea coast and promoted the establishment of fishery cooperatives. Yet the flood of initiatives during the early 1950s soon lost its impetus. Towards the end of the 1950s the EBK initiative to develop the fisheries dissolved when financial support was withdrawn (Bilecik 2003). Despite various state-lead initiatives during the 1950s and, to a lesser extent, 1960s to develop the fisheries, there was no significant increase in fish catches.

Some years later, fisheries were included in the five year plans, which were drawn up from 1963 onwards, with entire volumes devoted to 'water produce' (*su ürünleri*) in the VI Plan (Acara et al. 1989), VIII Plan (Acara et al. 2001) and IX Plan in 1989, 2001 and 2006 respectively. All in all, however, the 1960s saw fewer initiatives in the fishery sector. In 1971 the old fisheries law (Zabıta-i Saydiye Nizamnamesi) from 1879 was finally replaced by new 'water produce' legislation, after several drafts had been rejected by the parliament during the 1950s (Çelikkale et al. 1999: 290–1). At the same time the responsibility for 'water produce' (as the fisheries were hereafter called) was transferred from the Ministry of Trade (Ticaret Bakanlığı) to a newly established General Directorate for Water Produce (Su Ürünleri Genel Müdürlüğü) within the Ministry for Agriculture (see Figure 3.2 for the organizational structure of the Turkish bureaucracy). This General Directorate established ten regional water produce directorates. The ministry started to draw up and distribute annually a set of regulations for the 'harvesting (hunt) of water produce in the sea and internal waters for commercial purposes' (Denizlerde ve İçsularda Ticari Amaçlı Su Ürünleri Avcılığını … Sirküler). Since 1976 credit and grants have been distributed from a water produce branch (Su Ürünleri Kredilendirme Müdürlüğü) within the Agricultural Bank.

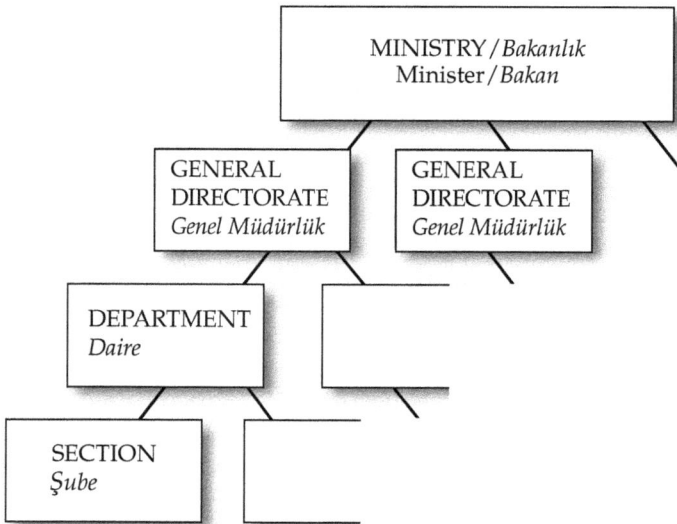

**Figure 3.2. Bureaucratic structure.** Simplified model of the hierarchical structure within a ministry.

# Marine Science

In an article entitled 'The Importance of Fisheries in the Feeding of our Population', a researcher calls for a strengthening of fishery research in Turkey (Baysal 1969: 77):

> Without knowing the results of research it is impossible to reach any favorable outcome from efforts aiming to give direction to the fisheries, in other words it is almost impossible to carry out fishery policies. In all countries research institutions show the way to those who administer fishery policy so that the measures taken will be advantageous. In Norway, for example, there has been continuous research for 60 years, all problems have been solved and fisheries are now part of the normal planning process.

Compared with many European states, including Russia who early established marine research stations on the Black Sea, marine science had a late start in Turkey. Prior to 1950 there were a few initiatives within Istanbul University (prior to 1933 this was named Darülfünun). These efforts were directed towards investigations of marine life forms. Within the Public Debt Administration a few initiatives were also taken to investigate fisheries. Scientists from various European countries played a significant role in these efforts (Bilecik 2003). Due to limited resources however research was very restricted and there was little academic continuity.

The trajectory of contemporary Turkish marine research originates with the Hydrobiology Research Institute (Hidrobioloji Araştırma Enstitüsü) at Istanbul University. The Institute, which EBK helped to finance, was established in 1951 under the leadership of Professor Kosswig, a German who had fled the Nazi regime in 1937. He was the prime motor in Turkish research on marine life forms until he returned to Germany in 1955. In addition, many foreign fishery experts visited Istanbul during the 1950s as part of the Marshall Plan and various FAO initiatives as well as a Turkey-Japan cooperation framework (Bilecik 2003: 43–52). EBK started their own Fishery Research Centre in Istanbul in 1955 and initiated the publication series *Balık ve Balıkçılık* ('Fish and Fisheries'), partly in collaboration with the Institute. The research activities of EBK and the Hydrobiology Research Institute levelled off during the 1960s. With the reorganizations in higher education after the coup in 1980, the Hydrobiology Institute in Istanbul was closed down, and its resources transferred to the 'Water Produce College' which was established as a branch of the Ministry of Education in 1973, but affiliated to Istanbul University in 1983.

During the 1960s and 1970s various smaller research units started within the Ministries. The activities of these various research bodies were pooled and strengthened in 1984 with the establishment of state water produce research institutes (Devlet Su Ürünleri Araştırma Enstitüsü). During the 1980s many more Water Produce Colleges (Su Ürünleri Yüksek

Okulu) were established within major universities. Most of these have since evolved into faculties or departments that provide degrees at both MSc and PhD levels (Ergüven 1983; Acara et al. 1989: 172–3; Özbey 1989). In 1999 water produce research in Turkey consisted of three state institutes and seventeen departments or sections at universities. At these university departments and faculties alone around five hundred academicians were employed in 1999 (Çelikkale et al. 1999: 316). Moreover, several university biology departments are currently involved in marine research. Thus, development in Turkish water produce science has since the early 1950s been intimately intertwined with state initiatives in the fishery sector. As indicated by the citation above, marine science was, especially during the 1950s and 1960s, regarded by the elite as a prerequisite for development and growth in the fishery sector.

## Development Ideals: Production and Proteins

One day in 1991 an old small-boat fisherman told me about fishing in bygone days. We were sitting on the sand among the small fishing boats and looking across the harbour at the large fishing boats and the factory of the Çarşıbaşı cooperative. I asked him whether he had been a member of the cooperative. 'No, that's not my business (*işim olmaz*),' he replied. 'The cooperative is only for the owners of the large boats (*mal sahibleri*, 'proprietors'),' and added, 'They call it the *water produce* cooperative. We used to say *fish!*'

In the Republican era the state's approach to fisheries had become framed within a new discourse, a framing that was indicated in Devedjian's work but only reached its 'mature' form and actually guided policy efforts after 1950. Since the 1950s the discourse about production (first *istihsal*, later *üretim*), proteins, modernization, development, progress (*kalkınma*), technological development, and the exemplars of Europe and Japan, has been pervasive throughout fisheries science and management in Turkey. For instance, there seems to be almost a template for the introduction to Turkish fishery texts. This template is adhered to by state personnel within the bureaucracy as well as by many scientists. Various permutations of this basic model can be found in the introductions to many different texts, including reports from the State Research Institutes (e.g., TFRI 1992); symposiums on water produce (e.g., Agricultural Bank 1982); planning documents (e.g. Acara et al. 1989; Acara et al. 2001); and to some extent in scientific papers (e.g., Düzgüneş and Karacam 1991). One example of adherence to this template is the table of contents of the first substantive chapter in a textbook on 'Fishing and Catch Technology' (Sarıkaya 1980):

II. THE STATE OF WATER PRODUCE IN THE WORLD AND IN TURKEY

1. The general state of water produce in the world
2. The state of water produce in Turkey
3. A comparison between our country and countries which are developed with regard to water produce
4. The importance of water produce from a nutritional perspective
5. The water produce policies in Turkey
6. The catch modes (*şekilleri*) for water produce

A second example is an extract from the opening speech made by the head of the Foundation for Economic Research (İktisadi Araştırmalar Vakfı) for a panel discussion organized in 1988 on the topic of hamsi fisheries in the Black Sea. The speech was made at a point when the hamsi fisheries had seen their longest sustained increases in catch (Dikmen 1988: 7):

> Actually, fishing is one of the undeveloped (*gelişmemiş*) activity sectors of the Turkish economy. Its share of the GNP does not even reach half a per cent. The annual catch of fish does not even amount to 600,000 tons. Per capita production is 10–11 kilos whereas consumption [only] totals 8–9 kilos. In countries like Norway and Japan where fisheries are developed, the per capita production and consumption amount to six to seven times these figures.

These two examples illustrate several characteristics of the Turkish modernizing approach.

First, the Western scientific-technological approach came to be seen as a guiding star at the expense of an appreciation of contemporary 'traditional' technology and organization. Fisheries was seen as an undeveloped (*gelişmemiş*) and primitive (*ilkel*) sector to be transformed – in terms of technology, organization, profile of consumption – in the image of a modern, Western prototype, and, notably, not a Russian/Soviet prototype. In the 1930s the Soviet Union developed a modern fishing fleet in the Azov Sea and the Black Sea, organized as state-directed collectives (*kolkhoz*), which regularly caught far more fish than the Turkish fleet (Knudsen 1997; Knudsen and Toje 2008). Yet, despite their 'production' success, they were discredited, like all Soviet models after 1950, because they were 'communist'.

Secondly, developing the fisheries was, and, to a certain extent, still is, considered by many within the state bureaucracy to be a national mission or duty (Özbey 1989: 5):[42]

> In conclusion one may say that – as one may also understand from the historic development to the present– it is a national task and necessity to put into operation as rational, scientific and economic a management as possible in the administration of this issue and in finding solutions to the problems that the fisher, the producer and the industrialist face in their use of the products of our seas and 'internal waters' – these waters that shall become our future food depot.

Third, concepts such as per capita consumption and 'production' (*üretim*) are central to gaining an understanding of the bureaucratic approach to the fisheries. Fisheries emerged, or was created, as a sector to be mapped, manipulated, calculated and researched; a sector contributing to the 'economy' of the national state, not to the tax revenue of a 'backward' state. The whole apparatus of 'modern' and 'rational' economic measurements and polices was mobilized to work on what now emerged as a 'sector'.

Fourth, one further quality was added to the discourse when fisheries administration was 'agriculturalized'. With the passing of the new law in 1971, and the transfer of responsibility for fisheries to the Ministry for Agriculture, 'water produce' and 'production' (*üretim*) replaced 'fish' (*balık*) and 'catch' (*av*) in the state approaches to the sector. 'Proteins', 'food' (*gıda*), (human) 'population', and aquaculture became important topics and concerns. The concept of 'water produce' was only mentioned before 1970 in connection with the draft law. In an edited book on Black Sea fisheries and water produce cooperatives (Çakıroğlu 1969), prepared by the Ministry of Trade (Ticaret Bakanlığı) that was at the time responsible for fisheries, 'water produce' is occasionally mentioned. Overall, however, the various authors write about 'fish' production, 'fishery' cooperatives, and so forth. The Ministry of Trade in 1968 prepared a report entitled 'Report on Turkish Fisheries' (*Türkiye Balıkçılığı Hakkında Rapor*). Yet, after 1971 the new vocabulary spread surprisingly rapidly and soon became ubiquitous. In the official Yearbook of Trabzon Province 1973 fisheries are discussed over (only) one fourth of a page under the heading 'water produce', as a subsection of husbandry within the sixteen page chapter on agriculture. In place of writing about 'catches', the fishery statistics started to list 'production' of the different kinds of marine and fresh water animals (though this is rendered as 'catch' in the English translation).

Most scientists adopted the new usage in their publications, and the universities started to train 'water produce engineers'. The water produce bureaucracy has until recently primarily employed agricultural engineers even though water produce engineers have been trained since 1973 (Bilecik 2003). Agricultural engineer is a type of training that has long been important and widespread in Turkey and most of the first generation water produce (or marine) scientists also received their degrees in agriculture, or sometimes aquaculture. In water produce research there is a significant focus on and resources allocated to fish farming[43] and 'internal waters' (rivers, lakes and so forth). While there are three (small) water produce research institutes in Turkey, there are almost sixty state research institutes conducting research on agriculture or husbandry. The Tea Research Institute in Rize opened in 1924 (Özdemir 1983: 266, 272–3), long before tea had become an important cash crop, while the first water produce research institute (in Trabzon) was not established before 1987.

How easily and willingly scientists changed their vocabulary to the new context and how suffused the water produce bureaucracy and marine science became with agricultural engineers indicate, I think, how strongly marine scientists, also at universities, have been connected to the state and its policies.

Fifth, the examples above indicate that the attention to 'produce' and 'production' in state policy is bound up with a concern about the citizens', or the subjects', diet. Many policy documents[44] and academic texts refer explicitly to protein deficiency in the diet when arguing for the development of the Turkish fisheries. The Republican bureaucracy had gradually become concerned with the nutritional composition of people's diet.[45] This was already evident in the days of Atatürk when, for example, he emphasized the importance of sugar production so that 'healthy children will not be a utopian ideal' (Alexander 2002: 74). This was a new way to 'treat' food, framed by a new discourse of scientific rationalization, once more modelled on Western templates. The state developed a nutrition policy that included nutritional education especially directed towards children since 'most of our people are not knowledgeable about nutrition' (Tezcan 1982: 130–131).

Together these five aspects seem to articulate a version of what James Scott (1998) has termed 'high modernism', a 'strong version of belief in scientific and technical progress'. Although not acknowledged by Scott, in Turkey, especially during the statism years and in the Kemalist ideology, we find an archetypical instance of high modernist ideals (Bozdoğan 2001). The focus on a national mission of stimulating the economy, raising production, and providing the population with proteins is indicative of, and was made possible by, a general shift in what the elite classes saw as the role of the state elite in society: agents of a radical restructuring of society. In contrast to the classical Ottoman state elite, the new Republican elite envisioned complete societal restructuring as the path to arrive at some ideal modern Turkish nation state. It had become the responsibility of the state not only to show concern about people's 'way of living', but also to authoritatively guide this. The state became increasingly concerned about its subjects' welfare, lifestyles and capacities. In order to reach the new goals, the people, especially the villagers, had to be guided and educated in line with rational scientific knowledge.

In employing the tactics of governmentality on the level of economy, Foucault writes, the family becomes an instrument rather than a model, and statistics the tool when considering the population at large (Foucault 1991: 101):

> [P]opulation comes to appear above all else as the ultimate end of government. ...[It] has as its purpose not the act of government itself, but the welfare of the population, the improvement of its condition, the increase of its wealth, longevity, health, etc. ... The new science called political

economy ... is accompanied by the formation of a type of intervention characteristic of government, namely intervention in the field of economy and population.

This analytical model has primarily been used to address the historical development of European states. Mitchell (1988) has argued, however, that many of the more radical tactics of governmentality were actually first implemented in the colonies, and in a similar vein, Mintz (1985) regards the old colonial world as a 'laboratory of modernity'. Yet, the distinction between a state based on sovereignty and one concerned with governmentality has also been fruitfully employed to analyse the changes within the Ottoman and Turkish states. In an essay on modernity, religion and the Ottoman and Republican state, Nalbatanoğlu (1994) notes that, contrary to the classical Ottoman 'art of statecraft' regime, 'population' was a calculable 'standing reserve' within a new 'science of politics' in the early Turkish Republic. But, there was no sudden change from sovereignty to governmentality with the establishment of the Republic. A change towards governmentality had been under way since the early nineteenth century. The first effort to quantify population came with the 1830 census. In the era of the Tanzimat reforms (1839–1871) the central government assumed responsibility for education, health and sanitation, all of which had previously been in the hands of the religious institutions (foundations) and local communities. Thus, inspired by European models as well by the success of Mehmet Ali's reforms in Egypt, the Ottoman state began to change its focus from territory to human resources and developed new powers to affect the day-to-day life of people. In this process the Sultans and the governments paid a great deal of attention to the 'power' of statistics as a means of obtaining information about the population (Karpat 1992).

In general, 'governmentality' started earlier in the Ottoman Empire than in many other 'non-European' areas of the world. Note, however, that this change towards governmentality took place well before the development of Turkish nationalism and the idea of 'one (Turkish) people'. The idea of 'governing a population' came chronologically before the idea of 'legitimacy based upon representing a people' (in other words, nationalism). Nonetheless the instruments that the late Ottoman State developed to influence the population, especially education and statistics, became important tools in the nationalist project of the Young Turks (1908–18) and Kemalists. When these instruments were combined with the development of indigenous social sciences from the end of the nineteenth century (Karpat 1992), a far more penetrating process of social engineering became possible. It was not just that science was seen as the best guide in improving technology; policy itself was being 'scienticized'. Social science played a prominent role in the reform process and legitimated a macro perspective on society and ideas of social change that focused on plans and projects, not on any 'inherent' dynamism of development (Mardin 1997a). The new Republican state elite went much further than those of the late Ottoman Empire in envisioning a 'new' society, an ideal nation, and new kinds of men and women to populate it. The elite went so far as to design policies that were directed at reshaping the subjects' selves. In one sense it is possible to say that the new regime was more populist; on the other hand, it was also quite paternalistic (or Jacobin).

What about fisheries? The first attempts at 'governing' them beyond taxation were taken by the semi-colonial structure of the Public Debt Administration, first by 'unimplemented' recommendations of the foreign expert de Bellesme in the 1890s. Somewhat later, the meticulous work by Devedjian exemplifies the general tendency of trying to map, register and quantify 'what there is', not only for taxation purposes, but in order to be able to stimulate economic development. A report prepared by the Istanbul Chamber for Trade and Industry in 1924, just after the establishment of the Republic, notes the 'need for development': fishermen ought to become enlightened, fisheries should be guided by natural science and technology modernized (ICC 2006: paragraph 26). In the statism years up until 1950, high modernity ideals concerning fisheries development were articulated, but not implemented. When the state finally started to implement fishery policies from 1950, and especially from the early 1970s, it did so to a large extent in accordance with the new idealistic plans and aims designed for the fisheries and at great financial cost. Rather than securing income through taxes, the new fisheries policies (especially from the 1970s onwards) became a drain on the state's economy through subsidized credit, grants, investments in infrastructure (harbours, cold storage halls), research and bureaucracy. The new Water Products Law stipulates that the total level of taxation on fish sales may not exceed three per cent and is only to be collected by the municipalities.[46] The priorities of this new policy comes out 'crisp and clear' in the 2001 report from the State Planning Organization where it is stated that 'in order to raise a healthy generation … the water produce tax rates should be decreased so that the consumers can buy water produce more easily' (Acara et al. 2001: 113).[47]

Most of the instruments, or tactics, employed to work on the fisheries have already been mentioned. They include statistics, the model exemplar organized by the state (the EBK initiative), establishment of cooperatives, education of the fishers, establishment of a fishery bureaucracy, extension of credits and grants, codification of laws and regulations, design of short- and long-term plans, arrangement of symposiums and conferences, stimulation of water produce science, and investments in physical infrastructure. All of this is new. Before 1950 these were imaginable and desirable, but were yet to be put into operation.

Of these new tactics, science has attained an instrumental position. Ideally, as expressed in the citation on page 57, the other tactics follow the lead of the sciences. At a large conference concerning the Black Sea a leading marine scientist addressed the audience: 'As everyone knows, the Black Sea is now exhausted (*yorgunmaktadır*) by a range of problems. How can we find answers, solutions, to these problems? *Who* is going to give the answers? Those who know (*tanımak*) the Black Sea very well, the *scientists* of the Black Sea countries, will provide the answers.'[48] The developmental ideals for the fisheries have been instrumental in instilling in the bureaucrats, managers and scientists the idea of a decisive break between past traditions and new developments. Indeed, the very existence of marine sciences as a profession in Turkey has been a result of state-initiated reforms. Marine scientists have, at least at the ideal level, subsequently been entrusted with the role of custodians of progress (and recovery) in the fisheries.

Although there had been some biological research on marine life at Istanbul University during the early Republic, a Turkish science of sea, fish, and fisheries started to develop and grow only when the state, together with foreign support, launched its initiative for developing fisheries. The sciences were part and parcel of this mission, and except for the impressive efforts of Kosswig there seems to have been little independent academic drive towards the development of marine sciences. During the 1950s the institutional linkages between the semi-autonomous EBK and the scientific communities were evidence of and speak to the role of science as an agent for development. However, although the water produce research and education sector has since become fairly large and the university sector is formally independent of the executive branches of the bureaucracy, the position of 'scientist' (*bilim adamı/insanı*) is seldom considered an independent and purely academic position. For most scientists and certainly for the 'man on the street' (or at sea) in Turkey, a scientist is first and foremost a state employee, a *görevli*, working on tasks assigned to her by the state. Of course there is some individual variation as to how scientists themselves perceive their role and their relation to the state, but the idea of the scientist as a state representative, a spearhead in the national civilizing project, is indeed widespread. Thus, there is often little difference between scientists and state bureaucrats, the former are simply seen as one kind of state bureaucrat (*devlet memuru*). The frequent movement of persons between positions in the ministries, the state research institutes and the university departments reinforces this impression.

## Unfulfilled Ideals

High modernist ideals have been influential in many modernizing states. But their influence varies by the degree to which the ideals have been transformed into plans and programs and implemented as practical policy.

Furthermore, as it is Scott's main concern to demonstrate, many of these high modernist ideals, when transformed into grand state projects, have not been successful. Foucault (1977) concedes that the tactics employed in a state-guided disciplinary society, exemplified by the change from punishment to reform as methods of social control, did not have the intended effect; the tactics did not work on the subjects, not as intended anyway. This has clearly been the case of many larger reform projects in the Turkish Republic, for instance the attempt to 're-dress' the people. The effort to work on people's bodies and tastes, gender and family relations, by banning the veil and prohibiting 'religious' dress for university students and public employees has been met by widespread resistance (Özdalga 1998; White 2002; Navaro-Yashin 2002; Saktanber 2002; Göle 1996). It has even been one of the rhetorical vectors that recently brought some of those that articulate this resistance into government office.

When it comes to the state schemes for reform of the economy there has been less public controversy, even though some of these programs penetrate deep into local social organization. The Turkish state implemented many far-reaching reforms in the agricultural sector and established a high degree of control or influence over the production and distribution of many kinds of produce. While agriculture was the main tax base for the Ottoman state, the state schemes in agriculture have made it one of the main burdens of the Turkish Treasury. The production of important crops such as sugar, tea and tobacco has been administratively controlled through state-owned enterprises, and sixteen Agricultural Sales Cooperative Unions, formally apex organizations of farmers cooperatives but effectively controlled by the government, have a strong influence over the organization of production. They also have had control over the procurement of the produce at prices fixed annually by the government (World Bank 2000). These policies have to some extent been reversed since the early 1990s with the IMF-sponsored structural adjustment policies.

In practice the state has not intervened to the same degree in the social organization of the fishing sector, except for its attempt to establish cooperatives. Yet a national union of water produce cooperatives was not established until 2004, formally because the fishers could not match the legal requirement for the seven regional associations of cooperatives. The water produce cooperatives have mainly been instruments for distributing credits and have had only very insignificant roles in organizing production and distribution (see Chapter 9). While the state personnel at district level generally include one or more agricultural engineers, none – not even among the district authorities in Çarşıbaşı, one of the more important fishing communities – have responsibility for water produce. Furthermore, as is the case with fishery administration in many developing countries (Hersoug 2004: 47), the state's ability to initiate concerted, integrated and planned action has been hampered by an increasing degree of institutional branching, both of the bureaucratic units within the ministries and of the research sector.[49] The General Directorate for Water Produce was dissolved in 1984 and its tasks distributed to several other units within the Ministry of Agriculture.[50] The various departments and sections within the Ministry of Agriculture and Rural Affairs do not share a common perspective or policy on fisheries. In addition, still other units are responsible for tasks such as planning and grants (State Planning Organization), licenses (Under Secretary for Maritime Affairs), registration of boats (Harbour Chiefs), and credit (The State Agricultural Bank).[51] The lack of cooperation between these institutions echoes the situation elsewhere in the state bureaucracy. The activities and policies of the institutions responsible for state-administered sugar production, for example, can at times be disparate and competitive (Alexander 2002).

Thus, the structure and activities at the institutional level fail to mirror the conceptual framing of the fisheries as one sector of the national economy. This lack of institutional integration, especially the lack of a Ministry or General Directorate for fishing, is seen by many familiar with the sector as the main reason for various problems in the fisheries. However, this perception is based on different premises: fishers complain about the lack of a powerful and just state that can implement and police laws, while the bureaucrats lament the lack of the panoptic view, the all-seeing integrating gaze. Recently, this lack of integration has also been identified by the EU as one major obstacle for aligning Turkish fishery policy with EU Common Fishery Policy (Knudsen, Pelczarski and Brown 2007). The situation in Turkey is, however, not unique. In developing countries fisheries administration is often placed in the Ministry of Agriculture 'with weak scientific and administrative competence, unclear lines of command and limited funds for the transport needed for control and surveillance' (Hersoug 2004: 47).

There may be several other reasons that the state has provided less 'guidance' to fishing than to most other 'sectors' that the state bureaucracy has identified. First, production and distribution of fish was only penetrated at a late date, much later than most agricultural commodities that early on came under direct (State Owned Enterprises) or indirect (but de facto through Agricultural Sales Cooperative Unions) state control. When the state eventually undertook to stimulate progress in the fisheries, the political climate was no longer conducive to heavy-handed state intervention. The political climate during the Democrat Party era of the 1950s, as well as the post 1980 neoliberal climate, probably did not favour any 'communistic' development in the fishery sector. Secondly, since Turkey imported almost no seafood (or meat, for that matter), fisheries were accorded little national importance within the import substitution strategy that was pursued up until 1980. Nor was water produce perceived as important export produce.

Trouble in managing fish and fishers is likely a third reason for the feeble state penetration into the fisheries. Mobile boats and men are not easy to govern, control, police or count. Also, since fish and other seafood are 'produced' daily most of the year and spoil rapidly, they are much more difficult to store, control, manage and standardize than most agricultural products. This is especially so in Turkey where there is a clear consumer preference for fresh fish and dislike of both frozen and canned fish. The seafood trade required competence, knowledge and networks that the state bureaucracy simply did not possess and was hard put to gain control of. Despite early aspirations to dispense with the 'capitalist class of middlemen' and establish a direct collaboration between the producers and the state – as well as similar ideas proposed by the political elite in the 1960s – the state seems to have made only half-hearted attempts to gain control of the trade. The abortive water produce undertaking of the EBK was probably intended as a step in this direction. In general the fish hall facilities have improved and fish trade has developed in scale and volume. But, to my knowledge, there is no tendency towards monopolization, state or other. Nor are there any kinds of price control or price regulation of the fish trade. There seems to have been no basic change in the structure of the fish trade in recent times. The basic outlines of the auction system in the fish halls with auction middlemen (*madrabaz*) and *kabzımal* display a great deal of continuity from Ottoman times.

Although state penetration into the fisheries has been feeble, fisheries nevertheless finally 'took off'. From the mid 1970s the statistics started to show the figures desired by the bureaucrats (see Figure 3.3). The rapidly increasing catch capacity of more mobile fishing, especially big-boat purse seiners and to a lesser degree trawlers, accounted for most of this increase while the dalyan fisheries were all but wiped out by changing environmental conditions and competition for space and fish.[52] While the basic operation of the purse seiners did not change, new and improved technology made fishing much more effective.

Several reasons can be cited for the 'production' success during the 1970s and 1980s. State investments in the sector were of central importance. From 1973 to 1983 investments in fishing harbours increased by a factor of five (in inflation-adjusted figures). During these years research received only around two per cent of total investments in the fishery sector. In 1983 state investments in the fisheries amounted to U.S.$42.2 million, including U.S.$15.8 million for harbours and U.S.$22 million for credits. While credits for the fishery sector totalled U.S.$4.25 million in 1976, it peaked towards the end of the 1980s (around U.S.$30 million annually), dipped to U.S.$23 million in 1995 before it peaked again at U.S.$46.2 million in 1999.[53] Many fishers were entitled to subsidized water produce credits, and the credits effectively reached the 'producers'. The interest rate on these loans was well below inflation and almost half

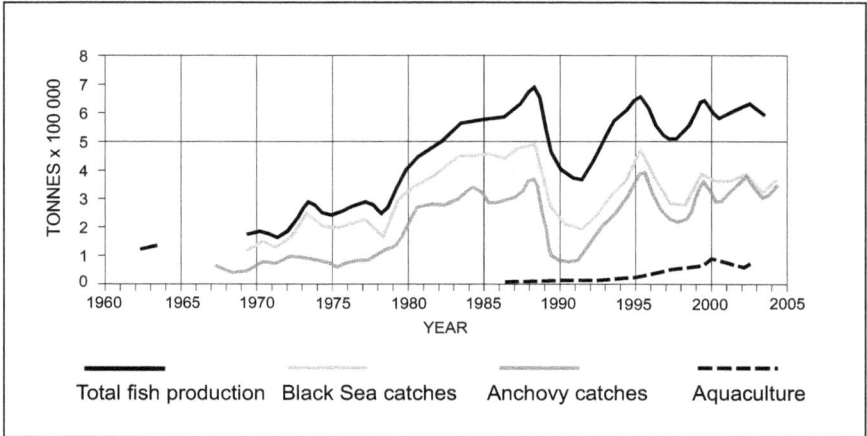

**Figure 3.3. 'Water produce' production Turkey 1960–2004.** Source: Created on the basis of State Institute for Statistics Prime Ministry Republic of Turkey (SIS) Fishery Statistics and Acara et al. 1989.

the level of the market interest rate.[54] Last, but not least, from the mid 1970s the state massively sponsored, with subsidized credits, grants and import tax exemptions, the establishment of fishmeal and oil processing plants. In certain circumstances the Development Bank of Turkey (Türkiye Kalkınma Bankası) provided very generous grants for the construction of water produce facilities (Çelikkale et al. 1999: 310–11). Construction of fishmeal and oil factories in the 'backward' Province of Sinop was entitled to a forty per cent investment grant. Starting in 1972, there was accordingly a surge in construction of privately-owned factories during the 1970s and 1980s (Doğan 1982; Zengin 2000). At the maximum there were, by the end of the 1980s, more than twenty factories. Most were located in the Black Sea region, and in 1990 the factories had a total daily production capacity of approximately eight thousand tonnes (Zengin 2000). While there is an upper limit on how much fresh fish the market can absorb in a short time, the high capacity of the factories and the possibility of delivering undersize fish meant that there was an almost limitless demand (albeit at a lower price) for hamsi and other small pelagic species, and it became possible to fish very intensively and profitably for a few weeks, especially for hamsi. As a sizable portion of hamsi catches were processed (see Figure 3.4), the growth of the Black Sea purse seine fisheries were stimulated. Some of the produce of the factories supplies part of the demand for feed in the growing fish-farm industry in Turkey.

Yet, factors outside of state initiatives to develop the 'fish production sector' were of equal importance. A general monetization of the economy from the 1950s onwards and the development of a new seafood consumer

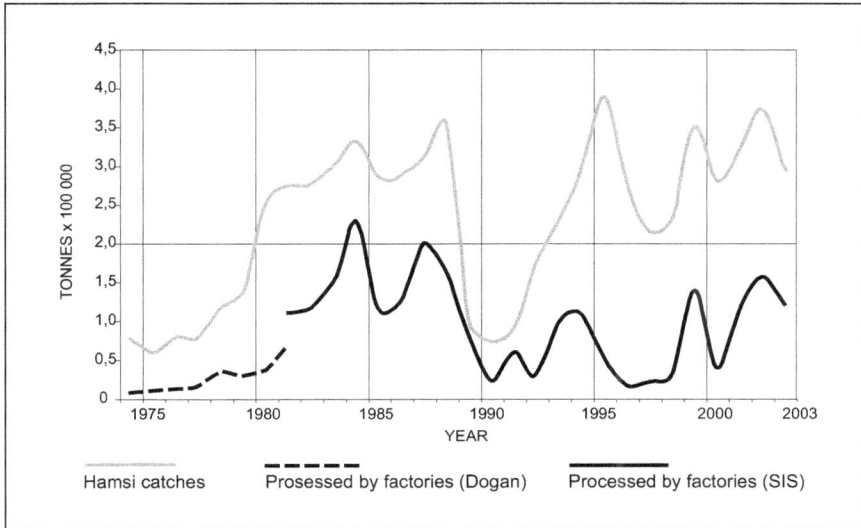

**Figure 3.4. Hamsi catches and amount processed by factories.** Created on the basis of State Institute for Statistics Prime Ministry Republic of Turkey (SIS) Fishery Statistics, Acara et al. 1989 and Doğan 1982.

culture greatly increased the demand for seafood. The construction of a national road network significantly improved market access and gradually transformed many regional seafood markets into one large national market. Marine research, however, seems to have played only a minor or marginal role in the success history: neither with respect to technology nor to knowledge of stocks were they able to guide development in the fisheries.

## Change in Scientific Priorities

Early studies (e.g., the EBK series) explored primarily the distribution of fish and the feasibility of using various new kinds of gear and boats. Foreign input in this period, particularly by the FAO, typically promoted modernization, technological development, industrialization and catch increase. This was no accident, since the 1950s saw huge sustained increases in catches globally and fishery policies internationally during this period focused on catch increases through technological development (Pauly and Maclean 2002; Hersoug 2004). With the collapse of the Norwegian herring fisheries in the 1960s and the Newfoundland cod fisheries in the 1970s and 1980s, focus gradually shifted towards rational and sustainable exploitation of stocks and new management tools based upon the science of bio-economics were developed. With regard to Turkey, however, I can see no trace of scientists and bureaucrats worrying about catch effort, stocks, population dynamics, MSY (Maximum Sustainable Yield) and so forth before the end of the 1980s. In the various long-term plans and seminar reports on the 'water produce sector', increased production remains the primary goal. Examples abound (e.g. GDWP 1974; Agricultural Bank 1982, 1984), but the following is typical: The IV Five Year Development Plan (1979–83) states that stock assessments will be undertaken, especially in the Black Sea, with the goal of an annual production increase of 7.7 % (Sarıkaya 1980: 26). The 'agriculturalist' focus on production may have made management and science less receptive to the new focus in international marine science and policy.

Things started to change towards the end of the 1980s. First, the collapse in the Black Sea fisheries during 1989–92 pushed the domestic and international discourse towards sustainability issues. At the same time international research bodies 'rediscovered' the Black Sea and it became easier to fund courses and scholarships for Turkish marine scientists. Turkish scientists received training under, among others, the auspices of FAO and the Japanese aid organization JICA in stock management, MSY, and the like. Second, the year 1989 was an important turning point in international politics, and the strategic interests of the U.S. and NATO may have played a role in the design of research programs. From 1989 onwards NATO initiated and funded stock-assessment studies in the Black Sea (Acara et al. 1989: 7), particularly at the Middle East Technical University. One of the NATO publications resulting from the studies is tellingly titled *NATO TU-Black Sea Project: Ecosystem Modelling as a Management Tool for the Black Sea* (Ivanov and Oğuz 1998). In 1993 the UN-funded Black Sea Environmental Programme was established. It has played a major role in promoting marine research with the objective of facilitating sustainable management of the sea.

Marine scientists in Turkey rather swiftly adopted bio-economic models during the 1990s. A survey of the 700 publications, mostly by Turkish authors, that are listed in the *Turkish Black Sea Bibliography* (Öztürk 1998), shows dramatic increase in publications dealing with population dynamics, stocks, and fishing effort from 1989 onwards. While only two or three publications dealt with such issues before 1989, as many as thirty-five works address such issues in the years 1989–97. Furthermore, new Turkish textbooks in basic marine and fisheries science (used at water produce faculties) concentrate on fishery biology, population dynamics and MSY (Avşar 1998; Evkoyunca 1995; Bingel 2002) and make extensive use of the models of internationally acknowledged scholars such as Beverton-Holt (population dynamics) and Gulland (stock assessment) and Schaefer (mathematical framework for explaining the relationship between fishing effort and catch). Such models have been widely applied in the management of many large-scale fisheries, especially in the North Atlantic since the mid 1970s.

Turkish scientists and managers alike believe that use of bio-economic models holds the potential for establishing a quota management system in Turkish fisheries. Most acknowledge, however, that there has been insufficient research on stocks and that efforts in this field should increase. Adaptation to the EU's Common Fishery Policy as well as the potential agreement on a Black Sea fishery convention will necessitate this. There is, however, no discussion to date of what a potential quota system would look like, whether it would work, and what the social consequences would be.

---

### SUMMARY OF FISHERY POLICIES SINCE 1950

| | |
|---|---|
| 1950s: | The EBK initiative – Marshal Plan and FAO supported attempt at creating scientifically guided state lead development in the fishery sector. Yet, little effect on catches. |
| 1960s: | Much of the initiatives of the 1950s were discontinued. Ambitious goals in five-year plans. Continued low catches. |
| 1970s and 80s: | New 'water produce' law, fishery administration within Ministry of Agriculture. Research dispersed, focus on fish farming. Susbtantial direct support to fishers and development of infrastructure. Rapidly increasing catches. |
| 1990s and 2000s: | Some move away from 'agriculturalist' production approach towards sustainability and bio-economic models. From early 2002 starting adaption to EU Common Fishery Policy. |

---

## What Role for Tradition and Privileged Access?

The international academic and management discourse concerning fisheries management is presently split. One line of thought emphasizes comanagement, participation, Customary Marine Tenure (Hviding and Jul-Larsen 1993), and the importance of local ecological knowledge (or indigenous or traditional ecological knowledge). The other, and the more influential in large-scale fisheries, is bio-economic models that focus on stock assessments, total allowable catch (TAC) and quotas. Both of these differ from classical modernizing fishery policies in that they aim at sustainable development and ecosystem management.

One might envision the first model as useful in the Turkish fisheries. The traditional framework of privileged fishing rights, rented from the state and still partly in place when the Turkish State undertook to develop the fisheries from the 1950s onwards, could have formed a basis for the development of communal usufruct rights in modern coastal fishing. Did laws and regulations stimulate or work against a system of privileged access, for example? The 1971 Water Produce Law (1380/3288, paragraph 12) stipulates that privately owned dalyans left unused for five years will be nationalized (*kamulaştırılma*). Furthermore, lease of 'production' (*istihsal*) rights to dalyans, volis, lakes and lagoons is primarily to be given to water produce cooperatives or village associations of men residing in the production region (Paragraph 4). This suggests that the state regarded as unacceptable the inheritance and possession of private dalyans and other kinds of privilege associated with the old fishery regime. Rental of production rights of dalyan, voli sites, and the like have seemingly been contingent upon the state which never designed a policy to 'develop' dalyan fishing. These 'traditional' modes of fishing were clearly perceived as 'marginal', as they surely were by 1971. Technological development as well as the destruction of good voli and dalyan sites along the Bosporus made this a less sensitive question than it could otherwise have been. Recently the practice of dalyan and voli fishing became even more restricted when the ministry decided not to grant any new permits. The bureaucrats discourage their use because they allegedly catch fish in the reproduction season. They indicate, however, that the practice of dalyan and voli fishing conflicts with other more important uses of the seascape.

While territorial rights connected to 'traditional' technologies were marginalized in the new law, what of such modes of fishing in practice? In 1955 the 'folk poet' Vasıf Hiç wrote: 'Along the Anatolian and European coast of [Istanbul] there are voli places, rented from the Evkaf [government office of foundations] or in the past offered someone as a favor by decree, where the renters or owners possess the right to execute the art [of fishing]; other boats cannot come from the 'open' and turn a voli there' (quoted in Koçu 1960: 2000). Thus, while the dalyan fisheries were in decline, and the more mobile purse-seine fishing (*gırgır*) gained ground, old practices continued in the seine fishing on the volis. Hiç noted that 'seine means fishing in one's own place', and 'each voli has its own borders for where the seine can be set.' There were 'owners' that were entitled to charge others for the use of their voli. If Hiç is correct, during the early Republic the privileged patrons (tax farmers) of the fishing rights disappeared and the fishers rented fishing grounds directly from the government-controlled Evkaf. In all likelihood, the dalyans, and especially the voli places, were not policed as stringently before. Fishers probably increasingly enjoyed 'hereditary' rights to voli places without the burden of paying a rent or tax for using them. Although the Republican fishery regulations include a long list of regional and place prohibitions, none of these are related to privileged access for individual persons, villages or the like. On the other hand, some Ottoman privileges were possibly retained well into the Republic. The large Beykoz dalyan on the Bosporus was rented out by the heirs of a certain Hüseyin Ağa who had received the right to the dalyan as a gift from the Sultan during the Ottoman age. The heirs retained this right until the dalyan was set up for the last time in the late 1970s (Pasiner 1993/94: 545).

While, on the one hand, 'modern' fisheries and Western models were idealized and 'traditional' practices were ignored in law and policy formulations, on the other hand received practice, including some privileges, was allowed to continue. The Republican policy had clearly not effected a decisive break with the past. There were continuities from Ottoman times at the level of fishing practice and even state-acknowledged privileged access. An explicit conflict between received practice and new ideology, however, does not seem to have emerged. When fishery development policies at last began to be implemented after 1950, the idealistic 'high modernism' discourse continued.

Thus, the Turkish authorities do not consider fishers' knowledge to be indigenous knowledge (IK) or traditional ecological knowledge (TEK). Such concepts are unknown, not only in Turkish fishery management, but in Turkey in general. In a report addressing intellectual property and traditional knowledge, delivered to the Convention on Biological Diversity, the Turkish authorities bluntly state that 'there are no indigenous people in Turkey' (GDEP n.d.) This indicates that IK and TEK are part of a larger discourse about knowledges and that the use, or not, of these concepts are conditioned by a range of external factors. They are not neutral concepts. The particular track taken by the Turkish modernization process privileged, and created, the emergence of marine sciences as an independent field of authoritative knowledge of sea and fish. When tradition was sought to be 'overcome', it would have been seen as reactionary to champion IK or TEK. This has clearly prevented the acceptance of alternative development models focusing on participation, comanagement, farmer first and the like, thereby blocking the main road through which IK and TEK enter policies and academic discourse.

At the same time, Turkish social science has not been ready to acknowledge informal and dynamic processes that are typically thought to be characteristic of IK and TEK. In a critical analysis of Turkish social science, Mardin has claimed that, due to its special itinerary, the language of Turkish intellectuals has given priority to a macro-sociology (1997a: 66). He asserts that one effect of this 'macro' focus has been dismissal of 'identity processes, the noninstitutional basis of religion, and personal histories as "colorings" of social processes'. He calls for more micro-sociological studies along phenomenological lines or inspired by themes such as 'lifeworld' and the 'everyday' in order to link 'micro' and 'macro' (Mardin 1997a: 72).

For various reasons it has not become common to make statements about IK and TEK in Turkey and the Middle East in general. This does not reflect a lack of indigenes or situations that could have been appropriately studied as IK or TEK. A complex set of factors has caused the lack of IK and TEK approaches in the policies and studies of the Middle East: the rise of Islam in political-academic discourse on the Middle East; a crisis of representation in Middle East anthropology; past and recent endogenous processes towards the standardization of law in the Middle East; the character of colonial policies; and a lack of natural resources with global importance 'protected' by a native population (Knudsen 2007). Some of these issues concern dynamics within academia and the frameworks through which scholars study and represent the Middle East. Other issues concern social change in the region itself and how it has been positioned with regard to colonialism and processes of modernization and globalization.

Although alternative ideals for fishery management that emphasize tradition, continuity and participation have emerged internationally during the last twenty-five years or so, fisheries management in Turkey now seems set to be designed according to 'modern' bio-economic models. While marine scientist in Turkey now rely less on modernistic 'production' models, the overall framework of rational exploitation and the important role of the sciences remain intact. The new bio-economic models require more of the social and natural resources to be legible (stocks, fleet structure) and may therefore even afford scientists a greater role in the fisheries than before. Bio-economic models coupled with EU-style management models necessitate and legitimize deeper penetration of the state into the social organization of the fisheries. The bio-economic approach promises to make manageable that which has hitherto been beyond the reach of the state.

## The State and Seafood Consumption

While the state's efforts at making legible and controlling fishing activities are set to increase, it steadily makes less effort to direct the culinary aspects of seafood, tastes. Concerns about production and taste were still interconnected during the late Ottoman era in the few articulations of ideals for development of rational and industrial fisheries. Yet, within a new discourse of scientific rationalization in the early Turkish Republic food was treated differently. The state became increasingly concerned about its subjects' welfare, health and material conditions and designed a nutrition policy along with a general policy to stimulate development within a range of different economic sectors. As the state's approach to the fisheries moved from tax farming to scientific and rational development planning, increasing production and maximizing proteins, rather than taste, became the main concern and challenge. Concerns about taste and production became disconnected. Interestingly, Devedjian, the head of fish auctions in Istanbul in the beginning of the twentieth century, was more explicitly interested in this. His detailed study (1926) of fisheries in Istanbul not only includes catch statistics, fishery technology and recommendations for industrialization, but for each species or kind (more than 160) that he describes he also notes their culinary value and primary mode of cooking, and often also supplies detailed descriptions of various modes of conserving. In contrast, the culinary value of seafood receives much less attention in post-1950 state approaches to fisheries. The book 'Our Black Sea Fisheries' (Çakıroğlu 1969), sponsored by the Ministry of Trade which at that time was responsible for fishery policies, includes some recipes, but, notably, only for hamsi. After responsibility for administration is handed over to the Ministry for Agriculture, the only way consumption enters the picture, as in textbooks on 'water produce marketing', is in the technical and formalized language of economic science, as 'demand' (*arz, talep*) and 'consumption' (*tüketim*) (e.g., Şener 1987). What the state indeed effectively managed to accomplish was increasing demand through stimulating construction of fish and oil processing factories.

The state has been less effective in influencing the culinary cultures of seafood. Lifestyles have been more impervious to state influences, and seafood cultures display a great degree of continuity, likely because they are more closely connected to daily practices of identity negotiations and morality management. Also, the main characteristics of the fishing sector are not predicated only on state modernizing efforts, but are also a result of the sector's adaptation to the culinary cultures of seafood. Thus, in certain respects, the post-1950 developments in the fisheries sector can be said to unfold at the interface of two different influences, namely the culinary cultures of seafood, and the state modernizing project.

The 'forgetting' of the culinary aspects was an effect of the particular road taken in Turkey in the creation of fisheries as a sector and the parallel emergence of the knowledge field of water produce science. There is reason to argue that this 'modernization' process also resulted in a 'forgetting' of fishers' practices and knowledges and created a wall between scientists and fishers. The severe resource crisis in the Black Sea during the early 1990s created social tensions, and the search for reasons for the disappearance of the fish was a pervasive concern for fishers and scientists alike. But they held very different opinions about the reason for the crisis. While Turkish marine scientists adopted the internationally accepted scientific position that the invader species comb jelly (*mnemiopsis leidyi*) was one of the major reasons for the resource crisis (GEF – BSEP 1996), this was totally unknown to the fishers (Knudsen 1997). In contrast, most fishers thought that the fish-finder sonar killed or scared away fish – an idea known to, but ridiculed by, the scientists. I will return to these issues in later chapters. While this chapter has dwelt on state discourse on fisheries, I will now turn to fishers' knowledges and practices.

# CHAPTER 4

# Fisher's Knowledges

26 April 1998. Around 5 A.M. dark shadows appear out from the groves, paths and houses along the busy main road that passes through the village of Keremköy. The day is just about to dawn. Young men, and a few middle-aged ones, still dizzy with sleep, converge on the open space between the main road and the local kahve. Not many words are exchanged; there are only a few comments about who's coming and who's not. When we have waited for five or ten minutes we look down the road and see the red minibus starting up. Yavuz, the local minibus driver stops his van by us and the men get in, ten or twelve of us. After driving two kilometres along the coast, we get out at the harbour near the centre of İskefiye.[55] Each man pays U.S.$0.2 to Yavuz who returns to the village to pick up the rest of the men, the latecomers. The men head for their boats. Most fishers from this village tie their boats to the longer of the two breakwaters that enclose the harbour. They jump onto their boats, mostly nine to twelve metre long wooden *alametres*, and immediately set quietly about their tasks. Some leave at once; others wait for a brother, son or friend among the latecomers. This morning I join the young men Cengiz and Kaya who are good mates. They also have with them Kaya's younger brother Arif who usually goes to school, but could come today because it is Sunday. Kaya's elder brother, Yaşar, usually comes with them, but this morning he has a headache, allegedly because he had been drinking. They all know me well and are eager to have me along. They expect me to take plenty of photos.

Cengiz enters the cabin (*kamara*) and starts the engine while the other two cast off and help manoeuvre the boat out between the row of boats. It is overcast but fairly good weather, with insignificant waves. It's rather cold though. We have hardly rounded the breakwater before Kaya and Arif change to some worn-out clothes that they keep on board. They also put on rain clothes and rubber boots. Thus prepared, they remain standing on the aft deck while the boat proceeds to the fishing ground. As usual, and like all the other boats from this village, we head northwest from the harbour in the direction of Vakfıkebir (See Figure 4.1). After approximately fifteen minutes we reach our destination, the 'whiting island' (*mezgit adası*) off Yalıköy where they keep their bottom net almost continuously during the winter. Once at the *ada* ('island', actually shallow waters or fishing bank) Cengiz has a quick look at the buoys marking others' nets as we pass them in order to determine the direction of the current. I had become familiar with this technique by now and felt I was almost able to figure it out for myself by looking at both the tilt of the buoy and direction in which the line stretches out underneath it. However, no one had ever told me that; they say simply 'we can understand the direction of the currents from the buoys.' Cengiz, in answer to my question, told me that today the *sular* (the 'waters', i.e., the sea currents) were *poyraza*, towards *poyraz* (northeast, here in effect east). The sular, he continued, are almost always either *karayel* (west) or poyraz here, almost never on or offshore. They cast their nets parallel to the shore therefore, in order not to damage them. I know, from previous conversations and trips with the fishers, that one type of damage is that the net may become filled with rubbish and rubble such as leaves, sticks and even branches of trees. Moreover, the net may be swept away by the current and lost if cast too near deep waters, a *kuyu* ('well').

They have an approximate idea of where they cast their net the previous morning and head in that direction. The ada is fairly wide, but the fishers use no 'sign' (*işaret*, or more uncommon here, *kerteriz*, bearing) in order to relocate their net. They soon spot one of the two home-made buoys, which have no personal markers, and Kaya catches it with a bargepole and starts pulling in the line. As soon as the line is taut he throws it over the hydraulic winch, starts it with a switch of the handle on its stem and continues to pull in the line, now with the aid of the winch. Arif arranges the line in a neat spiral on the cabin side of the deck. They have made sure that they lift the net on the leeward side of the current, i.e., from poyraz. That way there is no risk of the boat drifting over the net and making a mess of it or of the net becoming entangled in the propeller. A small anchor is brought out and placed side by side with the coiled line and the buoy. Cengiz keeps the boat engine running to keep the boat in position until the net enters the winch. Now he, also wearing his sea outfit, appears from the cabin to help his friends clear the net. Without any discussion each man finds his place for the clearing of the net. Cengiz takes charge of the winch, over which he now drags the net. Occasionally, when the net accumulates at his feet, he stops the winch and disentangles some fish from the net. The brothers each handle one end of the fathom-deep net, removing fish and sorting the net neatly into sinker-line and cork-line piles on the deck. The catch consists entirely of small (approx. 15 cm) whiting that are thrown into a corner of the deck. I had asked to borrow a raincoat and rubber boots and was able to give them a hand cleaning the net. By now I am familiar with the technique for disentangling the fish from the single meshed net, the first step being to stretch the net around the fish so that any pockets which may have formed around it open up. Often the fish is then left dangling by its teeth entrapped in the net. A mixture of rough pulling and manipulation of the filament between the fish's teeth is enough to set it free. If the fish is more badly entangled in the net, it is necessary to first pull any filaments out from between its teeth and then find a 'hole' (net opening, mesh) in the net to slide the fish through. It's all done in a matter of seconds. I had learned this partly by watching my fisher friends at work, partly by experimenting.

We continue pulling in and cleaning the net for almost an hour without any discussion. The noise from the winch makes conversation difficult anyway. I take some photos. Their net, not atypically, consists of four parts, each seventy-five fathoms long. Some parts are torn. But the work proceeds without difficulties today. Moreover, the catch is good. When net, second anchor and buoy are safely on deck, one of the brothers puts the fish into a bucket. Meanwhile one of the others cleans the debris from the deck that might become entangled in the net. Cengiz reenters the cabin and starts the engine. Without any discussion he steers the boat back to approximately where they started lifting the net, and turns the boat; without measuring the depth, one of the others throws the anchor into the water. The line starts running out as the boat makes headway at good speed; the buoy and then the net follow suit. It runs out smoothly on its own since it has been well cleaned, but one of the men watches attentively and now and then stretches the outgoing net to loosen tangles. After a few minutes they finish setting the net by throwing the second anchor and buoy into the sea. They will come back to lift the net the next morning. Or perhaps the morning after, depending on the weather.

Kaya now uses a hose to clean the deck thoroughly. They also use it to clean their rain-clothes. The fish are emptied onto the deck again and thoroughly rinsed with seawater. Damaged specimens are thrown into a corner for private consumption, and – since the catch is good – the rest are sorted into two cases, one with big and one with small fish. There is enough fish to sell large and small fish separately. That way the larger fish will fetch a higher price. They take care to arrange some bigger specimens on top. Cengiz is already guiding the boat for the harbour and we are soon approaching one of the boats tied up in the inner harbour. Arif, who has already changed clothes, leaps onto the other boat. I join him. The cases of fish are handed over to him. Cengiz and Kaya take the boat back to its place by the breakwater. There they change clothes and make sure the boat is properly secured: ropes tidily arranged, the engine cover securely in place, and the door to the cabin locked. Arif carries the plastic cases of fish across the main road. There we meet Ali who is also going to take his catch of whiting by *dolmuş* (minibus carrying passengers) to Trabzon. This is common procedure and they each take their own fish. Soon they stop a minibus and place the fish in the small rear luggage compartment, then we find ourselves seats inside. For a slight extra charge the minibus driver takes the fishers all the way to the fish hall after the last stop in Trabzon. There is no time to lose if they are not going to be late for the morning fish auctions.

We arrive at the fish hall around 8 A.M. They put their cases on a large scale in front of the office of their 'commissioner' (*komisyoncu,* also *kabzımal*) friend. Seven or eight inconspicuous men, arriving from similar auctions along the row of *yazıhanes* (offices) soon cluster around the fish. A man appears from the yazıhane and announces over a megaphone, 'Whiting sellers, whiting sellers' (*mezgitçiler, mezgitçiler*). In a book he writes the first names of the fishers, weighs the fish and starts the auction. The buyers, mostly small-scale fishmongers or peddlers, wink, nod or command, 'Write!'. The cases of large and small whiting are sold separately. Fish are auctioned by kilo price; small ones go for U.S.$1, 'large' ones for U.S.$2.4. The fishers are passive spectators. After the auction the buyers immediately take possession of the fish while the fishers drift around awhile watching other auctions. Then they enter the yazıhane of their komisyoncu friend and help themselves to some tea. At his desk one of the komisyoncus counts out their money, and gives it to them, together with a piece of paper where he has written the name of the fishers, the amount of fish, price/kg, as well as totals. From the total ten per cent has been deduced, the komisyoncu's share. Today they don't stop to chat with the komisyoncu. However, here at the fish hall they often learn of the first catches of migrating species that only appear seasonally. I return to Keremköy together with Ali, while Arif attends to some business in town. Halfway on our ride back to the village Ali checks on his pocket calculator the calculations on the piece of paper that he got from the komisyoncu. It's correct.

This simple fishing trip and subsequent market expedition involves a very wide range of knowledges. How can we adequately describe these knowledges? The following discussion addresses some general issues that will facilitate comparison with others' knowledge. This is not meant to be a comparison only of what they know, but of how they learn and keep knowledge. Fishers operate in a very complex world where the skills employed at sea and their knowledge about sea and fish are difficult to separate from other abilities and knowledges, such as familiarity with market, regulations, procedures for applying for grants and credit, and so forth. In the present chapter, however, I concentrate on fishers' activities at sea and their articulations of the sea and fish. Clearly, fishers themselves emphasize that their knowledge is based on being at sea, and this is certainly the primary experiential field with regard to fishers' knowledge.

What are the implications of this for fishers' knowledges? What kind of knowledge, or knowledges, is it? In what ways does it differ from other ways to know the sea and fish? Some epistemological and theoretical clarifications are necessary before I proceed with the ethnography of knowledges. What should we understand by knowledge? How should we approach a study of it?

## Towards an Anthropology of Knowledge

Is the kind of knowledge fishers in the case above employ indigenous or traditional ecological knowledge? The kind of close, implicit familiarity with the natural environment evident in this case is indeed often considered as typical of IK and TEK. These kinds of knowledges are commonly regarded to be characterized by being tacit or oral, eco-friendly, situated, dynamic, bodily, non-scriptural and subjective. I find, however, that these assumptions often lack theoretical grounding and that the vocabulary of IK and TEK does not allow for enough specificity in analysis. The most important defining characteristic of TEK and IK is, actually, their *dissimilarity* to science[56] which is characterized as general, formal, distanced, systematic and scriptural. Within the humanities and social sciences there has evolved a partitioning of work whereby different scholarly traditions focus on IK/TEK and science respectively.

Science and Technology Studies (STS) and Sociology of Scientific Knowledge (SSK) have been rapidly growing fields of study during the last twenty to thirty years. These scholarly approaches can trace their roots through Thomas Kuhn (1962) back to Ludwig Fleck who, inspired by anthropology, studied how the development of a blood test for syphilis was related to contemporary ideas within diverse 'thought collectives' (Fleck 1979). Fleck believed that all knowledge – including science – was socially constructed and emphasized cultural and historical dimensions in the establishment of traditions of knowledge (Gonzales et al. 1995; Nader 1996). With disciplinary origins in history, philosophy and sociology, recent work within SSK and STS has concentrated especially on studies of advanced science in Western societies and has generally employed a social-constructivist perspective that has worked to dethrone science from the pedestal of 'universal' knowledge.

Studies of IK and TEK have their intellectual roots in Malinowski's studies of 'native science' among the Trobriands (Malinowski 1922). Out of these studies grew the ethnosience tradition that particularly focused on classificatory systems. By way of a detour via structuralism (e.g., Levi-Strauss 1969) this tradition evolved into, among other things, studies of 'indigenous knowledge systems'. Generally, studies within this school have used models for classification and cognition derived from linguistics and have striven to document and analyse the cognitive or cultural 'content' of 'their' knowledge: people with IK 'perpetuate legacies of cultural knowledge' (Brush 1996: 1). From around 1980 this tradition has been partially appropriated by a new developmental discourse which holds that the success of developmental projects depends upon local participation and knowledge (empowerment, farmer first and bottom up etc.).[57] Increased attention, internationally, on democratization, human rights, civil society, NGOs and the like has further kindled interest in IK and made it into a politically correct concept.[58]

Studies incorporating this perspective have especially emphasized social and cultural processes in resource management, as is exemplified in anthropological contributions to the debate about Common Pool Resources (F. Berkes 1989; Bromley 1992; Cordell 1989; McCay and Acheson 1987). These studies tend to emphasize local-specific conditions like the adaptation aspects of local knowledge (Brush 1993: 659), as well as various ecological, technical and social conditions that make each case unique. Anthropologists and biologists have demonstrated that various 'producers', such as hunter-gatherers, fishers and pastoralists, often possess extensive ecological knowledge (e.g., Freeman and Carbyn 1988; Johannes 1989). A dichotomy or conflict between this kind of 'traditional (or customary, local or indigenous) knowledge' and 'scientific knowledge' is therefore often a main topic in studies of resource management (see, e.g., Feit 1988; Johannes 1989; Pálsson 1991).

Anthropology has been an important source of inspiration for both the STS and the IK/TEK research traditions. Fieldwork, including participatory observation, is among the methods of preference in both traditions. Nevertheless, there is today hardly any dialogue between these research traditions. There is almost a total ignorance of STS among those studying IK and TEK, even though, as discussed, science is often held as a contrast when IK and TEK are defined (see Ferradás 1998). STS have been braver and more innovative theoretically, but have still largely focused on 'Western' science. This partition of work, especially the categorization of certain kinds of knowledge as indigenous, results, as Pálsson (1998b: 52) has noted, in the reproduction of the distinction between 'us' and 'them', and – in the more relativistic approaches – of the myth that we live in different, incommensurable worlds. As such, this conceptual partition and accompanying division of work evokes the 'great divide' (Latour 1993).

During the last decades important new insights have been gained in anthropology by attending more carefully to embodied aspects of human action and knowledge. It is now widely accepted that it is insufficient to analyse people's knowledge of the world only in terms of their concepts and classifications, as do ethnoscience, structuralism etc. (Csordas 1999). We have come to acknowledge that especially people who are clearly involved in practical, manual tasks – such as dancers, craftsmen and fishers to name but a few examples – mobilize skills that defy being cast (solely) in a structural and linguistic idiom. It has thus become fashionable to let 'embodiment' bear the burden of explanation when knowledge is displaced from language and theory to practice.

These insights have however had little impact in fields of study such as IK, TEK, STS and CPR. Embodiment is sometimes evoked as explanatory factor, but often remains largely a black box in many studies. In the stereotyped partition of knowledges embodiment is easily seen as practical knowledge typical of IK, TEK and the like, while science, based upon language and theory, is perceived to be less 'personal', more 'distanced'. While this opens some interesting lines of inquiry, it also hinders others. For instance, in his article 'After Nature', Escobar (1999) acknowledges the important rethinking of 'local knowledge' as practical, embodied knowledge (in the vein of Ingold), but he reserves this approach for only one of three 'regimes of nature', namely 'organic nature' (i.e., rural, folk or indigenous kinds of knowledge); 'capitalist nature' and 'technonature' are to be studied employing other theoretical frameworks. I argue that we must not at the outset assume that science is less situated or embodied than other knowledges. This may be so, but that will have to be ascertained through careful ethnography.

Latour shies away from approaches that focus on cognition and experience since he is unwilling to look for 'cognitive reasons (abilities)' for differences between knowledges: cognitive explanations have hindered studies of inscriptions and networks and how knowledge is organized in time and space (Latour 1987: 246–7) and have ultimately reproduced the 'great divide'. Yet I would claim that while approaches to cognition that are inspired by Levy-Bruhl (see Tambiah 1990: 84–93) may often imply an asymmetrical tack (according 'them' prelogical mentality, and 'us' logical mentality), this need not necessarily be so. Lambek, for instance, defines objectification as 'features that have been externalized or that exist externally and at some degree of independence from particular bodies as signs, rules, effects, or constraints of personhood … [while e]mbodiment refers to features that have been internalized, or that exist internally or by reason of the fact that they are located within or as bodies' (Lambek 1993: 428n.1). These may be difficult to use as strict analytical concepts. I see them rather as indicative of processes in all human cognition and communication, with embodiment providing the experiential grounding of objective knowledge, and objectification making embodied knowledge graspable by others. Thus, these concepts may be used symmetrically, for example by focusing on how both fishers and scientists embody and objectify knowledge.

Other scholars have contributed to further elaboration of the embedded or embodied (or even ecological) character of cognition[59] and increasingly challenged the linguistic approach to cognition. Bradd Shore (1996) concurs with the overall outlines of Lakoff's (1987) theory of Idealized Cognitive Models (see Introduction), but seeks to expand the theory to include the social (or cultural) dimensions: 'Instituted models are the public life of culture, empirically observable social institutions that are available as resources for a community. Mental models, by contrast, are cognitive representations of these instituted models but are not direct mental mappings of social institutions' (Shore 1996: 68). He distinguishes between two main modes of cognition: 'analytical' ('propositional model' in Lakoff's scheme), based upon digital codes, and 'non-analytical', based upon analog codes (Shore 1996: 325). Shore thinks that instituted models may also be encoded as non-analytical concepts. I find that these distinctions, for a start, are more useful than a mapping along practice versus language or theory, and may also bring greater specificity to analyses of embodiment and objectification. However, I consider it imperative to look more attentively at how, and to what degree, mental models come to exist in public life as instituted models: what is the 'materiality' and context of these models, and in what ways are they inscribed?

The issue of instituted models, for example the 'water produce' model, was partly addressed in the previous chapters that focused on the shared discursive formations that both fishing and marine science are embedded in. Although there clearly are differences between the knowledges of fishers, marine scientists and bureaucrats, they are also historically connected, are part of the same social system, and relate to the same discourse of identities. Through the remainder of the book I will first identify the way in which knowledge is held and then gradually work my way back to the larger issues of historical context, identities and discourses.

Through focusing on the process of 'inscription', Latour suggests one intriguing approach to study how 'objects' or 'facts' are constructed and how knowledge becomes embedded in larger structures. He prefers to 'use the word *collective* to describe the associations of humans and non-humans' (1993: 4) instead of 'hybrid' which carries connotations of being 'put together' (from essences or pure forms from nature and society, respectively). These collectives are associations of 'actants', which are the forces or actors which are represented by 'spokespersons' (Latour 1987: 89). Science, or, as I would prefer to say, knowledge disciplines, construct and stabilize new collectives by bringing in, mobilizing, as many and as strong actants as possible and by extending the 'networks'. The 'universalism' of science is no more than one kind of local knowledge supported by particularly rigid and ever-increasing networks. Networks are enlarged as more actants are added to harden the facts. 'Relative size' (or scale), and not local-global, us-them, true-false, is therefore a pivotal criterion in comparing knowledges. For Latour (1987: 220), gaining knowledge means becoming 'familiar with things, people and events, which are *distant*' (Latour 1987: 220). Thus, he maintains, studies of the process of gaining knowledge should focus on how one is enabled to 'act at a distance' through the 'mobilization, stabilization and combination of inscriptions'. A hallmark of technoscience, he claims, is that it mobilizes everything that can possibly be inscribed and moved back and forth and piled up in collections. In studies of knowledges we should therefore be sensitive to the different emphases they put on inscription (Latour 1987: 218–228).

I here use many different analytical concepts to specify the 'movement' of knowledge out into interpersonal and transportable forms. We may distinguish between these concepts by saying that *articulation* of knowledge may occur in different forms of *manifestations*. It may imply varying degrees of *externalization*, movement away from the original quality (situation, context, form of manifestation) of knowledge. Different kinds of manifestation harbour different qualities as or potentials for *inscription*. In general, externalization facilitates, and is stimulated by, *objectification* – the making of something *as* something *for* someone.

## Situated Knowledge of Bottom Topography

Knowledge of bottom topography is one of the main assets in several kinds of fishing, including big-boat trawling and purse seining. It may be the well-kept secret of a single fisher who has found a big stone from which he regularly brings home good catches of croaker, or it may be the well-known and shared knowledge of a community of practitioners (e.g., the whiting adas) and thereby constitute an institutionalized cultural model. This knowledge is for the most part not inscribed. The sea charts, which the small-boat fishers seldom employ anyway, do not give sufficiently detailed information about the sea bottom to be of any use for this purpose, or in other kinds of fishing. On the other hand, small echo sounders in small-boat fishing, GPS-aided satellite maps in trawling, and sonars and echo sounders in purse seining have become increasingly important tools for knowing the bottom conditions. This technology does not remove the need for other knowledge of the bottom. Interpretation of the sonar display, for instance, is contingent upon familiarity with the local bottom topography. Some of this technology, notably the GPS-aided satellite maps, facilitate inscription of both general features and individual fishing knowledge, for example trawl 'tracks' that have proved profitable. There is also integration of knowledge across fleet categories. Small-boat fishers who work as crew on the purse seiners may be called up to the bridge to advise the skipper whether a potential spot for casting the net is 'clean' or not.

In most kinds of small-boat fishing familiarity with the general topography of adas (and other features of the bottom topography) is primarily accumulated through the use of a sounding line and net positioning. Adas are generally perceived as being relatively flat and can therefore best be translated as fishing banks. To the fishers in Çarşıbaşı it is common-sense knowledge that whiting, and to a lesser extent turbot, are more abundant on adas than elsewhere. Whiting is not among the most highly esteemed fish, but it can be caught almost year-round in a fairly simple operation. It will usually provide a stable income, but there is little possibility of huge catches. It's the business for the poor. In some places, and especially during winter, fishers depend almost solely on whiting fisheries on adas.

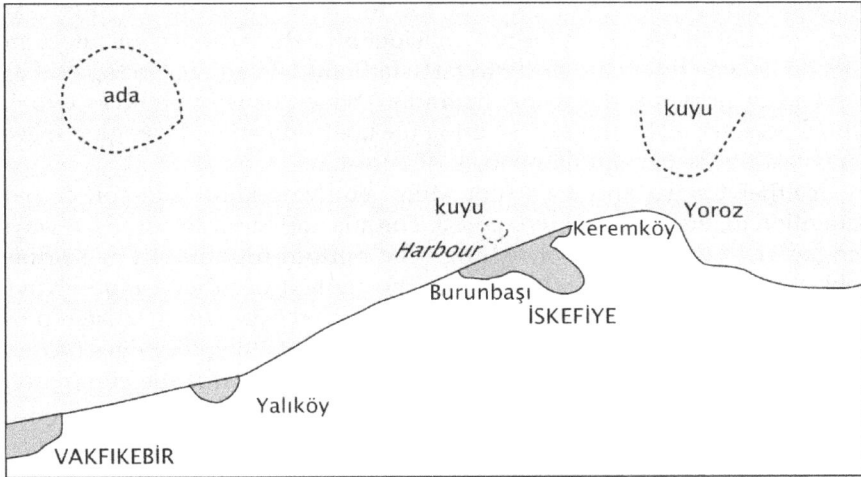

**Figure 4.1. Map of coastal region and sea bottom topography Çarşıbaşı.** Some elements of bottom topography along the coast of the District of Çarşıbaşı.

A group of approximately ten boats from Keremköy set their nets continually on the smaller ada off Vakfıkebir during most of the winter season (see Figure 4.1). That was as true in 1990–91 as in 1998 and 2008. Fishers from other villages or *mahalle* in Çarşıbaşı do not engage in this fishery on a regular basis. Many men in Keremköy have the basic skills necessary to participate in this activity. They can be said to constitute a 'community of practitioners' (Pálsson 1998b) with shared embodied knowledge of the basic operations. Thus, it is easy for Cengiz and Yaşar to find relatives and friends to work with in flexible constellations within the village networks. This makes it possible for the fishers to go regularly to the ada and work smoothly together – as in the case above – even though a son may be away for military service or a father very tired and unable to get out of bed one morning. For Kaya and Cengiz relating to the ada has become a routine practice. They know where it is, and they do not experiment very much. There is a whole procedural routine associated with the fishing trip which is a kind of embodied practice. Even though it is not objectified, fishers may very well share a fairly general model for the routine operation of setting whiting nets which is instituted in practice and not simply organized as concepts.

Sometimes individual fishers combine such general models with more creative, individual strategies. Once I went fishing for large (ca. 300–500g) whiting with Murat. In an otherwise undifferentiated seascape, except for the position relative to the straight shore, he was attempting to set his net at a very specific place, on the shoulder of a kuyu (deep water 'well'). To master that is quite a feat. First, he has to know where the kuyu is, take into account the length of the net, consider how the currents will affect the net on its way down the thirty to forty fathoms and so on. On top of it all he had to carry out the whole operation, which usually involves two or three persons, all by himself: steering the boat, adjusting the engine speed and casting the net simultaneously (Figure 4.2).

Neither Cengiz and Yaşar nor Murat cultivate knowledge of, or pay attention to, the ada and kuyu per se. The ada and kuyu are almost always engaged in the process of fishing. The bottom topography is seldom objectified and always related to in the context of other factors. Kuyu attracts Murat's interest because he knows from experience, bolstered by popular theories, that large whiting can be caught along the edges using a certain kind of net under certain current conditions. It is the cumulative

**Figure 4.2. Setting a whiting net around a kuyu.** Murat 1998.

familiarity with various elements – the bottom topography, the fish, the net, the boat and the engine, the sea currents, navigation, the weather, even other fishers' activities and market prices – which is typical of small-boat fishers' skills. Thus, Murat is not an expert on whiting, or weather, or market dynamics for that matter. He is an expert on how to catch whiting.

Since the operational models fishers employ are primarily 'hands on' knowledge implicated in situated, bodily practice and to a very limited degree externalized, it is difficult to say anything certain about how they are organized, and even the degree to which such models are shared. What model does Murat have of that unseen world below the surface of the sea? I cannot know for sure, but I became aware that I could draw upon my own experience as a hobby fisher using hook and line from a small boat along the Norwegian coast. It is, not unsurprisingly, three-dimensional vision created by a kind of extension from visual observations of the landscape on shore. But how does he 'perceive' the sea currents within this three-dimensional model? To what extent do fishers externalize and inscribe this knowledge?

I was usually only able talk with the fishers about bottom topography while on shore, most commonly in the kahve. At sea it was generally too noisy or the fishers were too busy. When prompted to explain what an ada is, fishers sometimes say that it is a fairly wide *sığ* (shallow waters), separated from the shore by deeper waters. It was completely impossible to get fishers to make a sketch (map) of ada or kuyu. I tried again and again to no avail. In most cases they would take pen and paper in hand, but then hesitate. Sometimes they made some vague short lines that indicated direction, but never any delimited entity. Yet, despite the fact that we could not discuss the topographical and other qualities of adas and kuyus on the basis of two-dimensional sketches, fishers had no problem sitting in the kahve and illustrating important aspects of the bottom topography, where fish gather, how currents flow, and so on. Most commonly they used their hands (sometimes one, usually both) to make a three-dimensional iconic representation of ada or kuyu. Accompanied by pointing to 'features' at their hand-icon, they then explained the rest verbally, referring to how fish behave as weather and sea changes with the seasons. Thus, the fishers are able to articulate some of the qualities of the adas and kuyus by means of hand symbolism and also couple this with highly standardized models of fish behaviour and seasonal changes. There probably is an element of convention involved here, of communication by means of conventionalized signs, but such signs may also conform closely to the fisher's own experience and imagination of the bottom topography. It is a very 'plastic' kind of sign that can be shaped to fit the individual ada or kuyu. This image is not linguistically organized and is activated and develops during continued interaction with gear, water bodies, and the sea bottom. Meaning construction here is by analogic prosessing that draws on a model that certainly is very 'bodily', but has elements of abstraction and distance. The hand sign is actually rather empty without verbal comment that can situate it.

Much knowledge is clearly embodied, lived, local and embedded in biophysical and social contexts. Yet, the 'way that the fishers know' seems difficult to capture and is not sufficiently explained by embodiment. While theories of embodied cognition may be of some assistance, a lot remains speculative. Although knowledge has its starting point in personal experience, I believe that the condition of situatedness cannot be reduced to 'being internal to the body'. It is more aptly understood as a certain attitude to the world, an immediacy that Merleau-Ponty has variously called the 'pre-objective', 'tending towards the world', 'a taking up of the world' (Csordas 1999; Merleau-Ponty 1962). Thus, embodiment is not about the body per se. '[C]ulture and self can be understood from the standpoint of embodiment as an existential condition in which the body is the subjective source or intersubjective ground of experience' (Csordas 1999: 181).

From a somewhat different perspective (at the crossroads between phenomenology and ecological psychology) Tim Ingold has directly addressed the issue of how to understand such practical skills. He makes a range of different distinctions, for example, between 'dwelling' and 'building' (Ingold 1995), between 'umwelt' and 'discourse/symbolic thought' (Ingold 1992), and between 'technique' and 'technology' (Ingold 1993a). I see all of these distinctions as representing basically the same theoretical agenda and will primarily be discussing the latter pair. Ingold defines technique as tacit, subjective, context-dependent and practical 'knowledge how'; in contrast, technological knowledge is defined as explicit, objective, context-independent and discursive 'knowledge that' (1993a: 434–5). He maintains that one can acquire technique directly in practice ('direct perception') without the knowledge being inscribed as symbols (1992: 53–54), while technology is 'encoded in words or artificial symbols' (1993a: 434–5). He claims that direct, (culturally) unmediated perception of the environment is not only common but also central to being (Ingold 1992). This reminds one of the division in praxis theories between embodied knowledge and theoretical/linguistic knowledge (Bourdieu 1977; Giddens 1979), whereby it is supposed that the practical, embodied skills cannot be 'translated' into symbols or language. In Ingold's model there is, however, a gradual shift or transition between these two ideal-typical oppositions. There may, for instance, by style and context, be clear 'technique' aspects to talk (Ingold 1993b, see also Borofsky 1994; Shore 1996). The existence of technological knowledge is only made possible by the imagination, or construction, of 'language' as a closed linguistic system with its written manifestation as a template (Ingold 1993b; Pálsson 1991: 15).

Ingold's assertion that 'technique' is 'pre-symbolic' and that norms and rules are linked to reflection and not to practice, can, though, be dubious, especially so because it becomes difficult to perceive how routine daily activities can be both structured by and give structure to underlying models, norms and rules. In his eagerness to do away with the Cartesian split, Ingold purges culture from the pre-objective (Merleau-Ponty 1962), from what he calls technique, umwelt and dwelling. In other words he regards the everyday unreflective action, the 'being in the world', as unmediated by symbols and language. To him symbolization and categorization are only post-hoc processes of meaning construction. 'Systems of cultural classification are not … a precondition for practical action in the world, but are invoked to recover the meaning that is lost when action turns reflexively inwards on the self' (Ingold 1992: 53). However, he only manages to eliminate culture from the pre-objective kinds of action (and it becomes plausible to do so) because the culture concept that he employs and criticizes is precisely the linguistically based notion of culture that Shore and Lakoff, for example, argue against. Others have argued that non-verbalizeable, implicit knowledge can also contain abstract principles and patterns (e.g., Borofsky 1994). That is certainly also one of the main insights of Bourdieu (1977) when he outlines how the habitus may be the materially and socially (and thus culturally) constituted and structured basis for practical knowledge.

There is indeed convergence between Ingold's ideas of technique and theories of embodied cognition. I will continue to be inspired by Ingold's (and Merleau-Ponty's) ideas, but identify the differences between different kinds of knowledges not in a simplistic distinction between direct perception and culture, between technique and technology, but by attending to the multiplicity of models, articulations and inscriptions that operate. For instance, fishers' knowledge of the bottom conditions is not only given by and in their direct, bodily engagement during fishing. That is not all fishers know about adas and kuyus. Fishers talk about them, have theories about fish, bottom conditions and water bodies, and reflect upon them at a distance. I strongly believe that there is no sharp distinction between these 'linguistic' models and the 'embodied' models employed during fishing operations. They readily come together both in practice and in the hand symbolism.

We cannot, Merleau-Ponty holds, separate speech, and more generally language, from non-linguistic ways of being in the world, from what we ordinarily call bodily practice (Merleau-Ponty 1962: 174–99). Speech is bodily practice, 'one of the possible uses of my body'. Words are brought forth from the body and are not expressions of the taught, but 'his speech is his thought' (1962: 180). Here bodily practice should not be understood in a conventional manner. For Merleau-Ponty embodiment signifies, in the same manner as the pre-objective, all non-objectified approaches towards the world, in other words a 'being in the world'. He compares speech with music in order to demonstrate that the meaning of speech does not inhere in grammar or vocabulary (the 'notation'), but in its 'doing', its practice. Speech is linguistic gestures. While Lakoff focuses on how language becomes possible through the bodily basis for cognition, he is still primarily interested in language (Lakoff 1987). Merleau-Ponty's perspective is different. For him speech is also a way of being 'pre-objective'. Or, put another way, speech, as 'being in the world', is at the outset prereflexive and preabstract (Csordas 1990: 10; Østerberg 1994: vii). Speech is also a kind of bodily practice.

If we accept Ingold's and Merleau-Ponty's perspectives on language, it is no longer possible to equate discourse with language[60] or theory with language. Language has different forms of manifestation: body language; speech; writing; print; screen images. What may legitimize a distinction between speech and other ways of 'being in the world' (or, 'being towards the world', as Merleau-Ponty may have preferred to say), is that speech may 'settle into a sediment' as an intersubjective acquisition. This takes place not with its transformation, inscription, into text, as music can also be inscribed in terms of notation. Rather, '[s]peech implants the idea of truth in us, loses sight of itself as a contingent fact, and ... provides us with the ideal of thought without words ... ' (Merleau-Ponty 1962: 190).

Jack Goody (1986), as well as Walter Ong (1982), argues that the oral and the written give rise to different forms of cognition; in other words, different forms of manifestation shape cognition and experience as well as social organization. Objectification, reason, and reflection are thereby easily seen as outcomes of the technology of writing. Merleau-Ponty approaches this somewhat differently. He claims that speech gives rise to the idea of the privileged position of reason. And when speech is fixed, primarily as writing or text, the idea of an independent reason and rationality, the pure thought, is affirmed. The leap from speech to text fixes the potential for abstraction that speech presents. But that formalization and abstraction can include maps, graphs, and the like underlines that it is not language *per se*, but formalization (or 'hardened objectification'), inscription, and literalism (Herzfeld 1992, see Chapter 7) that constitute this leap.

## Fish Behaviour: Narratives and Cultural Models

When the fishers are at sea, or when their attention is focused on fishing while on shore, they are guided by an ensemble of models. This often comes out in brief expressions such as, 'I should start preparing my grey mullet nets since it seems that the poyraz (northeast) is now blowing continuously' (in springtime). This is based on a very general model which seems to be widely shared by fishers; 'When the poyraz is blowing, the sun shines continuously, and weather tends to become warmer. The water heats up as well, and the fish, which prefer warm water, move towards the shore to spawn.' The case above also indicates that it is important to the fishers to learn and share such models, not only as 'post hoc' reflections, as Ingold would have it, but also as 'production technology'.

In the Black Sea ecology and in the regional fishing economy hamsi is the most important fish. There seems to be a very powerful and widely shared model among the fishers for the behaviour of hamsi, but they seldom explicitly outline this. However, during a longer conversation with one of the senior boat owners in Keremköy in the spring of 1998, the model of hamsi behaviour was more clearly expressed. I had known Hakan for a long time and he talked about the fisheries often and willingly. He is considered by many to be one of the best *reis* (skippers). On this occasion I met him outside the local kahve and we had a somewhat more formal conversation since I taped it.

Ståle: What is the life pattern of the hamsi?

Hakan: Look, ... Allah (Cenap Allah) has created such a law, the natural law – yes nature is such, look now: towards those months everything, the birds in the sky as well as all things below, flow from Africa, those warm, very warm places, and from the ice. Towards where? Towards the Middle East, towards the east, towards the south it flows. They come from the air, come out from under the weather, or, in other words, they move with the weather. It sets off the movements, the fish also set off from below. ... Yes, nature is such a great thing. Now, let's admit that whenever autumn comes, towards the tenth month, when it is coming towards the eleventh month, when the weather has started to turn cold, hamsi flow out through the Kerch strait; right from the Crimea they stream eastwards. The bonito, the lüfer – the migratory fish – in the east [of the Black Sea] start to flow straight in that direction [westwards]. The units intersect. When the hamsi come out of there, bonito and lüfer pass the strait [Bosporus] and enter [the Sea of Marmara]. Of those remaining the dying ones die, the ones that can live stay alive, because they, the bonito and lüfer, are animals without scales, no scales ... What is it necessary to do to live in the winter? One needs to wear thick clothes, isn't that so? There must be resistance against the cold.

... ... ... ...

Now, hamsi is an animal with scales. Ninety per cent of hamsi and other scaled animals cannot live in warm places; it gets difficult, they cannot take in oxygen; life becomes difficult. The hamsi has plenty of scales, so it can live in cold water. OK, let's admit that as the temperature of the water falls to six or seven degrees, not even the hamsi can survive. But the bells ring for bonito, *lüfer*, non-scaled fish, as it falls towards ten degrees, nine degrees, they are doomed to die ... ninety per cent die.

... ... ... ...

Now, from the kuyus the hamsi part by part (*parça parça*) come out, from here and there in the deep waters. From the places where it has gathered it goes part by part, package (*koli*) party by party, party by party, party by party o-o-u-t towards the sea. The weather will blow up and the hamsi spread out, becoming a grid. In other words, it thins out wide like this [shows by spreading the fingers on one slowly horizontally moving hand]. But as soon as the cold weather [starts] ... , when it is partly cold, it seeks, seeks, seeks and gathers, becoming like a clenched fist. It gets into a really crowded state, becomes congested.

... ... ... ...

Now, this year there was a lot of hamsi in the Black Sea, crowds of hamsi coming in towards the shore. However, the weather conditions were very unusual. For instance, when it was time for snow, when we should have had bad weather, there was summer, warm weather, and the hamsi couldn't gather ... It went continuously in 'grill' formation, diffused. ... In snowy and cold icy weather, when it is very, very cold, are you able to move much? No, you cannot; come what may you will be stiff with cold, become numb. But the hamsi moves quite fast in warm weather.

S: It can easily be caught in cold weather?

Y: Of course, of course.

[Discussion of weather conditions and the occasional occurrence of 'freezing' water off Sinop]

... ... ... ...

Water currents are very important ... yes, the natural conditions have a very great importance in the fishing sector. For example, for it being possible to catch hamsi, for the season to be long, there must be strong weather towards the eleventh, twelfth month or tenth month. There must fall snow because the temperature of the seawater must fall to seven degrees, to eight degrees, in order for the hamsi not to move, so that it moves down into the kuyus. There are a variety of kuyu, or deep waters, in the Black Sea ... and the hamsi will not enter these when it is scattered. The weather shall influence it; when it becomes cold activity falls, and what can it do then? It is forced to seek shelter (*zemin*) in deep waters. In this period it moves slowly, activity decreases. Let's say that the hamsi makes sixty miles a day. When there is a weather occurrence, what will it do? The deep water should be warm, but the water temperature falls and the hamsi must find a warm environment [implicitly: in the kuyu].

This story can, on the one hand, be seen as a fisher's objectification – seeing at a distance – of a reality partly beyond experience. As such it can be regarded as a theory and is comparable to, for example, scientists' models. On the other hand, the model(s) is also based upon personal experiences accumulated as a member of a community of practitioners. It is not completely distanced from fishing activities. Hakan has experienced time and again the changes in weather, felt the cold air of winter, enjoyed the coming of the hamsi, seen the density of fish near the kuyu on the sonar display or echo sounder, seen and felt the hamsi's scaled 'clothing' etc. That these models have experiential reality for him is also highlighted by his frequent use of analogies with human bodies and behaviour ('thick clothes in winter').

The 'fish behaviour-temperature-seasonal weather changes' model as well as the human body metaphors are very widely shared by fishers in all kinds of fishing and are routinely employed as both guiding models in the actual fisheries and when 'talking at a distance'. These metaphors in themselves involve very basic, experience-near models of body and temperature and maybe even of sociality, which Lakoff (1987), in theory at least, acknowledges as a field of primary experience. Although the narrative, as a linguistic expression, naturally depends upon digital codes, meaning is to a large extent constructed through analogies. This is not only apparent in the human body analogies, but also in the style, or technique of the narrative, such as the spreading of the fingers to demonstrate the dispersal of the hamsi, or the repetition of 'party by party, party by party' which mimics the actual separation of the hamsi into lots of 'parties'.

The narrative also includes elements that have no relevance at sea. Unlike most other fishers in Çarşıbaşı Hakan has attended (but not completed) high school and likes to demonstrate that he is knowledgeable (in 'book knowledge'). He often spices his talk with semi-scientific 'facts', therefore, such as the specific water temperatures different fish can tolerate; during the same conversation he claimed that all sea animals and fish spawn when the water temperature reaches 13–14 °C in spring. Such figures have little experiential reality or relevance for the fishers. I have never seen them measure water temperatures with a thermometer. They will usually put their hand in a bucket of sea water to assess its temperature.

The narrative of Hakan may be interpreted as a composite of various elements, models and concerns. The basic structure is provided by the model of seasonal hamsi movements, in accordance with changes in weather. This main model ('fish behaviour-temperature-seasonal weather changes') is fairly standardized. It can be said to be an institutionalized cultural model (Shore 1996). But it also in itself involves several interlocking models. Weather (or 'air', *hava*), especially temperature, is clearly seen as the main driving force of the seasonal changes and the behaviour of the fish. When the fishers during late autumn wait restlessly for the season to begin, they continually wander around muttering things like, 'The weather should make one [storm]' (*hava bir yapsın*). But, again, it is symptomatic that the story mixes various factors – weather, fish, bottom topography and geography; none are treated as isolated entities. On the other hand, references to Africa, temperatures, and the like draw in the larger world, the book knowledge, and helps give the story 'grandness'. It is an important story, a story so big that he invokes Allah, and Hakan himself is part of that grand story. It is difficult to interpret this story as only 'objectification'. There is a dynamics here in which embodied aspects of knowledge are actively involved, especially in the extensive use of analogies, particularly human body analogies, in a story that depicts aspects of the fishers' environment in such a way that it can be clearly seen and discussed and thereby objectified. It is an observer's model, but an observer's model that uses 'techniques' of actor's models in order to create meaning at a distance.

The analytical challenge, then, is to hold a focus on knowledge while keeping in mind that this knowledge is always situated and seldom becomes an explicit or independent pursuit for the fishers. For instance, different behavioural modes often go together. Once a fisher taught me how to remove small crabs from triple-walled nets: 'First you tear off these (tearing off the claws), then you take these (breaking off the legs), then you take it through like this – don't crack it (holding the shell and manoeuvring it through the meshes).' Talk and body movements point at each other and form a totality of both doing and showing. Verbal utterances can be used for many purposes, and this example is clearly one of 'doing' or 'being'. Hakan's narrative illustrates a greater degree of distancing or objectification, but also remains rooted in personal experiences and directed towards more immediate concerns: to tell a good story, to impress, or simply to have a 'sweet' conversation.

## Classifications

'Indigenous' people's efforts to classify their environment has been one of the main focuses in anthropological efforts to map other 'systems' of knowledge, especially within ethnoscience and structural analyses. These approaches have also fundamentally shaped major assumptions within the research agendas of IK and TEK. My ambition here is not so much to involve myself in those very specific debates about classification, as to explore what place classification efforts have in the lived world of fishing, and what an analysis of classifications can tell us about fishers' knowledges.

It proved to be very difficult to get fishers to be explicit about 'taxonomies', and even to classify. One fisher's response when I asked him about fish classification and taxonomy is typical: 'We catch the fish, the classification we leave to the scientists!' Fishers clearly found it difficult to outline context-free taxonomies or classifications. However, Şaban (real name), an easy going small-boat fisherman in his late thirties (in 1998), without much hesitation set about working out this interesting taxonomy for me (orally, I wrote it down, see Figure 4.3).

| I. Shellfish | II. Jellyfish | III.Fish | | | |
| *Kabuklular* | *Yalgılar* | *Balıklar* | | | |
| sea snail<br>sand mussel<br>black mussel<br>crab | | III.A.<br>**Migratory**<br>*Göçmen*<br>bonito<br>*lüfer*<br>red mullet<br>*hamsi*<br>shad<br>'Russian' mullet<br>garfish | III.B.<br>**Those always present**<br>*Devamlı olan*<br>horse mackerel<br>whiting<br>grey mullet<br>dolphin<br>angel shark<br>eel | III.C.<br>**Bottom fish**<br>*Dip balıklar*<br>*kaya balğı*<br>turbot<br>flounder<br>sole<br>whiting<br>two-banded bream<br>three-bearded rockling<br>croaker<br>umbrina<br>scorpion fish<br>thornback ray<br>stingray<br>piper | III.D.<br>**'Inshore' fish**<br>*Kıyı balıklar*<br>sea bass<br>grey mullet<br>goby |
| * Inclusive class of small 'rock fish' in shallow waters. | | | | | |

Figure 4.3. Small-boat fisher's classification of 'sea animals'.

The second level (III A-D) of this taxonomy of 'sea animals' relates to where or when the fish are to be found and seems to be based upon three different oppositions:

(1) migratory: permanent    (III.A vs III.B),

(2) bottom: pelagic    (III.C, the pelagic group has not been specified),

(3) coastal: open sea    (III.D, the open sea opposition has not been specified).

Since different tasks (using different gear, at different times of year, in different places) may involve similar species, both grey mullet and whiting are to be found in two of the groups. Fishers very commonly refer to distinctions (1) and (2). Division (3) is more idiosyncratic, however, and reflects the special interests and approach of Şaban who likes the hunt and prefers to operate near shore with his very small boat. While Şaban classifies hamsi as a migratory fish, Birol, a fisherman who has worked for many years as a skipper on big purse seiners plying all the seas around Turkey, casually – in a conversation not focusing on taxonomies – spoke about the hamsi as a *yerli* (local, indigenous) fish. This distinction is based upon the image that only fish that enter the Black Sea through the Bosporus are migratory. 'Here' therefore means very different things for these two fishers: for Birol the Black Sea; for Şaban the waters outside of Çarşıbaşı. The operating principles of their taxonomy evolve from their practice, and the world presents itself as different things to fishers with different practices. The second level of Şaban's taxonomy is based primarily upon personal experience and his particular way of 'being towards the world'.

Although fishers are not concerned with 'classification' and taxonymization as an independent pursuit, they *are* concerned with the differences and relations between fish, and the naming of fish as an integral dimension of their occupational practice. The importance of differentiating between and classifying the animals of the sea is set by the agendas of being able to assess the value of a fish, to decide on the appropriate catch technique, and so on. Categorization, and certainly taxonymization, is not an independent project or task, as it may be to science. To talk about fish and sea animals without the context in which they are encountered may be a violation of the fishers' perspective.

For fishers most classifications are involved in practice, therefore the classification must also be understood as such: embedded in situated activity. Thus, pre-objective attention to different aspects of their environment during practice may involve or even require classification and taxonomy, but in a rather ephemeral and unreflective manner. Good 'technique' requires effective but dynamic taxonymization. Thus I agree entirely with Ellen that identification, and not classification, is the primary concern of most people in most kinds of activities (Ellen 1993: 65). Efficient practice that involves identification and distinctions does not require a formal set of classifications (Ellen 1993; Ingold 1992). From a strictly taxonomic point of view, Şaban's talk was full of digressions, irrelevancies and contradictions. But, from a practical point of view his 'taxonomy' was very useful.

Worsley (1997) has argued that thinking is a plural phenomenon and therefore pluralizes 'knowledges'. The question is what the character of that plurality is. For most people categorization is a complex of multiple agendas and sources. I identify several different sources for the fishers' classification of fish and sea animals. The practice of fishing and interaction with the environment through the tools of fishing constitutes one important source for identification and classification of fish. However, unlike Ingold, I would maintain that fishing practice is embedded in social relations and informed by 'external' models (but these need not be in the form of 'linguistic representations'), taking place in an environment which is already to some extent culturally impregnated. In contrast to the second order distinction between different fishes, Şaban's first order distinction between shellfish, jellyfish and fish is not an objectification of structures within practice, but rather an institutionalized cultural model where the differentiating principle is primarily morphological features. Other distinctions Şaban made were also shaped in interaction within a community of practitioners, for instance he emphasized, like Hakan, the difference between scaled and unscaled fish.

Thus, classification activities of fishers may be directed towards other kinds of concerns than the manual or practical, such as what is edible and what is not. Here moral considerations make up a part of the 'constellation'. Fishers' differentiation of fish in practice is greatly influenced by categorizations prevalent in the fish market. This is to a large extent determined by trends in seafood consumption and food taboos. To this may be added the fishers' own seafood categories, based primarily upon the Trabzon fish culture. Furthermore, the names of many fish and sea animals reflect some physical or environmental attributes of the animal.[61] I accept that a human tendency to organize animals and plants into basic level categories (Lakoff 1987), as 'natural kinds with essences' (Berlin 1992), may influence the way fishers differentiate between fish and sea animals. Finally, the influence of the scientific codification of *tür* (kind, species) and *familya* (family, relative) may also be sensed here, linked with fishers' vague ideas about essences.

Fishers' knowledges are thus not only 'embodied' or 'situated', but organized in multiple ways, shaped in dynamic interaction with the environment, equipment, other fishers and the society at large. The community of practitioners constitutes an important intermediate level between practice at sea and extraneous models. Most fishers along the Black Sea coast share similar models of the sea currents, weather, bottom conditions, fish behaviour and the like. These models are filled with local content, for example about local ada and kuyu, which is knowledge that may be shared by only a small group of fishers. The next chapter focuses more closely on the social dynamics within the community of practitioners.

CHAPTER 5

# Informal Regulations
# in Small-boat Fishing

Fisheries along all of Turkey's coasts have developed considerably in both scale and technology since the 1950s. Parallel with the developments in the purse-seine and trawl fisheries, there has been a tremendous growth in the small-boat fishing sector. These fisheries have displayed significant technological development and a large expansion in the number of boats during the last decades. Small-boat fishing has proved to be a viable option for sustained livelihood for families with few other resources (such as land, capital, or education).

Management in small-scale fishing is often seen to be based upon traditional knowledge and rules (see, e.g., F. Berkes et al. 2001). Yet, it is difficult to characterize the small-boat fishing sector on the eastern Black Sea coast of Turkey as static and backwards. On the background of a description of development and changes in a couple of small-boat fisheries on the eastern Black Sea coast this chapter discusses what is 'traditional' in 'traditional knowledge'. Are fishers bound by customary law and traditional knowledge of sea and fish? What kinds of knowledges and rules are involved in these kinds of fishing? What is the degree and character of continuity? Who are fishers?

Turkish Black Sea fishers do not belong to a clearly identifiable cultural group different from the society at large. While a majority of the fishers in Trabzon, for instance, simply consider themselves ethnic Turks, in the Province of Rize some fishers are Lazi, a small group with a distinct language, and in the provinces west of Trabzon many fishers, while being Turk, will mention their Georgian or Çepni background. Fishers in the Province of Samsun come from all ethnic and regional backgrounds represented in the province (for a map of Turkey and the Black Sea, see Figure 5.1). Many fishers in small fishing villages at the river mouths in Samsun have Caucasian roots; the Yörük (settled nomads, coming from the southeast) have their own inland water produce cooperative near Bafra; one of the largest fishing firms in Samsun is owned by a Kurdish family from Bafra; and there are many Roma and Alevi fishers in Terme. Fishing in Samsun and elsewhere along the Turkish Black Sea coast is usually not strongly related to identities. There is no 'fishing people' with a characteristic all-embracing 'fisher's culture'. People of all backgrounds easily enter into or leave the fishing sector.

It is primarily economic and demographic factors together with settlement patterns and infrastructure for fishing (harbours etc.) which decide who is a fisher. In the mid 1980s there were almost no fishers in the District of Terme. By the early 1990s there were eighty small boats and many men working as crew, but no owners of large boats. With the construction of a harbour in 1994 and the increase in sea-snail catches since 2000, Terme has developed into an important fishing centre with nineteen trawlers and 331 small boats in 2005. Many have entered this sector because of lack of other opportunities, and especially the sea-snail sector has provided one of the few economic arenas open to poor people in the coastal region (Knudsen and Zengin 2006). The fisheries are thus characterized by openness, rapid change and dynamism. As will become apparent during this chapter, this openness is, however, mostly restricted to 'locals'.

Figure 5.1. Map of Turkey and the Black Sea.

This chapter focuses on small-boat fishing in the important fishing communities in the district of Çarşıbaşı. The district has a population of approximately 30,000, a third of them residing in the coastal district centre İskefiye (see Figure 5.2). The population in Çarşıbaşı as well as in Trabzon in general is more homogenous than in Samsun. Contrary to Samsun, Trabzon did not receive many new population groups but has largely experienced out-migration during the Republican era. Thus, fishers in Çarşıbaşı are mostly 'mainstream' Sunni Turks residing close to the coast. A noticeable development in Çarşıbaşı is the relative increase in the importance of small-boat fishing during the 1990s. I estimate that the number of small-boat fishers very likely doubled from 1990 to 1997. If one calculates the number of fishers in the district of Çarşıbaşı based on the numbers of boats,[62] there were in 1997 almost as many small-boat fishers (300) as fishers working on larger vessels (330). If we add on-shore activities, probably around 700 persons, or perhaps 500 households, in Çarşıbaşı receive their main income from fishing and fishery-related activities. Most of these would most likely leave and try to make a living elsewhere if it were not for the opportunities the sea provides.

In 1990–91 the main sources of income in small boat fishing in Çarşıbaşı were catches of red mullet, bonito and sea snails, but also grey mullet and whiting were important target species for many. Some, especially older

**Figure 5.2. Overview of Çarşıbaşı.** View of İskefiye and Çarşıbaşı from above the harbour in Burunbaşı, spring 1991. Keremköy is situated near the headland Yoroz in the background. Since the photo was taken, many new buildings have been constructed, among them high rises (up to ten floors), especially between İskefiye and Keremköy.

men, obtained an important part of their income by simple hook-and-line fishing of small horse mackerel. In 1990 the typical small boat was in the range of five to seven metres and had a 9 Hp engine. From 1990 to 1997 the number of small boats in Çarşıbaşı increased slightly from just under 100 to approximately 130. However, there was a dramatic change in the use of the boats. For small-boat fishers in this region sea-snail fishing became by far the most important source of income. The sea snails are mostly caught by dredges (one to three from each boat). To facilitate more effective operation and bigger catches many have built bigger boats (7.5–12 m), which are locally conceptualized as *alametre*, and installed more powerful engines (25–135 Hp) and echo sounders. In the coastal village Keremköy there was a total of about thirty small boats in 1990, but only a couple of them were of the alametre design. In 1998 the total number of small boats had increased to 45, including 30 alametres. Almost all of these alametres were constructed during the mid 1990s.[63]

## State Fishery Regulation and Small-boat Fishing

The fisheries regulations adopted and amended every second year by the Turkish Ministry of Agriculture contain few rules that apply specifically to small-boat fishing. Fishery management in Turkey includes a wide set of general rules with regard to fishing season, area restrictions, mesh size, gear, minimum catch size and so forth. These are relevant in principle for small-boat and big-boat fishing alike. Nevertheless, a variety of 'illegal' small-boat fishing activities are not policed at all, partly because supervision is difficult and partly because bureaucrats regard the sector's contribution to total catches as insignificant and acknowledge that small-boat fishers are poor people who need a livelihood. Thus, although one regulation states the minimum legal size of various species (all recent biannual regulative circulars, e.g., GDPC 1998), nobody inspects whether small-boat fishers adhere to this. In effect it is only the regulations that apply to the dredging for sea snail and the total ban on trawling in the eastern Black Sea that are considered by managers as pertaining to small-boat fishing. However, partly due to the political influence of owners of sea-snail processing plants, the various restrictions put on sea-snail fishing are not adhered to (Knudsen and Zengin 2006). Thus, most small-boat fishing can be said to be relatively sheltered from, or ignored by, formal state regulations.

As has been demonstrated many places in the world[64] fishers often manage local or communal systems of regulation which are independent of the officially sanctioned rules. This was precisely the kind of thing I was looking for during my first fieldwork when I was primarily interested in resource-management systems in the fisheries. However, formal or semiformal rules and regulations developed by the fishers themselves were very hard to find. The fishers characteristically presented their visions of the sea as free in initial conversations. Typically on a first visit to a fishers' kahve, I found that several men would gather around me and some outspoken skippers would take it upon themselves to reply to my questions. In their replies they categorically denied that small-boat fishers apply informal regulations. 'Here,' they would say, 'the sea is free for all.' Nevertheless, on closer inspection it became evident that there is a certain amount of what I call informal management in several kinds of small-boat fishing. I will here describe and discuss the evolution and workings of some of these, notably trammel-net *molozma* fishing for red mullet in the early 1990s and the net fishing for 'Russian' mullet that evolved during the second half of the 1990s. I shall more briefly discuss small-boat dredging for sea snails.

## Informal Regulations in Red Mullet Fishing

Every year during April and May, an intensive small-scale fishery of the highly prized red mullet used to take place off Çarşıbaşı and along the rest of the eastern Black Sea coast of Turkey. Since red mullet moves at right angles to the coast, the bottom trammel nets, locally called molozma, are most appropriately set parallel to the coast. The nets used are about one metre deep and between 100 and 500m long, and are fairly expensive (about U.S.$1 a metre in 1991). The red mullet is sold for local and regional consumption. Good catches may earn U.S.$60 per boat (two or three men) each night, which made this one of the most popular fisheries in the region. In the molozma high season, when fish were abundant and nets placed in shallow waters (5–15 metres' depth), both full-time fishers and part-timers went for red mullet. The nets were set just before sunset, pulled in later in the evening and set anew to be pulled in once more in the morning. Often the nets were left in the water for the day if they were not very dirty or in need of repairs which required them to be brought ashore. A special tool, a cup mounted on a pole, was beaten (*tokmak*) on the water surface to frighten the fish into the net. Some also practiced this kind of fishing in deeper waters during the winter season (then *tokma* is not applied). This implied very hard work for smaller catches. Only the poorest fishers had started deep-water molozma fishing in the early 1990s, as the relative value of fish had risen due to generally falling catches in the fisheries.

During the winter of 1991 Vahdet was the only fisher in Çarşıbaşı who kept fishing with a molozma net all winter. He set his net regularly in deep waters. As the weather turned warmer in April and it was expected that the red mullet would start moving to shallower waters, he started to place his net in the same spot every day – he was both 'securing a position' for the coming molozma season, and seeking the first big catches of red mullet of the season which would be more valuable and therefore result in a good income. A couple of days later, Yetkin, the store owner, was out fishing for pleasure. He set his molozma net between the shore and Vahdet's net. Observing this, Vahdet told Yetkin to remove his net. Yetkin pulled in the net somewhat later in the evening. When discussing this with me, Vahdet made it clear that the position of Yetkin's net was unacceptable because it was an obstacle for fish moving towards his own net. Yetkin and Vahdet knew each other quite well as they lived in the same neighbourhood and frequented the same kahve.

This is an example of the adjustment of behaviour in molozma fisheries with reference to a general 'rule'; a net cannot be placed alongside another, parallel to the coast, as the second net would catch fish otherwise heading for the firstcomer's net (Figure 5.3). Fishers should therefore place their nets in a line extending from the firstcomer's net. The kind of net positioning exemplified in the case above was described by one fisher as 'inappropriate' (*olmuyor*) and 'forbidden' (*yasak*). A net may be set parallel to another as long as it is placed at a substantial distance outside of the already occupied position, since fish are supposed to move away from the coast during the night (Figure 5.3).

Rules for appropriate conduct for fishers in the molozma fisheries produced a general pattern. During the evenings and mornings in April and May, the coastline would be lined with buoys marking molozma nets. Each boat would use the same position regularly and would claim the

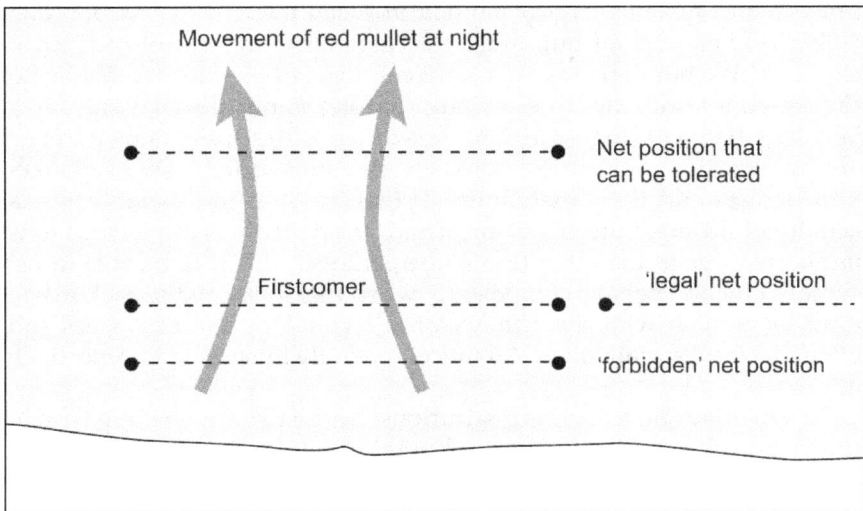

**Figure 5.3. Positioning of molozma net for catching red mullet.**

right to position their net in the same place every day during the season. If a fisher continued to set his net at the same site for several days, it would be regarded as *his* position. One part-timer conceptualized the general situation saying: 'Everyone has their obvious net-position' (*herkesin belli ağ kurma yeri var*). Moreover, even though fishers do not usually have clear conceptions of boundaries, the user-right positions are generally located close to fishers' home environs.

The principle guiding fishers' behaviour in molozma fishing is actually the outcome of adapting a more general 'rule' on which there seems to be common agreement, to the special conditions in this kind of fishing. This rule applies to all kinds of small-boat fishing all year round and may be summed up as follows: 'The fisher first occupying a location has the right to fish there for whatever resources, according to common knowledge, can be caught with the gear used. Other fishers must not go about their business in such a way as to threaten the firstcomer's right to maximize his catch'. But what is the status of this 'rule', what kind of knowledge does it involve?

## Embeddedness of Knowledge and Rules – Theoretical Approach

I have used the word 'rule' to denote certain guidelines for fishers' behaviour at sea. However, this 'rule', although shared, is not formalized or objectified, and certainly not inscribed. No fisher would spell it out, articulate it, in an explicit rule as I did above. The 'rule' is enacted in practice and remains largely implicit in social intercourse. As Bourdieu (1977: 19) has pointed out, much of 'customary law' is not codified in explicit rules, but depends on a different 'logic of practice'. Action is not the enactment of rules, just as talk (parole) is not the playing out of language (langue) (Ingold 1993b). How then is this 'rule' known? There are intriguing similarities between the embeddedness of fishers' knowledges and the situatedness of this 'rule' in the social-technical activity of fishing. Indeed, technical and social relations can be said to be implicated one in the other (Pfaffenberger 1988, 1992). To be able to fish successfully and behave competently when fishing for red mullet, fishers must be familiar with sea, fish, weather, technology, informal rules and, often, the local social milieu. All this is generally integrated unreflectively in practice.

To elucidate how 'rules/institutions' and TEK are coembedded in practice and how institutions emerge I couple theories of situated knowledge (Ingold) and embeddedness of rules (Varela). While Tim Ingold draws on phenomenology and ecological psychology to address the issue of how to understand practical skills, Varela leans on cognitive science and phenomenology to account for the embeddedness of ethics. Varela differentiates between 'ethical know-how' and 'ethical know-that' (1999). This plays on the distinction between embodiment and objectification, between the pre-objective and the reflective that I outlined in Chapter 4. When formulating this distinction, Varela takes his inspiration from Merleau-Ponty, the pragmatist John Dewey (know-how/know-that), and a 'non-information processing' direction within the cognitive sciences to which he has himself made important contributions. By applying these theories to interpersonal relations Varela thus makes an important addition to the insight established by Ingold whose perspective risks ignoring the social. It would seem that the actions of fishers when they behave decently towards each other at sea and elsewhere 'do not spring from judgment and reasoning, but from an *immediate coping* with what is confronting us ... Cognition consists not of representations but of *embodied action*' (Varela 1999: 5). He states that, '[e]mbodiment entails the following: (1) cognition dependent upon the kinds of experience that come from having a body with various sensorimotor capacities; and (2) individual sensorimotor capacities that are themselves embedded in a more encompassing biological and cultural context' (ibid: 11). This formulation situates Varela clearly at the intersection of the 'embodied cognition' theories, the language theory of Lakoff, and phenomenological theories of Merleau-Ponty and others.

Michael Lambek (1997) and Mark Johnson (1993) have both articulated ideas similar to Varela's concept of ethical know-how. I have chosen to employ Varela's concepts. The terms ethical know-how and know-that focus on the difference between the pre-objective and the representative in the domain of ethics and morals. Ethical know-how attends to 'what it is good to be', 'living wisely'. It is immediately perceived, unreflected ethical standards that 'spring from an immediate coping with what is confronting us'. Ethical know-that focuses on 'what it is right to do'. It is explicit, ideally context-independent, and often inscribed (e.g., as regulations and laws), standards for appropriate conduct. I view this as roughly the moral rules. I feel that these insights are very compelling and useful when I examine what kinds of knowledge are involved in small boat fishing.

## Ethical Know-how in Small-boat Fishing

I regard the 'firstcomer's right' as being a kind of ethical know-how. While there is no scheme for the overall organization in molozma fishing, and there are no moral precepts that apply specifically to fishing, interaction guided by ethical sensibilities – largely unarticulated values and norms – results in the described pattern in molozma fishing. The pattern is the result of the interplay, in fishers' coping, of such sensibilities with the technical and bio-physical environment. In molozma fishing the firstcomer's right is in effect for an entire season (between one and two months) and is connected to the fisher's home area. This is unique to molozma fishing. The application of the firstcomer's rule is not sufficient, therefore, to create a pattern of continuous user-right sites. The fishers claim user-rights to the same net-position only in the high season of molozma fishing. This is mainly because this is the sole period when limited accessibility is experienced and expected.

The autumn fishery for pelagic and migrating bonito involves perhaps even more fishers than the molozma fishery, and the fishers uphold rules of how nets can be positioned relative to other nets. Yet, no system of 'owned' sites operates (see Knudsen 1995). Why does the same pattern not emerge in both fisheries? Since the same basic 'firstcomer's right' principle, the same ethical know-how, applies to both, divergence in the aggregated overall pattern must be sought elsewhere. It is not space limitation, but fishers' behaviour in adapting to the different circumstances, that produces the dissimilarities between regulations in the two fisheries. Molozma fishing lends itself more easily to the emergence of continuous user-rights since:

1.  The nets used rest at the bottom and are in addition also often anchored, they are not easily moved by currents. Moreover, the nylon (monofilament) nets don't decay and can be pulled in and set again immediately and therefore left for long periods in the water without requiring drying. In this way, nets can easily occupy a position physically and, with their buoys, indexically signify occupation – or possession – of a position.
2.  Due to the outlined characteristics of the resource and applied technology, nets are most appropriately aligned in a single long row along the fairly straight coastline. Then, if the total length of nets that fishers want to set exceeds available space, there will remain no open places. Fishers will therefore have a great interest in securing the position they have already occupied. Available space tends to simply become filled up.
3.  Since the availability of red mullet is fairly evenly distributed and amounts do not vary greatly from day to day, fishers are generally content to use the same position.

When fishing for the Atlantic bonito fishers use drift nets tied to boats, nets are placed vertically to the shore, and, since it is a migrating species, availability of Atlantic bonito varies considerably. Thus, more fishers can always be accommodated, and fishers are not so eager to stick to the same position. The same ethical know-how induces the fishers to apply different 'rules' in different fisheries. It is not enough to be familiar with ethical standards. Fishers must also know the technology and the practice of fishing in order to act in an ethically sensible manner. That is precisely the point: ethical know-how is situated, context-dependent, and defies formalization in explicit rules. Technique and ethical know-how are tightly knit. You have to be a good fisher to be able to behave ethically or acceptably in the eyes of other fishers. Likewise, to be a good fisher your behaviour has to be ethically sensible. An inexperienced fisher may set his net in an inappropriate way because he does not know enough about local ecology and gear. When the shopkeeper Yetkin set his molozma net inside of Vahdet's it may have been due more to ignorance than to maliciousness.

I have no comprehensive knowledge as to the extent and kind of informal fisheries management along the Black Sea coast of Turkey. The very nature of the regulations – informal, manifest only in practice, lack of objectification – usually means that only those who participate get to know the inner workings of such regulations. On the other hand, I have also realized that once I could speak from experience, from practice, I have been able to engage fishers in conversations – although only in very informal contexts – about comparable forms or principles. Local fishers have told me that informal rules govern user-rights in fishing for shad off Çarşamba, in beach seining near Arsin (20 km east of Trabzon), and bottom-net fishing for turbot in many places. Beach seining (*barabat, manyat*), now of little general importance in the region, may be more subject to notions of territoriality. Villages or teams might possibly have laid claim to territories (stretches of coastline) and not crossed boundaries into other regions, expressed in saying such as: 'We mostly worked this area, and we never crossed the river.' Few fishers are willing or able to talk about privileged access in the important hamsi fisheries of former times. Yet one very old fisher did tell me that it used to be common to close places (*yer kapardılar*) a month before the hamsi arrived. More recently, informal regulations have evolved in fishing for introduced species such as Pacific mullet and sea snails (to be discussed below).

## Traditional Knowledge?

What I have described above may be only a small fraction of the informal management forms in small-boat fishing, and the variations between regions and even villages may be substantial. However, there is sufficient evidence that small-boat fishers along the eastern Black Sea coast of Turkey have a proclivity to work out informal regulations in various kinds of fishing, based primarily upon general principles of firstcomer rights and home areas. But to what degree can these regulations be seen as traditional? Are these forms of regulations handed down from their fathers and grandfathers? Are there any authorities or organizations that manage these regulations?

Nobody is in charge of or is imbued with the authority to organize and supervise the informal regulations in small-boat fishing. There is no formal and/or inscribed agreement stipulating individual fishers' positions or a village's territories and there has been no assembly of fishers to negotiate and plan the described pattern of regulations in these fisheries. Nor have the state bureaucracy or other extra-local agencies been involved in shaping the pattern of informal regulations. They (re-)emerge spontaneously on the aggregate level each season as the fishers adapt to the technoecological framework and interact – with other people who have business at sea – according to certain standards of ethical know-how concerning decent behaviour. It is not a consciously planned, defended and talked about system, but a 'lived' or 'enacted' system, worked out and experienced in practice. It was typical therefore that, even though I had asked whether informal regulations existed, it was not until I took part in molozma fishing myself for the first time that I started to learn about such 'rules'. Thus this knowledge is generally not verbally articulated and objectified.

Nevertheless, fishers are at times able to objectify such knowledge during informal conversation. Fishers referred to positions under continuous user-right in the molozma fisheries as 'owned' (*sahipli*). Moreover, the agreement on the principle of 'owned' positions was talked about, when I raised the issue, as 'our principle' (*bizim prensep*). However, such talk only occurs on the basis of shared experience of practice. The objectification presupposes prior familiarity with fish behaviour, fishing techniques, the impact of sea currents, and so on. On a visit to Sinop I was amazed at how much I could learn during an informal conversation with a fisher about how they go about their business at sea. This man, who also worked as an accountant for the local water produce cooperative, clearly had more schooling than the average fisher and had an unusually reflective perspective on the practice. He spoke easily of the various ways to position nets and illustrated these with simple pen drawings. While he could articulate aspects of the technical know-how, he found it difficult to explicate the social processes at work between fishers, for instance in informal regulations. In other words, he found it easier to lift aspects of the technical know-how to the level of conscious reflection than the ethical know-how.

Socialization into the knowledge of fishing is not separate from the local social structures. Young men learn the craft primarily by assisting older family members and relatives, neighbours and friends. Men without such options in their immediate surroundings may try to seek out prospective 'friends' to work with. Thus, one man from a family of carpenters learned fishing by joining an experienced small-boat fisher, assisting him at sea and on shore, and sharing the catch. But it was not a 'formalized' relationship. There is no concept by which to identify the relative positions of such partners, no 'esoteric' knowledge to be initiated into, no rituals to mark the completion of the 'initiation'. It is a very open, flexible and indeed informal process. Moreover, young men who are curious or eager to sign on the purse-seiners as crew may join for a few days as a 'friend', just for the 'tour' (*gezme*). He may lend a hand here and there, and at some point the skipper may ask him whether he would like to sign on. By then the skipper has noted his skills as well as personality and social relations to other crew members.

Unlike many other fisheries around the world, there are, except for the obvious fact that the skipper is generally more knowledgeable than the crews, no 'experts' in fishing and no traditional authority on the knowledges and practices of fishing. Individuals may be known, even renowned, for being good at special things: a crew member may be very skilled at net mending, a skipper may be very good at tracking the bonito, a small-boat fisherman may be an expert at catching mullet or turbot. The expertise is, however, not embedded in a social structure that is geared towards organizing such knowledge. Moreover, formal education in fishing is of practically no importance. Thus, at first sight the fishers' knowledges as outlined in these cases may not seem to amount to a 'tradition of knowledge' since there is no traditional governing authority and the system has not existed for a long time. Nor do fishers talk about fishing practices and knowledge as 'tradition' (e.g., as *gelenek*, *örf*), or as something 'received from our ancestors'. Yet, there are good reasons to argue that there exists a tradition of knowledge of molozma fishing: there is continuity in underlying conceptions of fairness and there is a long tradition of molozma fishing practice and gear use.

Molozma technology has long been known and used by fishers along the eastern Black Sea coast of Turkey. Nets used to be made of cotton and susceptible to decay if not regularly dried. When monofilament nets became available in the 1960s, fishers did not have to bring their nets ashore for drying and could therefore occupy a position by keeping the net more continuously in the sea. Fishers in the quarter of Faroz in the city of Trabzon then started to occupy the same position for longer periods in the molozma high season. In addition, the improved technology made possible the use of longer nets. This, together with the already high density of boats there, meant that the shift to monofilament nets led to more competition and the described pattern of informal regulations gradually emerged.

Fishers in Çarşıbaşı also started to use monofilament nets in the 1960s, but informal regulations did not emerge initially as there were very few (3–5) boats. The practice of informal regulations did not develop until ten to fifteen years later when the number of boats and fishers increased. I was told that during the second part of the 1970s fights and physical confrontations took place (at sea) between fishers from the villages Keremköy and Burunbaşı. High levels of intercommunal tensions connected to the political turmoil in Turkey during this period may have reinforced fighting at sea. Such confrontations have since become uncommon. These earlier conflicts may have consolidated a pattern of diffuse user-right territories in molozma fisheries. Previous bargaining over and subsequent establishment of territories may be the reason why fishers today abstain from fishing in areas that they do not consider their own.

One old fisher in Çarşıbaşı, who had made the shift from cotton to monofilament nets in the 1960s, told me that the molozma principle did not come into effect as a result of agreement (*anlaşma*) but emerged little by little as it became necessary (*mecburen*) for fishers to position their nets in the same place several days in a row in order to secure a place at all. Thus they also knew who operated alongside them, and who had used the same position the day(s) before. This can be illustrated by the following example. During the winter of 1991 Vahdet had been the only fisher from Çarşıbaşı using a molozma net in pursuit of red mullet. Other fishers eventually began molozma fishing on an irregular basis and in various locations, as the expected time for the red mullet's approach to the coast drew nearer. The weather was unstable, the work hard and the catches so minute that few regarded it as worthwhile. The best catches were still made at a depth of 25–30 metres. Spring was late that year, and when the weather cleared up and offered some warm days around 20 April, many fishers started the season while others shifted to molozma from other types of gear. The fishers began to stick more permanently to a single position. Vahdet could name six or seven boats/fishers using molozma to catch red mullet, and all of them operated close to his position just outside the harbour. They all knew each other well and all frequented the same kahve, which was associated with villages just west of İskefiye. At the same time fishers from Keremköy begun molozma fishing right off their village.

Although the pattern reemerges 'spontaneously' every season, it is something the fishers expect to happen and which they therefore adapt their strategies to, for example by planning 'where to position the molozma net this year'. Fishers came to conceptualize the regulations as a system of commonly agreed rules and expectations of the pattern's reemergence. This means that both the actual observed pattern of net positioning *and* the fishers' conceptualizations developed gradually and informally over many years. It was worked out through a multitude of informal encounters at sea and on shore and therefore evolved in an interplay between, on the one hand, changes in technology and the number of fishers and, on the other hand, fishers' responses and interactions.

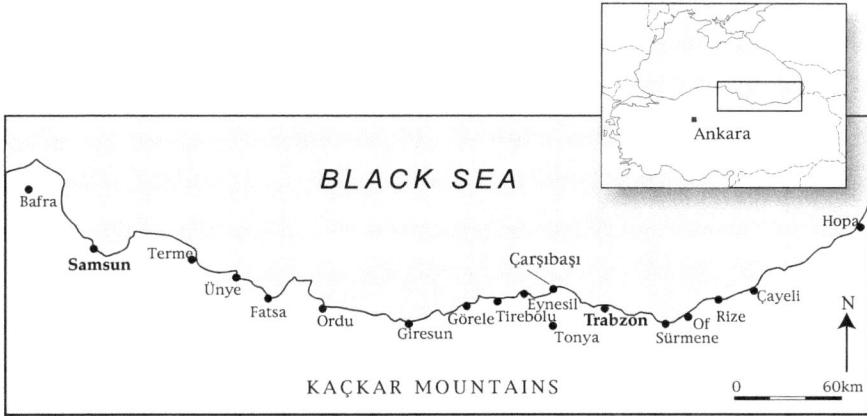

**Figure 5.4. Map of eastern Black Sea region of Turkey.**

There is also etymological evidence that there exist continuities (tradition) in the practices, and by implication in the knowledges, of the fishers. First, 'molozma' has its root in Greek (Kahane et al. 1958: 492), and its pre-First World War use in Çayeli (see map of eastern Black Sea region, Figure 5.4) is mentioned by Kazmaz (1994: 273). Second, the basic technology of purse-seine fishing has remained unchanged throughout this century, and the terminology for both operations and equipment indicate deep roots in a common Levantine marine language that was primarily based on Italian dialects, but with Greek and Turkish additions (Kahane et al. 1958).

Third, while some fishing grounds (ada) are named by proximate places onshore (*'Eynesil adası'*), a few also have their own proper names, such as two fairly wide shallow grounds off the city of Trabzon. These are important fishing grounds for small-boat fishers from Faroz. They bear the names *'Büyük* (the big) *Panavrası'* and *'Küçük* (the small) *Panavrası'*. The fishers say that the names are Greek and that they do not know their meaning. This indicates that fishers have set their nets on these grounds for a long time, and that there is continuity, and therefore a tradition, from the times before the First World War when many fishers in Trabzon were Greek.

## Rules and Tradition

Although the rules in molozma and other kinds of fishing are fairly new, I think it is reasonable to claim they are based upon 'traditional' knowledge and codes of conduct. However, if I were to try to identify tradition at the level of rule itself, it would hardly be plausible to regard the rules in molozma fishing as traditional. Fikret Berkes describes a similar development of new rules in coastal fishing in Mediterranean Turkey but finds that the rule making in question is not based on tradition (F. Berkes et al. 2001: 178). Elsewhere, Berkes has claimed that traditional ecological knowledge is 'both cumulative and dynamic, building on experience and adapting to changes' (F. Berkes 1999). However, it is less clear how this comes about. The TEK approach is less specific on how rules are embedded in tradition. How do management systems based upon TEK evolve over time?

As mentioned in the discussion about CPR in the Introduction, the NIE approach also has problems accounting for how rules come about. Moreover, NIE tends to ignore the larger context in which rules emerge and exist. How are the rules 'embedded' and emerge in society? What happens to a rule when a fishery declines or is discontinued? Sometimes it is though that the formalization of 'traditional' management institutions in small-scale fisheries safeguard and even strengthen the system (see, e.g., Bailey and Zerner 1992). But definitions of 'tradition' that pay too much overt attention to explicit rules and 'forms' (e.g., the pattern of molozma fishing) may be misleading and of little use. They risk being essentializing and reifying, and can give the impression of 'frozen' traditions; or of a complete collapse of or break with traditions although, beneath the surface forms, there are continuities.

This leads me to query at what level can we identify change and dynamic development? How much and what kind of change before some practice is not 'tradition'? Did the end of the aggregate pattern in bottom-trammel-net fishing for red mullet in the mid-1990s result in the discontinuation of traditional knowledge? In order to shed further light on these issues I will describe how the decline of the molozma fishery is followed by the development of another fishery in which emerge rules similar to those in the molozma fishery. Tradition, I claim, was not discontinued with the end of molozma fishing.

## New Tradition: Fishing for 'Russian' Mullet

In the spring of 1998 nobody secured fishing spots for molozma by leaving a marker. Red mullet were less abundant than before, very likely because the benthic ecology and fauna was degraded by sea-snail dredging and illegal small-boat trawling. In addition, the molozma nets to some extent compete with sea-snail dredging for space. Thus, the intensity of the seasonal molozma fisheries declined dramatically during the 1990s. By the late 1990s many fishers chose to invest their resources during the spring season in either sea-snail dredging or netting of the introduced species Pacific mullet (*Mugil soiuy*). The first examples of a new species were observed along the coast of the Turkish Black Sea in the early 1990s. In the beginning there were only occasional catches of and stories about a 'new' mullet. By the middle of the 1990s the general idea had developed that there was now a new fish, popularly called 'Russian' mullet. This name has humorous associations for most men with *'Nataşalar'*, 'Russian prostitutes', who also arrived in the beginning of the 1990s, coming down from the northeast, like the fish is supposed to do.

Was there any kind of continuity between the molozma and 'Russian' mullet fisheries? By 1998 the fishery for 'Russian' mullet had already acquired a certain degree of predictability, pattern and 'tradition'. Fishers prepared for the season in May-June and had fairly clear expectations about when the fish would arrive, how it would behave, and how to catch it. The mean size of the fish had increased to approximately one kilo and it came in large runs towards the shore. It was possible to make very substantial catches. Although unusual, one small boat could catch as much as one ton in a day. 'Russian' mullet is not very highly esteemed as food, but it has gradually found a market. The season continues for twenty to thirty intensive days, and for the fishers in Çarşıbaşı this fishery has developed into one of the main sources of income, on a scale almost comparable to the autumn bonito fisheries. A brief survey of the catch technique and social dynamics involved in this fishery will illustrate the ways in which and degree to which 'traditional knowledge' is involved.

First, with regard to catch technique, how did fishers go about catching this new fish? Basically they modelled their catch technique on the well-established and widely-known technique for catching the less abundant 'native' (*yerli*) grey mullet. Once this mullet has been visually observed

**Figure 5.5. Casting a net for 'Russian' mullet.**

fishers set a floating net around the small shoal of fish, enclosing as much as possible of them between the shore and the net. The ends of the net are curled to form *koltuk*s ('armpits', see Figure 5.6). Fish are considered to be able to see the net, and the koltuks are supposed to increase their confusion as they try to escape when the fishers attempt to frighten them into the net. The net, which like the molozma is a kind of trammel net (but with larger meshes) approximately two fathoms deep, is lifted immediately. Away from shore the net can be set in a circle, with the two koltuks coming together.

Fishers use the same kind of nets for catching the 'Russian' mullets and set the net with koltuks (see Figure 5.5). Most nets were set in the shape of the left-hand example in Figure 5.7. However, fishers tried out many different shapes in order to, as they put it, 'confuse' (*şaşırtmak*) the fish. The nets were invariably set towards the shore, with the 'opening' towards

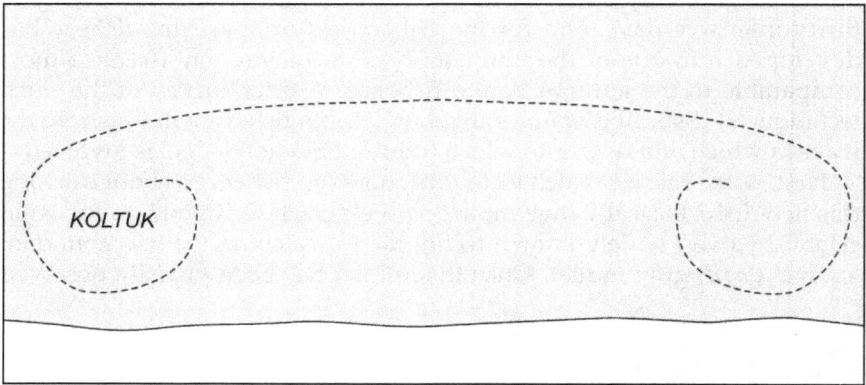

**Figure 5.6. Typical net set for grey mullet.**

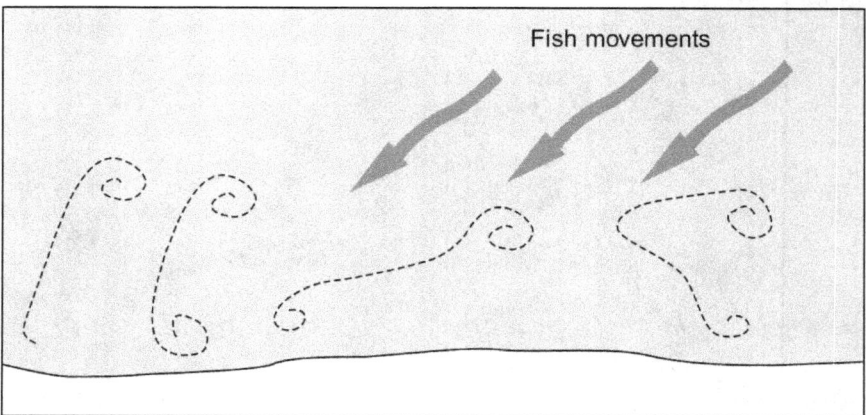

**Figure 5.7. Alternative ways to set nets for 'Russian' mullet.**

the east, since the fish are held to come from that direction. Experience has shown that most fish were caught in the koltuks.

During the preparations for the 1998 season many fishers were busy adding depth and length to their nets. Many held that fish often escaped under the nets, so it was considered important to close the gap between the net and the bottom. After the net is cast it is left for some hours before it is lifted. The net may be set and lifted several times each day and through the night. They do not attempt to frighten the fish into the nets, but some keep guard at sea and close the gap of the koltuk with their boat if they see fish swimming into the koltuk. These nets are very sensitive to winds and currents. Fishers often have to struggle to disentangle the nets in the koltuk, which may have folded completely in on itself. This heightens a need to keep constant watch on the net, so the fishers prefer to cast their nets close to their home area (house or kahve). Alternatively, they may go away for several days to fish in waters less influenced by the prevailing currents and winds.

Already ten days before the first 'Russian' mullets arrived, some of the most diligent fishers set out buoys in order to secure a good fishing spot for the upcoming season. Fishers clearly saw a parallel between this and the equivalent practice in molozma fishing and some said that they put the buoy there in order to establish ownership of the spot (*yer sahiplamak için*). However, not everyone did this. Only one of the around fifteen fishers in Keremköy who engaged in the hunt for the Russian mullet marked a spot, right off the small village breakwater. A few others later put out markers, one with a paraffin lantern, and kept to the same place during the entire season. Because the nets are mostly set from the shore outwards and it is acceptable to set them fairly close together, there is less competition for space than in the molozma fishery, although some sites may be more popular than others and occupied early in the season. However, as was the case in the molozma fisheries, fishers from Burunbaşı and Keremköy did not fish in front of each other's settlements.

Thus, to summarize, the knowledge of technique, fish and environment which fishers employ in their pursuit of 'Russian' mullet is developed in a dialectic process between the established knowledge of mullet fishing and creative experimentation to create a new rule or 'institution'. But, on the level of ethical know-how the same basic principles apply as in the molozma case. It is the same tradition of knowledge, the same local culture, which the fishers draw upon when they, in their handling of their nets, strive for technical perfection and ethical performance.

Although fishing for the 'Russian' mullet is new and shows a novel pattern, I would therefore claim that its practice embodies aspects of 'tradition'. It draws upon 'traditional' know-how of nets, sea currents, fish behaviour, and more particularly mullets. This is employed in a creative manner, together with established and shared know-how regarding firstcomer rights and place reservation – as in the molozma fisheries – making possible the swift and successful development of a new kind of fishing. I want to stress, however, that tradition is on the level of knowledge as know-how, as it is employed, involved, or enacted in practice, and not on the level of form, rule or institution, which is an emergent quality. The different patterns in molozma, Atlantic bonito, and 'Russian' mullet fishing conceal continuity in basic knowledges that are all part of a tradition of knowledge and of a tradition for the appropriate conduct of fishers. Tradition therefore only exists in so far as and as long as it is reproduced in the practice of fishing. Fishers' knowledge and the emergent pattern of informal regulations are neither fixed in any kind of inscription nor framed by any kind of formal organization.

The general pattern of regulations in molozma and 'Russian' mullet fishing is not formalized therefore but expected, and appears to imply some kind of custom or tradition. A tradition of knowledge exists as an enduring pool of fishers' experiences and knowledges of the sea, fish, and gear, which are often shared and common. Fishers' interaction is informed and sanctioned by shared ethical know-how, particularly ideals of fairness, decency, and reciprocity, which, when applied to fishing, manifests itself as informal rules regarding the firstcomer's right[65] and a tendency, but no 'rule', that fishers should have privileged access to 'home waters' for certain kinds of fishing, especially those that are closer to shore or in shallow waters, such as molozma fishing. Thus, fishers are restricted by a set of codes, values and knowledges, by ideas of the traditionally appropriate forms of interaction between people. These experiences, codes, sensibilities and knowledges are shared by various levels of communities of practitioners ranging from the fishing community at large (in Turkey, Black Sea coast), to the group of fishers regularly setting their net on the same fishing ground.

## Tradition, Conflict and Creativity

On the level of both ethical and technical know-how, continuity is supplemented with creativity and conflict. Fishers' experimentation with new net positions is not unique to the fishing for 'Russian' mullet, but actually occurs to some degree in most kinds of fishing. In addition, other developments suggest that what constitutes proper conduct at sea is not always agreed upon and static. There is not only tacit agreement, but also confrontations and conflict, quarrels, mutterings and slander, as well as negotiation. Until the middle of the 1980s, small-boat fishers in Yalıköy, a few kilometres west of Çarşıbaşı, that specialize in whiting fisheries, used to go as far east as Hopa in pursuit of this fish. But, when the locals started to chase them off, especially by cutting their nets, the small group from

Yalıköy left. For some time they also fought with the more numerous Eynesil fishers for access to the rich whiting grounds off Eynesil. Eynesil is much closer to Yalıköy than Hopa is, and after some time they came to an understanding that granted the Yalıköy fishers access.

There has also been an increasing degree of conflict over sea-snail dredging. While fishers in 1991 could range freely along the coast in pursuit of rich sea-snail grounds, communities have striven increasingly since then to restrict sea-snail dredging in their 'home' waters. Sea-snail fishers from Çarşıbaşı and Yalıköy have been driven away from Hopa and other places. Towards the end of the 1990s fishers from Çarşıbaşı decided that it was 'comfortable' (*rahat*) to dredge for sea snails only between Trabzon and Görele, even avoiding some areas within this region. In the homogenous small-boat fishing community of Gerze (Sinop Province) small-boat fishers chase trawlers from their home waters. Fishers in the small-boat fishing communities Eynsil and Faroz are both less well equipped for sea-snail dredging and oppose it because they believe it to be harmful. They enforce informal restrictions on fishers from their own communities and try, partly in cooperation with state supervising bodies, to keep strangers out of 'their' waters. Thus, some fishers are actually trying to work out a new rule for which there is no prior tradition and which is highly controversial among fishers. Interestingly, trying out a new location or enclosing a territory can also mean testing out a moral border. Morals or ethical sensibilities are an integral part of the practice of fishing.

## Social Organization and Ethical Behaviour in Small-boat Fishing

In the district of Çarşıbaşı most inhabitants living in rural coastal communities were born and raised in the community where they are presently living. Migrants coming from the mountainous interior mainly settle in the township centre. Almost all men, including fishers, have long-established and complex local relationships to the other men through kinship, neighbourhood, friendships, patron-client relations and work. Social relations among males are articulated above all in the closeness of interaction and perception of 'all as equal' in the local kahve. In this arena different kinds of fishers also mix with local people who make a living in other ways, such as teachers, bus drivers, carriers, shop keepers, farmers, traders (*tüccar*s), and so on. Sometimes the kahve clientele and the village identity overlap (as in Keremköy), but most often they do not. In any case, it is unusual for fishers to socialize with fishers outside of their immediate group.

In Çarşıbaşı there are two primary reasons for interaction between small-boat fishers: cooperation and assistance in the work, and exchange of information. The most important and immediate of these tasks are ideally handled within close family relations. Descent in Çarşıbaşı is rigorously patrilineal and settlement virilocal. Small fishing boats are either owned individually or in partnerships between father and son(s) or brothers. The family-based work on the boat is also the primary context for socialization into fishing and sharing of information. When the team composition requirement cannot be met within the close family circle (father, sons and brothers), more distant relatives, especially patrilineal cousins but also affinal relations, may together constitute stable teams. Although families ideally constitute close-knit units with a large extent of sharing and little internal conflict, there is sometimes conflict between the ideally absolute paternal authority and the real desire of the son(s) for independence and esteem. I know also of several cases where brothers have fallen out with each other and discontinued joint fishing activities.

Cooperation and pooling of resources also occur between friends. Fisher friends within 'diffuse user groups' exchange information, support each other's user-rights in certain fisheries, assist each other when extra manpower is needed (e.g., pulling a boat on shore for repairs), and occasionally form more or less enduring partnerships. In small-boat fishing friends seldom share ownership while it is more common for friends to pool resources in big-boat fishing (yet, without renouncing the individual family-owned companies). Teamwork among friends is not only facilitated by but also seems to be contingent upon the partners continually articulating and reconfirming the friendship. In 1990–91 neither Murat nor Şaban, two small-boat fishers, had sons or other family members or relatives able to assist them at sea. For an extended period in the autumn of 1990 they worked together continuously in mullet fishing. They used Murat's net and Şaban's boat and shared the catch fifty-fifty. Their personalities are very different: Şaban is an easy-going man who likes a drink; Murat is more introvert and religiously conscientious. Despite this, they spent a lot of time together in a kahve in the township that catered to all of Çarşıbaşı and was a kind of 'neutral' ground. This socializing was partly required by the logistics of fishing, but two brothers who worked together in the same kind of fishing spent much less time together; their allegiance did not need constant reconfirmation since they were brothers. After a couple of months, relations between Murat and Şaban became strained and they stopped working together. After that they did not sit together at the kahve. Murat returned to solitary work while Şaban started to hang around with his new fishing partner Ahmet in Ahmet's regular kahve.

Most fishers in Çarşıbaşı are 'locals' with established and complex relationships with family, friends and neighbours. There are many new fishers with no or little family background in fishing, but entry is in practice not open to everyone. I know of only one case of a stranger moving into Çarşıbaşı and trying to establish himself as a fisher. In 1990 Mert brought his family from his native town near İskefiye. He set up a small store selling equipment to small-boat fishers, but business was slack so he tried to supplement his income by fishing. Although he did not violate the informal fishing rules, he was, however, not accepted by the locals. His problem was that he failed to become a 'local'. He felt increasingly uneasy in Çarşıbaşı; his net was cut in the sea at night, and he became more and more isolated in the neighbourhood kahve. It probably annoyed others that he portrayed himself as generally being more knowledgeable about fishing than the locals and that he dared to characterize them as being lazy since they, in his opinion, spent their time complaining about the political situation instead of taking advantage of the potential the sea provided. Mert not only lacked local kinship and long-standing friendship bonds, he also lacked the ethical know-how or sensibility that could have helped him to take more careful steps into the community. After having spent one year in Çarşıbaşı Mert, resentful and disillusioned, eventually moved back to his native town. Success as a fisher is just as much dependent upon ethical know-how as upon technique.

When people interact at sea, they have to take into consideration the fact that they also mingle with some of these men at other times and in other situations. That is why Yetkin so readily acquiescence when Vahdet asked him to remove his molozma net. Ethical sensibilities in fishing are part of the general 'code of conduct' among people in the coastal communities. The ability to find partners and to acquire information from others depends critically upon an individual's moral standing in the community. Thus, what are the bases for evaluations of people's moral standing?

First of all, moral standing is not strictly individual, but is to a large extent a reflection of the moral standing of the family. Indeed, the family is *the* moral unit. The moral standing of one family (parents and offspring) may also reflect upon other close kin. The small boat fisher Metin regularly worked together with his unmarried son Aydın on their small boat. When popular slander had it that Aydın was responsible for the theft of some valuable coils of telephone cable, Metin's paternal cousins and neighbors Vahdet and Fuat, as well as his brother's son Osman – all small boat fishers – distanced themselves from him. They established a *konuşmaz* ('no-talk') relation. While Osman and Vahdet exchanged certain information about fishing after this incident, Vahdet and Metin never did. Vahdet distanced himself from Metin and his family not in spite of, but rather because, they are close relatives. He did not want to be tainted by the bad reputation that Metin's family had recently acquired.

The more important fishers tend to socialize with men outside of their neighbourhood and even outside of Çarşıbaşı. However, for the small-boat fishers the world centres on the local clique of friends who habitually meet in their local kahve. Friendship between men is symbolized by generosity and sharing (tea, cigarettes, etc.); by physical gestures such as holding each other's hand, even stroking an intimate friend's hand for half an hour or more; through ironic humiliating jokes; and simply by spending time together. Mutual trust, respecting the other's family and possessions, and not trying to 'profit' from the friendship are among the valued qualities.

On the other hand friendships are clearly regarded as strategic relations, and most people try to establish new friendships that can expand their sphere of action. It is not an alien idea to get in touch with complete strangers, because if individuals can, as White (1994) has so vividly demonstrated, trace some line of connecting relationships, if only at the outer fringes of their individual circles, a relationship may be established. People try to establish a link through a series of intermediary face-to-face contacts. Friendships are often seen to include a potential for reciprocity and mutual indebtedness (White 1994). Thus, friendships embody an integral tension between the ideal companionship and the instrumental. The instrumental dimension may never be realized, or may alternatively be 'over exploited' so that the 'friend' aspect of the relationship is ruined. The friend becomes a trickster, swindler or charlatan (*dolancı, üçkağıtçı, şarlatan*). The very great importance placed on (male) friendship relations, and their vulnerability, has been claimed to be a pervasive feature in many Mediterranean (Davies 1977; Herzfeld 1992: 173) and Middle Eastern (Bates and Rassam 1983: 244–5) societies. Friendship in Çarşıbaşı and beyond may from one point of view be conceived as 'techniques' for influence; the wider the circle of friends a man commands the more power he possesses.

The population in Çarşıbaşı is, relatively speaking, religiously very devout, and religiously derived norms are obviously important in assessing people's moral standing. Nevertheless, as exemplified by the cooperation between Şaban and Murat, the degree of religiosity had little influence on interaction in fishing. Whether one fisher is able to get along with another depends more upon whether he respects him as a 'good man', than on whether he keeps his fast or is conscientious in all his five daily prayers. The most successful purse-seine fishing company in Çarşıbaşı, the Can Kardeşler (real name), is owned and managed by a group of brothers who are religiously very devout. Nevertheless, they cooperate with whomever it makes economic sense to interact with, and at the time of fieldwork their accountant was a self-declared secularist.

In Çarşıbaşı many certainly see moral conduct as inherently *Muslim*. However, I find it difficult to subsume all moral standards and ethical know-how under the label of religion. As was seen in the conversation with the accountant-fisher in Sinop many standards for interpersonal interaction remain unarticulated as they seem self-evident. Such evaluations are only summed up in standard expressions such as 'He is a good man', 'He is a very stubborn (*inat*) man', and 'What an "asshole" he is!' While religiously stipulated moral conduct is generally regarded as crucial for a man's standing, only excesses are sanctioned among fishers. There is thus reason to speculate whether all ethical standards for interpersonal interaction are actually framed by the vocabulary of Islam and the codes of honour, shame (*şeref, namus, ayıp*) and so on. This position is echoed by the findings of Gilsenan (1996) in his study of authority, hierarchy and violence in a Sunni Muslim community in Lebanon and in Tapper and Tapper's study (1991: 62) of the confluence of Islamic and Republican ideology in a town in western Turkey. A moral universe of ethical sensibilities wider and more diffuse than Islam is mobilized by fishers when they evaluate others' moral qualities.

In Çarşıbaşı the informal regulations in small boat fishing – and more generally interaction between fishers and among the population at large – are based upon local and customary values, a body of ethical know-how which is lived, embodied and situated in social practice, as a kind of 'social poetics' (Herzfeld 1985), but only rarely spelled out in explicit rules. Fishers' knowledge is socially embedded in a universe of morality and is interestingly at conflict with the ideally neutral knowledge within science. Fishers' ethical sensibilities are an integral part of the fishing practice, not just something drawn in from the outside, post hoc and reflexively, in order to evaluate the practice. I would claim that, not only does morality impinge upon knowledge and knowledge become a resource in ethical or moral discourses, but knowledge is *already* ethically impregnated by being socially constituted. This ethical knowledge comes into play in appreciation and evaluation of family life, friendships and allegiance to locality and community. It is a tradition of knowledge that is not objectified, and in conversation only diffusely codified in characterizations of people by expressions such as: 'He is a good/bad (*kötü/iyi*) man', 'He is a self-seeking man/opportunist (*menfaatçı*)', 'He is a man with good intentions (*iyi niyetli bir adam*)', and so on. What is interesting about these concepts is that they refer to a moral universe and standards that lack clearly defined rules and scripts. They are inherently negotiable. When you set your molozma net you are safer if those setting their nets close to you are friends. But there are no formal criteria for belonging or membership, such as those found in fisheries in many parts of the world, and those documented in Alanya on the Mediterranean coast of Turkey (F. Berkes 1992).

## Conclusions

The outline of the practice and knowledge of small-boat fishing above demonstrates the degree to which ethical and technical know-how are intertwined, tacit and not easily objectified as 'rules'. Interaction between small-boat fishers builds upon both (1) their knowledge of the marine environment, and (2) upon highly traditional values and rules (custom) for accepted behaviour between neighbours, relatives, and friends. There is no one single set of values or codes that is drawn upon to direct and evaluate behaviour. Ethical sensibilities as well as moral rules from models as diverse as manhood, kinship, family, neighbourhood, village, friendship and Islam guide people's behaviour. But these models are not separate, nor is there a 'segmented hierarchy' of models.

Technological change and expansion of the scale of fishing should not blind us to continuities in fishing skills and ethical sensibilities. In the cases described here there is tradition in the sense of continuities at the level of know-how as it is employed, involved, or enacted in practice. There is less continuity at the level of form which is an emergent quality that conceals continuity in basic, socially embedded, knowledges. Tradition therefore only exists in so far as and as long as it is reproduced in the social practice of fishing. Ethical know-how does not constitute rules that are easily 'transported' to other contexts, nor easily 'designed' by outside agents or agencies, as the NIE approach sometimes seems to imply.

The approach chosen here does not imply a rejection of generalizing ambitions, but intends to qualify the NIE and TEK approaches. It is difficult to precipitate out traditional institutions and norms without specifying cultural depth and context. Although accepting the importance of informal rules, approaches to resource management inspired by NIE tend to limit their view to cost-benefit considerations directly related to the resource in question. These approaches easily ignore how rules and knowledges are embedded in persons and in society and may therefore also fail to appreciate the complex interplay of natural environment, technology, skills, and ethical know-how. In small-boat fishing on the eastern Black Sea coast of Turkey we cannot identify a set of rules pertaining particularly to each fishery.

Even unorganized communities of fishers can have the capacity to develop management rules for their fishing activities. And even when there is considerable change in technology, practice and scale of fishing, 'traditional' codes of conduct and 'traditional' knowledge may inform the management regime. On the other hand, the 'tradition' I have described is a dynamic continuity, open to innovation and adaptation to new circumstances. Traditional standards for ethical know-how can be challenged through conflict and negotiation. New technology and changes in markets or resources encourage fishers' creativity, as in their experimentation with nets in the fishing for 'Russian' mullet. There are also creative dynamics on the level of the social organization of the fisheries, as exemplified in the working out of new informal rules of access. The 'emergence' of rules and management practices will be more easily understood if we include in our analysis fishers' ethical know-how and their dynamic adaptation to changing contexts of fishing.

The informal and non-inscribed (e.g., in local or state legal codes) character of rules ensures the potential for dynamism. Excessive formalization may be unresponsive to new management needs as adaptations change (see Knudsen 1995 for an elaboration of this). Traditions of fishing must be understood in a diachronic perspective. There may have been continuities in certain aspects of traditions of knowledge over the last hundred years or so despite radical technical, economic, social and political changes. There has probably been more continuity at the level of fishers' ethical sensibility than in the state's approach to fisheries and fishers.

I find that conventional understandings of IK and TEK are unable to account for the complex qualities of knowledge that I have described in this and the previous chapter. A rendering of these knowledges as IK/TEK versus science is simplistic and insufficient to grasp their social and cognitive complexity. Although fishing practice clearly involves 'traditional knowledge', adoption of advanced technology and rapid change in fishing practices means that fishing on the Turkish Black Sea coast also depends upon ways of knowing that are not easily described as IK or TEK. Furthermore, the widespread assumptions that people's ecological knowledge is part of their 'tradition' or 'custom', and that IK and TEK is associated with a special group of people – either ethnically or geographically distinct – do not fit well with my observations. Fishing is one of many ways to make a living within the complex and dynamic communities of 'ordinary' Turks, with a variety of religious, geographic and ethnic backgrounds, along the Turkish Black Sea coast. Fishers do not make up a distinctive ethnic group or a separate population unit, except for very specific (fishing) purposes.

CHAPTER 6

# Fishing Careers, Family and Friendships

This chapter tells the story of fishery development in the district of Çarşıbaşı since approximately 1950. The focus here is particularly on big boat purse seine fishing. By way of narrating individual fisher careers I discuss the role state initiatives in fisheries, improved infrastructure, general economic development, and seafood consumption have had for the developments in the fisheries. I explore how the economic, technological and social changes in the fisheries have affected the kinds of knowledges fishers employ. Of particular importance for fishers' knowledge are the extended social scale of the fisheries and the increased importance of politics. In the second half of this chapter I take the discussion of friendship and networking, initiated in the previous chapter, one step further.

The discussion will here proceed by focusing on three conceptually distinct ideal-typical fisheries adaptations which I regard as overlapping in time, but which are still typical for different stages in the recent development of the fisheries. The types will be exemplified by the men, the entrepreneurs, who were among the first to pick up new practices which were in time generally accepted and adopted. It is my own categorization and not one prevalent among the fishers. Since the fisheries have undergone rapid changes, a heuristic focus on 'entrepreneurship' to specify the interplay between contextual changes, agents, and aggregated effects makes it easier to identify the changing dynamics of the fisheries. The material for this chapter largely comes from conversations and interviews with fishers.

Like many other fisheries of the world, the Turkish fisheries have also become increasingly capital intensive, large scale and dependent on advanced technology. In Trabzon fishing was consolidated into two often conflicting sectors: small-boat labour-intensive and large-boat capital-intensive fishing. In the rural and semi-rural communities in the province of Trabzon small-boat and large-boat fishers generally live in the same communities and interact on a daily basis. The large boats are not owned by foreigners or large metropolitan (i.e., Istanbul) consortiums that come from the outside and extract the resources from under the noses of the 'indigenous' people, as is the case in many of the third-world fisheries. The situation in Turkish fisheries at present is not an example of some neocolonial situation, but rather resembles similar developments that took place earlier in the North Atlantic. There has not been a technological 'great leap', but rather a gradual (although swift) appropriation of new technologies through the career of individual teams.

## Type 1: Labour Intensive Fisheries

According to old fishers in Faroz, in the city of Trabzon, there were in the 1950s only around ten teams (*takım*) in the eastern, or possibly the whole, Turkish Black Sea region: one in Fenerköy (the Lahoğlu team) two or three in Sürmene,[66] one in Kalecik (east of Trabzon) and five to six in Faroz, City of Trabzon. Crew were, however, recruited from a wider region, especially the Çarşıbaşı-Fenerköy area. In Çarşıbaşı, many claim that Ali Reis[67] was the first local boat owner (*mal sahibi*) to form a team. He hunted dolphins during the 1940s and probably started to use shotguns for this purpose when it was legalized around 1950. The pursuit of dolphin by medium-sized boats (10–12 m) often took the fishers far off shore. Locally, this hunt was one of the few options for cash income. Later on, Ali Reis switched to *ığrıp* (seine), to catch pelagic fish such as hamsi. Two boats ten to fifteen metres long were employed.

During the 1950s some fishers started making use of engines, thereby increasing the area of operation considerably; one motorized boat could pull two others all the way from Trabzon to Fatsa where for months they would fish hamsi, which tended to stay in deep kuyus, often also called *yatak* (bed). This fishery was very strenuous. Nets were small, approximately ten to forty fathoms deep and one hundred fathoms long. Since they were made of cotton, nets were heavy and required many men to lift them. Drying the nets (because of the danger of their rotting) also required substantial labour. A fishing team would typically comprise approximately forty men on a main boat (12–15 m) and a couple of supplementary vessels (reserve or carrier and net boat). In the beginning of the 1960s purse-seine fishing was still very labour intensive and, except for the engines, based upon locally-produced technology. In addition to the boat owner's locally-based social position that enabled him to raise funds and recruit crew, his personal involvement in the fishing and his *reislik* (skipper-skill) – especially his ability to seek out and spot shoals of fish – was critical for the success of a team.

Ali Reis was regarded as the 'big' fisherman in Çarşıbaşı during the 1940s and early 1950s. But he was big because of his skills as skipper, not because of his material assets. He may have been – here I can only speculate – an innovator and a risk-taking skipper at sea. Nevertheless, the cultural emphasis on reislik and the fact that there was no one to carry on Ali Reis' business when he died in 1965 (his sons had long since moved to Faroz to pursue small-boat fishing – a common move to get closer to the market), indicate the relative low importance of accumulated capital in this adaptation. He didn't head an innovative and expansive enterprise that went into a spiral of growth.

Until at least the early 1960s catches of most species were primarily sold in local urban centres. For fishers in Çarşıbaşı this primarily meant Trabzon. With thirty-five thousand inhabitants in 1950, it was the only major city and the main market in the region. Fish, especially hamsi, could be offered for sale in rural areas on local market days, but since the economy of the region was mainly of a subsistence character, fish was difficult to market. Surplus catches of hamsi were delivered to the EBK fish oil and meal factory in Trabzon for a very low price, or used as fertilizer, especially for the tobacco crops in Akçaabat. There was both a domestic and an international demand for dolphin blubber. Nevertheless, marketing the fish was a prevalent problem. Thus, in the era of Ali Reis, resources were abundant, but lack of demand made investment in new technology, beyond perhaps a small engine, unfeasible. The main assets in fishing were labour and personal abilities and skills, especially those of the skipper-owner. Monetary investments were less important and profits limited. One old fisher put it succinctly: 'One didn't work to become rich but to survive'. Initially, the fisheries were primarily locally embedded with regard to capital, resources, technology, knowledge and market (except dolphin export). Until some important contextual changes took place, there was simply no potential for expansive, innovative fishing businesses.

## Type 2: Capital Intensive Fisheries

Several of Ali Reis's younger contemporaries later developed expanding businesses. Selahettin Özdemir, the father of Hakan Özdemir (see Chapter 4) from Keremköy, started his career as beach seiner and dolphin hunter, but turned after some years to hamsi fishing, having in the early 1950s bought his first large boat (12 m) and an appropriate net. Through subsequent purchases he acquired larger boats. A turning point of great symbolic importance in his career was his investment in 1971 in the first steel-hulled boat in the eastern Black Sea region. While the usual size of the wooden vessels in those days was twelve to sixteen metres, this boat was twenty metres long. Soon afterwards, Selahettin Özdemir retired from business, but Hakan and his younger brother kept the business going and expanding. In 1984 they sold their boat, bought a bigger one and invested in more advanced equipment, such as echo sounder, sonar, and larger purse seine.

Many teams entered spirals of growth similar to Selahettin Özdemir and his sons. They were able to take advantage of new opportunities offered by better infrastructure, subsidized credit, expanding market and new technology. While few of the state's initiatives in fisheries in the 1950s were of immediate relevance for the fishers, from the early 1970s state fishery policies started to make an impact on fisheries in the eastern Black Sea region. Subsidized credits, establishment of EBK cold-storage facilities and fish-processing factories in Trabzon and Fatsa, tax exemption on import of engines and gear, construction during the 1970s and 80s of a number of harbours along the exposed Black Sea coastline with few natural harbours, and the establishment of fishmeal factories facilitated the investment in, use of and profitability of larger boats and nets. The general economic development and dynamism staring in the 1950s, with increasing monetization of the economy, nascent urbanization and higher demand for seafood also contributed to expansion in the Black Sea fisheries. The construction of a national road network facilitated transport of fresh fish to larger urban centres. The first road along the eastern Black Sea coast was built in 1957.

The general post-war technological development in fisheries internationally, with advances such as monofilament/nylon nets (from 1952), fishmeal technology and electronic fish finders, resulted in dramatic increases in worldwide fish catches. The introduction of nylon nets made the cumbersome drying process, which had been necessary to prevent the cotton nets from rotting, superfluous. Around 1960 the first echo sounders were imported and the fishers became less dependent upon weather and light conditions. All these innovations facilitated more continual fishing. The teams started to use special carrier vessels (*taşıcı, yedek motoru*) that would take the catch ashore while the main vessel (*ana motoru, ağ motoru*) continued fishing operations. When the fishers were allowed to use radiotelephones and coast radio during the latter part of the 1970s, communication between the mother vessel and the carriers, between the teams, and between the teams and their contacts ashore was made much easier. In the 1970s the introduction of the powerblock (for mechanical lifting of the seine), the fish pump (for mechanical transfer of fish from the net to the carrier vessel) as well as radar (enabling the fishers to see other boats and shore), the adoption around 1980 of the fish finder sonar, and in the early 1990s the legalization of GPS-guided map systems, further increased catch capacity.

In the 1950s and early 1960s there were some ten freighter (*taka, çektirme*) owners in Çarşıbaşı, making this a more important business locally than fishing. During the 1940s Zekeria Ertuğrul (real name), from Kaleköy, west of İskefiye, owned a freighter together with his father. In 1954 Zekeria sold the freighter which had operated between Trabzon and Istanbul, and invested in his first fishing boat. He was in partnership with Ali Reis from 1957. Since then he has been in four more partnerships. Commencing in 1962, he received credit several times. Prior to 1983 he had invested in new and larger boats thirteen times. In 1990 he was the owner of one of the largest purse seiners in Çarşıbaşı. Zekeria and others who made the risky investment in an engine in the 1950s may have been the entrepreneurs who sparked a new trend. Some fishing families still keep their first 5 Hp engines, as a token of the seed of their career growth. These innovators had typically been young men during the 1960s and 1970s when some important contextual changes took place in state policies, as described in Chapter 3, and in economy, infrastructure and technology, which I shall turn to below and in Chapter 8.

## Local Ecology and Household Structure

The way household structure in Çarşıbaşı has adapted to local economic and ecological circumstances seems to have had implications for who had the capacity to succeed in fishing. A household would have to command both enough male labour and be able to raise sufficient funds for investments. In the 1950s the modest funds necessary to launch and manage a team were mostly raised locally: a few sold land or freighters, many borrowed money from relatives, invested the shares earned as crew in fisheries, and from the 1960s a few invested earnings from work as transient labour migrants in Western Europe. For many, partnerships with other households were indispensable in making the first investments. Yet households, and not established firms or corporations, were the financial actors in the fishing sector. Except for komisyoncu in Trabzon that gave fishers credit, urban capitalists played only a minor role as investors in the fisheries in the Black Sea region. Most of the new careers evolved in rural and small-town societies along the coast, effecting a regional shift away from Faroz/Trabzon to Çarşıbaşı and other rural areas and small towns along the Black Sea coast.

From the 1960s onward there was a turn in Çarşıbaşı from subsistence farming (horticulture, maize, and cows) to the cultivation of hazelnuts for the international market. Because of the limited need for labour in growing hazelnuts, a nuclear family possessed sufficient labour. Since the fields would be too small if split by inheritance, they were often kept by one male member of the family while the others left for western Turkey and sometimes Germany. Thus, households with substantial income from hazelnuts tended to become nucleated and with few agnatic relatives in the community. At the same time, compared to growing hazelnuts, fishing was risky and exhausting work. Thus, it was mostly households with insufficient possibility of planting hazelnut groves that were pushed into fishing.[68] These fisher households also tended to be extended since all available male labour was needed. When the attractions of the fisheries became apparent with the growth and profits during the late 1970s and 1980s, the comparatively well-to-do agricultural households had no experience in fishing and not enough able males to put into fishing. The households of Zekeria Ertuğrul and Selahettin Özdemir, on the other hand, had a suitable family structure and commanded the necessary assets, especially capital, manpower and knowledge about fishing, to evolve into successful family enterprises.

Due to the limited potential for subsistence agriculture and cultivation of hazelnuts (steep slopes and small fields) in the coastal villages on the eastern side of the district of Çarşıbaşı many successful careers in fishing had an early start here. In 1990 people living in the villages Keremköy, Gülbahçe and Fenerköy, with seven per cent of the district's population, owned and managed approximately seventy per cent of the large boats in the district.

## The Emergence of a Capitalist Sector

The expansive adaptation of Selahettin Özdemir and some others early on provided an ideal and a model for other teams' development. They clearly emerged as innovators, being willing to take risks, including mortgaging their house to obtain loans and exploring new resources and technologies (like trawling and steel-hulled boats). Almost all of the existing teams that I know, both in Çarşıbaşı and elsewhere, have evolved through a gradual development similar to that of Zekeria Ertuğrul and Selahettin Özdemir. The continual adoption of new and expensive technology, however, demanded successive increases in investments, and the enterprises that were not able to follow suit were easily outpaced. While the value of boat and gear for a team in 1967 was equal to one to two thousand tonnes of hamsi, this had increased to five thousand tonnes of hamsi in 1990.[69] Thus, to start fresh in this business continually required a much more substantial investment than earlier. In purse-seine fishing, investment and expansion have been prerequisites for maintaining a viable business. There are several reasons for this.

First, in addition to each boat's increased catch capacity and mobility, the number of teams also rose, at least initially. By 1967 there may have been as many as 175 teams in the eastern Black Sea region (Çakıroğlu 1969) and by 1990 there were thirty-seven large boats in the District of Çarşıbaşı alone. This intensified competition. Secondly, the biggest boats with the most powerful engines, the best electronic equipment, and with different kinds of very expensive purse seines used for catching different fish were, and still are, in the best position to spot fish and land large catches. Because of the general advance in technological sophistication, each family firm had to continually reinvest to attain the high level of capitalization that was necessary in order to stay in business. Some fishers have not managed to keep up with these developments. For instance, four brothers who operated a very profitable trawler business during the 1980s were on the brink of managing to make the investment in a purse-seine team when cooperation between them broke down. As individual units they were too small to invest in purse seiners and they ended up as owners of small boats, trawler and a carrier vessel.

The last fishers in Çarşıbaşı to successfully make the transition from a labour-intensive adaptation to a capital-intensive one were the brothers in the family firm Can Kardeşler (real name). Sons of a poor small-boat fisher in Keremköy, four young brothers from this family took up beach seining in the middle of the 1970s, followed soon by purse seining on a modest scale: a ten to twelve metre long boat, small seine, no electronic equipment and few men. Earnings Yakup, the eldest brother, brought home from his six months stay in Germany covered half the cost of their first big boat (15 m), which they used for very profitable trawling off Eğreli in the western part of the Black Sea. Before replacing this boat with a bigger one, they also did some mid-water trawling for hamsi. In 1983 they bought larger purse-seine nets and rented a big (steel-hulled) boat. Catches were bountiful, they made huge profits and paid generous shares to their crew – and for the first time bought a boat appropriate for purse seining. Only a couple of years later they bought another and supplied both vessels with the best and most expensive sonars in Çarşıbaşı.

By 1990 Can Kardeşler had become the largest firm in the fishing business in Çarşıbaşı. During the 1990s they elongated the sterns of their boats, constructed new boats, bought several new seines and new, expensive sonars. By 1997 they possessed three purse seiners, four carriers and a fishmeal factory and had become one of the largest fishing companies in Turkey. In the early 2000s they stared exporting conserved and frozen fish to Europe. This rapid progress to a very large degree depended upon state financial support. In 1987 the central authorities covered forty per cent of the investment costs of their first fishmeal factory. In 1991, their total debt stood at approximately two-thirds of their estimated total assets (US$1.05 million).

In the course of only fifteen years Can Kardeşler had undergone a spectacular change from poor villagers to the level of regional elite.

Starting from scratch and working your way up in the fisheries, as Can Kardeşler once spectacularly did, may simply no longer be possible.[70] There are several reasons for this. Until the onset of the general resource crisis in 1989–90, it was possible to switch to other resources to offset the problems created by tougher competition and decline in a specific fish stock. Moreover, trawling was an important stepping stone for many of those who began a big-boat career at a late date. Trawling requires only five or six men and lesser investments than purse seining. However, the value difference between a trawler and a purse seiner increased, and trawling was no longer a feasible route for making the transition from a work-intensive small-boat adaptation to capital-intensive purse seining. The gap between the successful and unsuccessful big-boat fishers has also been cemented by the fact that the purse-seining technology utilized in the 1970s, or even a few years back, is no longer competitive. With powerful engines and far-ranging sonars the large, more mobile new purse seiners can spot and catch the hamsi long before the older vessels would (Figure 6.1). Finally, since labour migration to Europe has been restricted due to changes in the economies and immigration policies in recipient countries, fishers seldom raise funds to invest in fishing by working abroad.

Thus, it has generally become much more difficult for fishers to achieve upward social mobility. The change in options is also reflected in people's attitudes. In the 1990s small-boat fishers and crew no longer considered continual reinvestment in fishing a realistic path by which to leave their

**Figure 6.1. Purse-seine fishing boat.** In 1998 Ergün Kardeşler was, at forty-five metres, one of the largest purse seiners in Turkey. Yet the style, rigging and general organisation of the boat is typical of Istanbul and Black Sea purse seiners. Note the *bot* on the aft deck.

labour-intensive adaptation. They looked to international shipping, to labour migration to states in the Middle East and above all, in a more extended time-frame, to the prospect of their sons having higher education in order to escape their partly stigmatized and strenuous adaptation.

The gap between the owners of large purse-seining companies and other fishers has continued to grow. The resource crisis in the beginning of the 1990s intensified the general structural developments in the purse-seining sector. While the number of purse seiners in the district of Çarşıbaşı has decreased (see Table 6.1), the catch capacity has probably increased due to more large-scale and efficient equipment. The most successful family companies expanded by increasing the size and number of boats. A tendency towards ownership concentration can be seen all along the Black Sea coast as well as in Istanbul. Some of the larger family-run companies may employ as many as two hundred men. Many of the owners of purse seiners who have been forced to sell out are still in the fisheries sector as owners of carriers, trawls or small boats, and as hired skippers and crew. By 2004 Zekeria Ertuğrul had died and his son had become a small boat fisher. Hakan Özdemir had sold his boat and worked as a skipper for Can Kardeşler.

**Table 6.1. Big boat ownership Çarşıbaşı 1990 – 2002.**

|                                    | 1990    | 1998  | 2002    |
|------------------------------------|---------|-------|---------|
| Purse seiners                      | 14      | 9     | 9       |
| mean length purse seiners, m       | ca. 30  | 40.2  | ca. 42  |
| Carriers                           | 19      | 15    | 13      |
| Trawls                             | 4       | 5     | 2       |
| Families* owning big boat(s)       | 28      | 14    | 9       |
| Families owning purse seiners      | 12      | 6     | 8       |

Source: This table is based on detailed information on every single large boat in the District of Çarşıbaşı, gathered directly from the fishers during fieldwork. Figures here are not congruent with official figures. *'Family' can include groups of adult brothers, and sometimes their father, each with their own household.

## Type 3: Organization, Business Management and Political Entrepreneurship

There may be reason to argue that, for the fishers in the eastern Black Sea region of Turkey, the 'onshore' (Durrenberger and Pálsson 1987) social processes of the fisheries have increased in relative importance. Initially, fisheries in Turkey were fairly local. By the 1990s all teams and companies took part in the same national fisheries, competing for fish, markets, crew, and credit. Knowledge of and power to influence the bureaucratic game has become more crucial in maintaining a viable fishery business. This is partly an effect of there being a fishery policy and fishery bureaucracy: it opens the possibility for fishery politics. The ensuing social webbing stretches into governmental offices and the central bureaucracy, and is therefore indicative of a growing interchange between localities and the state. A new kind of entrepreneur – the administrative and political entrepreneur – has emerged, contributing to still further changes in the field and creating new kinds of linkages to other social spheres. Moreover, while fishing was once a survival strategy, it has, for big-boat owners, increasingly become the economic backbone of projects with broader aims. Earlier, politics was primarily involved in to helping one fish successfully, whereas now fishing gives resources for political projects, for some companies at least.

This change can be exemplified in a further elaboration of Can Kardeşler's success. The resource crisis from 1989 onwards dramatically changed the context for the fishers. They had to adapt to a new, more challenging, situation. Can Kardeşler were one of the very few firms which managed to make a profit through the years of resource crisis. They had the clout to exploit both well-known and new fields. In the autumn of 1990 the start of the hamsi season was disappointing with small catches and, more seriously, fish size mostly below the legal minimum (9 cm). For a long time the authorities refrained from interfering, but eventually in the beginning of December, it was decided to put the foot down. In protest at this decision, owners of big fishing boats and some fishmeal factories went as a group, formally defined by the cooperative structure, to meet with bureaucrats and politicians in Ankara. Yakup, the elder brother of Can Kardeşler, was widely held – also in statements to the press – to be the initiator of this mobilization. In the deliberations they were supported by MPs from the region. The authorities conceded to their request, reducing (temporarily) the legal minimum size to 7.5 cm. This decision was given legitimacy by referring to scientists' disagreement about the size of hamsi when it reaches the reproductive state. One scientist believed that the hamsi reach maturity at 7 cm. Subsequently, the fishing of hamsi, even as small as 5–6 cm, continued, though with small catches.

The persons and companies who led this political mobilization were generally those who were better placed technologically and organization-ally to make a profit despite dwindling resources. Can Kardeşler had, due to their reputation as one of the most profitable firms, a full and well-qualified crew. Furthermore, they possessed superior electronic equipment and could deliver catches to their own factory. The two purse-seining teams of Can Kardeşler travelled widely, cast their nets often and came out among the leading teams of the season (1990–91). They caught ten per cent of the total hamsi catches in the Black Sea that season and

3,500 cases of bonito in the Istanbul area. Profits amounted to U.S.$600,000 and their crew received decent shares of U.S.$1600 to 2400. In addition, the company earned a considerable sum from hamsi processing in their factory. While most other fishing firms pursued a cautious strategy and many were halted in their spiral of growth, Can Kardeşler diversified their activities by investments in lorries, real estate, a petrol station and fish farming.

The continued success of Can Kardeşler is not only based on hard work and new technology. They have also realized the importance of administration, politics and a wide web of social relations. In contrast to Hakan Özdemir and his brother, Can Kardeşler coordinated their businesses from a central office in Çarşıbaşı where Yakup, who never participates in the fishing, is the undisputed leader. He commands substantial political influence, having a wide network of contacts and holding during the 1990s the leading positions in both the local water produce cooperative for a period and the influential district branch of the Islamistic Welfare Party. He is also active in the local branch of the religious brotherhood Süleymancılar. He has used this influence to put pressure upon the scientists to confirm that their new vessels were suitable for 'open sea' fishing (to circumvent a ban on construction of new fishing boats) and, allegedly, to remove the director of the Agricultural Bank in Trabzon from his position when he refused to accept that their carrier vessels be counted as net boats (which would allow them much more credit).

Although no other fishers in Çarşıbaşı have ventured as far as Can Kardeşler in seeking to influence bureaucratic and political decisions, there are other very influential fishers and factory owners in the region, some of whom were able to mobilize local MPs to approach supervising bodies and effect the annulment of fines received as a result of being caught with undersized hamsi. Such cases indicate the growing importance of information, politics, and coordination and administration. Knowledge of laws, regulations, standards for receiving credit, and so on is also essential. I was told that the Can Kardeşler brothers, at the beginning of their career, put a lot of effort into learning all the relevant laws. Thus, despite their lack of formal schooling above the primary level, they started to relate more actively to the inscribed rules and procedures of the state bureaucracy. Paperwork, including writing formal letters themselves, became increasingly important. They hired an accountant to assist them with the formal procedures and in contact with the bureaucracy. The office, with its files, computer, telephone and reception hall, and not the captain's cabin, became the social centre of the business.

Although of increasing importance, abilities and resources such as textual skills, a willingness to take risks, economic clout, a wide network and access to information cannot replace skills in the more practical aspects of fishing. In the beginning of the 1980s a rich and influential man in Çarşıbaşı with no experience as a fisher invested in a purse-seining team and hired skipper and crew. It was generally acknowledged that the lack of family control over operations at sea was the reason he made no profit and abandoned the business after only a couple of seasons' operation. The Can Kardeşler business is owned as a corporation. In the late 1990s two of the brothers were skippers on one purse seiner each, another was manager of the factory and Yakup general manager while his eldest son was in charge of operations on the third purse seiner. Skill in fishing is now more than reislik, but these skills are often differently distributed within a family company. Can Kardeşler's achievement is a result of a combination, within the same company, of a range of assets and kinds of competence and knowledge. Both family organization of their business and a competent management of a wider web of social relations are important for success.

## Trust in the Family

Partnerships between brothers or father and sons is definitely seen as, and often demonstrated to be, the most trustworthy and stable unit for organizing business operations in Turkey (Buğra 1994: 207–218). This is borne out in both small-boat fishing, trawl fisheries and purse-seine fishing along the eastern Black Sea coast of Turkey. The importance of having many sons and being many brothers is particularly important in big boat fishing. All small as well as almost all large fishing companies[71] along the Black Sea coast and in Istanbul, including the most successful ones (e.g., Can Kardeşler, Kuloğlu, Akgün Kardeşler, Aktaşlar, Malkoçlar, Kıyak Kardeşler, and Fatoğlu) are organized as family firms. Brother-brother/father-son relationships undoubtedly ensure more trust and obvious lines of authority.

As mentioned, a breakdown of relations between brothers will often imply a break in the spiral of growth in the fisheries sector. But in household cycle and structure lies also one of the main limitations to growth in the fisheries, both because the number of operational units (factory, office, boats) a single family can handle is limited to the number of male adults in the family, and because people tend to quit when 'on top'. Relations between patrilineal cousins when their fathers are not active in the company usually seem not to be strong enough to ensure a stable foundation for managing a fishing business. There is no 'natural' authority (father or elder brother) and they prefer to keep separate economies. This partly explains Faroz' decline as a centre for purse-seining teams: sons of successful boat owners in Faroz did not learn the business but received extended schooling and found employment in good positions in Ankara and Istanbul, while others, through accumulated family capital, set themselves up as fishmongers and kabzımal. One of the early, more profitable family-based teams in Çarşıbaşı also, and for the same reasons, sold out in the second half of the 1980s and invested in a store in İskefiye that sells electronic goods. In the early 2000s they invested in a fishmeal and oil processing plant. After the Can Kardeşler brothers in 2007 split the business into four independent and smaller family companies, continued success could be seen to depend upon continued good relations between the brothers and – as their sons mature – their ability to integrate the next generation into the business.

In contrast to friendship bonds, families are seen locally as 'natural' relations, relations that one does not cultivate, but that one has a moral obligation to support and confirm unconditionally. The bond is 'already there'. Unlike the cooperation between the fiends Murat and Şaban (see Chapter 5) brothers do not need to spend time together in kahves in order to be able to cooperate in fishing. The family is clearly experienced as an economic, symbolic and moral unit. For instance, the belief in the power of the evil eye (*göz*) is connected to an idea of the family as a moral unit. Many people in Çarşıbaşı believe that if one eats fish which has been cut while alive (i.e., not left to die), the women of the family may give birth to deformed children. Thus, misfortune, as well fortune (wealth is ideally shared within the family), is focused on and distributed along lines of family membership. One day during the last days of Ramadan in 1991 I was sitting together with a group of men – fishers and others – on the sand between the small boats in the harbour area of Çarşıbaşı. It was one of the first warm and sunny days of spring. Mahmut, a poor shopkeeper, complained that for fifteen years he had stuck to the word of the Koran; he had given up drinking, 'but where is the money? (*ama hani para*?)'. One of his friends objected to this by indicating that he had seen that Mahmut's (adult) son, a small-boat fisher, was not fasting, implying that this made the whole family 'impure'. Friendship relations, or kinship relations beyond the core family for that matter, are not sanctioned by this kind of external forces; they are not 'sacred' like the family is.

## The Social Web

The model of society for most people in Çarşıbaşı is made up of three main levels: the family, the social circle, and the state. Beyond the family, social relations are commonly conceptualized as friendship. The social web of friendship relations is also of great significance during operations at sea. Exchange of information primarily takes place within one's circle. The inner circle of trusted and intimate (*samimi*) friends may consist of only a few other teams. Conversations with acquaintances, those who are not intimate friends, take place over the open channels and follow very stereotypical patterns. In order to avoid being overheard when transmitting more accurate and important information, communication between close mates is increasingly conducted on mobile phones. On one occasion an unknown captain operating near Samsun called up on the radio the purse seiner I was on board near Çarşıbaşı to ask for news. He had probably heard rumours about good catches near Hopa. The captain only gave inconsequential answers and quickly closed the conversation. Afterwards, those present in the cabin criticized the caller severely for getting in touch and requesting information without having an established bond or connection to them.

A person's set of friendship relations is in Çarşıbaşı commonly talked about as a person's *çevre* (surroundings, milieu, circle), especially when referring to influential persons. Once when talking about a former 'big man' in Keremköy, my friends noted that he was not very rich, but his çevre was wide (*çevresi geniş*). To have a wide social circle or web is therefore seen to be a source of power in itself. Social webbing and the formal politics related to the state and authorities are very much interwoven. Local political units may be regarded as 'clusters' within the social web – social circles that attain some degree of 'we' reference. Although many may talk about 'us' and about becoming 'one of us', such social clusters are often unnamed and their 'membership', or rather allegiance, diffuse and floating. During the 1980s and 1990s Keremköy was more readily identified as a village social cluster than most other villages and *mahalle* (quarter) in Çarşıbaşı. The reason for this was probably not because the social border, or geographical border for that matter, was more clearly defined, but because there were more important persons at its node, resulting in both a higher density of relations within the 'group', and wider circles extending out from it, thereby giving it a clearer identity. Since the mid 1980s, when a man from the village was elected MP for the Motherland Party (ANAP) of Özal, men in Keremköy talked about the Motherland Party and its local branch as 'our party'. However, the party label is only a surface phenomenon. They talk about the pre-coup (1980), far right Nationalist Action Party (MHP) as 'our erstwhile party' (*eski partimiz*), and the current 'strong man' in Çarşıbaşı, who used to head the district branch of the Motherland Party, entered the 2004 elections as Justice and Development Party (AKP) candidate for the position as head of the municipality.

Associated with the idioms and models of social webbing is also the powerful image of *torpils*, literally 'torpedoes', people who have influential positions as bureaucrats or politicians and can help 'friends' (or clients/followers) to cut through or side-step bureaucratic procedures. Poor and 'unimportant' people cultivate relations to patrons in order to attain the services of *torpils*. A man is regarded as well-connected if he has an *adam* (man) or *dayı* (maternal uncle) (both euphemisms for torpil) in 'Ankara' (i.e. the central bureaucracy). Torpils are extensions of a person's çevre into the domains of bureaucracy and political authority. I had the general impression that successful entrepreneurs and big men in Çarşıbaşı – not only in the fishing business – all command a wide and influential çevre, with extensions outside of Çarşıbaşı and Trabzon extending to Ankara, Istanbul, Izmir and beyond. To be in the wrong faction after changes in the political party in power, will often result in lack of contact in the central bureaucracy, restricted access to information and resources and limit one's influence. Although the use of torpils is generally regretted in explicit discourse, most people try, however, to activate torpil relations when necessary. A young man, a self declared 'socialist' with some experience in construction work, was asked to paint the house of the current Motherland Party MP from Keremköy. He mentioned to the MP that he wanted to obtain a job in the state Deniz Yolları ('Sea Lines') and he didn't charge anything for the painting, thereby trying to establish a debt on the part of the MP. However, he never got a job in the Deniz Yolları.

It has been common to claim that networking, friendship relations, and patron-client relations constitute fundamental aspects of Turkish (see, e.g., Stirling 1993; White 1994) and Mediterranean (Boissevain 1974; Gellner and Waterbury 1977; Davies 1977) society and culture. In current social sciences, a lack of formal organizations – governmental, NGO or other – is often seen as leaving a void which is filled by networks, patron-client relations, family, tribes, ethnic corporations and the like. Social networks based upon friendship and patron-client relations, therefore, easily fall within an evolutionary and moral framework. To counter the evolutionary assumptions underlying this approach it has become increasingly common to elevate social networks to the status of 'organization', conceptualized as civil society (Hann 1996; White 1996: 151–2).

There is thus reason to take care when using vocabulary derived from social-scientific discourse, such as 'civil society', 'traditional' and so forth. This is even more the case in studies of Turkish society since by marking social life as structured by networks, patron-client relations, or civil society the scholars position themselves within a 'native' Turkish discourse of societal development, and implicitly bolster the authority of one position or interpretation. The Republican State adopted and stimulated a 'scientific' approach to society. Partly through the work of the early twentieth-century ideologue Ziya Gökalp, the young Republic's elite was very strongly influenced by current social science. Gökalp wanted to replace local forms ('communalism') with more 'societal' forms ('solidarism') of solidarity, in line with Durkheim's image of society. In this framework, patron-client relations and networks based on friendship, as well as certain kinds of institutions, do not conform with modern solidarism and will easily be seen as 'backward' or even 'reactionary'.[72] It is not simply that this evolutionary framework is implicated in social-science discourse; in Turkey the discourse and practice of policy and politics draw heavily on such models.

Putting the label 'civil society' on social-webbing practices may imply rendering practices based upon ethical know-how as more rigid structures based upon ethical know-that. Practice thereby easily becomes objectified into structures, representations. This is the social interactions of others as seen from a distance. Catherine Alexander, considering the usefulness of the concepts 'informal' and 'formal' organizational structures in Turkey concludes that she prefers to use the term 'alternative' rather than 'informal' since 'the informal is … often only a different form, maybe an older form, by another name' (Alexander 2002: 176). At the phenomenal level, on the level of personal experience, I believe it is a mistake to regard the social networking of the Black Sea fishers as simply one alternative form for organizing social life. The social web is not experienced as an 'alternative' to cooperatives, political parties, or state institutions. Instead, social life is in the main perceived as a web of personal relations, and organizational frames or structures are incorporated into this understanding: organizations are nodes of resources and positions, but allegiance is still vested in persons, or families, not organizations. The social web is the social life per se.

The quality of social life I observed in Çarşıbaşı and among fishers on the eastern Black Sea coast of Turkey bears a strong resemblance to Rosen's characterization of social life in Sefrou, Morocco (Rosen 1984: 164–5,188):

> The central feature of social organization in Sefrou is the interpersonal contract. Since corporate groups are virtually nonexistent, individuals forge personal bonds according to conventions that are as well recognized as they are fraught with leeway for maneuvering. … [W]hat the people in Sefrou share … are the concepts and procedures by which relationships may themselves be negotiated. It is in this process, more than in the arrangement of its resultant forms, that we must seek the regularity and distinctiveness of Sefrou culture.

## Can a 'Big Man' be a Local?

An important development in the fisheries is the degree to which success, as described in Type 3, is increasingly dependent upon investing in extra-local large-scale social webs. This puts fishers into positions that entail moral and strategic dilemmas since diffuse ideas of local belonging continue to play an important role in the construction of self and others. The social skills that are involved in fishing thus imply managing social relations by balancing ethical considerations with economic and political profit. One of the most outstanding entrepreneurial aspects of Can

Kardeşler's strategy is their readiness to violate the local code of conduct, or norms of local belonging. They cross a moral boundary (Barth 1963, 1967) and are thereby in a position to profit economically. Firstly, they do not conform to some of the more pervasive local ideals of manhood and friendship. The Can Kardeşler brothers, and in particular Yakup, hardly ever enter a kahve, the main realm for expressing and confirming local loyalty, friendship, and manhood. Instead they adopt an ideology of hard work and family values. To them, killing time in kahves is a symbol of idleness and laziness. One covillager commented upon the eldest son of Yakup, that 'he is like a woman, he never enters a kahve'.

I do not think that this critique about being 'feminine' hit very hard. Rather it indicates resentment connected to a second, related critique levelled against them: that the Can Kardeşler brothers do not share their lives with fellow villagers. Can Kardeşler earned a reputation early on for being stingy, giving little fish to neighbours and friends who lent them a hand. Once, as I enjoyed the hospitality of a poor man in his modest home in Keremköy, I commented on a television program and said that wealth does not necessarily bring happiness. The man, a covillager of the Can Kardeşler brothers, responding, regretted that 'although I worked six years with Can Kardeşler [as crew], we never sat together at home like this and had a nice, friendly chat (*böyle evde oturarak güzel muhabbet hiç etmedik*)'. Happiness is *muhabbet* (sweet, friendly conversation) and 'sharing' (*paylaşma*). Ideally, muhabbet is not an expression of sharing, but rather *is*, in itself, sharing. It means living, or doing, sharing through taking part in each other's lives and activities. Demonstrating ethical sensibility through sharing implies more than distribution of goods. Sharing and closeness, involving emotion, time, ideas, money, cigarettes, allegiances, and so on, is the content of friendship and is important in maintaining a good reputation locally.

Sharing is considered an ideal that is often difficult to live up to; it is perceived increasingly as something out of the past, of the pre-corrupt bygone days. Now money has distorted this; 'Money is the best friend' (*en büyük dost para*). Personal relations and trust become critical and problematic. When important men are too busy or consider themselves to be too important to hang around their local or village kahves they estrange themselves from their 'original' friends, their local following. It is a frequently heard complaint in the kahve; 'He does not come here any longer', 'He does not greet us since he became important'. Also, higher education is seen as creating a distance, since it directs the educated into other life courses (urban, cultivated, and wealthy) that separate them from their original comrades.

For the Can Kardeşler brothers and other successful men there are alternative sets of values that can be elaborated in place of local intimacy and sharing. These options include the articulation of the prestige of material wealth, of technological superiority, of being well-connected, or of learning and cultivation. In the case of Can Kardeşler, their partial failure to employ ethical know-how to conform to local codes of conduct is offset by a strong emphasis on the more universal and explicit (as well as inscribed) moral rules and values prescribed by Islam, a structure of ethical know-that. For example, the brothers have all been to Mecca at least once, take great care to perform their daily prayers, are very strict with regard to the behaviour of female family members, have no television, and emphasize rhetorically the importance of *zakat* (religious 'tax'), prayer, abstention from alcohol, and so on.

The moral force of Islam is attested to by the fact that people seek Yakup's advice in difficult times or about moral dilemmas. One day in March 1991 I was hanging around in the office reception room of Can Kardeşler. Yakup liked me to come in and discuss religion. Yakup had come under the influence of the influential Turkish Muslim organisation Milli Görüş while in Germany and had become an Islamic (unofficial) authority in Çarşıbaşı. Ali, the office manager of the cooperative, came in, together with a middle-aged owner of a purse seiner (at that time Yakup was leader of the cooperative). The resource crisis had hit the man hard and in the spring of 1991 he was on the brink of bankruptcy and people had started to talk about him as 'unsuccessful'. He now gave the impression that he wanted advice about the sale of the boat. Yakup told him that he thought that he should continue fishing, try to manage. 'If you don't manage, you just leave it to me', probably indicating that he would offer to buy his boat and seines. Yakup continued by criticizing the boat owner and Ali (who was known to be a follower of Ecevit, at the time the leader of the secularist and left leaning CHP) for being secular (*laik*). He also hinted at the possibility that fishing was not going well for the visiting fisher because of a lack of religious merit (*sevap*). Ali, agitated and flushed, pointed at me and yelled that Norwegians are not Muslims, but still catch a lot of fish. Yakup then pointed at the Koran, read a few paragraphs and asked whether Ali accepted that. Ali responded by muttering, 'I do accept, Allah the compassionate, Allah the compassionate (*Kabul, Allah Rahman, Allah Rahman*).' Yakup also criticized the boat owner for not paying zakat of his incomes from fishing and hazelnuts. The visiting fisher was not argumentative, simply bowed his head. Like most other men (except the elderly) he generally attended only the Friday prayer. However, after this meeting he often performed the *namaz* (ritual prayer) in Yakup's office. He may have been particularly humble and concerned about his religious 'credentials' during this period since the meeting took place just before the start of Ramadan.

Not all that goes into the local elaboration of what it means to be a Muslim is based upon or refers directly to ethical know-that, to explicit rules. Many would include being honest, hard working and modest, as well as many of the other values that I have earlier described as ethical know-how, as qualities signifying a true Muslim. What it means to be a good Muslim is clearly negotiable: some think that good Muslims should not eat seafood at all, others think it now acceptable to bring their family to the new 'meat and fish' eating establishments. Although the moral concerns connected to seafood consumption are based upon a fairly clearly inscribed rule that bans the consumption of wine, the assessment of which contexts and meals are acceptable or not rests upon largely unarticulated and negotiable ethical know-how of appropriateness. There is, of course, a kind of dialectic in Islam between objectified knowledge and moral rules on one hand, and situated practice and ethical reasoning on the other. Within this heterogeneous universe of Islam, the Can Kardeşler brothers choose to present a certain version, a certain kind of Islam, that is often claimed to have become increasingly dominant in the public discourse about Islam in Turkey since the early 1980s: an orthodox Sunni Islam that is often intermingled with a political agenda. But the Can Kardeşler brothers also emphasize less formal rules of (Islamic) behaviour, for instance by placing hard work and family life before the 'idleness' of kahve sociality. All in all, they articulate a kind of Islamic Puritanism reminiscent of the protestant ethic as described by Weber (1930).

Indeed, there is a heterogeneous set of moral or ethical models and associated vocabulary, ranging from Islamic prescriptions to deep-seated but diffuse ethical sensibilities about being a good or bad man. Family and social webbing are articulated in idioms that give them different significance: the family as a moral unit, the personal relations as social intimacy. Good personal relations, and personal qualities, are commonly evoked by a set of metaphors of closeness, warmth and liveliness (*yakın, sıcak, canlı*, etc.). Muhabbet entails sharing, closeness and warmth. These are the kinds of personal and social qualities that should be expressed in relations with family members and friends. Another model, or models, often – but not necessarily – more directly associated with Islam, concerns honour and shame or moral standing (*ayıp, namus, şeref*, etc.).

It is noteworthy that enacting ethical know-how, or moral reasoning in Mark Johnson's (1993) terms, proceeds to a large extent through metaphorical (or analogical) reasoning. People draw upon their basic experience from similar situations and from other domains (heat, family relations), as well as general models of family and kinship, in order to evaluate the actions of a 'friend'. Such metaphorical usage also extends to patrons and the state: 'NN did us a lot of "fatherliness" (*babacılık*)', 'The father state (*devlet baba*)'. These are not models inscribed in texts, rules, or laws.

Friendship ties do not blind small-boat fishers to inequalities, unfairness and exploitation and the moral vocabulary also includes 'bondedness' (*bağlılık*), 'exploitation' (*sömürge*), accusations of big men acting like 'kings' or *aga*s (lords) (Meeker 1972), and the image of 'eaters' (*yiyici*, corrupt ones). During the second half of the 1990s, often associated with the Susurluk scandal[73] and other revelations that placed the issue of mafia on the national agenda, it was very common to criticize influential men in terms of a highly standardized idiom, an eating analogy: 'In Turkey everyone, from the politicians downwards, "eats" (*yer*)'. The critique against 'eaters' could be levelled against almost every 'big man', and the worst eaters were often associated with the mafia. This vocabulary was frequently used in Çarşıbaşı during the 1990s to criticize in particular powerful men, including the Can Kardeşler brothers. This discourse is further elaborated in Chapter 10.

CHAPTER 7

# State Representatives:
# Elite Lifestyles and Knowledges

While in Chapter 3 I outlined general changes in state policies towards the fisheries, Chapter 6 detailed to some extent the effect of policy initiatives in the district of Çarşıbaşı. In this chapter I look closer at another result of state fishery policy initiatives: the emergence of a class of water-produce scientists and bureaucrats in Trabzon. The chapter starts with charting what kind of social world the water-produce state representatives in Trabzon live in. Marine science and state water-produce bureaucracy demonstrate considerable overlap with regard to careers and social life. I specifically chart the background, careers and practices of marine scientists at the Sürmene Faculty of Marine Sciences at Karadeniz University in Trabzon and at the state Trabzon Fisheries Research Institute. On the background of this and a description of some scientific practice I gradually approach an examination of what kind of knowledge marine researchers in Trabzon possess.

## Institutional Structure and Personnel

Although it is one of the major fishing centres in Turkey, the Turkish State had no fishery or water-produce representatives in Trabzon before 1950. The Hydrobiology Institute in Istanbul posted a few technicians to Trabzon during the 1950s, and the provincial branch of the General Directorate of Water Products and the EBK had up to fifteen water-produce technical experts (primarily at their fish-processing plant) in Trabzon during the 1960s and early 1970s (FAO 1975). With the establishment of Regional Fisheries Directorates (Su Ürünleri Bölge Müdürlükleri) in 1972 there were for the first time ministerial bodies at regional level dedicated exclusively to water produce. The unit located in

Trabzon, while responsible for most of the eastern Black Sea region, was staffed by only six agricultural engineers. With changes in ministerial structure in 1984 this unit was discontinued and responsibility for water produce was embedded within province agricultural directorates. During the 1990s and early 2000s, two or three agricultural engineers at the Trabzon directorate administrated affairs related to water produce. There have never been water-produce state representatives at the district level. While the district administration in Çarşıbaşı includes several agricultural engineers responsible for agricultural development in the district, none are authorized to work on fisheries in the district. Credits to the sector have always been distributed through local branches of the Agricultural Bank, including the branch in Çarşıbaşı.

With the establishment of the High School of Marine Science and Technology at the Karadeniz University in 1984 the Black Sea region had its first institution dedicated to water-produce research and teaching. It was upgraded to a Faculty of Marine Sciences in 1991 and located in Sürmene east of Trabzon. Only one of its three departments, Fisheries Technology, with an academic staff of approximately ten, explicitly directs its research and teaching to fishing. In 1987 the General Directorate of Agricultural Research established, at the same location and partly with the same personnel as the former Regional Fisheries Directorate, discontinued in 1984, the Trabzon Fisheries Research Institute (TFRI).[74] TFRI has grown rapidly and employed thirty-five researchers in 2004 (twenty-seven in 1999) out of a total staff of one hundred persons.

The main difference between the Sürmene Faculty and the TFRI is that the former is responsible for education at all levels including PhD (*doktora*), while the second, in close dialogue with the ministry, undertakes research aimed at developing fishing and aquaculture in the region. In general, the TFRI is regarded as being better supported than the university faculties in terms of equipment, infrastructure and supporting personnel while the most prominent scientists work at the Sürmene Faculty.

## Becoming and Being State Civil Servant

The critical steps in the process towards becoming a full-fledged university academician with a permanent position include first passing the university entrance exam, which is often dependent upon extensive preparation within one of the private, and often expensive, *dershane* (private teaching institutions) that train the student exclusively for these university entrance exams. The next step is becoming a 'research employee' which gives one the opportunity to complete master and doctoral degrees. Third, receiving ones doktora, and then usually automatically becoming a research associate (*yardımcı doçent*), depends, most crucially, on the thesis being accepted by a scientific committee. Finally, the acceptance of a candidate as doçent (associate professor) is contingent on the decision of a scientific jury that reviews one's publications and scientific credentials. A few years after becoming doçent one automatically attains the position of professor. The TFRI does not follow the above procedure. Formally candidates enter national exams which, together with their training and experience, are evaluated when the Institute selects a new employee. In practice many of the research staff at TFRI come from positions within the regional bureaucracy of the Ministry for Agriculture. Staff are often shuffled around between TFRI and positions within the Trabzon Province Agricultural Directorate.

The dean at the Sürmene faculty and the director at the TFRI each directs much of the research activity, decides who will work on which task, be sent on assignments, or receive permission for leave. The very hierarchical structure within the institutions means that the work practice is thoroughly suffused with an experience of doing a task on behalf of the institution. Thus, the daily activities as well as the careers of scientists are profoundly structured by the state. Unlike in fishing, what is 'good' or 'correct' knowledge is to a large extent dependent upon the formalized structures of academic degrees and levels/positions. Being a scientist, in the cases at hand, not only means 'doing science', but also 'being with the state'.

The majority of employees in both institutions are trained as agricultural engineers, but the younger generation is increasingly trained as water-produce engineers. About half of the water-produce researchers in Trabzon and at the new 'water produce' faculty in Rize have degrees from the Trabzon Karadeniz University. A majority of the scientists in Sürmene have completed a higher degree abroad (USA, UK, Canada, Germany), are quite fluent in English and most tenured staff hold doctoral degrees. Only two had doctoral degrees at TFRI (in 1999). A handful of researchers at TFRI have attended courses abroad, but foreign language competence is poor, and unlike researchers at Sürmene they hardly publish internationally and rarely attend international conferences. There is relatively little scientific cooperation between the two institutions.

Marine scientists and bureaucrats generally have very little practical experience at sea. The education at the water-produce faculties is supposed to produce graduates that can go into the fishing sector. However, I know no example of this happening – those with a higher education are too 'fine' to work on boats. Moreover, employees of the state, including staff at both Sürmene and TFRI, are guaranteed a range of attractive benefits. First, most are guaranteed lifelong employment and salary. This is of utmost importance in a society with virtual no unemployment benefit. Other perks include insurance, pension, subsidized lodging, orderly work hours, transport to work, and lunch. For these reasons, many will choose a position with the state even though the income may be lower than in alternative occupations. Thus, no small-boat fisher would hesitate to accept an offer to fill the lowest remunerated *memur* (civil servant, bureaucrat) or labour position with the state. Small-boat fishing is generally something a man does when he cannot support his family in other ways.

Income differences are generally huge in Turkey, with the upper quintile securing fifty-five per cent and the lower quintile receiving only five per cent of the total national income in 1994 (SIS 1997). Within this picture most bureaucrats and scientist typically belong to the middle class. During the spring of 1998, while the official minimum wage was U.S.$140/month and workers in places such as Çarşıbaşı were paid as little as U.S.$100/month, salaries of water-produce bureaucrats and scientists ranged from slightly more than U.S.$400 to U.S.$1600 (for some full professors). Since living expenses are much lower in Trabzon than in cities in western Turkey, most higher civil servants and scientist manage quite well on this income, especially so since many are married to professionals with incomes in the same range. Thus, for most people being a scientist means success in life. Although a career as a civil servant agricultural engineer is generally, and especially in the larger cities in western Turkey, not seen as attractive as it once was, civil servants and, in particular, scientists are generally accorded much cultural capital. Their relative success and status is also attested to by an upper-middle-class lifestyle, as expressed in culinary preferences and in such material wealth as fairly high-quality apartments and clothing. Many also own cars (no small-boat fishers or crew have cars) though not, however, the posh types that the factory owners and a few of the rich fishers can afford to zip around in.

More than half of the researchers at these institutions hail from Trabzon or its immediate surrounding and of those I know well and/or have interviewed, about half come from memur families (military, teachers, lower local bureaucracy), the other half from rural families that have their main income from agriculture (some rich, some poorer). Thus, most of these scientists have been upwardly mobile. I know about only two who have a background in fishers communities, and none with a family background in fishing. There are very few women among the researchers and technical staff at the Sürmene Faculty of Marine Sciences and the TFRI.

## Deniz: From Poor Village Girl to Educated Elite

Deniz is one of the researchers at Sürmene. Her story is not typical, but illustrate very well some of the crucial concerns, lifestyles and worldviews prevalent among this class of people in Trabzon. I had met Deniz on several occasions and had had glimpses of her life. In 1998 she told me on my request her life story. We sat in her office and she started out in her near fluent English, but almost immediately switched to Turkish. The story is extracted from a taped interview of one and a half hours and later conversations.

Deniz was born as a poor villager in a coastal rural area in Trabzon in the early 1960s. While her mother came from a somewhat wealthy family, her father was very poor and went to Germany to work. In practice she came from a broken home. But she was a good pupil and the teacher wanted her to continue her schooling. Her mother, however, would not let her; she wanted her help in the fields and in looking after the cows. 'No matter how successful I was [at school], it did not matter. Then I realized that I would have to fight.' When the day came to sign on for junior high (*orta*) school around the age of twelve, she protested when her mother did not want to let her go. Thus, together with her elder brother she went for the first time beyond the small market town close to their village, to a larger town nearby, to have her photograph taken. This was a necessary step to get admission to the junior high school. 'When I started at the junior high school, the city (*şehir*) dwellers – well, although not yet a city, even though only a small town (*kasaba*) – the children of the families living there saw those coming from the villages as small (*küçük görürler*), in other words they were looking at our clothes, they looked down on us (*küçümselerdi*). I was fighting that.' She was lucky because she was seated next to the daughter of the school director. Deniz helped the director's daughter with the homework and in return she got Deniz accepted among the other pupils. 'Yes, the rich children went [to the junior high school], the children of the poor families could not go. Or, more correctly, their families did not send them. Then, there was also the culture issue (*kültür konusu*). It was difficult, but I was a successful pupil.'

During the fifth grade at primary school she had already entered the exam for a boarding high school (*lise*) in Istanbul. At the beginning of the second grade of the junior high school she received the news that she had 'won' the right to study at the lise in Istanbul. Again, her family did not want her to go. '"You have only been once to the town [where she had her photo taken]". Once more I put up a fight. I realized that if I stayed here, no matter how successful I might be, I could not win [the right to enter] the university. … The quality of the school …, the teachers may be good, but how good? I thought that there [at the boarding school] the opportunities will be better, and I put up a fight, I opposed my mother. … I did not envisage a very important job, but I did want to have a job, to have some power (*güç sahibi olmak*), to acquire the "right to talk" (*söz sahibi olabilmek*), to have material opportunities in accordance with this, I wanted to win my independence, and I fought for that.' As she left for Istanbul her mother tried to stop her by throwing herself in front of the bus.

Only a minority of the poorer classes are admitted to such state-sponsored high schools. The first month at the boarding school in Istanbul was difficult. There were people from many places, and even more than in the junior high school people looked down on her. But she had luck on her side. With regard to clothes, they used school uniform (or rather a 'cover' or apron, *önlük*). Speech was very important, but she rapidly and easily picked up the 'Istanbul accent'. She stayed. The educational level was very high, 'so advanced that the English teacher never spoke Turkish.' The school was so good that she managed to 'win' university even without having attended dershane. 'The school was very disciplined. The political atmosphere was very bad [this was during the conflict-ridden late 1970s]. I lived far away from that. For five years on end I lived behind closed gates.' When making her choices of universities and studies, she was greatly aided by her 'successful and *efendi* (gentlemanly) *dayı* (maternal uncle)' who was living in Trabzon. She was persuaded to apply for the university in Trabzon. She had become fond of painting and music and wanted to study that. But she realized that the employment opportunities were very limited. She ended up with a priority list that had architecture at Karadeniz Technical University (KTÜ) at top, forestry at KTÜ at second, and biology teacher at the Education Faculty at KTÜ as third choice. She got the third, started her studies, and came to like her new profession.

Although the lise in Istanbul formed a very closed or segregated milieu, she 'picked up some culture' there, for instance she began wearing trousers. 'When I returned to Trabzon and went to the village I did not wear trousers, and it was necessary to cover my hair. Even when arriving in Trabzon [city] I covered my hair. I just didn't want to uncover all of a sudden here. Because I knew that also after me families would send their daughters away to schools, and so it happened [mentions examples].' She wanted to wait until others little by little started to uncover and wear trousers. She became an example, and it was important that the villagers did not find anything to criticize. She was especially stringent as regarded contact with men since this was very important from the perspective of honour (*namus*). The villagers found that she had not changed (she also switched back to native dialect). But she could not enjoy her youth (*gençliğimi yaşayamadım*). That was her first sacrifice (*fedakârlık*). Her second sacrifice was giving up the arts. In Trabzon both her dayı as well as her maternal grandfather, a very pious man, gave her some financial support. At the university she was among the five best. She also, unusually for women, got responsibilities such as being class head. 'I was not timid in front of men.' She had learned in Istanbul to talk to men, and to persons of higher standing. 'There I learned how I can defend myself, to speak for myself, to not be restrained, to be in control of oneself (*rahat*). Thanks to my friends in Istanbul, thanks to the milieu there.'

She was urged to apply for a position as 'research employee' at the Sürmene Faculty of Marine Science when the position was announced. Also here her being a woman was an issue, but since she was the only one who passed the exams, she had no competition and got the position. Two years later a series of coincidences suddenly left open a YÖK (Yükseköğretim Kurulu, Council of Higher Education) scholarship for PhD study abroad and she was asked to go. Again the family opposed the move, and, again, she went anyway. She successfully completed her PhD abroad, had her first boyfriends, realized that Islam was important to her and returned with more confidence: 'The family culture that I had earlier acquired, that was given me, restricted me in doing certain things. *That* I could never break and throw away. Well, perhaps I wanted to throw it away, but something restricted me. This continues. In other words, be as free as you possibly can, but some things restrict your behaviour. Perhaps my family also knew this, but I am not sure. After I returned here from abroad, it was as if some things finally opened up, everybody accepted it, I could easily go on holiday on my own, I could dress as I wanted … it did not bring any criticism.'

During her first years as a 'research employee' before she went abroad she started to wear a bathing suit (*mayo*) when swimming. The social circle (çevre) was very *modern*, everybody used mayo. However, she wore shorts over the mayo, she could not manage otherwise. They made fun of her, joked about it. Several years later, when Deniz was back from her studies abroad, one of those modern women who criticized her then, wanted to wear shorts over her mayo. Deniz then joked about it, said it was comical and shameful (*ayıp*) and reminded her of her earlier criticism, which the 'modern' woman did not remember. 'That woman felt uneasy (*rahatsız*) there. Why did she feel uneasy? Because she had lived for a long time in Trabzon. There was something about the life in Trabzon. For example, another very close female friend. She studied in Istanbul, her father is from Izmir, Giresun [on the Black Sea coast] is a somewhat *modern* place, she lived there. Her father was a [medical] doctor. She was the daughter of a *modern* family, but here [in Trabzon] she did not manage to dress very uncovered (*açık*, 'open').'

She stresses that she herself had acquired the ability to be 'open' by fighting for it. She knows both societies (*toplumlar*), the different cultures, and can assess how things are seen from both an open and a closed/covered (*kapalı*) perspective. 'Since they [the modern ones] have been raised exclusively within one culture, they feel a desire to imitate others (*özenti duyuyorlar*), sometimes they strive to exaggerate.'

We touched on religion, and she stated that she is a very religious (*dindar*) person. 'Very few know that I am religious. That's because someone who [only] looks at the outside appearance would assume that I in my lifetime haven't made the namaz prayer. But I may have made the namaz many more times than that person. I also keep the fast. In my life I have skipped the fast only one time, and that was during my first year abroad. I do this because I believe. It's a thing between me and God (*Tanrı*)… I am both a Muslim and an Atatürkist, even a passionate

Atatürkist. Anyway, this was really what Atatürk wanted.' She mentions the well-known principles of laicism, that religion and state should be separate and that belief is a private matter. This reference to laicism is a defence of her belief, and she concludes the issue with 'some of my friends ask me "as a scientist, how can you believe?" Yes, that criticism [was levelled against me]. But I reached a decision by thinking, not by being influenced by anyone.'

Towards the end of our conversation, I brought her attention to the distance between the scientists and the fishers. We had talked about this during an earlier conversation and she recapitulated and elaborated some of her points. She admits that the fishers with their extensive experience (*tecrübe*) may make wide-ranging observations, but the difference, she says, lies in the fact that scientists ask about the reasons and study them in detail. On the idea of having better communication between fishers and scientist, on the scientists better being able to serve the fishers, she says that fishers could request education (*eğitim*). They may for example organize a 'fishers education program' at the Sürmene Faculty. But she does not have much belief that this could really happen. Either the state must perceive the need, or the fishers must request it. But the fishers think that they are educated, they do not believe that they are uneducated. And, when it comes to the state, 'those in the leadership, because they have come there for political reasons, think as ignorant persons (*cahil düşünen insanlar*).'

Deniz lives alone in a fairly spacious flat at the university campus and she possesses a small car. Relations with her closest family remains strained. She has had several boyfriends, both foreign and Turkish, but has never married and is childless. She sometimes speaks of this as her third sacrifice. She actively participates in chat groups on the internet and maintains close academic and personal bonds internationally. Since the interview was made in 1998 she has spent many months as a visiting scholar and research employee in both Japan and the USA.

Deniz's life history illustrates what hurdles had to be cleared, what sacrifices had to be made to make this improbable transformation from poor village girl to top academician. She sees this transformation as an acquisition of modern culture, a modern lifestyle. The mapping of culture/town/rich versus ignorance/village/poor is apparent already at junior high school. Education is that which enabled her to 'achieve' another lifestyle, the modern lifestyle. The modern lifestyle is a package of traits that goes together: having a medical doctor as father, higher education, being açık and rahat, wearing trousers and mayo. On the other side of the divide there are, among other things, lifestyle traits such as being *kapalı* ('closed', being covered) and namus (modest). Geography is also part of the staging, with Istanbul and Izmir being centres of modernity and cultivation. Here the same kind of West/Istanbul/modern versus East/Anatolia/traditional opposition as was evident in the semiotics of seafood consumption comes into play, not as poles within a continuum, but – in her own words – as two different cultures. The same opposition is copied at regional Black Sea level, with an increasing degree of modernity as one goes from Rize towards Samsun. Islam is often also part of this mapping, but Deniz departs somewhat from this. Her belief is the kind of belief that is accommodated to the 'modern' Turk.

The change of lifestyle has not been easy for Deniz. Her transformation has clearly involved not only intellectual, but also bodily and emotional training. As acquiring 'culture' has implied such things as new ways of dressing (wearing trouser as 'picking up culture'), there has been bodily resistance against embodying the culture. It probably never would have been possible without her resocialization in the 'total institution', the closed girls' lise in Istanbul, during a very formative phase in her life. In order to become cultivated, she had to both adopt a new body hexis, and at the same time, when visiting the village, make sure to behave according to 'traditional' ideals of female decency.

## Education and Lifestyle

Traditionally, higher education in Turkey has been the privilege of the urban middle and upper classes; this is still the case at the prestigious universities. Memur families have typically put more emphasis upon education than others have. But offspring of the growing private-sector bourgeoisie now make up an increasing portion of universities' student bodies. Even the poorest families, including small-boat fishers, will usually make great efforts to get at least one of their offspring into university education. Education is increasingly seen as a prerequisite for successful career.

For Deniz and her colleagues, education is not only about securing a good income and is not only an intellectual transformation, but also a transformation of ways of living. That was also Deniz's motive for continuing her education. It was not yearning for knowledge, but the desire to make for herself a kind of life other than that her mother had that motivated her. She wanted to be master of her own life. Her achievement would not have been possible without her own determination and courage and her willingness to make sacrifices. She has been socialized into a world that makes her see education as the solution to all kinds of problems. For instance, she believes that fishers and scientists can come closer to one another by fishers receiving water-produce education. And the politicians are bad because they are *cahil* (ignorant).

In Turkey, to read, to study, generally means much more than learning the knowledge provided by the university courses and acquiring some professional skill. Higher education, in particular, is regarded as a training or cultivation that ideally transforms the self of the person and is to be expressed in a whole lifestyle, a cultivated, yet 'relaxed' (rahat) lifestyle. Being a state employee with higher education, and in particular being an academician, is a question of lifestyle and the gulf separating them from the *kaba* (coarse) and 'unclean' *taşra/köylü* (provincial/villager) is experienced as being huge. This creates a barrier for scientists and white collar memur against participation in the lives of fishers.

Women in this social environment are generally not covered (kapalı) but 'open' (açık), dressing and keeping their hair in a moderate 'Western' style. Hair, hair-covering and dress are continued sensitive and politicized topics in Turkey; they are issues which the researchers have got to relate to consciously somehow, especially as state employees who are subject to very strict codes of attire and appearance that aim at restricting 'excesses' in both directions, i.e., both in Islamic and 'indecent Western' styles. At the workplace, women are not allowed to cover, but neither are they allowed to wear skirts above their knees. Men are not allowed to grow beards and are barred from wearing shorts. Attire should be formal, clean and fairly neutral. These rules have become especially important at the universities since they were the major scenes of the *türban* (headscarf) protests of the 1980s and 1990s (see, e.g., Göle 1996; Özdalga 1998). Yet, at TFRI and the Sürmene Faculty there did not seem to be any serious conflicts over attire and general appearance. The 'Islam-West' conflict is not very pronounced within these institutions. Most regard themselves as religious, and for some the Islamic faith, rituals and life-style precepts are indeed very important. On the other hand, I do not know of any who are active members of Islamic brotherhoods or political parties, and few draw attention to their beliefs or proselytize (as many fishers as well as lower bureaucrats do).

Concerns about attire and bodily behaviour that partly transcend the 'Islam-West' opposition have profound importance in self-presentation and social practice. These revolve around concerns of cleanliness and good manners: *kibar* (refined), *terbiye* (well-mannered), *nazık* (polite). Most researchers, as others of the middle classes, pay great attention to the cleanliness of their clothes and shoes and make sure that they do not appear worn or unironed. The transport by official car service, available to the director, or researchers on special duty, gains an added importance in this context: when compared to travel by packed public buses or the (private) *dolmuş*es (minibuses), it is easier to stay clean from the muddy streets. Yet, appearance, including ability to dress 'well', is believed to reflect more than economic status; it is a result of cultural competence associated with breeding and education. Dressing is a subtle way to express tastes appropriate for a certain lifestyle. Added to this are other elements associated with body posture, eye contact, and use of socio space. For instance, scientists to a much lesser degree than fishers express friendship through physical contact. A concern for both men and women is the cleanliness of food and service. Many avoid eating at cheaper lokanta because they are perceived as unclean (both the food and the environment, socially and physically); some always make sure to wipe thoroughly drinking glass and utensils with tissue paper before eating. No fisher bothers about such 'niceties'. Most scientists prefer to do their shopping, even of foodstuffs, in the 'modern' and supposedly clean stores in the city centre's main shopping area, rather than in the cheaper markets just beyond these streets.

During one lunch at a riverside 'meat and fish' eating establishment near Maçka, a professor and a 'research employee' that he supervised (for the doktora) spoke about their undergraduate students. They found that the students from western Turkey (specified upon my request as the regions of Marmara, Aegean, Ankara, Black Sea and Adana) had more easy-going manners (*daha rahat*, 'more relaxed') than the students from the east. They specified that '*kültürlü* (lit.: cultured) is not the same as *sosyal* (social) or *rahat*. The students from the west are more sosyal, rahat, since they ask questions more freely in class, and so on.' Many that oppose the Islamic and conservative forces in Turkey emphasize precisely that they themselves are more sosyal. But this – exemplified for example with refined versions of Istanbul style seafood consumption – may be as much a way of distancing oneself from 'backward and village' style interaction, as an opposition to Islam (although Islam may of course be seen as one 'backward' trait). The ideals of being rahat and sosyal may equate with being urban and *kosmopolit*, being good at and desiring social intermingling – what Gökalp termed 'solidarism' (see Chapter 6).

The style of a person's interpersonal behaviour among scientist and bureaucrats should be fairly self assured and not overtly deferential, but polite with colleagues and superiors. She must be sensitive to striking the right balance. Even people working together, and even in informal situations, usually address each other with the polite *Siz* ('You'), which fishers and other 'simple' people reserve for strangers and superiors, though not for socially close *reis* or village head. Alternatively, scientists and memur may use other polite forms of address, such as *hoca* (teacher), *hanımefendi* (lady, madam), *müdür bey* ('Mr Director', if appropriate).

## Language

Speech is indeed one of the most important practice domains where style and manner are expressed. Most, although not all, researchers at TFRI and at Sürmene speak, as Deniz learned to do, with the national style 'Istanbul Turkish'. Also, most of them make sure to use the correct Turkish neologisms (e.g., *eğitim* for education), and not the Arabic words (e.g., *tahsil* for 'education') that are still common vernacular among the less educated. The scientists generally speak more softly and plainly, without the changes in pitch and 'power', without the swearing and rich use of metaphors that 'simpler' people employ. While the taped conversations with fishers are difficult to transcribe, those with the scientists are more easily turned into linear text. I suspect this is so because the scientists tend to take the written text as a model for oral styles, using longer grammatically correct sentences, with little implicit meaning, that are phonetically clear and not too hastily spoken. Thus, the 'clarity' of the scientists' speech style may be an effect of the fact that their thinking is structured by a high involvement in writing and reading (cf. Ong 1982: 56–57).

I believe, however, that there is more to this than simply the 'technique' (skill) of speech being moulded by the 'technique' of writing. There is a level of meta-communication in this style, precisely by being seen as a style. It is part of the lifestyle of the 'educated', a style for which they have a taste. The purity (correctness) of the style and of the language is, as Deniz stressed, in itself an important identity marker that demonstrates sophistication. It takes a special kind of breeding, training, and skill (technique) to be able to master the correct style. This literalism (cf. Herzfeld 1992) of the oral style may be an expression of a more general fetishizing of language as text. The 'rational' language of the scientists (and bureaucrats) is an aspect of their lifestyle that connects them with the 'grand narrative' of Turkish modernization. Educated state representatives both represent and embody this state-governed modernization process that is, as I noted in Chapter 3, ideally to be guided by rational, scientific thinking.

At a seminar concerning hamsi fisheries, organized by the Foundation for Economic Research, Professor Çelikkale, who was then director at the Sürmene Faculty, gave a talk about the hamsi for the assembly of bureaucrats, scientists, businessmen, and some fishers. The talk included a scientific perspective on hamsi migrations (Çelikkale 1988: 27–29):

> The catch capacity of hamsi, which in the Black Sea generally is caught between the beginning of November and the start of April, is strongly related to atmospheric conditions (*atmosfer koşulları*). In particular, the formation of shoals is connected to water temperature. The hamsi migration is undoubtedly the fundamental component in this fishery. In March and especially from April-May towards July the hamsi moves towards the upper water layers. During the summer months it approaches shallow waters, dalyans and bays, and even enters lagoons. In the autumn, from September until January, it stays at deep and warm waters. It has been established that in the Black Sea the hamsi stays at a depth of 70–150 metres at a temperature of 8°C. In the eastern Black Sea hamsi primarily winters along the Caucasian shores. In the spring it migrates northwards and spreads out all over the

Black Sea. In the summer the hamsi is found above the thermocline stratum. The wintering areas are limited to special depth conditions; to underwater valleys (*vadi*) that cross the shallow waters (20–30 metres) on the continental shelf. Streams are slow in the valleys where the hamsi gather. The size of the shoals changes continuously. Hamsi is found at 45–55 metres depth during daytime and at 20–25 metres during the night. Many such wintering areas have been identified in the Turkish territorial waters, e.g.; the Bay of Fatsa.

The main focus of this narrative is largely congruent with the fisher Hakan's narrative (see Chapter 4): weather and water temperature as 'movers', seasonal changes, and the importance of water depths and bottom conditions, such as underwater valleys. When it comes to categorization and taxonomy the differences between the fishers and scientists are more pronounced. Scientific words such as *atmosfer* and *termoklin* readily find place in Çelikkale's text, and he does not use the fishers' term (kuyu) for the underwater valleys. Although Hakan tries to quantify things, there is clearly a greater degree of quantification in the scientific text (especially in the discussion of life span, spawning, etc.)

Hakan's narrative is oral whereas Çelikkale's is written (although presented orally, it was probably inscribed beforehand in a written document). However, as I will discuss in more detail in the next chapter, the significant lack of human body analogies and metaphors in general in the scientist's text is not prescribed by the kind of articulation (text, not oral). If Hakan's use of analogies is a technique to imbue the story with experiential reality and situate himself in the narrative, one may counter that Çelikkale probably had neither need nor desire to make himself part of the story. His rhetorical strategy is the opposite. As a scientist he would wish to 'keep a distance'. Through the text he stresses clarity, transparency, and the decontextualised meaning of language. This conforms to the 'correspondence theory of meaning' that Lakoff criticizes (see Introduction), and which Herzfeld disclaims as a 'myth of representability' and a 'literalist dream of clarity' (1992: 111,118). The style, character and context of Çelikkale's presentation rather inscribe his talk into another narrative: the grand narrative of Turkish modernization.

Skills such as cleanliness, refinement and literalism are kinds of ethical know-how that are to a large extent tacit and embodied, but still very much a defining characteristic of what it means to be a man or woman of learning and good breeding. These skills, like the fishers' ethical know-how of interpersonal interaction, defy to a large extent being defined as either 'Islamic' or 'Western'. To wipe the fork before eating, is that 'Islamic' or 'Western' style? Most academicians, irrespective of how much they emphasize religious precepts, will find that the new style of 'fish and meat' eating establishments, brightly lit, alcohol free, and so on, is fully acceptable and even attractive. There have emerged competing claims to elite style framed within the opposing idioms of 'Islam' and 'Secular'. Chic head-cover stands in opposition to 'styled' hair (White 1999; Navaro-Yashin 2002). But both of these are styles that distance a woman from 'village styles'. The stress on being rahat, sosyal, and kültürlü could be interpreted as composing an 'ethos' of 'solidarism', a cosmopolitan social code that stands in opposition to *mahalle* (community) 'ways', as expressed for instance in patron-client relations, blood-feuds and ignorance concerning the edibility of non-fish seafood.

Concern with manners and style, with cleanness, sophistication, literalism and being rahat, is found throughout Turkish society, and these are important aspects of scientists' lifestyles. The unwillingness to expose oneself to 'dirty' environments, people, places, and food often results in people living very segregated lives. One researcher at TFRI regretted having been assigned to stay in the small town of Çayeli (east of Rize) for a couple of weeks since she found the people there to be very *kaba* (coarse, without manners). The same consideration also makes research cruises, especially prolonged stay on fishing boats, highly problematic for most researchers (especially female) and few have much maritime experience. Thus, lifestyle-related preferences put restrictions on practice and hamper interaction and contact with the 'common man', of which fishers are widely regarded as being among the most ignorant (cahil) and kaba. Both the social and physical dimensions of the fishing sector are considered 'unclean'.

At the research institutions there is lack of resources for undertaking journeys and field trips. Neither are there inspectors regularly coming with fishing boats. However, the task of some researchers requires them to interact more routinely with fishers and other people in the sector, and a couple of scientists have spent some time on fishing boats while pursuing their research on fish population dynamics. Below I chart in some detail a case that illustrates the character of daily life of scientists doing science. In the daily activities of the scientists there is a fundamental separation between office life and 'data collecting' activities. The relatively formal attire of office life is changed for more convenient clothes when one goes to the field. All visits to the field are structured by a purpose and regulated in time and space.

## A Research Survey

Japan International Cooperation Agency (JICA) has since mid 1990s supported a project at TFRI that aims to develop competence in rearing turbot for fish farming and stock enhancement. During 1999 to 2002 TFRI released 30,000 marked juvenile turbots in various locations along the Turkish Black Sea coast to enhance the seriously depleted turbot stock. In an effort to register the development, and hopefully success, of this stock-enhancement project, TFRI conducted field surveys along the entire Turkish Black Sea coast. One of their senior researchers, Mustafa Zengin (real name), with a doctoral degree on turbot, carried out this survey in several legs during the summer of 2004. He invited me to come along to their survey in the Sinop-Samsun region in May that year.

We spent three days together 'on the road'. In the Institute pickup van there were, in addition to Mustafa and me, the long time institute driver, and Mustafa's close colleague Yaşar (real name), who came along to have a break from the office routine and do some preparations for a survey he would later undertake in the region. While still on the road Mustafa used his private cell phone to call the owner of a sea-snail processing factory to confirm the agreement to meet at a seafood restaurant in Samsun that evening. In Samsun we drove to the University campus to deliver some equipment that the institute had sent to be used in a joint project. We visited a professor at the Department of Biology, an acquaintance. Mustafa also went to the office of an assistant professor working on the age assessment of fish, including turbot. They knew each other well, but they did not talk about 'personal' issues such as family. She asked Mustafa for some information to include in an article she was working on. Mustafa also promised to look through her draft article. We briefly went to her small office to look at some pictures of turbot otoliths (stony inner ear used in assessing age of fish).

While we were at the university İbrahim, the factory owner, called. He was waiting for us at the restaurant. We drove into the city centre, Mustafa jumped off in the environs of the restaurant while the rest of us drove to the Samsun Province Agricultural Directorate's guest house not far away. We waited for the porter to show up, then it transpired that they had not registered the reservation that Mustafa had made by telephone earlier that day. We were offered one room for three while the fourth had to share a double room with some stranger. None of us liked that. Without consulting Yaşar, the driver picket up his cell phone and called a friend, 'our leader' (*başkanımız*) – the leader of the regional office of Türk İş (Confederation of Turkish Workers Syndicates) – and requested his assistance. After twenty minutes he showed up, in a posh car and immaculate suit. He was, however, unable to alter the sleeping arrangement and did not offer us any alternative. Rather, he stressed that the guesthouse was newly renovated, and reluctantly we had to accept the deal. We each had to register with minute personal detail and paid U.S.$3.25 each.

Mustafa called up. They had started to eat. We had some problems finding the seafood 'restaurant' which was camouflaged as a social club. In addition to the four of us coming from Trabzon, and İbrahim, a middle-aged fairly calm man, the company included the Türk İş leader and a technical specialist working for İbrahim. Another round of fish was ordered. Some drank moderate amounts of alcohol – rakı and beer – while conversation circled almost exclusively around fish, fishing, sea snails and so forth. İbrahim, disclosing the real purpose of the meeting, told us that he was organizing experiments with three different kinds of traps to catch sea snails. The harmfulness of the *algarna* dredging for sea snail, the prevalent catch method, had long been a matter of concern, and the scientists at Sürmene had already started experiments with traps. Now İbrahim offered to finance five thousand traps to be distributed to fishers, on the condition that fishing with algarna became prohibited. Mustafa and Yaşar stressed that their authority is limited, that all they can do is to inform the ministry of their advice. When the party broke up after two hours İbrahim paid the bill without even symbolic gestures of negotiating over the bill (restaurant bills are never split). We were offered lodging by İbrahim. Three of us had already settled in the guesthouse, while Mustafa accepted the gesture and spent the night at a nice three-star hotel.

When we got up next morning the Türk İş leader waited for us. He had arranged for the kitchen (which usually serves lunch for 3–400 staff at the Province Agricultural Directorate) to serve us a very nice (and free) breakfast. Afterwards we walked over to the Directorate building next to the guesthouse were we met Mustafa at the water-produce section. This was clearly mostly a visit to pay their respects. Then, finally, the real business of this trip could start. First stop was at the office of the successful Balıkçıoğlu family trawl fishing company at the fish auction halls in the Samsun harbour area. Mustafa knew the four brothers well from earlier visits. Over the universally served tea Mustafa conducted the survey questionnaire interview, was handed over copy of their list of catches, and joined in small talk concerning turbot, sea snails and so forth before all present in the office, including a range of diverse visitors to the busy office, were lined up for a group photo. The tone of interaction was warm and personal.

**Figure 7.1.** Scientist interviewing fishers in Toplu köyü, Samsun.

After an hour we hit the road and headed west. In the small seaside village Toplu at the Bafra delta we met a few fishers by a shed they had put up near the beach (Figure 7.1). Mustafa went through his questionnaires: one listing all small-boat fishers catching turbot (technical data, catch data details), and one more detailed questionnaire for an expert turbot fisher. If there were no expert turbot fishers present Mustafa always commanded one to be summoned (*çağırır!*). We continued to the larger fishing harbour in Yakakent where we sat down outside a teahouse with members of the small-boat fishing cooperative. Mustafa knew some of them from before. After small talk and interviews the cooperative leader invited us for a meal. The fisher brought us to the best lokanta. We were all very enthusiastic about the inventive dish of scorpion fish (until recently not usually consumed) that we were served. The fisher paid for the meal. Another brief interview was conducted before we set off again.

We made a short visit to a fishmeal factory in a valley between Yakakent and Gerze where a range of the larger fishmeal factories are located. There was no activity in the factory, and we declined the management's dinner offer and continued for Gerze. In this small town of small-boat fishers cum lower memurs we were not warmly welcomed and Mustafa had problems finding someone to conduct the interviews with, probably because the issue of opening up the waters near Gerze to trawling was currently on the agenda. The cooperative leader was sent for and business was eventually conducted. Back in the car Yaşar and Mustafa agitatedly condemned the Gerze fishers for not telling the truth, for underreporting their catches and not disclosing that they have caught marked turbots, for not being true fishers but teachers and retired memurs. They argued that in general it is hard to work with fishers: 'They don't tell the truth, they are kaba and cahil.' They think, however, that it is not too bad in the provinces of Sinop and Samsun. They were not looking forward to working from Perşembe and eastwards: 'The further east you go the worse it becomes.'

We arrived in the town of Sinop just before sunset. The office of the water-produce cooperative was closed, but the cooperative leader was sent for by some fishers mending their nets in the workshop below the office. Mustafa spoke with the cooperative leader for a while, starting filling in the questionnaires. Then we went to a nearby fishers' teahouse to do the expert turbot fisher interview. Back at the cooperative office the cooperative leader treated us to *pide* ('pizza') that he had ordered from a lokanta. Informal conversation continued until 11 P.M. A long day's work was rounded off with a few beers in a nearby *birahane* (pub).

We stayed overnight at the spacious and all but empty basic and run-down Province Agricultural Directorate guesthouse. First on the agenda the next day was a visit to the Sinop Agricultural Directorate where Mustafa became excited when he was handed over a large preserved marked turbot that fishers had delivered to the Directorate. We made another visit to the cooperative where Mustafa completed his questionnaires. Ali, a young successful owner of a trawler, had accompanied us since we arrived in Sinop. He was a remarkably well-informed and educated man and Mustafa and Yaşar liked to converse with him. Ali kept our company when we left the cooperative and went to a seaside restaurant to have lunch. We ate some more of the scorpion fish. Nobody drank alcohol. Ali paid for the meal.

Now we could afford some leisure. Sinop's once dreaded and famous prison had a few years back been transformed to a museum. We toured the cells and spoke about its famous, mostly left-wing, prisoners. Mustafa sang a beautiful song which a famous prisoner had composed when imprisoned there.

Before leaving Sinop we drove up to the new Sinop Water Produce Faculty building, some distance from the town, where Mustafa and Yaşar had some interchange with colleagues and friends working on turbots and bioeconomics. On the return to Samsun we visited the harbour in Dereköy on the Kızılırmak delta. We also learned about Kumcağız, another fishing village nearby. In both places Mustafa made sure to meet the cooperative leaders. It was nine o'clock in the evening before he made the last interview. We trailed our way on small village roads through the delta towards Samsun. Mustafa was exhausted, but also excited. Addressed to Yaşar he spoke about the beautiful diagrams he would extract from the interviews.

Back in Samsun, Mustafa had dinner with his childhood friend and now Coast Patrol commander while the rest of us ate a simple meal at a lokanta after we had checked into the guesthouse. Next morning we had breakfast at another lokanta, where the Türk İş leader showed up. I parted with them here. They continued with visits to several harbours and cooperatives on the Çarşamba delta seafront before returning to Trabzon the following day.

Both Mustafa and Yaşar were informally dressed and travelled lightly. They received from the TFRI U.S.$9 per day to cover expenses. This is not much, but because of the generous hospitality with which they were often met, they actually spent less than this. On the other hand, they had expenses for which they were not reimbursed, for example use of their private mobile phones to make appointments and even follow up on other projects, communicating both with colleagues at the TFRI and with superiors in the Ministry.

During the few days' survey Mustafa relates to many different categories of people: bureaucrats, fishers of different kinds, the institute driver, scientists, a water-produce capitalist, even a leader of a workers' organization makes his contribution to the logistics of the survey. Moreover, the survey is set in context of the project, which again is set within a still wider network of social relations, including relations to a range of people at the Institute, to people in different sections in the ministry (both Control and Protection and the Directorate for Agricultural Research), to the Japanese partners in JICA and to a professor at the Sürmene faculty. His professional work on the turbot also involves him in relations to the GEF (Global Environmental Facility, UN)-funded Black Sea Environmental Recovery Project and to scientists around the Black Sea also working on the turbot. Moreover, in a still wider perspective, Mustafa's research and career has involved international relations and experiences, including attending courses in Rome (FAO) and Japan (JICA) and participating in an EU project (through me).

Thus, Mustafa involves himself in and cultivates a range of different social relations to get things done, to produce scientific knowledge. He is conscious that the way he acts affects the kind and amount of data he is able to gather. While the 'truth about turbot stocks and turbot stock enhancement', as yet not stabilized and calibrated, is the emerging collective (Latour 1993) to be produced by the research project, Mustafa is at its social centre. The work requires Mustafa to relate skilfully, according to different standards for interpersonal behaviour, towards strangers, acquaintances and friends. His ethical know-how is critical for the success of the project and the character of the collective. Mustafa and many of his fellow state representatives in the water-produce sector depend upon the cooperation of fishers. They sometimes acknowledge this and talk about the need for having experience (tecrübe) in handling relations with fishers.

Even during research which does not directly address fisheries or fishers, researchers often depend upon relating to fishers. Lack of research vessels, almost no funds to reimburse fishers for samples taken from their catch, together with very limited per-diem payment during research surveys result in scientists and bureaucrats depending upon fishers being generous and forthcoming. Mustafa has for many years kept close relations with certain fishers and factory owners, including the Balıkçıoğlu brothers. For several projects, including his own doctoral project on turbot, he relied on the Balıkçıoğlu for samples, research surveys and test trials of new technology. However, the research institutions have no strategy or explicit ethical code for how such relations are to be handled. There is generally neither any formal cooperation with fishers nor funds set off for these purposes.

Almost a year after the research survey, I went with Mustafa to Ankara where we had several formal and informal meetings with personnel in various sections that deal with fisheries within the Ministry of Agriculture. During these visits Mustafa brought up three different cases on behalf of fishers: for a fish-processing firm in the Marmara region, for some fishers near Istanbul who were dissatisfied with the activities of the local veterinarian control, and for the Balıkçıoğlu family who disputed the current interpretation of a regulation pertaining to mid-water trawling.

When bringing up this last case Mustafa excused himself, stating that he is an envoy (*elçi*) for the Balıkçıoğlu, but that he also has his own view on the issue. He stressed that he does not let anything pass his throat (i.e., he is not 'eating'). The officer opened a detailed map on his computer screen. Consulting the map they discussed the case and concluded that the current interpretation of the regulation was correct. Mustafa again said that he was sorry for bringing up the issue, but explained that he has personal relations (*kişisel ilişkiler*) with the fishers, that he feels indebted (*minnet*) to them.

To me he expressed that he is fed up with the Balıkçıoğlu being on at him. Other fishers criticize him for his strong bonds with them. The Balıkçıoğlu, knowing about Mustafa's business in Ankara, called him on his cell phone just after the end of working hours. They probably assumed that the issue had been discussed and wanted to learn about the result. Without answering the call Mustafa resignedly closed the cell phone. What was he to tell them? Nevertheless, his relationship with the Balıkçıoğlu was soon back on track.

To a large extent state representatives share with fishers and others codes of hospitality, generosity and politeness, the quality of which are important techniques for demonstrating one's status in the local community and to create bonds with social circles of wider social scale. Fishers and other actors in the fishery sector try to create bonds with scientists and bureaucrats. There might not be much tit-for-tat services or blatant corruption (*rüşvet*), but rather attempts to create indebtedness on the part of the state representatives. As was mentioned in the previous chapter, this is a common strategy when relating to potential torpils. However, the bonds created are vulnerable and the strategy does not always work.

Just as much as fishers may involve in the use of torpils although they regret the practice, state representatives may accept services that may be intended to create a debt on their part although they may dislike such social practice. Scientist and bureaucrats take the hospitality and generosity to a large extent for granted, and will act similarly to the fishers when they themselves receive visitors. They often criticized the Japanese JICA representatives living in Trabzon for not expressing personal intimacy and, when meeting Turkish co-workers visiting Japan, for failing completely to be hospitable and generous. Staff at TFRI and at the Sürmene faculty are concerned that relations should not only be purely instrumental. The ethical know-how of investing 'instrumental' relations with friendship qualities, giving due attention to the individual and the mutual relation among humans, is highly cherished. But, unlike the fishers, they are, as Mustafa indeed was when meeting fellow scientists as well as higher bureaucrats, more familiar or, as Deniz said, *rahat* (comfortable) with 'impersonal' relations.

Although Mustafa and Yaşar, unlike many other marine scientists, do relate to fishers, share standards for interpersonal behaviour with them and adapt their behaviour to the situation for example by using the 'traditional' address *Selam Aleykum* (which scientist do not usually use among themselves), fishers can hardly be said to be included among their significant others. Unlike fishers, in their time off work, the researchers do not hang around in local kahves. Some occasionally visit the Teachers House in Trabzon in small groups (of men) to play a game of cards. Some have access to the Kalepark ('Castlepark') military social club where they can have high quality food and alcoholic drinks at a low price in a 'civilized' environment. Generally, however, they spend more time with their families and make a point about that. The unmarried, often in mixed company, sometimes meet after work for a meal at a café or a cup of coffee at a *pastahane* (patisserie).

## Politics in Science

Bureaucrats or politicians are the driving force behind many of the research projects at TFRI and even at the Sürmene faculty. Yet, the scientist to a certain extent see their role and knowledge as being independent of the central administration and government and often regret that politicians and bureaucrats do not listen to their advice. They believe that the politicians think primarily in the short term (*günlük*) and are too much concerned about their vote potential. The scientists, apparently in contrast to politicians, have a firm idea about 'rational management' based on scientific knowledge. Thus, they embrace easily the ideal of stock management. One marine scientist explained: 'What happens to an unmanaged (or non-administered, *yönetilmeyen*) stock, or an unmanaged human society? In the end it will enter a crisis.' Fish, like people, are to be 'managed'. Connected to this is a belief that people involved in water-produce activities 'unfortunately' do not see the need for scientific knowledge and a 'professional, technical' approach.

Although scientists regard themselves as belonging to the elite, that does not mean that they can direct everything or that they feel secure in their elite positions. Indeed, they feel just as much as everyone else does that they are restricted and influenced by politics and that their elite status is constantly challenged. This is especially so in post-1980 Turkey where the relative salary of state-employed scientists and bureaucrats has decreased and alternative elite groupings, elite symbols, and power wielders have 'proliferated' (Göle 1997). Many scientists lament the degree to which they perceive science, especially recruitment of staff, being unduly politicized. This seems to be more pervasive in administrative positions. Since 1990 the director's chair at TFRI has been filled by seven different men. Most of these were backed by a political party and change in government therefore often resulted in change of director. Many of the directors came from or continued their career at the Province Agriculture Directorate. Before a new director was appointed in 2004 none had been trained as a water-produce engineer and none had held a PhD.

Politics is thought also to influence: the allocation of position of 'research employee', which in many cases is a de facto decision about who is to become an academician; allotment of attractive grants to study abroad; and decisions of juries that decide whether a post-doctoral fellow (*yardımcı doçent*) is eligible for a permanent position and higher status and salary. There are also intense 'local politics', running along local lines of personal relations and allegiances, of deciding who is going to be included on the list of authors, and in what sequence. Thus, with its local politics, the importance of social webs, the readiness to mobilize torpils and the importance of party politics for filling positions, the kind of social interaction scientists and bureaucrats are involved in is not too dissimilar from the social world of the fishers.

Marine scientists readily reconceptualize politics as 'personal relations' (*kişisel ilişkiler*). This implies a de-ideologization of politics, to some extent putting the blame on individual persons and not groups or the political system. This position also contains elements of a critique that politics is invaded by 'mahalle' norms instead of being based on reason and rationality and is therefore embedded in the discourse of rational modernization and nationalism. A common way of conceptualizing the situation in Turkey is to say that 'in Turkey politics enters everything', thus implicitly holding up an ideal of bureaucratic rationality that is thought to have been deviated from, alas, in Turkey.

The marine scientists in Trabzon are ambiguously positioned relative to the state. On the one hand they embody and represent the state and the moral project of modernization policies. On the other hand they criticize the state for dictating the science, and the politics and bureaucracy for being corrupt and irrational. For instance, marine scientists uphold the ideal of independent, free and universal science and many find the overt emphasis on 'water produce' and aquaculture an imposition by the state, yet they pay lip service to it.[75] Many scientists regret that their recommendations for fishery regulations are overturned by the politics and lobbying activities of the fishery sector.

This ambivalence is, however, mirrored by and embodied in scientific and bureaucratic lifestyle and practice in itself. There is an implicit ambivalence between, on the one hand, state representative's styles and manners that tend to separate them from fishers and other 'simple' people and, on the other hand, the practical, daily activities of bureaucrats and scientists that, through concrete projects, networking, friendships and politics, induces them, as we saw in the Samsun-Sinop survey case, to interact, cooperate with and sometimes become indebted to fishers and other actors in the sector. Apart from being with the state, what separates marine scientists in Trabzon from fishers is the way the experiences 'in the field' are, by the scientists, transformed to standards for 'scientific knowledge'.

## Making Science: Inscription and Models

The survey Mustafa undertook was only one aspect of the scientific work. Everywhere he filled in forms, counted, noted numbers, etc., on paper (the institute cannot afford to provide him with a laptop). Already 'in the field' he started to distillate knowledge/information from a complex practice. Latour defines knowledge as the ability to be 'familiar with things, people and events, which are distant' (Latour 1987: 220). By this definition, only what was left from the survey counts in the construction of knowledge. What was left? The questionnaire, reports and forms, and the turbot. Of course, the turbot remained only a potential at this stage; it had to be worked upon and transformed into various inscriptions. Back at his office Mustafa or one of his subordinates entered the numbers into Excel or more specialized data-processing programs that could provide him with 'results', either as numbers or as diagrams.

Almost all observations are transformed and inscribed into quantities, in other words digital codes. This, according to Shore (1996: 339), eases 'information processing'. Yet, once analysed or 'processed', information is often transformed again, for presentation and interpretation, into analogue codes in the form of graphs and diagrams that Mustafa could almost visualize while still in the field. Analogue codes ease understanding or 'meaning construction' (Shore 1996: 339). Since we generally take our basic level perception to be unshakeable, the visual analogue representations are usually more readily accepted as 'real' knowledge of primary data (Lakoff 1987: 298). It is possible to 'read' the figure, to extract meaning from it, without understanding the underlying models and assumptions.

The marine scientists in Trabzon firmly distinguish – as is common in science internationally – between material, method and results. The repeatedly visited 'station', for example the harbours visited by Mustafa time after time in his surveys, is an important part of the methodological design, and the results contribute, by comparison and design of models and theories, to knowledge proper, the *bilgi* (knowledge, information).

Despite, however, the emphasis on scientific methodology, a research cruise I participated in relied on practices that are fairly similar to the fishing practices: routine skills of navigating the boat (done by the researchers), using the trawls (done by the crew, but assisted by the researchers), interpreting the echo-sounder display (done by the researchers), and so forth. The importance of skills such as knowing English, interacting smoothly with fishers, or steering a vessel is formally or informally acknowledged. These are primarily embodied skills, technical and ethical know-how, that are not inscribed or otherwise externalized/objectified during or after operations, but nonetheless are a part of and even a prerequisite for this science. However, among the marine scientists such 'hands on' skills are generally not regarded as knowledge (*bilgi*), but rather as tecrübe (experience). Scientists find that they are well qualified in the theoretical aspects of navigation, which is being taught at the Sürmene Faculty, but have had too little practice. They have, as one researcher expressed it, 'sufficient knowledge, but insufficient experience (*bilgi yeterli, tecrübe yetersiz*).'

In many contexts the researchers actually prefer the term *uygulama* (putting into practice) to tecrübe for such practical skills. This terminology draws on a model which considers practice as the execution of theoretical knowledge, the latter being prior and primary. Science orders them hierarchically, placing 'technology' over 'technique' (Ingold 1993a). This is a reflection of the language-based knowledge concept (*langue* as the basis for *parole*) that I criticized in Chapter 4. For the fishers, knowledge is what it takes to successfully catch fish, and they explicitly regard 'being at sea' skills as knowledge (bilgi). For the scientists, bilgi is the output, the product, of the process. Observations and experiences only become knowledge when it can be transported, manipulated, and accumulated, when it, by being inscribed, becomes separate from any individual possessor.

Unlike fishing, in a scientific project it is an end in itself to construct collectives that are as stable as possible and ensure that they can easily be combined, transported and mobilized. That is what makes observations into 'knowledge', and that is what science is about. This is rather self-evident, but has far-reaching implications. Fishers do not strive to build stable collectives. Rather, their situated 'technique' should precisely be unstable, undecided, and elusive in order to be useful. To catalogue it, freeze it, would be to remove the dynamism, situatedness and flexibility upon which their adaptation strategies depend. Thus, one of the primary differences between fishers' and scientists' knowledges may inhere in the very definition of knowledge that Latour supplies: 'to be familiar with things distant'. Such is the aim of science, not of fishing. Although fishers may know 'things at a distance', more important is familiarity with the immediate.

## From 'Production' to Bioeconomic Models

Scientific results are meaningless without a context. Results must be processed by means of established models in order to have meaning and be accepted as 'knowledge'. In Chapter 3, I described how there was, during the 1990s, a shift in Turkish marine science towards bioeconomic models as the major framework for organizing scientific knowledge. Marine scientists in Trabzon partook in this change. By the end of the 1990s, calls for monitoring of stocks and quota regulations became more widespread in reports and academic publications by scientists at TFRI and the Sürmene Faculty (e.g. Çelikkale et al. 1998; Zengin, Genç and Düzgüneş 1998; Zengin, Genç and Tabak 1998: 47).

There are good reasons to believe that the increase in computing power at the research institutions has facilitated the use of bioeconomical models and made it possible to build a wider network than previously feasible. In 1990–91 TFRI had very few computers. By 1998 many of the staff had at their disposal up-to-date computers, in part financed by project support from the World Bank and from JICA, capable of running advanced programs. At the Sürmene Faculty researchers seem to have enjoyed similar developments. Thus, by the late 1990s a lot of the daily research activity now consisted of, for example, making population estimates by plotting field data into either plain Excel spreadsheets or into predesigned 'forms' of some specific program that according to an established equation will 'automatically' 'process' the 'material' and generate some 'findings'. This implies that not only the model, but also the 'processing' becomes black boxed. The importance of such black-boxed models is indeed very great, as is exemplified by an excerpt from a paper by a professor at the Sürmene faculty on population dynamics of hamsi (Düzgüneş et al. 1995: 60):

> Growth was determined as length and weight by absolute values and rates (Beverton and Holt, 1957). The length-weight relationship was derived using the formula given by Pauly (1983). Fulton's condition factor was calculated according to Ricker (1975). Von Bertalaffy growth equation for length and weight at a given age were determined (Ricker, 1975). Survival rate from age series was used for calculations of the instantaneous total mortality coefficient (Z) (Nikolsky, 1965; Gulland, 1969). The instantaneous natural mortality rate (M) was calculated with the formula given by Ursin (1967).

The growing complexity and authority of the taxonomic system and the advent of bioeconomic models has increasingly distanced scientists' models from fishers' models. Pálsson has noted a similar change in the Icelandic case with the scientists' shift to a modernist paradigm with bioeconomic models (Pálsson 1998a). Marine sciences in Trabzon may now be more influenced by imported scientific models than before. But these 'external' models that the Trabzon scientists lean on and draw on have attained such a degree of sophistication that for the most part local sciences in Trabzon lack the capacity (human and technical resources) to challenge or adjust their basic premises or design. The increased complexity of bioeconomic models also makes peripheral science increasingly dependent upon models that are designed in the scientific metropoles. Thus, the content of science may be more black boxed at this peripheral level than in the frontier of science.

I have stressed here that scientists are incompletely understood if one limits analysis to 'rationalities', 'ideologies', 'knowledges' or the 'construction of facts' (Latour 1993). Indeed, Latour's approach is insufficient not only for studying fisher's knowledge but also for analyses of science and bureaucratic knowledge. There is a need to balance the analyses of the 'life of the facts' with an analysis of the 'life of the scientists (or bureaucrat)'. In the life and practice of the scientist, the focus is not always the project at hand and the knowledge gained, but rather the dynamics of having a degree or position, in effect a career. This is intimately connected to lifestyle and manners. Lifestyle and an academic career are both dependent upon and facilitate the other. Skills in managing social relations and engaging in 'politics' are, just as in the fishers' world, critical for success. And it is precisely through politics that science and fishers meet. At this level knowledge is often an important resource but is also frequently contested. One of the cases in which this comes out most clearly is in the controversy over the sonar.

# CHAPTER 8

# The Controversy over the Sonar: Does it Harm Fish?

The lives and knowledges of fisher and scientist meet in the case of the conflict over the use of the fish finder device sonar. Sonar use has remained a controversial issue among fishers since its introduction in the Turkish fisheries in 1980. Most fishers claim that sonars scare away or kill fish while local marine scientists and some fishers contend that sonars have no such effect. In this chapter I discuss ways in which fishers and scientists know the sonar. What is their involvement with the sonar and with one another in the context of sonar use? I discuss these issues by surveying multiple aspects of people's relation to the sonar.

I mentioned the conflict over the sonars to a leading English marine scientist who had been working in the Black Sea. 'Well', he said, 'I suppose the difference is one between knowledge and belief.' This is a supposition that I do not want to make. In my view, an anthropological approach to the way in which fishers and scientists know this new technology should try not to privilege any position. My purpose is to develop a more sound understanding of the conflict and incongruent positions by focusing on how different people relate to and think about the sonar. What kind of a 'thing' is it to them? I will not restrict myself to an analysis of the different views and arguments as different claims to 'truth'. Rather, I will work to grasp some of the underlying factors that shape those claims; the practices, experiences, reasoning and metaphors involved.

In studying the culture of science and technology, feminist cultural analysts have demonstrated that science/technology fetishisms are pervasive in Western popular discourse (see, e.g., Franklin 1995). Such approaches demonstrate the ways in which technoscience is embedded in wider cultural contexts. I follow such lines of enquiry in this study of the sonar, but believe that these approaches risk producing interpretative 'surface' analyses; they have a tendency to slip into a style that focuses primarily on history, texts and discourse and that privileges deconstruction (and critique) of the technoscientific 'constructions'. In other words, they tend to be extremerelativist with regard to science and technology. I find that Latour's (1987, 1993) approach is less extremerelativist because he does not privilege the social. His focus is on the 'collective', the piece of technology or fact as it is made up of associations of humans and nonhumans alike. Although I support Latour's deconstruction of the nature-society dichotomy in studies of things/facts, I contend that we should work beyond that: 'facts' and technology can only be understood through people's engagement with them. Admittedly, technology is not fully explained as subjective experience and social construct. On the other hand, it is impossible to precipitate out the purely material aspects of technology. It is a composite, or a 'collective'. I want to heed the possibilities and limitations that the material aspects of technology engender, but that can only be done within a perspective that regards technology as a 'total social phenomenon' (Pfaffenberger 1988). Although I am interested in understanding this highly complex technological object, I do not focus primarily on the technoscientific production of the sonar. I do not limit my perspective to a 'Latourian', 'How is the sonar constructed?', but ask 'How do the fishers and scientists know the sonar?' What is their involvement with the sonar and with one another in the context of sonar use?

## The Sonar Controversy

The first sonars were used in the Turkish fisheries around 1980. Some larger and more expansive Black Sea family-fishing companies spearheaded the development. The sonar made more of a difference to them since it facilitated observation of hamsi but not of other, larger pelagic fish. Istanbul fishers raged against this development and argued that the sonars harmed the fish. They lobbied successfully for a regulation that made use of sonars illegal. Some Black Sea fishers owning large purse seiners, with the assistance of MPs from the region, mobilized against this decision and managed to bring the case before the Turkish military for a final decision.[76] The Military deemed the sonars not harmful; thus, only a few days after the initial ban on sonars had been issued, a counter-statement was issued in the Official Gazette. Nonetheless, sonars remained a heated issue. A few years later the national television channel broadcast a discussion about the sonar among elder skippers, sonar salesmen and scientists in the Kumkapı fishing port in Istanbul.

During the 1980s and 1990s the use of sonars became steadily widespread. The sonars used in these fisheries are of the latest model, technologically very advanced, and similar to the sonars used in technologically developed fisheries around the world. The sonar is now indispensable in the hamsi fisheries and fishers must reinvest continuously in better and more expensive sonars in order to stay in the game. Sonar has become emblematic of success within the pelagic purse-seine fisheries. Most of the larger purse seiners involved in the hamsi fisheries are now equipped with sonar; not having a new model is a clear indicator that one is in the process of being sidelined. A good sonar may cost as much as U.S.$220,000 (1998) and is, together with the net(s), boat and engine, one of the main investment costs in the purse-seine fisheries. Most sonars are now imported from Japan and marketed by agents in Istanbul. Since 1997 a new kind of sonar, introduced by the Istanbul fishers, has gained currency and further increased the capitalization of this sector. This new 'large pelagic' sonar can see not only small pelagic fish but also the larger pelagic fish. It has especially transformed the fisheries of the bonito, which is fished during its annual migration from the Sea of Marmara into the Black Sea.

The use of sonar has remained a controversial issue since its introduction (Taner 1991; Knudsen 1997), and, for the fishers, science has not settled the case. It is clearly one of the most important and most discussed issues in these fisheries. Among small-boat fishers and crew on the bigger boats in the Black Sea region, as well as in Istanbul, it is the most cited reason for the ecological crisis and low catches of the first half of the 1990s.[77] As a kind of concession to the sceptical Istanbul fishers the government has crafted a regulation that rules use of sonars with frequencies of 60 KHz and below illegal in the Sea of Marmara (GDPC 1997).

## The Scientists' Sonar

To the marine scientists in Trabzon the sonar is essentially a scientific product, a piece of technology. They rely primarily on the scientific discourse of other centres of scientific knowledge, especially Norway and Japan, for their own knowledge. A 1980 textbook in fishery and fishing technology (Sarıkaya 1980) includes an extensive chapter on electronic fish finders in which the operating principle of sonars is briefly outlined. As the text relates little to actual conditions in Turkish fisheries, it is better seen as a general summary of the potential and possible uses of electronic fish finders. Most of the technology outlined in the textbook has not found application in Turkish waters. Some of the scientists in Trabzon, either through training courses or during longer stays in Japan or England, have observed that the effect of sonar on fish is not a controversial issue in other countries. But they are well aware that many fishers are concerned about the effect of sonars and regret that most fishers seem unable to understand the 'facts'.

In contrast to the fishers, scientists use sonar only occasionally in their research and their research vessels are equipped with outdated sonars. The scientists' involvement with sonars has thus been limited and, overall, the sonar has not been an investigative priority. Scientists at the Sürmene Faculty have undertaken one limited study of the effect of sonar on fish. This study, together with the informal comments on it made by many of the participants, give valuable insight into the scientists' approach. The report from the study (Çelikkale et al. 1988a) outlines three lines of work they did on the sonar. In the first, horse mackerels in an aquarium were exposed to waves similar to those emitted by the sonars. The sonar pulses were 'translated' to sound audible for humans so that the scientists would know when the fish were exposed to the waves. The experimenters then watched the fish react to different kinds and strengths of sonar pulses. They noted no changes in behaviour except when the frequency was below 12 KHz '[I]t was seen that the individuals in common made 2–3 powerful whips with their tail and fled into the other corner of the aquarium' (Çelikkale et al. 1988a: 12). The study implicitly assumes the 'truth' that the sonar emits 'sound'. In the international scientific literature sonar pulses are understood as sound and the authors accordingly describe the properties of sound in water in great detail (FAO 1980; MacLennan and Simmonds 1992). Fish are regarded as deaf above approximately 2 KHz. Most sonars operate in the range of 15–200 KHz.

In the second component of the study, scientists observed, again visually, fishes' behaviour when they were exposed to sonar pulses from fishing boats. They hired a fishing boat (with crew) from one of the larger family fishing companies near Trabzon. In the first five runs the scientists watched the behaviour of free-swimming schools of small pelagic fish (hamsi and horse mackerel) on the sonar display. In a sixth experiment divers stationed at three different depths inside a half closed purse seine watched entrapped hamsi as the sonar of the research vessel 100m away was turned on and off. No change in behaviour was observed (by the scientists? fishers? the report does not specify) and the report concludes that the fish were not scared off by the sonar pulses. In its conclusion the report gives most weight to this last experiment, most likely because it involved direct visual observation.

The last component of the study is a survey of the international scientific literature on fishes' ability to hear sounds in water. Here the emphasis is put on arguing that while the two first parts of the study have shown that sonar does not scare off fish, other studies from the literature indicate that engine noise and the like may. In accordance with accepted convention for writing papers in natural sciences, the report lists the different 'materials' used. This includes detailed taxonomic identification of the relevant fish species, but only a vague identification of the sonars (by general brand name, such as FURUNO). No attempt is made to explain the general working of the sonar, nor is there any discussion of the specifics of the sonars involved in the experiments. For the scientists the focus moves away from the sonar to the fish. The question becomes: 'Do fish hear the sonar?' The fishes' capacity for hearing, and not the sonar and its emissions, is constructed as the 'unknown'.

I did not observe these experiments myself, but I know both the fishers and scientists involved. Their informal comments give insight to their approaches to the sonar. In independent informal conversations with me, the scientists' statements on the issue were rather uniform: in 1990 the researcher who led the study referred primarily to the experiment during which divers had observed fish inside a net and argued that sonars absolutely do not scare away or kill fish. However, he added, they know nothing about potential hormonal or biochemical changes. The technical expert, an electronic engineer, was most concerned about the fishers being 'ignorant' and said that they do not know what KHz is. Also, he maintained, they are further confused by the regulation that stipulates that use of sonars above 45 KHz is forbidden in the Sea of Marmara (which was not consistent with actual regulations).

One of the Faculty's lecturers who participated in the experiments as a diver also based his position on the experiment during which the divers observed the fish directly. Being socially closer to the fishers than most of the other marine scientists in the region, he could explain the fishers' alleged misperception of the sonar. He explained that the fishers know that light scares fish and that the same generator used for powering the sonar is also used for the powerful spotlights that illuminate the work area on the boats; therefore many fishers have concluded that the sonars emit light or powerful electricity. Yet, he pointed out that the manuals that accompany the diving equipment they receive from the U.S. recommend not diving near operating sonars because they may, without perceptible sensation, damage your heart. He commented: 'Biological effect is another matter, it was not part of our study. We studied the effect on fish.' A senior researcher who works in the same faculty but did not participate in the study, referred to the same part of the study as the others. He furthermore questioned any potential harm to fish since the sound waves emitted from the sonar are reflected when they hit the fish. Although supporting the general findings of the study, he claimed that 'it was not very scientific, they conducted it badly. When the divers were in the water strong gales were blowing and the fish were difficult to observe. It would have been better if they had done it in an aquarium.'

Each of these scientists supported the main findings of the study and referred to the 'diving' experiment when arguing that sonars do not harm fish. But, most of them also commented that the study did not answer the issue of possible biochemical or reproductive changes in humans, and by implication, in fish. At the end of the 1980s a memur with the Water

Produce Section at the Samsun Province Agricultural Directorate proposed a study to ascertain the influence of sonars on fish reproduction. His superiors within the Ministry turned down the proposal. This, together with the one scientist's claim about the unscientific nature of the experiment, indicates an undercurrent of reflection and argument among scientists that make the sonar a less 'solid' and well-defined thing.

## The Fishers' Sonar(s)

Unlike scientists, fishers relate to sonars during daily practice. To understand what the sonar is to the fishers I will therefore first explore this practice and ask: how has the introduction of the sonar altered fishing operations? In order to identify what has changed I compare contemporary practice with an account of purse-seine fishing in the region during the early 1960s. It will be demonstrated that while there certainly have been some fundamental changes in fishing operations, the personal skills of skipper and crew remain crucial for success.

In 1961 the Turkish journalist Fikret Otyam published an essay that includes a fairly detailed account of the actual fishing operations in the Black Sea off Giresun/Espiye during this era (Otyam 1982: 284 – 286).

> We were five persons in the bow, our eyes on the sea. The skipper gave my shoulder a nudge [skipper's conversation in dialect]:
>
> - Do you see the fish?
>
> I thought he was kidding. No, I didn't think so; the fellow was certainly kidding. I grinned stupidly. He nudged my shoulder again.
>
> - Let me say to the right, you see the fish, don't you?
>
> - What fish, skipper?
>
> - Just fish, hamsi, you see?
>
> I started to look more attentively.
>
> - Well there, huge fish.
>
> He wasn't kidding. The waves cast up on the two sides of the bow were a bright, sharp green from time to time. The lights were like pebbles, the water was phosphorescent. It was a greenness difficult to explain, a luminousness.
>
> …
>
> - Heey, work the engine!
>
> The engine ran at full speed, the bow was turned towards the open [sea]. All eyes hung with full attention on the sea. From the depths of the sea there was a stream of phosphorescence.
>
> …

The skipper suddenly sprang up from the bow where he was lying and shouted:

- Heey, stay ready.

We were ready. There was someone else at the helm of the boat. The skipper lay down again in the bow. The eyes of the man at the helm remained fixed on the signs given by the skipper's right arm. There was a commotion aboard the boat. We had found the hamsi 'bed'.

By the late 1990s the process of searching for fish had become very different on the technologically advanced purse seiners. In 1998 Ergün Kardeşler (real name), one of the teams from Çarşıbaşı, invested in a new purse seiner. With a length of 46 m the boat was regarded as one of the largest in Turkey (See Figure 6.1). It had plenty of space for both fishing operations and the crew. With its modern amenities life on this boat was certainly much more comfortable than aboard the crowded boats of the times of Otyam's essay. The crew's quarters were forward, while four cabins and a bathroom on the second floor were reserved for the owners, hired skipper, and one or two senior crew. The bridge, or 'upper cabin', was spacious, heated by radiators, and floored with wall-to-wall carpet. In the after portion of the cabin several of the skippers and often a visitor or two would sit on deep sofas and relax, sometimes chatting about the fishery. There were three men to take turns at steering the boat and searching for fish: the skipper-owner, his eldest son, and the hired skipper working for shares. This is a typical composition for the leader team. During the search one of the skippers would sit leisurely in a comfortable chair at the helm, shoes off (as had all others in the upper cabin), feet on the desk, sonar remote control in hand, surrounded on three sides by various types of electronic equipment. No lying out on the bow deck during cold winter nights to spot the fish!

A full description of the multitude of activities that make up the search and catch of hamsi is beyond the scope of this discussion. I prefer to concentrate on the search process because it is seemingly at this stage of the operations that the qualitative change brought on by the adoption of electronic fish finders has been most dramatic. Net operation per se has been enlarged, but the main principles and operations are the same as thirty years ago. A change in scale may of course amount to a qualitative change; indeed the current operations involve working more machines and depending on a wider variety of specialized equipment. Yet, the skipper's leap from the bow deck to the reclining chair in the upper cabin is the most striking change. While the skipper/owners know well the practical operations of the seine, the crew members are less familiar with the practice of searching for fish – the search is the responsibility and privilege of the skipper. Usually only the skipper and owners and possibly a senior member of the crew follow developments on the sonar- and echo-sounding displays during normal operations. Thus, the crew generally have almost no experience with the sonar nor know how to operate one. Crew members generally do not hang around in the upper cabin but socialize or watch television in the 'living room' on the main deck.

During the week I 'signed on' to the *Ergün Kardeşler* they cast the seine net two or three times a day. When the crew had finished cleaning up, rewinding the wires, and so forth after a seine they had set near Çarşıbaşı one day, Mahmut (real name), the skipper-owner, slowly started a new search, westwards. After a mate told him via radio that someone had set seines to the east of Çarşıbaşı, he turned the boat around and headed eastwards. He first switched on the echo sounder, then the sonars, and after the sun had set, the radar to 'see other boats' in the vicinity. Now and then he glanced at the screens. Others present in the upper cabin talked about other things and did not look at the screens. Mahmut saw some fish on the echo sounder and started to search along a zigzag course, but soon continued a straight course without comment. I wondered why, with such powerful sonars, they needed to zigzag during a search. The skippers told me that the (kuyus) make it impossible for sonars to 'see' everything. They generally had the 'large-pelagic' sonar fixed on a range of 450 m (maximum range 600 m), tilt 8°, and the 'hamsi' sonar somewhere between 2200 and 3200 m (maximum range 4000 m), tilt 3–5°. While both sonars can detect hamsi, the 'large pelagic' sonar is preferable to the 'hamsi' sonar for observing the track of the boat during setting of the seine (Figure 8.1).

Both sonars, as well as the echo sounder, showed fish on otherwise black screens as fields of yellow, greens and reds, deep red indicating the highest concentration. The 'large pelagic' sonar usually showed a red field in the upper section. That red field, I soon learned, was bottom. The hamsi sonar showed a more confusing picture, with many small, moving fields of yellow and green. Only stable red fields attracted interest. When a red spot (other than the one always present on the top of the screen) appeared it was crucial to know whether it was a 'hill' (*tepe*) or fish. Sometimes one of the skippers would claim that he knew the bottom conditions at the location and could safely conclude 'hill'. If they were unsure, they might adjust the tilt up and down in order to see how the field appears. If the field gradually became wider when tilt was adjusted downwards it was most likely a hill. Otherwise it was fish.

Next, Mahmut, the skipper-owner, adjusted the tilt of the 'large pelagic' sonar up from 8° to 6°, probably because the echo sounder showed the fish near the surface. He already knew from the echo sounder that it was fish. When he spotted some fish 'upwards' (i.e., seawards), he made radio contact with a purse seiner seaward of us and asked why they had not set their seine. When he learned that they did not intend to set their seine, Mahmut headed seawards. Red fields became visible on the echo sounder.

**Figure 8.1. Knowing the sonar.** A skipper instructs a boat-owner's son in the use of sonars. Above right is the 'hamsi' sonar, to the left the 'large pelagic' sonar (switched off), and below the echo sounder. Note the charm (*nazarlık*) protecting against the evil eye on the bottom of the echo sounder (photograph manipulated to enhance the image). There are similar charms protecting the sonars as well (not visible on the photograph).

Other men approached and watched the screens attentively. They then used the 'large pelagic' sonar to move in on the shoal and the echo sounder to evaluate the shoal's size. Birol, the hired skipper, commanded Mahmut: 'go like that', looking out over the sea and pointing on the screen. Mahmut pressed a bell. One man jumped into the bot (a small boat used to hold one end of the seine net in place during a cast) and the rest of the crew made themselves ready. Mahmut gave full speed to the engines, the bot was let go, and the seine was dropped into the water. Only a few minutes later the boat had come full circle and come back to the bot. One hour later the purse was pulled almost completely together. The carrier vessel had arrived (called on by Mahmut). The small purse remaining, full of silvery glittery fish, was now between the net boat and the carrier. Haul upon haul of hamsi were lifted from the 'pan' of hamsi into the carrier with a large scoopnet, a ton at a time. This was always the climax, always the time the crew and skipper most expected me to shoot photos. That was the moment when the red fields on the sonar materialized as fish.

This was a fairly typical search and setting of seine. Variations and disruptions certainly occur. The slightest lack of attention, lapse of concentration, might lead to breakdown of the normal procedure. Once the skipper-owner set the seine too wide and the hamsi escaped through the gap in the net, another time one of the crew had not fastened the bot properly. Such mistakes result in substantial financial losses. This points to the continued importance of skills at all levels, both of skippers and crew. For skippers to recruit competent crew, and for crew to ship with skippers renowned for their skills, are therefore of great concern to owner and crew respectively. What, however, has happened to fish finding skills? What kind of change has there been from the direct watch for *yakamoz* (phosphorescent glitter) to the 'distant' watch via sonar screen?

## What is the Sonar to the Fishers?

I have argued that both the fishers' and scientists' knowledge is embodied, lived, localized, and embedded in biophysical and social contexts. This is not to say that I strictly separate bodily 'precultural' practice from linguistically organized culture. I have accepted Ingold's claim that all knowledge may be regarded in some respects as skill, but I do not view skill as being separate from cultural models. Models are implicated in skills, and skills play their role in representation and objectification. In earlier chapters I have sought to show that both the fishers' and scientists' knowledge are based on or have their starting points in personal experience, but both are also involved, albeit in different manners, in objectification. I have described how (or the degree to which) the sonar is engaged in practice. Below I analyse this engagement as I question whether it has stimulated new ways of perception. One might assume that the adoption of sonar in the Turkish fisheries has resulted in fishing practices becoming more like practices in other technologically advanced pelagic fisheries. Any similarities are assumed to be not only technological, but also lie, possibly, in the perception of the hunt: with sonar all fishers look at comparable images on fairly similar screens. What does this 'technologization' of fishing, or any other kind of activity, actually do to practice, perception and knowledge? For instance, can one say that the transformation in search technique/technology has implied a transition from 'being' to 'seeing', from situated practice to distant, neutral observation, from 'technique' to 'technological knowledge'? I will expand on this by discussing the ways in which the sonar's symbolic significance and articulation in narratives (oral, texts) indicate how it has come to be different things to scientists and fishers.

How do the fishers know the sonar? They know by using it, by engaging with fish and seaspace through it. I claim that fishers experience themselves as being within the screen picture, they are positioned, situated, not outside watching. They integrate perceptions of the changing fields of colours on the screen with their observations and knowledge of the immediate surroundings, the weather, and sea currents. The skipper must know much more than simply the technical use of the sonar in order to mobilize its power of 'seeing'. To interpret the display fishers often need to know the local bottom conditions. Even though the best sonars can scan a circular area with a diameter of 8 km, knowledge of local conditions is still important. This is attested to by, among other things, the preference of skippers for operating in home waters.

The sonars currently in use offer a wide range of options including measuring the weight of a school of fish. The sonars can also be connected to an autopilot. However, fishers use almost none of the possibilities for numerical (digital) information that the sonars provide and rely on their own interpretations of the changing fields of colour on the display (analogue codes). In this respect use of sonar does not imply a radically new way of seeing for the fishers. The type of perception has not changed much. Pálsson (1998b) has made similar observations with regard to the use of electronic technology and artificial intelligence in Icelandic fishing. In the Turkish purse-seine fisheries, there is still an attention to colours, to the intensity of colours, even to the same colours that used to be most important during direct observation; red and green. Moreover, it was and still is important to be able to add three-dimensional visualization to the observed fields of colour. How does a fisher know how to interpret these changing fields of colour? There are no 'transportable' inscriptions of them, no carrying over from situation to situation of experience by external means such as printouts or the like. Moreover, the sonar display units are equipped with a confusing set of buttons, often with no clearly identifiable icons to indicate their use.

The fishers have neither formal schooling nor training courses in the operation of sonars (or in any other aspect of fisheries, for that matter). Neither do they refer to manuals to learn how to operate the sonar or to find guidance for interpreting the fields on the screen. The sonar manuals are in English only and so packed with technical jargon as to be unintelligible to a layperson anyway. Although I had read some general technical literature on sonars, I could not make sense of most of the manuals; nor could the local English teachers who had been asked to assist the fishers. Even when a fisher does have an instruction book in Turkish, for his radar for example, he does not use it. Thus, fishers have learned how to operate their sonars and radars through trial and error and by demonstration. They do not relate to inscribed knowledge about their technological equipment, nor create it themselves.

Sonar operating skills are precious knowledge – big money and prestige are at stake. Some have so much trouble adjusting their new 'large pelagic' sonars as to render them essentially useless. Owners that themselves do not master the art of sonar use may, therefore, work hard to sign on a competent skipper who can both ensure effective searches and teach sonar operation and interpretation to the hopeful younger ones among the owners, especially sons growing into the business. Fishers observe the actions and verbalized interpretations of others. More than one may adjust the sonars and comment on the picture when something interesting appears on the screen. As of old, the skill is learned and sustained through common shared practice. I claim that even though fishers now employ very advanced technology, for the most part they do not relate towards it with technological knowledge, or a 'technological approach'. Skill is learned, transferred to new situations, and accumulated through embodied and engaged practice. Use of sonars hardly involves much new knowledge or modification of perception. Thus, on the level of experience, new technology does not necessarily imply any dramatic departure from past practices.

This should not be surprising. Use of advanced technology certainly does not require technological knowledge, a distanced or reflective view. We use bicycles and cars to move faster, but use them effectively only after we stop thinking consciously about what we are doing, and immerse ourselves in it so that our knowledge becomes procedural, implicit and embodied (Bateson 1972; Borofsky 1994; Bloch 1994; Shore 1996). Think also of developments in computer software: more advanced technology is steadily mobilized in order to facilitate more direct, immediate and non-reflective use of the programs. Some of the newer technologies may even facilitate 'oral' communication and come therefore ever closer to everyday forms of communication.

The increasing dependence on sonars (as well as other electronic equipment and engines) means that the fishers increasingly depend on scientific-technological knowledge created in other places in the world. In some respects these new 'things' are 'black boxes' to the fishers; they have only very diffuse ideas about how they work. However, they do not simply adopt rigid, external models. They actively engage in and contribute to shaping these knowledge-technology clusters. For instance, the 'large pelagic' sonar in use in Turkish waters was developed upon request from Istanbul fishers to the importers of Japanese sonars. Japanese experts arrived and puzzled for several days on board a purse seiner at sea. Sonars for large pelagic fish existed, but special adaptations were needed for the Marmara and Black Sea waters. In this situation, the Japanese experts, possessing both practical skills and technological knowledge, needed to function as mediator or 'translator' of a sort between the skippers' practical skills and the 'technological' knowledge developed by their company in Japan.

There must certainly be differences in locating fish by sonar than by other means. But the differences may be at levels other than where we first expect to find them. First, there may be less likelihood of overlooking fish, and thereby less room for both chance and personal skills. Once the first hurdle of learning sonar operation has been cleared, there is probably little difference in search skill between skippers, or at least less than before. Furthermore, the use of sonars has meant a change from waiting or searching for the fish near deep waters close to shore during the night, to an active search for fish, sometimes up to 25–30 nautical miles offshore. However, the greatest change that the sonar constitutes and symbolizes lies, I believe, in one question: who has the possibility to search for fish? The main difference the sonar has facilitated is *not a change in perception, but in social differentiation.*

In the beginning of the 1960s, purse-seine fishing was characterized by the traits I described as Type 1 in Chapter 6. These were the main skills the skipper needed; his locally based social position than enabled him to raise funds and recruit crew, and his skill as skipper. Since then, and especially after 1980, the competitive game in the fishing sector has been radically transformed. Whereas it used to be a game open to many, with luck/chance and skill/hard work as the defining characteristics, it has evolved into a game of the few, with money/technology/power as the defining resources. To be successful, the boat owner must increasingly be a successful 'politician'. In this situation, where it is no longer possible to advance from small-boat fisher to owner of big purse seiners, the sonar has become somewhat metonymic for the success of the rich and the powerlessness of the poor. Thus, the main difference the sonar has created is not a difference in perception, but a difference among people. While the skipper used to be on deck, among the men, exposed to the 'elements', he now sits in the comfortable upper cabin, which increasingly resembles the reception room of local 'big men'.

Boat owners still socialize with their crew, and the younger of Mahmut's sons generally mingle with the crew, who incidentally for the most part are co-villagers, relatives and schoolmates. But, the activities of the boat owner increasingly draw him away from the crew and into other social webs and practices. The sonar is among the main symbols of this gap. For the fishers the sonar is very much embedded in a social universe. Boat owners are often eager to show visitors their sonar and brag about its range and price. Most other fishers, including crew on purse seiners equipped with sonars, are more than ready to criticize the use of sonars. It is often perceived as creating unfair competitive advantage and clearly creates envy. Most crew accordingly view the introduction of the sonar as diluting the importance of the skipper's skills; they commonly claim that there is 'no skipperhood any longer'. Another common claim since the advent of the sonar is that 'There is no chance any longer!' These claims play into a general discourse where monetary and material riches are regarded as morally suspect. Sonar has become suspended in an indefinite position between fetish object of prestige and metonym for morally dubious riches.

The incorporation of new technology into traditional and well-proven ways of fishing has been gradual, not some sudden import of a total package. The skills needed to operate sonars have become integrated with other skills in the fisheries. Certainly, fishers need outside experts to install, calibrate and repair the sonars, a limitation that, to a large degree, applies to a lot of their other equipment as well. The local skipper nonetheless remains the expert on sonar operation. The fishers, or rather a certain class among the fishers, have remained in control and new technology has been appropriated into their ongoing projects. Thus the meaning and use of the sonar is shaped as much in local contexts as by the 'inherent' qualities of the sonar itself.

## Narrating the Sonar

Further insight into the fishers' understanding of the sonar can be gathered from the way they articulate their views. All sorts of fishers, in my main fieldwork site Çarşıbaşı and in many fishers' villages or harbours along the Black Sea coast and in Istanbul, have over the years addressed this issue during informal conversations and in semiformal interviews. Their narratives about the sonar are invariably oral. A tale from one man or a discussion around the cafe table will often include many different arguments made in an eclectic manner. Very similar stories about personal experiences are told along the coast, such as: 'The fish I was catching by hand line disappeared when a purse seiner passed'; 'Dolphins who frequently follow the boats flee as soon as the sonar is turned on'; 'The fish is not as lively as before when hauled into the boat'; and so forth. Except for some of the skippers, nobody talks about the sonar pulses as sound. The sonar pulses are generally explained as or compared to 'light' (*ışık*), 'rays' (*ışın*), electricity, and, more seldom, X-rays, laser and radioactivity. One fisher told me: 'The rays hit the fish and return. There must be resistance in the fish since the rays do not simply pass through it. Something happens.'

'Social' metaphors are also invoked to explain the effect of the sonar. 'If the police continuously crack down on the kahve where you usually hang around, what will you do? Yes, you will go to another cafe, or you will escape to Russia.' 'If you enter a kahve waving a shotgun, what will people do? They will flee'. Fishers furthermore often prop up their arguments with the popular idea that sonars have been banned in Japan (which they have in a limited fashion), and some also use semi-scientific models, for instance claiming that the sonars send charges of 220 volts into the water. In general, fishers' stories about the sonar are very popular and have standardized elements. But, unlike narratives about the state, corruption, politicians and so forth, many different concepts are used and the situational details vary widely. This may indicate the importance of personal experience as a foundation for the fishers' stories.

Many fishers have heard about the scientists' experiment and comment that it was not set up properly. They are especially critical of the fact that the divers wore diving suits. Fishers claim that the sonar pulses cannot pass through rubber. This is in line with a general idea that shellfish are protected from the sonar by their shell. In other words, the fishers think that the response of the human body to sonar pulses is a good indicator of how fish bodies are influenced. Some fishers told me about a similar experiment set up by fishers in which the divers had no diving suits. The men were allegedly stricken by electricity and severely harmed (some said one died). I have also heard a story about a wealthy small-boat fisher who offered an owner of a purse seiner a large amount of money if he dived beside his boat when the sonar was turned on. The skipper did not accept the offer.

These cases, as the narratives and metaphors used to explain the effects of the sonar, conform to a general concern with fish and human bodies sharing many qualities of 'life'. Fishers along the Turkish Black Sea coast commonly use human body analogies in order to explain the behaviour of fish. Small pelagic fish, for instance, are believed to gather in dense shoals in cold water in order to stay warm, 'just as we gather around the stove in the teahouse during cold winter days.' Once, when the fifteen year old son of a boat owner proudly showed me the room in the boat's hull where sonar transducers were installed, he commented that 'Actually it is harmful. Fish are live creatures like us. They are influenced.' I think that all fishers, even the boat owners, harbour some uneasiness about this object: they do not know for sure how to understand it. Those who contend that sonars scare or harm fish will often round off their arguments with the comment 'and anyway, even if it is not harmful, it leads to excessive fishing.' Boat owners often ask my opinion, what the situation is in Norway, and so on. During a long, spontaneous conversation with a skipper (not boat owner) he asked me what scientists in Norway think about the sonar. I told him that they think that the fish cannot hear the sonar. He replied that he was bewildered. 'Whatever is emitted from the sonar, it has an effect on the fish.' The insecure, ambivalent and precarious yet important role of the sonar is underlined by the fact that there seem to be charms protecting against the evil eye attached to almost all sonar displays.

The crew and small-boat fishers' critique of the sonar may also be interpreted as a language of resistance towards mounting inequalities within the fisheries. The 'traditional' objects of critique and envy, the fish traders, have always been easy to criticize on a general basis as being a group of usurers and rentiers. Since the owners of the large purse seiners, crew and small-boat fishers all live and work together in villages, small towns and urban neighbourhoods along the coast, critique is deflected from a direct attack on the boat owners to the most potent symbol of their success: the sonar. The engine could also have been an object of opposition and envy. Indeed, many fishers acknowledge that the big engines scare fish. But it has not become an object of conflict. Why? Perhaps because use of more powerful engines, contrary to the sonar, has not led to a transformation of the fisheries. Although once a critical factor of change in the fisheries in the 1950s and 1960s, the engine has not changed the game of luck and chance. The current need to install more powerful engines is in part simply a secondary effect of the use of sonars.

The sonar, on the contrary, has a special role in seeing, in finding the fish, previously the role of the experienced and talented skipper. Just as the evil eye, its working is more mystical and obscure. What is it? What are the powers it embodies? It strikes its object and hurts it, as the evil eye does. I have not observed any direct, explicit oral coupling or analogy between the evil eye and the sonar, but the model of the evil eye may reinforce or support the understanding of the sonar as having the force to deform and kill. Crew and small-boat fishers feel so utterly powerless in the face of new techno-magical instruments. But there is no organization to voice their opinions and interests. So the critique is informal, on the level of widely shared but personal opinion. Moreover there is no 'action', no sabotage of sonars. I have not even heard such a thought voiced.

It seems as though the critique of the sonar in some social contexts gives the crew and small-boat fishers an upper hand and empowers them to turn the hegemony upside down, if only temporarily. Once, while sitting around a table in the kahve during the off-season, a group of primarily small-boat fishers were discussing the sonar. As usual they held it to be harmful. The only boat owner at the table, himself in possession of a sonar, remained mostly silent. Although usually very talkative, bad catches and economic problems had made him rather sulky. He was confronted by one of the small-boat fishers: 'The sonar is harmful, isn't that so?' He didn't answer, but responded with a quiet nod.

## Global Technology Confronts Local Morality

On the purse seiners, work has not been 'rationalized'. There is not a radical change in subjectivities. Capitalist relations are still embodied as friendship and the like. But there are tendencies. Can Kardeşler (see Chapter 6) formally present themselves as a 'company' (*Şirket*), and Yakup, the eldest of the four brothers, is not 'skipper' but 'director' and spends most of his time in their main office. They are not only fishers. What is most important in this case is not that there are tendencies of changing relations of production, but that the character of the capitalist economy of the fisheries has changed. It was once a sector of possibilities, where chance and fate, skill and hard work, were the differentiating factors. To some degree chance and fate were seen as the results of 'good morals'. Now success has been engulfed by monetary power and politics, which are morally dubious. While a moral personal character and having a 'clean heart' may have been regarded as important to success in bygone days, now the opposite is seen as necessary: success is not possible without involvement in politics and corruption. This resonates with a general nostalgia and complaints about the loss of 'sharing'.

The critique of the sonar articulates a connection among fish, people, technology, and moralities. Together this constitutes a universe of continuities and connections among the natural world, humans' bodies and morals. The working of the evil eye is based on the same kind of connections among morals, human reproduction and envy. Thus, it is notable that fishers try to protect sonars against the evil eye with charms (*nazarlık*). In addition, the frequent use of human-body analogies to explain fish behaviour operates on the same tacit assumption of connections. Thus, I believe it would be wrong to regard the analogy with human bodies as 'merely' a metaphor. For the fishers the human body and the fish body *are* similar, are of the same quality. Certainly, if fishers were to articulate a cosmology they would employ concepts that are at least as Cartesian as those employed in the West, stringently separating humans (*insan*) from nature (*doğa*) and animals (*hayvan*), primarily on the basis of humans' capacity for reason (*akil*), which they separate from feelings (*duygu*) and body (*beden*). However, in their everyday discourse, fishers are more prone than scientists to think that they have a bodily continuity with fish and the sea. For them it is not only possible to extrapolate the sonars' effect on human bodies to fish, it is seen as perhaps the ultimate test of the sonar.

Scientists, on the other hand, give priority to visual observations of fish behaviour and in the report discussed above write in passive, subject free language: 'it was seen that (*görülmüştür*)' – thereby emphasizing the 'seeing as'. Neither in the report nor in the comments on the experiments does the idea appear that the sonars' effect on human bodies should have any relevance for its effect on fish. They are familiar with the sonar's potential for numerical information and think that, since it emits sound, sonar waves are simply reflected by the fish body as an echo. Although there is nonetheless an undertone of uncertainty among scientists, they try to reframe this uncertainty as 'another' question, as a 'biomedical' issue. This uncertainty includes the realization that they lack practice, and that what cannot be seen cannot be trusted. Science thus upholds a distinction between object and subject and between nature and culture.

The sonar is clearly a very different thing to the fishers and to the scientists. In text, the official discourse of the scientists, the sonar is a black-boxed technological object (Latour 1987) that emits sound. In contrast to many other issues or objects, it is rather peripheral to the world of these scientists and they relate to it primarily through scientific texts. The sonar is not as critical to the lives of scientist as to the lives of fishers. For the fishers the sonar is implicated in a moral discourse. It is a social thing that looms large in the fisher's world. Contrary to the scientists, they struggle to conceive what it is that the sonar emits. The sonar is not black boxed, it is an unknown hard to grasp, and for many, hard to accept.

## Local Science in the Politics of the Sonar

The fishers and scientists both know well that at the end of the day the actual use and non-use of sonars is not decided by knowledge alone. That is rather an outcome of the brutal politics of money, votes and social webbing. But officially sanctioned knowledge can be one vector in the political game. Fishers and scientists realize this. It was fishers who owned and supported the use of sonars that in 1988 persuaded marine scientists at the Sürmene Faculty to undertake the sonar study. Thus, contrary to most research projects that are initiated by bureaucratic decree or by scientists themselves, the scientific study of the sonar was encouraged by some better-positioned fishers, who tried to achieve 'closure'of the controversy by referring to the ideal of 'sound scientific knowledge'. One party in the internal controversy among fishers mobilized science to strengthen their position, not necessarily against other fishers, but in face of the authorities. This may have settled the debate in the eyes of the scientists, bureaucrats and politicians, but among the fishers the controversy has continued unabated.

In science there is more pull towards 'certainty', the absolute truth. I am therefore sceptical of making the question of 'truth' or 'right knowledge' a central issue when comparing science with other traditions of knowledge. That more than 'facts' or the 'truth' are at stake in contemporary disputes over technoscientific projects is readily apparent in the case of consumer scepticism with regard to genetically modified food, and in the general critique of the Human Genome Project. This is most likely so because these projects directly challenge understandings of what the human body, and in a wider sense, what the human is. It may be more difficult to see that the sonar challenges fundamental ethical sensibilities such as ideals of equality, locality, sharing and intimacy, and gendered use of socio space.

For the fishers, the controversy over the sonar is not a knowledge conflict, but a conflict over practice and morality. The controversy about the sonar cuts across the fishing communities, yes, even through boats. It remains an unresolved issue. For the fishers the sonar is not primarily an object to be known. It is an extension of the technique of seeing, and its use or non-use is not settled by knowledge, but by money and power. 'Usefulness' or 'result', and not 'truth', may be what are most important to the fisher.

Some fishers acknowledge that fishers and scientists have different priorities and are involved in dissimilar projects and that different criteria apply to scientific practices. Accordingly many fishers criticize the scientists not for being scientists per se, but for being bad scientists. Birol, hired skipper aboard the *Ergün Kardeşler*, was in charge aboard the fishing boat used when the scientists undertook their study of the sonar. He is sympathetic to the scientists' view on the sonar, but says that he would not accept the findings of the scientists until their study had received international recognition. As many others, he criticizes the way the experiment was set up. Talking about the experiment which involved the divers he said that 'It only lasted for half an hour, and that was it.' He thought there was not enough time given to the experiments. Thus, fishers claim a voice about how science should be practiced. However, they are not heard. Fishers' jargon, with its emphasis on personal experience and the body, with the lack of fixation of their knowledge into texts, together with the social barrier created by mutual constructions of ignorance, to be further discussed in the next two chapters, ensure that their voice is mute in the politics of officially accepted, 'high' knowledge.

Actually, both sides claim to be the more knowledgeable. Scientists think that the fishers are cahil ('ignorant') since they do not understand what KHz is, are unable to use the full potential of the sonars, and still tend to trust the gulls more than the sonars. Fishers say that they have learned the use of sonars themselves and know more about (the use of) sonars than the scientists do. Yet, since the sonar is a product of technoscience, scientists are therefore easily seen as the legitimate experts, and they do not think they can learn anything from the fishers. It would be different with, for example, fish behaviour or bottom topography which from the outset have not been scientific 'constructs' (but may of course be appropriated). In contrast, scientific knowledge is included and claimed in fishers' eclectic narratives. As was evident in Hakan's narrative about hamsi migrations (Chapter 4), reference to 'scientific facts' is precisely one of fishers' narrative strategies and reference points for authority. But such reference to or mobilization of science is prone to gross oversimplification or distortion (for instance, one fisher claimed that the sonar sends a charge of 220 V into the water). In this game the fishers lose, as they can easily be proven wrong in relation to the accepted standards of scientific truth. In effect, their effort to sound knowledgeable leads them to reconfirm unwittingly their stereotype as ignorant.

Thanks to the bureaucrats' textual tradition, some of the dialogues between fishers and scientists have been preserved. During an exchange about various issues at a 1988 seminar on the hamsi fisheries, fishers expressed their views on the sonar. One elderly fisher, owner of purse seiner without sonar, claimed that a net with eighty tons of hamsi caught without sonar were pulled with only the hand power of the crew, while a net with twenty five tons of hamsi caught with the aid of sonar is impossible to raise only with manpower. The sonar, he said, 'had put the hamsi in a state of shock, killed it' (İktisadı Araştırmalar Vakfı 1988: 136). Another boat owner asked (ibid.: 137–138):

[I]s sonar advantageous, or is it harmful? It is harmful in three ways: One, I did not buy, therefore it is harmful. Two, it quickly finishes off the fish in the sea. Three, it scatters light on the sea bottom. But I cannot know whether this is right or not, whether it is studied and to what degree it is correct. But I observed that my friends receive exceptional results on this topic [i.e., by using the sonar]. We also entered the sonar business and bought one.

These two statements, particularly the last one, aptly summarize the positions and dilemmas of the fishers. They do not quite know or understand what it is or what it does, but the dynamics of their adaptation forces those who still want to join the race, and have the resources, to use the sonar. While fishers thus express uncertainty, scientists tend to advocate scientific certainty. At the same seminar Professor Çelikkale at the Sürmene Faculty commented (ibid.: 144):

[T]he sonar is not harmful to the fish. I don't conjecture this. I state this on the basis of the results of a study [the study discussed earlier in this article] that I did with five researchers and was supported by the University Research Fund. The fish ear hears a maximum sound (*ses*) of 12 thousand hertz. The frequency of our sonars starts at 38 thousand hertz. It is the military sonars that affect the fish, the large trade sonars, but those you cannot remove. The sonars used by our fishers do not have the effect of scaring or making substance-less. If you believe in science, this is the result.

Yet, despite the general scientific claim that science constitutes universal knowledge achieved through peer review and openness, with regard to the knowledge of the sonar, the scientists seem to have been less than open. The report (Çelikkale et al. 1988a) from the study on the sonar was not widely accessible. First of all, it is written in Turkish and unpublished. I only managed to get a copy thanks to my personal relationship with and the generosity of scientists at the Sürmene Faculty. This implies that the report has not been exposed to the scrutiny of the larger scientific community and indicates that the rationale for this work was not so much 'scientific' as local politics. This is substantiated by the fact that the study was initiated upon 'requests' from some owners of large fishing boats. The report was not distributed to the fishers (except perhaps a few boat owners) – even the skipper Birol did not receive a copy, even though he sides with the scientists and, with his high school education, is better able to understand such a text than most boat owners. This contrasts with fishers in countries such as Norway, Canada and Iceland where boat owners' associations have hired marine biologists on a permanent basis to undertake their own analyses of scientific data (Pálsson 1998a: 216).

In Turkey the issue of the sonar is hardly addressed in newspapers and other public forums. Unlike fishers in Norway and Iceland, for example, Turkish fishers do not have their own magazine/newspaper nor do they write letters to the daily newspapers. The only time I have seen the sonar mentioned in the newspaper is when a journalist decided to do a feature story about fishers. Fishers lend themselves easily to such feature stories since they are generally considered exotic figures. The results from the scientists' work on the sonar have entered popular discourses about Turkish fisheries, but only as oral narratives. The scientific articulation of the result – the report, the text – has been appropriated by the scientists. On the other hand, scientists often rely on the practical knowledge of the fishers when conducting experiments at sea, although the fishers are not credited in texts. In the second half of the 1980s, Sürmene Faculty studied the dolphin stocks in the Black Sea (Çelikkale et al. 1988b). Four boats travelled in parallel along the coast as dolphins were observed visually through binoculars and counted. In the report this is described as a neutral technique (variation/deviation is admitted, but is implicitly ascribed to coincidence). By chance I learned many years later that the scientists had hired elderly dolphin fishers to spot the dolphins. With their bare eyes the fishers could spot the dolphins at a much greater distance and count them more accurately than the scientists could using binoculars. In Chapter 7 I point out that for the success of their projects scientists often depend upon their own ethical and technical know-how. In this case, the lack of acknowledgement of expert fishers' knowledge is probably not due to the expert being fishers, but to the fact that it is a kind of knowledge that is not easily externalized and objectified.

The fishers' and scientists' different understandings of the sonar are not totally independent of one another and should not be seen as two totally distinct and internally consistent cultural models. Each position is grounded in both embodied practice and external models as well as by articulations between them. There are indications of convergence: all sides accept that the experiment is the relevant technique to test an idea. But, while fishers and scientists use and rely upon each other's practices and knowledges, these connections are partly obscured by mutually exclusive constructions of knowledge etc. It would be possible to reframe the whole dispute and move towards a convergence in knowledge/perspective. If all parts could allow for uncertainties in their knowledges, they might be able to approach common ground along the lines of: sonars are heard by dolphins and may possibly have some effect on fish, and engine noise may scare away fish. Why is there no such common understanding? One reason may be that for the fishers the sonar is overdetermined by its role as fetish/metonym for (dubious) riches. And for the scientists it is difficult to accept arguments beyond the confines of scientific discourse.

## Conclusions

A rendering of these knowledges as IK/TEK vs science is simplistic and insufficient to grasp their social and cognitive complexity. The fishers' and scientists' different understandings of the sonar are not totally independent of one another. But, while fishers and scientists use and rely upon each other's practices and knowledges, these connections are partly obscured by different metaphors for understanding the working of the sonar and by mutually exclusive constructions of the others' identity and knowledge.

I hold that facts and technology can only be understood through people's engagement with them and I have situated the study of the sonar in the life, experiences, politics and cultural models of the people studied. Instead of focusing solely on 'different rationalities' with competing truth-claims, we should direct more attention to the role technology or fact takes up in peoples' lives: as practice; as tool; as symbol; as a social thing. This is, therefore, not an ethnography of two ontologies, but of scientists' and fishers' engagements with their biophysical and social environment, with the sonar and with each other.

The use of the technologically advanced sonars in the Turkish fisheries has not led to a major change in how fishers perceive the hunt – it has been appropriated into the 'local' dynamic tradition of knowledge. It has not resulted in a shift from 'being in' or 'technique' to 'seeing as' or 'technology'. Rather, it has effected a radical change in the character of social differentiation in the fisheries. This most likely accounts for the widespread criticism of the sonars. The sonar is, for the fishers, a social thing that exists in a world where there are continuities between peoples' bodies, morals, fish, technology, politics, and so on.

What has the role of local science been with regard to the sonar? What can this tell us about how scientific circles are positioned within the global fields of science and technological production? First, as is the case with bio-economic models discussed in Chapter 7, it is evident that Turkish marine scientists have no role in the initial design and production of the sonar. Neither can they assist in the calibration of the sonar to the local ecological conditions. They are simply not competent to do that. Yet, their role in the local *re*production of the sonar is not insignificant. They are called upon to defend the use of sonars and reestablish certainty when conflicts over the possible harmfulness of the sonars threaten to disrupt the social relations of production in the fisheries. The agenda of science is in large part local, and not even of local science's own making. It was the politics of the powerful big-boat fishers that got science involved. These same fishers also interact directly with the representatives of the Japanese sonar-producing companies, when technical experts calibrate their sonars, or when boat owners visit Japan at the companies' expense. There is no direct relation between metropolitan and local scientists; but locally powerful fishers interact with both.

Marine scientists in Trabzon build their own very local networks to support their knowledges and must therefore not be understood as yet another permutation of international/universal science. They constitute a community of practitioners that addresses first and foremost local concerns. Thus, science may take on more roles than only metropolitan producers of facts and technology. Scientists may be local spokespersons, or warriors, of science. While they interact with international science in this work, the 'science' that is expounded may be deeply implicated in local ideological and political projects. In Turkey the enlightened, educated elite has been entrusted the heavy burden of implementing, representing and guiding the grand, national modernizing project. This has, for instance, been manifested in efforts to organize fishers into cooperatives.

# CHAPTER 9

# Water Produce Cooperatives and the Cultivation of Ignorance

While the idealistic fishery policy in Turkey tended to emphasize the importance of western technology to increase production, state elites also envisioned fishery organization to be modelled on a western template. Hence, the state took a range of initiatives to organize fishers into cooperatives. This chapter surveys these initiatives and shows that the idealism inherent in the state development effort meant that the focus was on what was to be achieved, while traditional and contemporary social structures in the fishing communities were ignored. In explaining the failure of the water produce cooperatives, state representatives have ignored structural explanations and instead put the blame on fishers' ignorance.

## A Persistent Ideal

According to early draft plans for a new fishery law and fishery development, fishing activities were to be organized as fishers' sales cooperatives, fishers' credits cooperatives and fishers' production cooperatives under the umbrella of a central Fishery Bank (*Tan Gazetesi* 1936). Although there were attempts to establish fishery cooperatives in 1942 – as part of an effort to increase food production during the wartime years (Acara et al. 1989: 77) – and in 1949 (TKK 1997: 33), establishment of cooperatives was intensified during the early 1950s when the Marshall Plan promised fishers monetary and technical aid if they organized into cooperatives (Çakıroğlu 1969). During most of the 1950s responsibility for fisheries development, including the cooperatives, was in the hands of the EBK where the primary emphasis was on technical developments. Thus, the young cooperatives received little attention and most of them disbanded or fell into the hands of the kabzımals (Çakıroğlu 1969: 99–100).

When a new initiative to develop fishery cooperatives was taken in 1968, a delegation from the Ministry of Trade toured the eastern Black Sea coast and enlivened eleven 'sleeping' cooperatives and stimulated the establishment of fifteen new ones. Most of these cooperatives were 'persuaded' to go together into an 'Association of Black Sea Fishery Cooperatives' (Karadeniz Balıkçı Kooperatifleri Birliği) (Çakıroğlu 1969: 85–93). From this time on cooperatives have played a central role in the structured interaction between the fishers and the Turkish state, and the official number of water produce cooperatives has shown a fairly steady increase (Table 9.1).

**Table 9.1. Number of water produce cooperatives**, eastern Black Sea region 1969 – 2006.

| Year | Cooperatives | Source |
| --- | --- | --- |
| 1969 | 24 | Çakıroğlu 1969: 97 |
| 1973 | 20 | GDWP 1975: 65 |
| 1980 | 32 | DMP 1982: 31 |
| 1987 | 43 | Acara et al. 1989: 80–82 |
| 1998 | 38 | Personal communication, staff at Ministry for |
| 2006 | 53 | Agriculture and Village Affairs |

This growth in the number of fishers' organizations and the increase in credit (see, e.g., Acara et al. 1989: 67; Knudsen 1997: 8–9) channelled through them may suggest that the fisheries are well organized and that all fishers have access to established organizational channels to market their fish, further their interests and present their views. However, like the change in dress codes, or the establishment of women's rights, and unlike the emergence of the cooperative movement in for example the Nordic countries, the formation of Turkish water produce cooperatives was the result of deliberate top-down organizing efforts by the state elite. Said Bilal Çakıroğlu, a local of Trabzon who worked within both the regional and the central trade bureaucracy and who himself took part in the 'mission' along the Eastern Black Sea coast in 1968, writes in great detail about the work of the Ministry of Trade delegation (1969: 85–93). The delegation got fishers to organize general assemblies where the delegation members took an active part (ibid: 86–87):

> [O]ur delegation participated in the General Assembly and helped make the necessary decisions for bringing the dealings of the cooperative into order. During this section real cooperative *espiri* was related. A description was given of the advantages expected to be brought about by the association and the partners present were persuaded (*ikna edilmek*) to decide to let their cooperative be a member of the association.

Bureaucrats and scientists in Turkey have observed that in the more developed fishery nations of the West and in Japan, cooperatives played an important role in organizing various activities within the fisheries. Therefore, along with the adoption of technical aspects of the more developed fisheries, stimulation of fishery cooperatives was seen as a precondition for success in development of this sector. The ideal of cooperative organization in the fisheries has been put forward in numerous writings and symposiums in Turkey during the last thirty-five years, and the lack of organization within the fisheries has been regarded as a major cause for the perceived lack of success in the fisheries. The central role of the cooperatives, especially as channels for credit, is established in the Fishery Law, No. 1380/3288, Paragraph 15. The pivotal role to be played by cooperatives has been further emphasized in various annual programs (Devlet İcra Planları) and long-term (five years) development plans (see, e.g., Çakıroğlu 1969: 109–110). My survey of these texts reveals that among managers, politicians and scientists there has been some variation in the perceived aims and advantages of water produce cooperatives. Aims ranges from solidarity and escape from capitalists, securing social security and education of members, advantages with (rational) large units in production and marketing, to serving as suitable vehicles for credit extension and interaction with state bureaucracy. In 1969 a Trabzon MP wrote that (Orhon 1969: 116):

> To rescue our fisheries from the lack of guardians and organization, an offensive for fundamental change is necessary. Our position is as follows: The cooperativization as foreseen in our Constitution should proceed quickly. Fishers should be saved from the hands of exploiters and capitalists (*sermayedar*). ... The fisher should get used to managing, organizing and making forward leaps himself. This is the solution.

During one phase cooperatives were also seen as important to bringing the organizational structure in the Turkish fisheries in line with the cooperative structure which prevails in the EU in order to ease future Turkish entry into the Union (Acara et al. 1989; Çıkın and Elbek 1991). However, cooperative efforts in production and marketing have invariably been regarded as the water produce cooperatives' main work and function.

The formation of water produce cooperatives can be said to be a clear expression of the strong modernizing or westernizing spirit and ambition within the Turkish development elite and bureaucracy. It is notable that the texts that champion cooperative organization are suffused with tropes of rationality, modernization, and large-scale industrial operation. The sixth five year development plan states that (Acara et al. 1989: 71–72):

> As is well known, in the fisheries ['water produce hunting'] it is necessary to work together. ... In order to secure the continuity of this cooperation and partnership, the producers' [i.e., the fishers] financial opportunities should

be brought together within cooperative units and with the united power this should enable communal large-scale hunting [i.e., fishing] and attain abundant produce by the use of modern gear and equipment as in large-scale systems and methods. To fulfil this aim the Agricultural Bank undertakes the required work and in line with this gives credit support.

From these and other texts, one gets the impression that the cooperatives ideally should organize all and every activity in the 'water produce sector'. An adult education textbook on cooperative activities includes a short section on water produce cooperatives. Three photos of fishing activities are accompanied by the text: 'The activities of water produce cooperatives' (Aydın et al. 1995: 28–29). No fisher would perceive these as activities of cooperatives.

## The Water Produce Cooperative in Çarşıbaşı

The water produce cooperative in Çarşıbaşı was first established in the late 1960s (Çakıroğlu 1969: 90). By 1990 it had 146 registered members, of which forty-seven had loans through the cooperative, but before this the number was much higher since membership facilitated migrant work in Germany. In the beginning of the 1970s the cooperative constructed a building that housed offices, a production hall and cold storage facilities, and in 1986 it invested in a fishmeal processing plant (Zengin 2000).

During most of my fieldwork in 1990 and 1991 I lived in one of the empty rooms in the cooperative building at the harbour and had the opportunity to monitor the activities of the cooperative. The facilities were then, and in total for a decade, used by a private company, based in Izmir, but headed by a local entrepreneur, for buying, processing and selling sea snails. In the late 1990s the cooperative sold the building. Due to internal bickering and the fact that many of the members chose to deliver their catches to other plants, the cooperative fishmeal processing plant was not profitable and was in the early 2000s sold to a local (non-fisher) entrepreneur. Before the cooperative representatives go to Ankara there are seldom local cooperative meetings, but rather informal consultations with some of the most powerful men. When Yakup, the leader of Can Kardeşler, led the mobilization to change the hamsi size regulation (see Chapter 6), he formally went to Ankara as head of the Çarşıbaşı cooperative, but privately he said: 'The cooperative is not important, I go as a firm. '

Formation of user-groups that regulate access in certain kinds of small-boat fishing in Çarşıbaşı (Chapter 5) is not connected to any formal organizations at all. The small-boat fishers' position in the local communities makes this difficult. Very few small-boat fishers in Çarşıbaşı were members of the water produce cooperative and none were involved in the running of it. Nor did small-boat fishers establish their own cooperative. The following case illustrates the powerlessness of the cooperative to influence the activities of the small-boat fishers.

Large trawlers owned by men in Çarşıbaşı usually fish around Samsun. During the 1990s it became increasingly common for small fishing boats (designed for the purpose of fishing sea snails) to be involved in illegal (small-boat) trawling in the province of Trabzon. All trawling is forbidden in this region, and all fishers, including those who practice trawling, concede that it is a harmful and undesirable activity. This illegal trawling was a sensitive issue, both in Keremköy and among fishers in other communities along the coast of the province of Trabzon.

One day in 1998 the local headman (*muhtar*) of Keremköy sat down near the Çarşıbaşı cooperative headman (owner of a large trawler) in the warm spring sun outside of the village kahve and exclaimed loudly that, 'You are the headman of the cooperative. Organize a meeting and stop the trawling!' The muhtar, himself owner of a large trawler, stressed that various bottom nets were in the sea and were often damaged by the trawls. One or more of the small-boat fishers who was not involved in the trawling had probably complained to him. However, none of the small-boat fishers present spoke up during the ensuing discussion. The cooperative headman didn't say very much. He agreed that it was a problem and said that they would soon organize a meeting. However, there was never a meeting called to discuss the problem. Some of the committee members were allegedly very busy and no action was taken.

The cooperative in this case proved to be an ineffective instrument in fisheries management. During the days following the above conversation, I asked many small-boat fishers whether they knew about the initiative. Nobody did. While only twenty-one out of 130 small-boat owners in this cooperative's region were members at that time, most small-boat fishers in *this* particular village were members. However few identified with it. Some said that the cooperative was 'empty' (*boş*) or that 'It has absolutely no function'. It was claimed that 'There has never been a proper meeting'. There had been no genuine election and they had never been to any meetings. The activities of the cooperative were said to take place only 'among themselves', in other words, among the rich big-boat and factory owners who were in charge of the cooperative's dealings. Leadership rotates among the most powerful men in the fishery sector.

Many bureaucrats in Ankara believe that this particular cooperative is one of the most successful. They base their assertion primarily on the capital (holding) and economic activity of the cooperative. Yet, I think it is clear that the Çarşıbaşı cooperative fails to fulfil the aims of cooperatives as formulated by bureaucrats: there is little internal solidarity, no distribution of profits, no engagement in marketing and processing, no role in fishery management, and no contribution to education of its members. Assets have been sold out, there is no involvement of small-boat fishers, and no regular meetings.

## Informal Social Organization

Small-boat fishers' relations to others, within the general workings of heterogeneous local communities, makes it difficult for them to develop more comprehensive, extensive and formal organizational structures. Small-boat fishers involved in illegal sea-snail dredging cooperate in an alarm system warning of approaching supervision vessels. However, this system is organized by the sea-snail factory which posts one of their cars and local employees in a position to observe and report (by cellular or vehicle telephone) advancing controllers.

The Keremköy fishers who regularly cast their nets for whiting on the ada outside of Yalıköy (see beginning of Chapter 4) exchange information and advice among themselves, assist one another and work on each others' boats. They may gather informally in the harbour while mending nets or at their local kahve, typically after they have returned from sea. Nevertheless, except when focusing on fishing activities, fishers do not differentiate themselves as a group. Informal groups of small-boat fishers have no leader, no meetings, and no decisions are taken.

Although men from the different groups know each other and exchange a few words if they meet at the harbour (some used to be schoolmates), the flow of information between the groups is very restricted. During the autumn of 1990 many small-boat fishers who were regulars at the Burunbaşı kahve made unexpectedly good catches of red mullet off Vakfıkebir and Beşikdüzü for ten days in a row. However, they made sure that this was kept relatively secret and they stressed that I should not tell the men in Keremköy where they were setting their nets, and especially not how good their catches were.

The user groups in small-boat fishing are not clearly codified or even spoken of as groups, but change according to who participates in the different fisheries and may more appropriately be termed 'diffuse social clusters' (cf. 'social clusters', Acheson 1988). The fact that one is a small fisher (*küçük balıkçı*) is of relatively little importance in establishing and managing social relations. In a social environment where the men easily change occupation and often pursue several parallel income strategies, occupation is usually not the main social marker and imperative criterion for sociability and social support. Owners of big fishing vessels, captains, small-boat fishers and crew maintain local identities and bonds of solidarity with each other as well as other men within diffuse groups of men. The lack of formal organizations is a pervasive aspect of social life in Çarşıbaşı.

During the autumn of 1990 small-boat fishers in Burunbaşı were concerned about the monetary situation and the fact that the sea-snail factory was very slow to pay for the catches. Nobody could come up with a good solution, but a disillusioned young 'socialist' fisher said that the problem was that the cooperative didn't work. He thought that it could have organized the sea-snail trade, but the others did not agree. Small-boat fishers sometimes note that they cannot handle their activities collectively because they lack a leader. Their notion of a leader is someone who is not a small-boat fisher, someone with a base of influence and money. Influence is usually pursued through local notables such as village heads, owners of factories, leaders of fishing companies or other politically and economically influential men.

Small-boat fishers in Çarşıbaşı generally do not have sufficient confidence in each other to establish their own cooperative, for example for management of sales. They depend on local dealers or on making a tiresome thirty to forty-five minutes bus trip to Trabzon to deliver their catch to their regular komisyoncu. Small-boat fishers maintained that they can not cooperate on marketing since they cannot trust anyone to do an honest job. They especially distrust fishers from other 'diffuse social clusters'. Experiences with and rumours about corrupt water-produce-cooperative leaders have helped to undermine the trust in cooperatives. A water produce cooperative close to Trabzon had problems rebuilding the members' trust after a former leader had enriched himself with incomes the cooperative had from the kahve it owned and then moved to another part of Turkey. Similar stories can be told about many fisheries (and supposedly other) cooperatives.

Trust, not necessarily strongly felt but often strategic, is often vested in patrons, influential local leaders who are also seen as friends, as 'one of us'. Instrumental relations of dependency/loyalty are conceptualized and 'performed' as friendship relations (cf. Campbell 1964, referred in Herzfeld 1992: 175). The ideology of friendship, of mutual affection and respect in an equal relationship, glosses over stark inequalities. Sometimes this is only a gloss, 'performed' on front stage, but denigrated back stage, as when small-boat fishers regret that they are 'bonded' (bağlı) to a patron who they may derogatively call a 'king'. At other times, men from very different walks of life really do stick together as 'equal friends'.

A 'big man', the manager of the sea-snail factory in Keremköy – a local and a friend, but also a man highly influential in the whole region – had distributed credit to many of his fellow villagers so that they could invest in bigger boats and better equipment that would increase the catches of sea snails. The fishers thereby became 'bonded' to the manager and had to deliver all their catches to him. During one period the fishers became increasingly dissatisfied with the price paid for their catches, with delayed payments, and the discontinuing of advance payments. Although most men would still talk about the manager as a good man, and a close friend, as being helpful and cheerful, there was a subdued discourse of dissent evolving. Bent forward over the kahve table, and looking round to ensure that nobody was listening, and without mentioning any name, they complained that there was now one 'big man' (*büyük adam*) in Keremköy, 'somebody' that wanted to be *aga* (lord) (cf. Meeker 1972) while others become *köle* (slaves); 'The inequalities (*dengesizliği*) in Keremköy have increased.' To these critiques were also added comments about his past, about the illegal activities that made him rich.

The negative mood among the small-boat fishers did not go unnoticed by the manager, and – I was told – one day he showed up in the kahve and loudly exclaimed: 'Let one person rise [and speak]! (*bir kişi kalksın!*)' Nobody rose and the critique remained muted. The small-boat fishers were likely afraid of exposing themselves, of bringing down upon themselves the wrath of the manager, who was their main link to the outside world, to torpil (middleman broker) services and the like.

Despite disagreements, conflicting interests, anger and fear, people go to great lengths to give relations a veneer of 'friendship'. For the small-boat fishers and other men without influence, the dilemma remains: a leader should be one of us, but then he will be powerless. And if he is powerful, he joins the (relative) elite and becomes morally suspect. Power is a resource (money, positions in the state) to be drawn in from out there.

## Water Produce Cooperatives in Turkey

Most fishers I have spoken with along the Black Sea coast and in Istanbul relate similar stories about the impotency of the cooperatives. The cooperative associations (*kooperatif birlikleri*) show almost no activity. Most cooperatives are either 'sleeping', or controlled by a little clique of big-boat fishers. In a study of Istanbul fishers Taner (1991: 136) notes in the same vein that fishers 'transmit their problems or requests through the Chamber of Commerce or by personal relations which is definitely more influential than the union of coops.' Some of the lobby activity has been framed within new organizations outside of the cooperative structure, such as The Turkish Foundation of Fishing, Research, Development and Recovery (Türkiye Balıkçılık Araştırma Geliştirme Kalkındırma Vakfı) founded by the bigger purse-seiner family companies in Istanbul. The Istanbul Fish Producers Society (İstanbul Balık Müstahsiller Derneği), established already in 1923, is regarded as one of the oldest civil societies in the Republic. The Society organizes a social security system for its members, primarily owners of and skippers on the big boats, but also serves to a certain extent as an arbiter in conflicts between fishers (Taner 1991: 107).

Overall, however, institutionalized social bodies with rules for membership and operation are not active in shaping fisheries management policies in Turkey. There is no organization that represents the interests of the crew, and outside of a few cooperatives that are dominated by small-boat fishers, there exist no structure that represents small-boat fishers' interests. Fikret Berkes (1992) describes several cases where small-boat fishers along the Mediterranean and Aegean coasts of Turkey are able to formalize restriction on access by using the local water produce cooperative to give decisions and rules legitimacy. Such cases are difficult to find along the Black Sea coast. The cases discussed by Berkes are unique in that they are uniformly small-boat fishing communities and that their fishing territory is not attractive to trawlers or purse seines. The small-boat fishers in Çarşıbaşı do not constitute one single, homogenous group and their marginal position in the local community makes it difficult to organize their own cooperative. When there are owners of big fishing boats in a community, they will usually monopolize the cooperative. The current legislature makes it impossible to establish more than one cooperative in each locality thereby making it impossible in heterogeneous communities for, for example, trawlers and small-boat fishers to organize into separate cooperatives. Moreover, cooperation between small-boat fishers will clearly be easier where the shared identity as small-boat fisher is supplemented by other shared identities and bonds of solidarity (as Berkes' Alanya case clearly reveals). In Çarşıbaşı, relations between small-boat fishers do not take precedence over relations to other people. It is uncommon to forward one's interests through 'horizontal' interest organizations with voluntary membership. This is an aspect of social life that has also been noted by other scholars that have studied Turkish society, for example the working of political parties (Güneş-Ayata 1990) or in petty-commodity production (White 1994).

Evidence from a few small-boat cooperatives on the Black Sea coast, such as in Gerze, Sinop and Faroz (City of Trabzon) indicates that cooperation is facilitated where members share the same interests. In both Sinop and Gerze the cooperative organizes sales at a fairly large scale and works actively to protect the official ban on trawling in their proximate waters. Both cooperatives include many memurs or retired state employees and have been headed by former leaders of the local workers union. This has made it possible to successfully operate a sales cooperative in Sinop even though there are also quite a few owners of purse seiners in the town.

Towards the end of the 1990s there remained fewer incentives for fishers to keep the cooperatives alive. Previously, fishers could only import equipment through the cooperatives and obtain credit from the Agriculture Bank if they were cooperative members. This has now changed. Moreover, the customs union (1996) with the EU has removed

202 | Fishers and Scientists in Modern Turkey

import taxes on engines and the like, thereby diluting the other important rationale for coop membership. If fishers could have secured credit or grants as well as tax exemption on imports without being members of cooperatives, there probably would not have been a role for most cooperatives during the 1980s and 1990s. But the development in the fisheries would likely have been very much the same! And the distribution among the fishers would not have been very different. Since the end of the 1990s there has been an increase in number of cooperatives in the province of Samsun. This seems to be related to the construction of new harbours and the discount on boathouse rent given to cooperative members. Nevertheless, in 2005 only approximately ten per cent of fishers in Samsun were members of water produce cooperatives. The recent increase in number of cooperatives in the eastern Black Sea region is linked to the establishment of a central union of water produce cooperatives and a sense that the cooperatives may be accorded a more important role when Turkey adapts its fishery policy to EU Common Fishery Policy.

## Explaining the Failure: Cultivation of Ignorance

The relevant authorities have at times acknowledged that the cooperatives have not taken the position in the fisheries that they had expected (e.g., GDWP 1975: 32). However, my own experience, from interviews and informal conversations with bureaucrats who are responsible for the fisheries within the Ministry for Agriculture and Rural Affairs, indicates that they still see the cooperatives as the main organizing structure for representing (vis-à-vis the bureaucracy) and empowering (vis-à-vis the fish traders) the fishers. When Mustafa and Yaşar toured fishing communities between Samsun and Sinop they typically preferred to meet with cooperative leaders, and where there was no cooperative they criticized the fishers for having missed an opportunity.

General studies of cooperatives in Turkey emphasize that the lack of success of the cooperatives must be understood within the context of the national political system (Mülayim 1997; TKK 1997). After 1980 the state put greater restrictions on the activities of cooperatives and brought them more firmly under state control. At the same time the importance of cooperatives were downplayed in government programs and policy (TKK 1997: 17). Cooperatives became the victim of widespread negative stereotypes (TKK 1997: 53). In the neoliberal atmosphere after 1980 water produce cooperatives were sometimes looked upon with suspicion. Until the second part of 1990s small boat fishers in Sinop had problems establishing a working cooperative since it was stigmatized as being 'communist'.

The bureaucrats' and scientists' explanation for the unsuccessful development of water produce cooperatives focus on a perceived lack of organization at the local level and the failure to establish regional associations (*birlikler*) and, especially, a national union of water produce cooperatives. One professor stated that 'One of the most critical problems for the producers who are active within the marine products sector in Turkey is their insufficient level of organization (*yeterli olarak teşkilatmamalarıdır*)' (Demirci 1986: 172). A cooperative representative responded to the professor's presentation by exclaiming that: '[O]ur teacher counted and found that today there are quite a few cooperatives. But the doors of most of these are locked. And they are only unlocked for the general assemblies. Yes, these are indeed only cooperatives in name (*isim Kooperatifleri*). Cooperatives made to make it possible to receive credit' (Agricultural Bank 1986: 180–1). In his reply to the various discussants, the professor did not comment upon this.

The official explanation for cooperative failure is, however, not based upon detailed studies. In the few government studies of the activity and position of the water produce cooperatives (see especially GDWP 1975 and DMP 1982) data was gathered primarily through questionnaires and interviews. Although these studies have included some comments on the actual workings and problems of the cooperatives, later commentators (e.g., Çıkın and Elbek 1991; Demirci 1986) have focused primarily on the increase in the number of cooperatives and amount of credit directed through them in an effort to demonstrate their increased importance within the fishing sector. Yet, they conclude that '[O]ne should undertake detailed studies and assessments of the cooperatives, and the socioeconomic factors which inhibit the workings of the cooperatives in this sector should be identified' (Çıkın and Elbek 1991: 177).

When explaining why the fishery cooperatives remain inefficient, rather than citing changes in socioeconomy, politics and policy or bad fit with 'local' organizational culture, scientists and bureaucrats tend to blame the *cehalet* (ignorance) of the fishers. During an informal conversation among bureaucrats in the offices of a water produce branch of the Ministry of Agriculture in Ankara, one man claimed that the perceived inadequate development of the cooperatives was a consequence of a lack of cooperative spirit among the fishers. 'We didn't manage to teach the fishers. Among the fishers there is no compassion (*şefkatlık*), they don't trust each other.' He thought that the fishers quarrel and compete and therefore remain in the clutches of the middlemen. The fishers are not able to 'add value' to their catch – they do not process and market the fish in 'modern' ways. One top bureaucrat claimed that the cooperatives did not work well because the leaders were not knowledgeable (*bilgili değil*). Another common claim is that fishers do not organize since they do not think about the future. During a (taped) informal conversation with a marine scientist in Trabzon, I raised the issue of the ignorance of the fishers. He responded by claiming that

> [O]ne of the weakest matters in Turkey is that because of the low cultural level of the fishers there is no unity and cooperation. They think individualistically (*ferdi*). For instance, if I have my profit today, let come tomorrow what may come, that's of no importance at all. Because they do not act within unity and cooperation they enter a race.

He illustrated this with an example of fishers not being able to cooperate about diminishing effort when catches of hamsi surpass the demand for fresh fish, bringing 'ruin' to all. He said that the cooperatives 'haven't taken roots because both our members and our leaders are cahil people. It is very difficult to do business with such cahil people.'

The most frequently used terms to describe the ignorance and lack of civilization of fishers and other 'common' people include uneducated (*eğitimsiz*), cahil, *bilinçsiz* (unconscious/without foresight), *kültürsüz* ('lacking in culture', uncultivated) or having a reactionary mentality (*gerici zihniyeti*). Rather than being based in detailed study, such claims seem to draw both on a general model of the masses as uncivilized and immature because of lack of education, as well as on personal experience and reflection. This reason for lack of success in cooperative organization is frequently evoked also in reports and the like on water produce cooperatives. In effect, the blame for the lack of efficient cooperatives in the fishing sector is put to a certain extent on the fishers themselves. It becomes a problem of culture, not of policy and politics.

Several issues are involved in education. There are the more concrete skills and knowledges that schooling develops, such as writing, mathematics, and so on, and which is seen as a prerequisite for running a cooperative. Yet, as came out in Chapter 7, what really concerns the educated elite is the fishers' and other uneducated people's insufficient adoption of the cultivated, sosyal and rahat style of interpersonal interaction that is required for the smooth working of a modern, civilized society. The idealistic models of the educated elite require people to develop selves that are responsible and put the interests of the society ('solidarism') before individual, family and mahalle interests ('communalism'). The discourse about cehalet is shared in wider sectors of the Turkish society and the reference to cahil is a common explanation for many undesirable phenomena: the widespread practice of trawling, over-fishing, and illegal practices among fishers; fishers' failure to use new technology efficiently; the common man's support for the Nationalist Action Party; Kurdish support for the PKK; the alarming number of traffic accidents and deaths; people's preference for whole, uncut fish; and so forth.

It is as if underlying all these claims is a general understanding that Turkish society and culture is in a process of change, development or progress, towards a more civilized condition, and that the main instrument for bringing this about is education. The Turkish modernization discourse has been and is still largely imbued with the sense that society is not (yet) as it should be and that institutions and individuals should be transformed to reach those goals. What those goals are, and the means needed in order to reach them, have increasingly been challenged, but that one is striving to reach an ideal, and that education is the prime means and agent of this change, is hardly challenged in the public modernization discourse. While education plays a primary role in the development of most nation-states, in Turkey the stress has been on education as an instrument in attempts at transforming individual selves and modernizing the culture of the people. The 'technical' aspects of education have received less attention.

One important attempt at integrating practice and theory, industry and schools, in Turkey was the establishment of twenty-one village institutes (see, e.g., Karaömerlioğlu 1998). With the intention of improving contact between the village people and the banner-bearers of the new republic – the future teachers – the village institutes were very formative institutions during the 1940s. The village institute in Beşikdüzü, close to Çarşıbaşı, included theoretical and especially practical training in fisheries and brought teachers, students and fishers together (Özer 1990). Some of Ali Reis' (see Chapter 6) contemporaries and mates were associated to this institute. The institute, like others of its kind, was closed down towards the end of the 1940s after allegations by the Democrat Party that they were centres of communist propaganda (Zürcher 1993: 224).

Concerns with technology and material outcomes were important in parts of the early Ottoman sciences (e.g., medicine) (İhsanoğlu 1992: 38). The Young Ottoman thinkers and intellectuals of the late Ottoman period were, however, inclined to abstract thought and paid little attention to practical aspects of reform, such as, for example, economic theory or strategy (see, e.g., Crofoot 1993). In the new Ottoman schools that were to train the new officials, students studied (directly from books, often in French) 'principles and laws which were abstractions from reality, and had an artificial internal consistency. … Science then appeared to the students in the form of abstract models of reality, a characteristic also emphasized by the lack of experimentation and the parlous state of laboratories' (Mardin 1997b: 205). Thus, the idea of science that the Kemalist regime inherited from the Young Turks was an idealistic one (Kasaba 1997: 26). This idealistic approach was fairly devoid of experimentation and geared towards the mental manipulation of models to form internally consistent systems often by importing wholesale blueprints from industrialized countries, evident in the ideas about technological and organizational development in the fisheries that bureaucrats endorsed during the 1950s and 1960s. In a short article entitled 'The use of factory vessels in the Black Sea should (also) be considered', the EBK transport director presented detailed sketches of a large Russian factory vessel (Gedik 1969: 128–130). In contrast there is a telling paucity in the work of water produce bureaucrats and scientists concerning kinds of crafts and technology that were actually used by the fishers. That Devedjian's study (1926) remained the main reference work until the 1980s and 1990s, when the new water produce faculties slowly started to come to grips with the technological developments in the fisheries, attests to this idealistic approach.

In this picture 'mahalle (quarter) norms' were seen as undesirable as they were directed towards small groups and not society. The mahalle norms, specifically those associated with Islam, were considered to inhibit individual development; a prerequisite for a dynamic, progressive society. Therefore tradition and Islam had to be stamped out, and new selves created through education. In 1928 a Turkish government-appointed committee stated that 'religious life, like moral and economic life, must be reformed on scientific lines' (cited in Kasaba 1997: 25). Education was a tool for 'uneducating' tradition and preparing people for change, for accepting 'useful' knowledge and practice (N. Berkes 1998: 401–3).

When the educated elite claim that the fishers do not manage to organize cooperatives properly because they are cahil, they implicitly base their argument on the model of individual, society and education outlined above. The fishers have allegedly not received enough education to have had their selves sufficiently transformed; they are not mature enough to interact in accordance with 'society ethics'; they behave according to 'backward' mahalle, or rather *köy* (village), ethics and, therefore, do not trust each other and lack cooperative spirit. Guided by this 'idealism' the study of the reality of the water produce cooperatives has been deflected to a critique of fishers being cahil. It is thus symptomatic that Bayram Öztürk, one of the leading marine scientists in Turkey, writing in a popular overview article about fisheries in Istanbul, asserts that the fishers have contributed much to the decline of the fish stocks in the Bosporus since 'organizational development has been slow and educational level insufficient.' This claim about 'lack of culture', so to say, among fishers leads Öztürk to write that Turkish fishers 'have, unlike fishers in European countries or in Japan, absolutely no tradition (*gelenek*) for protecting the fishing grounds or controlling fishing areas' (Öztürk 2000: 84). The historical and contemporary practices I have described in some detail in Chapter 3 and Chapter 5 counter the content of Öztürk's assertion. What, then, makes statements like Öztürk's possible in the context of modern Turkey? Why have customary practices of restriction on access in the fisheries not been incorporated in the Republican state's approach to fishery management?

## Official Ignorance of Custom

Evidence from other regions indicates a possible correlation between legal pluralism and high formal/state acknowledgement of customary law, on the one hand, and the recognition of customary practices on the other. Reification or formalization of local practice, rules and litigation as 'customary law' clearly facilitates codification of terms such as IK and TEK. In comparison with ethnographic studies in Indonesia, for instance, the lack of scholarly attention to customary law and IK/TEK in the Middle East is striking.[78] In colonial Indonesia the Dutch administrators codified customary law as *adat*, which also become incorporated in the new national ideology (Geertz 1983). Although the continued pervasive use of this in the new Indonesian State has been criticized for stimulating reification of local practice and 'invention of tradition', it seems very plausible that the discursive space opened by the adat law facilitates establishment of indigenous organizations and a concern about indigenous knowledge in Indonesia (Warren 1993: 299; Benda-Beckman 2001; Bowen 2003). Here and elsewhere there exist public discourse (e.g., *Kastom* in the Oceanic context, Keesing 1989, 1992; Hviding 1996) that works as a legitimizing frame for claims to authenticity of local practices. Why could reference to 'tradition', to 'customary law', and so on not be mobilized as a strategic or rhetoric resource for legitimizing local practices in the Turkish fisheries?

Whereas national culture has to a large degree been folklorized and idealized in most nationalisms (Gellner 1983; Anderson 1991), in Turkey this process may have been extreme. While Devedjian in his book about 'Fish and Fisheries' (original Ottoman edition 1915) wrote widely about what he in the French 1926 edition termed *us et coutumes* in the fisheries (Devedjian 1926), later official approaches to the fisheries have largely ignored this aspect. The state representatives have principally focused on the 'developed' sector of the fisheries and documented, and conveyed in teaching, idealistic models and the technology and catch technique of big-boat fishing.

The Turkish Republic has, at an ideal level at least, chosen to try to completely reframe or recreate the fisheries. Even though cooperative organization is claimed by the cultural elite to be a continuation of traditions of *imece* (voluntary communal work) (TKK 1997: 7), cooperative organization was not presented to the fishers as such. It was, rather, introduced as a modern structure that should replace traditional structures and thereby contribute to development and progress. Implied in many Turkish scientists' and bureaucrats' discourse of development is, thus, a denial of 'local' culture as a possible ideological foundation for cooperatives. The relevance of 'traditional' practices, even of practice per se, has been ignored within the official framework. Practices of local regulation and privileged access, which were not only acknowledged by the Ottoman State but an integral part of the tax system, have been increasingly muted or suppressed. When the formal system disintegrated, the informal practices that it encapsulated became invisible to the state.

This contrasts with the development of Japanese fishery cooperatives which have explicitly incorporated local traditions and practices. While fishery policy had clear parallels in Japan and the Ottoman Empire, traditional privileges and rights, unlike development in Turkey, were incorporated in the first Japanese Fishery Law (1901) and sustained in modified form in the second Fishery Law (1949). The laws upheld to a large extent the coastal communities' privileged access to fish in their immediate coastal territories. Fishing cooperatives were allocated substantial responsibility and authority in the management of the fishing rights (Ruddle 1985, 1987; Kalland 1996). Since the Japanese modernization process took place at a time of empire expansion, local and traditional culture was not perceived as an obstacle to but as an integral part of successful modernization (personal communication, Arne Kalland). In contrast, the Turkish Republic was created against the background of imperial decline and, ultimately, collapse; modernization, therefore, came to be premised on forced change away from tradition and towards an idealistic, Western model. Therefore, the social engineers of the Turkish Republic were, unlike their Japanese colleagues, unable or unwilling to base the design of these cooperatives on local customary culture and institutions.

Around the world it is not uncommon that fishers' and other groups' management of natural resources is formally based upon customary laws associated with IK or TEK. There did, and do, exist terms for traditional practices and institutions in Turkey, such as *adet*, *örf* (or *urf*, customary law) *aneane/gelenek/görenek* (tradition), that could have been developed along the same lines as, for example, adat in Indonesia to give recognition and legitimacy (e.g., as IK or TEK) to local practice and law. Elsewhere in the Middle East, in places such as Al-Bahrain and Kuwait, fishing has been subject to 'highly complicated and sophisticated customary laws' sanctioned by the local Shaik or the state, often codified as *shar*, which is not related to Sharia, but rather means *adah* (custom) (Serjeant 1966, 1968; Serjeant and Adams 1980). No such conception of custom, however, fell within the new, idealistic scheme of a national mission of Western-style development and enforced social and cultural change in Republican Turkey: tradition and custom were contrary to rationality, reason, logic and science.

The colonial experience may explain why 'customary law' was to a larger extent acknowledged and codified in places other than Turkey. While Islamic law acknowledges custom and customary law (*adat, urf*), customary law and Islamic law have been separated in the Middle East to a much lesser extent than in, for example, Indonesia and Africa. The Middle East was generally occupied and controlled by colonial powers to a lesser extent than regions such as Africa, Indonesia and India. Where Western powers did establish colonies in the Middle East, they did not – with the possible exception of Morocco – encourage the inscription and cataloguing of local law comparable to the *adatrech* movement in Indonesia. They did not promote customary law as an alternative to Islam. Rather, Islam and tradition were generally merged in the colonizers' picture of the societies they administrated in the Middle East. While Turkey was never colonized, the Republican elite had internalized a Western perception of their society whereby custom and Islam were roughly synonymous and the 'other' of modernization and 'progress'. Kemalists were, and are, ardent moderns and have, except for folklorized local culture, rejected tradition and custom in toto.

## Open Access

When bureaucrats and scientists recently started to consider devolving managerial fisheries rights to local-level fisher's villages or organizations, they used the concept *oto kontrol* (auto control) (e.g., Mert 1996). Thus, their approach frames the issue of fisher's participation within a 'Western' scienticized discourse of fishery management instead of elaborating the prerepublican tradition and/or incorporating contemporary local practices and codes. While 'auto control' has recently emerged as a rhetorical figure, fishery management discourse in Turkey has definitely been dominated by the notion of open, free and unrestricted access to the sea and fish, or more correctly, of the illegitimacy of privileged access (see Chapter 3). This was an ideal, however, created not by the state alone. Development in the fisheries created powerful actors within the sector that preferred an 'open access' regime. Because fisheries came so late onto the development agenda, there was a legal void that, except for some seasonal and regional limitations,[79] gave almost free reign to more mobile fishing technologies such as purse-seine and trawl fishing that gradually outstripped the kind of fishing for which the state acknowledged privileged access. Since it was likely also in the interest of the skippers and owners of the big fishing boats to support a concept of 'open access' to seascape and fish, the idea of the sea as an unrestricted commons was gradually consolidated.

That fishing was increasingly seen as 'free' (*serbest*) may also be connected, especially after 1950, to the anticommunist rhetoric of 'freedom'. When asked about restrictions on access, some fishers forcefully express such views, saying that 'We are not like Russia (in other words, the Soviet Union), we are free'.[80] Thus, the conception of fisheries as being 'free for all' is not a representation of a 'pristine' or 'natural condition' were 'ignorant' and 'atomistic' fishers selfishly and unconsciously go about their business. The state cocreated this regime, partly through ignorance of traditions of restriction on access, partly through deliberate policy. Furthermore, international institutions as well as national organizations have, through their sponsorship of research, for example, supported the ideal of governmentality, the reference to the Western model, and the 'open access' regime.[81]

## Ideals and Pragmatics

The state has not infiltrated the social organization of the fisheries to the depth intended in the ideals and plans for fishery development. As described in Chapter 7 and 8, in practice the state representatives accept and involve themselves in social and political arrangements that diverge from the ideal. At one level 'traditional' practices, knowledges, local rules of restricted access as well as codes of conduct persist. Although neither marine science nor fishery cooperatives have played any major role in fishery development, the state was certainly instrumental in creating opportunities through credits and infrastructure developments. But most of the actual developments and dynamics were unanticipated and remained partly illegible for bureaucrats and scientists. Actually, while officials of the state have some knowledge of boats, equipment, and catch, expressed especially in the annual fishery statistics, they are, at the formal level at least, ignorant of the social processes and codes of conduct in the fishing. There is no Turkish social science of fishing. I contend, however, that without these invisible processes within the fisheries, the fisheries would not have experienced its success during the 1970s and 1980s and their resilience during the resource crisis years of the early 1990s (Knudsen 1997).

The unseen social processes in fishing include the exercise and reproduction of traditional, but dynamically changing knowledge and dexterity of the fishers; a social organization based on family enterprises that is flexible, resilient and has its 'natural' authority structure; and a willingness on the part of entrepreneurial rural small farmers to take risk. The success of many small family-fishing firms that typically started in the 1960s and 1970s as small-boat fishers lies in their ability to manoeuvre within the state-imposed framework. A pragmatics of state – fishers relations is at work here, as in Mustafa's dealings with fishers and bureaucrats or when powerful fishers and factory owners lobbied successfully in 1991 to reduce the legal minimum size of the hamsi when catches and income were reduced by a severe resource crisis (see Chapter 6).

Most fishers pay lip service to cooperative organization so as to satisfy zealous bureaucrats keen on the proper development of the fisheries. In many cases this formal interface for interaction with the state is appropriated by a few influential men leaving many fishers to feel alienated by the new world of 'water produce' (see fisher statement, beginning of 'Development ideals', Chapter 3). In most cases, a hierarchy of local and regional 'big men', interacting according to codes of conduct and along informal network structures that only partly parallel the official framework of cooperatives and the like, come into play. Before the change in hamsi regulation in the winter of 1990–91, quite a few boats were caught catching too many undersize fish. Many fishers, however, managed to acquit themselves with the help of MPs who intervened on their behalf. The same pragmatics has been at work in an ingenious circumvention of official bans on construction of new fishing boats after 1994, or in the successful pressure levied on the ministry to postpone or cancel payment of outstanding loans after seasons with below average catches. While fishers have had little influence on the design of the development ideology, they certainly contribute to shape the state fishery policy. Chris Hann (1990) has noted similar processes in the development of tea production in Rize where 'officials aspired to control every aspect of the business' but where the rural population 'domesticated the State' by multiple strategies that affected the authorities' policies.

This is a level of action that state representatives must actively be involved in, but often regret the existence of, criticizing the prevalence of 'personal' relations, 'corruption', torpil and so forth. Officially, the bureaucrats make the decisions, based upon information gathered from scientists as well as the perspectives and interests presented by various stakeholders. Thus, scientists have only an advisory role, and often do not have extended involvement in the decision process. The scientists see as political the way the knowledge they produce is manipulated or side-stepped by the bureaucrats who let politics get in the way of scientific management of the resources. State strategies for development become difficult to pursue when local initiatives can circumvent plans, laws and regulations. In this pragmatics of state policy, however, concerns other than the development schemes and reforms are of critical importance. For individual MPs, political parties or the government, extension of credit is a means of attracting followers and political support. Likewise, establishment of new water produce faculties is often an outcome of concerted action by local businessmen (who donate construction land and perhaps cover some construction costs) and the province MP, rather than the result of a planned strategy for the development of water produce science. Harbours have often been constructed as the result of successful lobbying by 'big men' and MPs that want to favour their men and their district.

Thus, there is a clear difference between ideological justification (for example GNP, nutrients) and pragmatic justification for individual state initiatives and decisions concerning the fisheries. Pragmatic justification primarily relates to the need for 'getting things done' and keeping and acquiring followers – both regional 'big men' and voters. Thus, at a pragmatic level certain groups within the state are guided to a great extent by their need to sustain support for themselves and the government. Governmentality may be the ideal, but the term 'popular sovereignty' perhaps better describes the activities of particularly those that depend upon the new political mechanisms of party politics and representative government for their position and influence. The break with Ottoman sovereignty may therefore not be as decisive as the rigidity of Nalbatanoğlu's interpretation of Foucault's model suggests (see Chapter 3). As Michael Meeker has argued, continuities from Ottoman times may be found in the play of interpersonal relations, both locally and vis-à-vis state representatives, according to a 'discipline of interpersonal relations' (Meeker 2002). The state is not homogenous. Different modes of state ideals and policies seem to coexist, and the distance between Öztürk's claim and the fishers' traditions may correspond with a parallel distance between bureaucratic ideal and the pragmatics of fishery policies. The civil servant, like Mustafa, who is put in a position where he has to relate daily to both the ideals and the pragmatics, has to negotiate the distance between them and resolve the ambivalence through skilled switching between roles and situations. However, dilemmas and ambivalences cannot be fully solved. They are partly embodied.

## Conclusions

A sustained 'futurism', including a period of high modernism, guided the Turkish development experience. Those who have been inspired by the futurism have aimed to radically restructure Turkish society and selves. Although fisheries were perceived by the elite to be of minor importance in the Turkish modernization process, ambitious ideals for reform and development were formulated. Yet, when the state finally undertook to implement reforms in the fisheries from 1950 onwards, changes in the political climate together with the nature of the resource prevented the deep penetration into the production and distribution process that was to some extent achieved in some sectors of agricultural production. In the anticommunist conditions of the postwar years the Turkish State was not willing to implement their development ideals by authoritatively forcing a transformation of productive organization, for instance by forcing a change from family- and community-based production to 'collectives'.

The continued prevalence of family-based production in the fisheries facilitated the growth and resilience of the fisheries. By the mid 1980s fishery policies were a partial success in terms of 'production'.

Technologically Turkish fisheries have come to resemble more closely the Western ideal. But, in terms of process and structure the state policy was, by its own modernizing standards, a failure; the state did not take sufficient command of the sector and the fishers did not behave as presupposed by the development plans. Networking and 'personal relations' remain the main modes of interaction both within the fisheries and between fishers and the authorities. Save for the, largely unsuccessful, cooperatives there are no representative organizations through which fishers can forward their interests. Moreover, there are no mass media such as newspapers or professional journals that specifically give voice to fishers.

There is nothing new in state schemes failing to meet their ends. What is significant is the wide distance between the ideals – the high modernity models – and the pragmatics of fishery politics. The resilience of these ideals is probably sustained by the social distance between the water produce bureaucracy and the fishers. There are not many like Mustafa who daily have to negotiate complex relations with scientists, bureaucrats and fishers. The bureaucrats' and scientists' insistence on the ideals is likely also an expression of their powerlessness in face of the reality of a pragmatics of politics where powerful fishers and factory owners can override bureaucratic ideals. Öztürk's statement is representative of a common characterization of fishers as ignorant and prone to act irresponsibly. This discourse works to divert attention away from the state's role and the actual workings of its policies and places the responsibility for problems in the fisheries solely on the fishers themselves.

There is a limit to what the state can, and should, know about natural resources and local society. It is simply impossible to engineer in every detail micro-social and natural processes. I claim, accordingly, that Professor Öztürk's mistake is not that he is ignorant about local practices and traditions. There will always be informal social processes, often vital for the survival and sustainability of communities and natural resources, beyond the state's gaze. But, to make empirical false statements about local practices based upon simplified and ideologically informed conceptions of fishers and 'people' in general I find objectionable.

If the state representatives were to be more informed about the tradition of fishing, this would most probably be knowledge of 'forms'. Yet, definitions of 'tradition' that pay too much overt attention to 'forms' (e.g., the pattern of molozma fishing) may be misleading and of little use. They risk being essentializing and reifying, and can give the impression of 'frozen' traditions/practices; or of a complete collapse of or break with traditions although beneath the surface forms, there are continuities. But the 'tradition' I have described is a dynamic continuity, open to innovation and adaptation to new circumstances. The non-formalized and non-inscribed (e.g., in local or state legal codes) character of practices and knowledges ensures the potential for dynamism. Excessive formalization may be unresponsive to new management needs as local adaptations meet changing circumstances (see Knudsen 1995 for an elaboration).

Both the idealistic 'production' models of fishery development, and the new, again Western inspired, bio-economic models fail to account for the social organization and power structure in the fishery sector and the fishing communities. 'Western' models continue to influence Turkish fishery policy. The current process of adapting Turkish fishery policy and management to EU Common Fishery Policy implies, for instance, that fisheries are termed 'fisheries' and not 'water produce', and 'cooperatives' are substituted for by 'producer organizations'. The new policies induced by Turkey's EU accession process promise to make far-reaching changes in the way fishing is monitored and controlled, for example with the implementation of port offices that will register all catches, and the deployment on large fishing boats of GPS-aided vessel monitoring systems (Knudsen, Pelczarski and Brown 2007). If Turkish fishery management moves in the direction of stakeholder involvement, comanagement and ecosystem management, it will again be based upon Western models.

Neither the development of marine science nor the effort to establish water produce cooperatives have had much effect on the actual course of development in Turkish Black Sea fisheries. However, marine science and water produce cooperatives, and their failure, created and sustained a particular influential discourse on fisheries. With the growth of the water produce sciences, for the first time the position from which Professor Öztürk speaks became possible. Thus, Öztürk does not talk from the position of independent intellectual, but as state representative, or as a moralistic representative of the Turkish modernization project. And when state representatives tap into the nationwide discourse on education and ignorance to explain the failure of cooperatives they are similarly moralistic. How interaction between fishers and state representatives are shaped by discourses of morals and identity is further explored in the next chapter.

# CHAPTER 10

# Articulation of Knowledges through Moralities and Politics

The term *cahil* has its origin in the Islamic cultural universe. The search for and reproduction of *ilm* (learned and rational knowledge) has been a critical focus in Islam since it keeps alive the knowledge of how to avoid the *cahiliyet*. This religious meaning of cahil was still the primary frame of reference when Stirling (1965) did his fieldwork in an Anatolian village in the 1950s, but the concept has gradually moved from an Islamic context into a more 'neutral' one. While bureaucrats and scientists in reports and other kinds of texts may prefer to use the term *eğitimsiz* (uneducated), in the vernacular it is now common to use cahil to indicate ignorance in a general and not only a religious sense. Today defenders of Kemalist modernity still evoke Atatürk's sayings. One of these demonstrates precisely how he tried to redefine cehalet. 'The truest guide in life is science and technology. To search for guides outside of science and technology is carelessness, *cehalet*, wrong thinking.'

I have indicated that scientists and bureaucrats tend to perceive a connection between studying (*okumak*) and education (*eğitim*), on the one hand, and manners/cultivation (kültürlü, sosyal/rahat), on the other. Eğitim is widely seen as necessary for cooperation and civilized interaction. A university graduate should also have good manners. A young woman in Çarşıbaşı told me that she tried to 'continue' (*devam etmek*) even though she had recently finished her schooling as a nurse. As examples of the 'continuation' (of training) she mentioned going to cinema and theatre. As became evident in the interview with Deniz (Chapter 7), a whole range of manners and skills – bodily, social and intellectual – are seen to come with education. A marine scientist in Trabzon opined that people should receive behavioural (*davranış*) education, sosyal education, in order to teach them to feel shame when they break rules. A marine scientist, one of the very few with origins in a fishing community, said about a small-boat fisher that was a mutual acquaintance of ours that he probably did not get involved in nocturnal small-boat trawling, because he is more kültürlü than most other fishers (since he has completed lise). We may say that these codes of conduct, which ideally come with higher education, constitute a stock of ethical know-how of how to behave in an elite manner and express an elite lifestyle.

So, what is really the level of formal education among fishers? In their surveys of fishing cultures, both Acheson (1981) and McGoodwin (1990: 25–26) point out that fishers are generally less educated than the non-fishers. This is also the case in Turkey (see Table 10.1).

**Table 10.1. Level of formal education among fishers.** All figures in percentages.

| | 5 years primary education or less | Lower secondary, 8 years | Higher secondary, 11 years (lise) | Higher education |
|---|---|---|---|---|
| Fishers Keremköy 1998[1] | 78 | 7 | 15 | 0 |
| Total men Keremköy 1998 | 54 | 8 | 20 | 18 |
| Fishers (skippers/managers) Black Sea region 2005[2] | 60,7 | 14,9 | 20,9 | 3,6 |
| Fishers Samsun Province 2000[3] | 80,4 | 10,0 | 5,8 | 1,5 |
| Fishers Samsun Province 2005[4] | 74 | 13 | 13 | 0 |
| Male agricultural workers Turkey 2003 (Çakmak 2004: 8) | 84,7 | 8,0 | 6,7 | 0,6 |
| Total Turkey 2003 (Çakmak 2004: 8) | 58,8 | 11,4 | 18,8 | 11,0 |

1 See note[82] endnotes.
2 See note[83] endnotes.
3 See note[84] endnotes.
4 See note[85] endnotes.

The educational level of fishers is substantially lower than among most other occupational groups except agricultural workers. The situation is roughly similar in the Marmara region (Güngör 1998: 318). In Keremköy more fishers have completed lise and the percentage of men with higher education is very high. The reason is most likely the village's relative wealth (making it possible for people to educate their offspring) that stems from success in fishing and from so many men being state employed thanks to their good political connections. There is a tendency for big boat owners and skippers to be better educated than crew and small-boat fishers.

According to the fishers themselves it used to be fairly popular to work as crew, and until 1985–86 they often had to have a torpil in order to manage to sign on the attractive teams. Tempted by high shares young men chose to leave school and even permanent work on land. After the crisis in the early 1990s fishing became less attractive. The boat owners have increasingly had to pay advances, cover marriage expenses, and the like in order to bind the crew. It is the aim of most, if not all, fishers – even the wealthy big boat fishers – to educate their sons and daughters. Contrary to what Erginsoy (1998: 143) has observed in Istanbul, sons of boat owners in Çarşıbaşı only settle for a career in fishing if and when they fail to pass the university entrance exam. Thus, sons of the successful fishing families tend to have higher education and have a career outside of fishing, while for young men with little resources (land, capital) and education, fishing is one of the few options for income in the region open to them. Educational level is thereby kept low and the fishery sector remains 'cahil and uncultivated'.

Articulation between fishers' knowledges and the 'formal' knowledges of the bureaucrats and scientists is also compounded by the hesitation fishers feel towards transforming their speech to writing. Fishers generally relate little to 'inscribed' knowledge. All fishers know how to write and read, but they generally do very little writing (or reading for that matter), seldom write catch logs, or relate to textual guides to their equipments. Although they see a recurrent cyclical or seasonal pattern in the life of fish and in their own activities, they keep no notes of past activities to help prepare for upcoming seasons. Instead they have mental associations with important days or seasonal occurrences such as festivals or weather. Although their knowledge is generally not inscribed in text, some knowledge is inscribed in rhymes. For instance, the knowledge of how the poyraz (northeast) wind blows in different places along the coast is summed up in the following saying which is transmitted orally within the fishing community:

| Dialect | Standard Turkish | English |
| --- | --- | --- |
| *Poyraz rüzkarı* | *Poyraz rüsgahrı* | The *poyraz* wind |
| *Yoroz'ta eserim* | *Fener burunda eserim* | I blow at Cape Fener |
| *Yason'ta tuterim* | *Yason burunda tutarım* | At Cape Yason I gain force |
| *İnce 'te kaptan secerim* | *İnce burunda kaptan seçerim* | At Cape İnce I choose captain |
| *Keremb'ta anacuk sikerim* | *Kerempe burunda anacık sikerim* | At Cape Kerempe I fuck your mother |

Models inscribed in practice or rhymes require active reenacting. Like the models articulated by hand-signs used to signify sea-bottom conditions (Chapter 4), they are not to the same extent as writing or other easily transportable manifestations inscribed outside of the individual and specific situations. Thus, to use Latour's (1987) conceptual framework, most of fishers' knowledge is non-inscribed, representing phenomena that from the outside may be seen as unstable collectives, held together only in practice within fairly small communities of practitioners.

Fishers' articulations of their knowledge often take the form of creative sayings which it is hard to get them to write down since they sense that their oral language is too different from the accepted scriptural norms; it's too saturated with swearing, sexual metaphors, irony and grammatical deficiencies. One fisher had seen a state representative of Somalia in the Kumkapı fish halls in Istanbul. Addressing a group of fishers and me around a table in the kahve he commented that: 'Somalia has got a ministry for fisheries, we have not. We have got a ministry for cunts!' Here 'cunt' is an ironic reference to Western female tourists, signifying the Ministry for Tourism. This is not 'literal' talk, but an oral style that furthers social intimacy, a kind of 'poetics of manhood' (Herzfeld 1985). Fishers and other men with little education cherish such play on words and their verbal style differs significantly from the literalist style of the educated elites.

Since the emphasis on 'correct' language is inculcated by the state on many levels of Turkish society fishers are conscious about their 'language deficiency'. During a class in Turkish at a primary school in Çarşıbaşı I noted that one child was put right by the teacher when he said that he intended to serve the state. The pupil said *yardım* (help, assistance), while he should have said *hizmet* (service). Yardım is part of the locals' vocabulary for interpersonal relations and morality. The educated elite may, however, see this as an expression of introvert 'mahalle culture', and advocate hizmet as a kind of impersonal service that is directed towards the society, in accordance with ideals of 'solidarism'.

There is in general almost no education that directly targets fishers. Yet, when state representatives do try to address the skills fishers have, or should have, the approach is very textual and formalistic. The 'skippers exam', required to gain the right to pilot the larger boats, is entirely a textual affair. Fishers' practical knowledge at sea has no relevance whatsoever in this exam. Furthermore, a recent regulation requires all fishers to show their primary school (five years) diploma in order to receive the license that entitles the holder to work at sea.

The way the processes of Westernization, modernization and nationalism were introduced in Turkey has had far-reaching consequences for the condition of knowledges. The very elitist and idealistic approach to education, together with its politicization, has resulted in the neglect of technical training, a Jacobin approach to societal development, and accusations of ignorance being readily invoked for explaining all kinds of evils or undesired phenomena.

In the educated elite's comments on the failure of the cooperatives, fishers are construed as immature, as egoists, and as being non-social. Advocating a positivist vision of scientific objectivism has been done in opposition to Islam and tradition. For the Kemalist elite the whole project of modernization/Westernization/nationalism depended upon this vision of science. Therefore, when marine scientists in Trabzon go to such lengths in order to present their knowledge as objective, the institutional context of their statements is not only science proper, but the larger project of Turkish modernization. To admit to a flaw in the scientific set-up of a concrete project may amount to opening the door for extensive critique of the Turkish modernization project and thereby the authority of the educated elite. In the metropolis of Istanbul, and among the students and the intellectual elite, there may have been a tendency to give way on this rigid conception of science and modernization. But in the provinces this combining of positivist science, Turkish modernization, and educated elite still remains in force. But how is this framework actually worked and drawn upon in interactions between marine scientists and fishers? Do the fishers passively succumb to such discourse?

## An Unwelcome Memur

Although fishers and educated elite share some codes of conduct, for example, as pertaining to hospitality (see Chapter 7), the different language styles, kinds of training and dissimilar interests can make interaction problematic. In the spring of 1998 Ömer, one of the researchers at TFRI, came to a regular sampling visit to Çarşıbaşı. I was at sea, lifting whiting nets with Keremköy fishers Metin and his father, when he arrived early in the morning. When we tied up at the harbour, Ömer was already busy interviewing the fishers on another small fishing boat. We all assembled in the cabin of the boat Ömer had already boarded. I knew Ömer and all the fishers fairly well, and they knew me. I kept a low profile and said almost nothing, feeling somewhat ill at ease with this unusual double set of allegiances. Ömer and the fishers did not know each other. The encounter had a very businesslike character, though tea was served. Ömer stressed that he had a *form* that he was to fill in. The *form* contained issues relating to fishing activity, gear and catch. He first filled in the form for Metin, which was largely a fairly straightforward business. But there were some misunderstandings. Ömer asked whether they had used *uzatma* nets. This left the fishers confused. The fishers usually apply this term to the long, floating gillnets, normally wide meshed, that they use to catch bonito and other large pelagic fish. They do not use uzatma to catch whiting. 'Did not this man even know what nets catch what kinds of fish?' However, the term uzatma is used differently among scientists. For them it is a generic that includes all kinds of common passive nets that are set straight, including the bottom nets that are used to capture whiting. Further confusion arose when Metin was telling that they also were dredging for *midye* ('mussel', the concept most fishers in Trabzon use to denote sea snail). Ömer did not understand this at first, and they could only proceed after they had agreed that they were talking about *deniz salyangozu* ('sea snail').

Filling in the form for the other boat proved much more difficult. Ömer had seen the plastic bags on deck filled with fish such as whiting, flounder and turbot, and had written on his form that they had been fishing with molozma (a 'catch all' bottom trammel net, see Chapter 5). It was evident to me, however, that they had been trawling illegally. Otter boards (*kapı*, 'door', to keep the trawl open) and the trawl net were stuffed away somewhere out of sight. But the rigging and the coils of thick rope on deck clearly showed what they had been up to (they could have been dredging for sea snails, but that season had not started yet). Most of the catch probably had already been dispatched to Trabzon. The fishers were very vague when giving information, preferring to answer in the general and not giving details about that night's trip. The fishers clearly saw him as a state representative, and did not perceive any difference between him and those policing the fishing. Neither did Ömer clarify his own position. A young fisher addressed Ömer. 'Did you ask us whether we have got bread at home?' Although this is a very common expression of poverty among fishers and other 'villagers', Ömer did not understand, and the young man had to explain that 'We stay hungry (*aç kalıyoruz*)'. I had known this young man since he was a boy. He comes from one of the poorest families in Çarşıbaşı and took up fishing very early on to earn some money. He was now working as crew. Although he probably did not lack bread at home, he was nonetheless 'justified' in raising the question. As a response, Ömer stressed that they had to think about tomorrow.

Other small-boat fishers arrived, and the encounter soon developed into a tirade of complaints, focusing especially on the harmful nature of the sonar. After a little while Ömer turned sour and shut off the discussion. Instead he directed attention to a more immediate concern: the fish on the deck. He politely requested (*rica ediyorum*) samples from the 'molozma' catch, but the fishers claimed that they had put it aside for a friend. After some discussion about this Ömer was fed up: 'Now it's enough! I must use some of my bureaucratic authority (*memur emrim*).' He then, after some more haggling, got the larger of the two bags.

As was evident in Mustafa's dealings during the survey in Samsun and Sinop (Chapter 7), owners of the largest family fishing companies, cooperative leaders, water produce factory owners, as well as large kabzımal often have some extended interaction with state representatives.

For most fishers, however, including the small-boat fishers in the case above, the presence of the state fishery bureaucracy and marine science representatives in their daily life is negligible. That partly explains why, when meeting a water produce memur, they are so eager to present their complaints and questions to the 'state'. They also feared that he could be an agent of supervision. But complaints were not what the 'state' wanted to hear. Ömer's agenda was different. The encounter was also suffused with misunderstandings because Ömer and the fishers use different terminology and have dissimilar language styles. The encounter reinforced existing antagonisms: the 'water produce memur' did not know his business, the fishers are cahil.

In discussing the sugar contracts between the state factories and villagers in nearby Erzurum, Catherine Alexander points out that the agricultural engineers who represent the factory 'would enact familiar roles of respect to facilitate the sense of intimacy … [and] visit some farmers for lunch, or take their wives with them, all of which encouraged the farmers to trust them as individuals rather than faceless representatives of the factory.' That the Erzurum villagers speak of the engineers with great affection and respect was due to the engineers showing respect to village custom and hierarchies and to the farming origin of all the engineers (Alexander 2002: 199).

Although water produce bureaucrats and scientists may occasionally develop friendships with fishers in the intimacy of a teahouse or *gazino* (nightclub) during surveys, the close and intimate interaction between state representatives and villagers that Alexander describes is hardly found in the fisheries. For the most part state water produce representatives do not depend on continued interaction with the fishers. The fisheries, to an extent greater than agriculture, constitute an alien physical context: it is less accessible, involves more travel, lacks regulated work hours, and so forth. Few water produce *memur*s can capitalize on some shared occupational or (quasi-) lifestyle background with fishers. This difference is exacerbated by the lack of a local fisheries bureaucracy. While there are no water produce officials living or working in Çarşıbaşı, there is an office for agricultural affairs at the District Administration in İskefiye, and agricultural engineers mingle with and befriend the local population in kahves in the town. The water produce bureaucrat is not a 'familiar face', not a friend to tease.

## Fishers' Response: 'We are Unconscious, They are Corrupt'

Fishers are aware of the accusations levelled against them that they are cahil. How do they relate to this discourse, how do they respond? What accusations do they make? At one level they partly internalize the discourse and accept that fishers, in general, are cahil. Small-boat fishers in Keremköy told me that 'Since the fisher lacks education, he does not think about the future'. One old fisher in Trabzon city explained to me that fishers could not cooperate because of lack of reason (*akıl yok*). He maintained that there was no solidarity (*dayanışma*), no belief in each other because of ignorance (*birbirine inanç yok, cahillikten*).

Does this internalization of the elite discourse close the possibility of alternative views? No, but they may be muted somewhat in certain contexts. Rather than accepting that they are *cahil*, most fishers tend to say that they behave bilinçsiz ('unconsciously'). It has been a challenge for me to understand the import of this widely used concept. In many contexts it seems to be used synonymously with cahil. However, bilinçsiz is often explained as 'not thinking about the future' (*geleceği düşünmemek*) and being irresponsible (*sorumlusuz*). Thus, a man behaves bilinçsiz when he knows that trawling is harmful, but still does it. The capacity to be *bilinçli* (conscious, have foresight) is most often seen as a kind of knowledge, primarily emanating from education. For fishers, however, *bilinçli* can lose its association with book knowledge. Once when I was at sea lifting turbot nets with a small boat fisher from Keremköy we were discussing turbot behaviour and positioning of nets. He stressed that 'the sea cannot be learned from books, only when doing the practice. But you will have to be bilinçli when doing the practice.'

In this native discourse, reason and reflection are seen as possible without extensive schooling. However, underlying this may be an idea that there is a difference between the 'practical' knowledge (tecrübe) and the knowledge that they are aware of, the reflexive knowledge that they can reason about. And, it is this last kind of knowledge that can be elaborated and extended in formal education. In Chapter 8 I argued that fishers tend to stress a model of knowledge that gives priority to experience (tecrübe) and externalization in terms of body metaphors. Yet, as came out in Hakan' hamsi narrative (Chapter 4), when fishers articulate their knowledge and their models of knowledge they switch back and forth from a model derived from scriptural or bookish definition of knowledge (*bilgi*) to an alternative model of knowledge (tecrübe, body metaphors). The effort at appropriation or redefinition to legitimize their own skills and knowledges is apparent in the following account. I was talking with some of my fishers friends in Keremköy about the scientists' knowledge and we touched on the concept of *alim* – the old Ottoman-Arabic concept for being educated, being a scholar – which they found to be a good characterization of fishers' broad and general knowledge. They illustrated this with what they called an 'old saying': 'As there emerge cahil people from among the educated, there emerge alim from among the uneducated.' This proverb is by all accounts a simplified version of one of Atatürk's famous sayings:

When we say cahil, then we are not talking about those who have not read in the *mektep* [school]. What we talk about is to know *ilim*, the truth. Otherwise, as the most *cahil* may emerge from among the educated, there may emerge from among those who cannot read at all real alims that can see the truth.

While this saying was originally a critique directed against the religious scholars ('those who have read in the *mektep*s'), the fishers use the very same proverb to shatter the authority of the secular scientists. Yet, despite this willingness to criticize the hegemonic discourse on knowledge, fishers regularly claimed that they engaged in unwanted practices because they were bilinçsiz or cahil. I had some trouble understanding this. For instance, most big-boat fishers are accustomed to bookkeeping and bureaucratic procedures, and most fishers have a fair idea of how a cooperative ideally should work. Moreover, fishers knew better than anyone that the processes of competition, capitalization, technological development, and so forth lead to overfishing, diminishing resources, and in the long run, 'ruin' for all.[86] I saw a paradox: since they could articulate this, they were conscious (i.e. 'bilinçli') of it after all. I presented this paradox to one of the reflective (but not very educated) among the younger small-boat fishers who very explicitly said that trawling is harmful and that he did not like to do the illegal small-boat trawling that he and his brothers sometimes undertook. He said that fishers being cahil was the reason for previous overfishing, that it is responsible for the difficult situation that they have run into. Now, however, it is poverty (*aç*, 'hunger') that forces them to illegal practices such as trawling. I often heard the claim made by fishers that aç led them to bilinçsiz fishing. They construct the bilinçsiz fishing as a situation that has been forced upon them. Perhaps bilinçli/bilinçsiz is used to characterize actions, while cahil is a characterization of the person, of a lifestyle, a mode of being in the world? Fishers often admit to being bilinçsiz but generally deny being cahil. They say that they are 'forced' to behave bilinçsiz by circumstances.

One day during the spring of 1998 I visited the village Akçakale between Çarşıbaşı and Trabzon. The fishers there did not know me, but after I had presented myself to some men outside of a kahve, a group of mostly small-boat fishers quickly gathered around me, as in so many other places I had visited. During the (taped) conversation many topics pertaining to fishing were raised, such as sonar, dolphins, adas, and so on. They also discussed how the rich manage to get laws changed, for example by prolonging the season for sea-snail fishing.

- This government is a corrupt (yiyici) government. The sea snails bring dollars, the prohibitions are not logical, the punishments (*ceza*) too lenient, but the government closes their eyes.

- The fishers should show respect for the prohibitions (*yasaklara saygılı olmalı*). If the government had wanted, it could have caught both [they were talking about specific but unnamed corrupt rich men in the fishing business].

...

- The fishers sector is generally cahil. Such things [illegal trawling, dredging for sea snails] are being done. Wherever a man sees profits…in other words one is chasing after the profits.

- That's it, There is no law (*Kanun*), the punishments are too low.

- The coast guard controls, but it cannot take the man, it's not possible.

- All the faults lie with the 'water produce'.

Ståle: Who do you mean, the scientists?

- Yes, the researchers. Those people that make the laws of the sea. They do not manage to put it right.

- The control bureaucrat (*kontrol memur*).

Ståle: Well then, not the researchers?

- Both researcher and control.

- They do it themselves, those men do both research, for instance, and according to that make the laws (*kanunları*).

- They even give the punishments. Anyway, there is no research. Research takes place on shore, not at sea. They are afraid of the sea.

- If you go to them with a kilo of fish, its OK (*tamam*) [i.e., bribe].

- There is the *red mullet* [remember that this is a very prestigious fish]. If you give one case of it, everything is fine (*her şey tamam*). 'I did not see you', 'I was not here'.

…

- There is the system, the system. It makes the rich (*zengin*) rich, the poor (*fakir*) poor.

- There is a plain word for Turkey: torpil. The one who sees to the business of the rich (*Türkiyenin açıkçası var ya. Torpil. Zenginin işi yürür*).

- Prohibited means prohibited for the poor, for the rich there is no prohibition.

- They all receive everything on a silver platter. Take, eat. (*Hep hazırcı oldu. Al, ye*)

…

- Do you know who does not comply with the laws? The big fishers do not comply. The small fishers always comply. … Who does not comply with the laws here? The rich ones, the persons with education (*tahsil*), persons in politics even. … Not the cahil ones, the learned ones (*okumuş*) do not comply. That's the condition of Turkey. The man of the cahil society (*toplum*) complies in every respect (*her yol uyar*).

…

- In our Turkey, the cahil ones are the rich.

- Those you call cahil are those who do not comply with the law (*kanun*), is that a lie? But all the poor ones here always comply, because they are afraid.

The 'legitimate' hunger, as articulated by the young fisher in the encounter with the unwelcome memur, is often implicitly contrasted with the morally suspect 'eating' by those with money and/or positions who do not comply with the laws. As was alluded to towards the end of Chapter 6, according to the fishers the most striking and pervasive characteristic of the elite is that it is corrupt, yiyici. While ethnographies set in Turkey have paid some attention to bribery and torpils, I have seen no mention of the idioms of 'eating' and 'eater'. Yet, in my experience it is a very widespread figure of speech. It was certainly common when I did my first fieldwork in 1990–91, and issues such as *mafya, yiyicilik* ('eating', i.e. corruption), have for many years been standard topics in the national media.

The concern about the yiyicilik has become so pervasive, so widespread and shared, that it can effectively be drawn upon by ads on television. In an ad for an insurance company insurance is explicitly contrasted with bribery and the ad ends with a man looking into an aquarium with fish and saying 'now *gluk-gluk* remains only here'. The gluk-gluk is onomatopoetic for swallowing and a common way to express 'eating' (*yemek*), thereby a metaphor for yiyicilik. It is also common to invoke the saying that 'Big fish always eat the small fish'. 'That's how nature and the world (*dünya*) is', says one old fisher, 'everyone, from politicians downwards, "eats".' Accusations of yiyicilik are not directed only towards state representatives, but towards businessmen and others that 'eat' the produce or toil of others, such as big fishers and factory owners, especially those who are seen to have close connections with politicians. It is very common, as expressed in the conversation in Akçakale, to say that the 'big men' do not comply with the laws, and connect this to the prevalence of yiyicilik. Small-boat fishers in Keremköy claim that there is no point in cooperating or having a leader because everything is directed towards politics (*siyasi amaçlı*) and based on money-power (*para gücü*). In Eynesil, a community where all small-boat fishers oppose illegal trawling, the fishers assert that there is no point in filing a lawsuit against those that they sometimes capture trawling in 'their' waters. The trawlers will be protected by 'big men'. Corruption (*yedirme*) and bribes (*rüşvet*) will 'solve' the case. They cannot police the waters near Eynesil themselves because, they say, they would be accused of being a band of rebels (*çete*), which is illegal.

Fishers often disclaim the scientific knowledge on the ground that when there is so much yiyicilik and *politika*, knowledge does not count. Sometimes the scientists themselves are accused of being 'eaters', but on a minor scale. The 'eating' can be very literal, as when the water produce officials are offered red mullet as an appeasement. It is also said to be common to bring the 'water produce', or inspectors (*müfettiş*), coming to inspect factories, to a good lokanta and offer them a meal. What Mustafa and Yaşar (see Chapter 7) may see as tokens of hospitality and generosity can alternatively be interpreted as bribes. The ambivalence of friendships between intimacy and instrumentality provides space for interpretation.

Similar metaphors of 'eating' have been used in many societies, from India, to medieval Russia and the Ottoman Empire, and generally connote greed, corruption, appropriation and bribery.[87] A few prominent ethnographies from the eastern Mediterranean indicate that 'eating' may be a fairly common figure of speech in the region. Herzfeld (1985) portrays how Cretan mountain dwellers demonstrate manhood through stealing, articulated by the metaphor of 'eating'. Gilsenan (1996) emphasizes that in Lebanon the wealthy and powerful ones are those who 'know how to eat', to 'eat' others. While the metaphors of 'appetite' and 'eating' are used to explain the success of the powerful on the Lebanese Marches, among the mountain Cretans 'hunger' is used to legitimate the deprived ones' 'eating'. However, in both cases hunger and eating seem to be part of a 'poetics of manhood'. And the 'eating' is at the expense of others, it is 'consuming' others.

In Turkey 'eating' is also seen as an integral part of being or becoming powerful and rich and behaving 'powerful-like'. But contrary to its use in Crete and Lebanon, 'eating' has mostly negative connotations in contemporary Turkey. The idiom of 'hunger', on the other hand, is – as in Crete – used to give legitimacy to actions. When the young fisher in the encounter with the scientist stated that 'We remain hungry' he legitimized his involvement in illegal trawling. In both Turkey and Crete the discourse about 'eaters' and 'hunger' is intertwined with people's regrets about the violation of friendship bonds, the moral failure of the leaders, the increasing individualism and egoism, and the commoditization of social relations.

## Politics, Pollution and Morals

Keyder claims that the way the state and the economy were restructured in Turkey during the 1980s and 1990s enlarged the scope for corruption, particularly for turning political position into economic advantage (Keyder 1999: 21).While corruption and the like had been the subject of nationwide discourse in Turkey for a long time, these topics received especially focused attention in the second half of the 1990s. The 1996 Susurluk scandal (see end of Chapter 6) more than ever before put corruption on the national agenda. It resulted in the huge 'civil society' campaign 'One minute of darkness for enlightenment' (*Aydınlık için bir dakika karanlık*). In all the major cities during early 1997 people shut off the lights for one minute.

In the spring of 1998 I had a long informal conversation with a fisher about fish and fishing. Towards the end he criticized the corrupt and immoral MPs for using their positions to enrich themselves and keep lovers, for not working, not making new laws. When we finally rose from the pier within the harbour, he reflectively commented on our conversation: 'We started at sea and ended up on politics.' This reflects a very common conception: 'Everything is politics.' One of my fellow hikers, a young mid level memur, during a day's hike in the Kaçar Mountains south of Trabzon, told me that the hiking was so fine; it helped him to reduce the level of stress and tension. I though he meant being away from traffic, busy work schedules etc., but he stressed that it felt so good to get away from politika, since 'everything is politics'. And politics are, of course, to a large degree about moralities. It is not only that so much is political. Politics were during the 1990s increasingly perceived as a 'dirty' activity: MPs care only for their own wealth as they use their position to 'turn the corner'; politics, corruption, and Mafia activities are blended; and the politicians' elite manners are suspect. A 1994 newspaper cartoon in *Milliyet*, one of the major daily newspapers, shows a 'politician' turning the 'corner' of a building while an obviously pitiable man, the 'people', is squeezed into the corner.

The rhetoric of corruption is a discourse most people can share in without regard for political position, whether they are Islamists, secularists or nationalists. On one level, accusations of corruption are accusations of impurity, of moral defilement. Many issues of lifestyles and morals involve some idea of cleanness and pollution. Concerns about alcohol or refined manners, to name a few, address moral standards and social borders. Knowledges are also framed by this, since they are not usually separated from the 'knowers'. A scientist must be socially and morally acceptable in order to 'be right' in the eyes of colleagues and others. Consequently, both parts construe the other's (lack of) knowledge as connected to the other's lack of moral virtues', be it their lack of education or 'social training', or their immoral consumption and corruption. And their respective rhetoric styles have little persuasive force with the 'other'.

In Chapter 5 and Chapter 6 I sketched some of the more prevalent models for morality and ethical know-how in fishing communities in Çarşıbaşı. Generally, models may constitute very concrete alternatives of interpretation in many contexts. 'Ignorance' and 'corruption' are only two of many possible moral models that actors can draw on in identifying and characterizing others. There is for instance the *devlet baba* (father state) model, where the 'father' both provides for but also directs and punishes his 'sons'. In fishers' discourses about knowledges and illegal fishing this comes out in expressions such as 'The state must enforce prohibitions. That's education! (*Devlet yasak koysun. O eğitim!*).' On the other hand, defying the state through smuggling (rampant during the 1970s) and possession of guns, as well as small-boat illegal trawling, can be articulated as claims to manhood in the Black Sea region.

The accusations of ignorance or corruption may be a logical consequence of scientific objectivism and bureaucratic rationality and is likely typical for modern nation states (Herzfeld 1992: 164), including Turkey. But although there may be structural similarities, I believe that in each nation state the rhetoric is differently constituted and coloured. With the propensity to denigrate 'villagers' as cahil, scripturalism – according texts a higher truth-value than other techniques of articulation due to the fetishisation of writing (e.g., Goody 1987: 299) – attains a very central position in the Turkish elite's articulation of their privileged status. Because the elite themselves to such an extent integrate scripturalism with other elite ideals and practices (good manners, language, refined taste, etc. – a whole lifestyle in essence) attacking bureaucrats' and scientists' moralities, manners and lifestyles, such as their consumption patterns (e.g., Istanbul seafood culture), becomes a feasible and pertinent criticism. Hence, one of the most frequently heard criticisms that fishers direct at scientists (and water produce bureaucrats) is that 'They only know how to eat the fish!' Once during a meeting at the Ministry offices in Ankara in the mid 1990s, I was told, one fisher held up a 'Russian' mullet – the new, introduced species – and yelled at the minister directing the meeting: 'Do you know what fish this is? No, you only know how to eat it!' This is a kind of critique I very frequently heard fishers expressing. During the conversation at Akçakale I asked whether the 'water produce' sometimes come there to do research:

> There came someone on our boat, students probably. Those people do not know the fish. You know there are poisonous fish here, scorpion fish, stingray. Well, about the *tekir* [very similar to the red mullet] a man asks if it strikes men. The tekir! Only think, the state of the 'water produce' is not good … ['everybody' knows that tekir is not poisonous].

Fishers in other countries (see, e.g., Pálsson 1991: 152) make similar claims about politicians and bureaucrats. But in Turkey, such a critique is especially weighty. It sums up several of the distinctions fishers draw between themselves and the politico-bureaucratic or scientific elite: (1) the memur knows only how to eat the fish: he does not know the practice of catching it. He has no bodily experience, no substantial knowledge. His knowledge is only 'pretence'. He is not even competent according to science's own standards (a scientists should know that the tekir is not poisonous); (2) the only way the memur knows the fish is through 'immoral' Istanbul-style consumption (with its associations with alcohol etc.); (3) the expression harbours a claim that the memur is an 'eater', he is corrupt.

Styles of fish and seafood consumption practice thus constitute one context that defines relations between fishers and state representatives. The bureaucrats and scientists alike are state agents who aspire to the upper-class Istanbul culture, including the culture of seafood, but are simultaneously entrusted with the implementation of a program of fisheries development, which in its emphasis on proteins and universal/national consumption goes against their own subjective experiences with seafood, namely the culinary pleasure (not the proteins) and the exclusiveness. It is not uncommon to hear water produce bureaucrats expressing a greater interest in how fish tastes than in fisheries policies. The marine scientists are among the agents, the engineers, of the modernizing efforts in the fisheries, but they continue to express their class position, or their status – their refinedness and so forth – by, among other things, associating with the Istanbul way of eating fish and demonstrating elite manners. While being, or aspiring to be, among the privileged seafood 'eaters', they simultaneously try to develop Turkey into a country of common 'fish eaters'. This puts water produce scientists and bureaucrats in a peculiar position at the intersection of two seemingly incompatible discourses: the one is a discourse of development and egalitarianism, its aim being the ideal of a culturally uniform Turkish people; the other is a discourse of sophisticated social praxis and hierarchy, the civilized, Istanbul style, the gentlemanly (*efendi*) manners, which has been partly excluded from ideological formulations of 'Turkishness'.[88] The gap is, I believe, partly bridged by the civilizing or educating mission the state elite accords itself, but it also makes the elite exposed to critique.

Yet, what does the discourse of 'hunger' and 'eating' do or effect? Is it 'only talk'? Such rhetoric is not the only way of expressing hostility or dislike of those in/with power: as mentioned towards the end of Chapter 6 'big men' may be criticized for trying to become aga and make all the rest 'slaves' (*köle*); and criticism may be raised against acts of violence. Through the discourse about 'hunger' and 'eaters' fishers and others construct an alternative frame of reference. Much the same can be said about the moral discourse engaged by fishers when criticizing state elites and others for their 'Istanbul ways'. It is a discourse that sets up a moral hierarchy of social honour where the standards of lifestyle, scripturalism, wealth, and so on are side-stepped, but not overturned. It is thus significant that while these idioms articulate 'symbolic or ideological resistance' (Scott 1986: 22), none of them seem to stimulate any kind of social mobilization, organized and collective acts of opposition, except being channelled into support for political parties and organized Islam.

Although not effecting collective acts of resistance, this rhetoric may be enough to create contexts in daily life in which the speaker can be in control or experience moral superiority, as when the purse-seine boat owner quietly admitted that the sonar is harmful (Chapter 8). Such discourse may create spaces of experienced moral community among the 'suppressed', where everyday practices can be framed by local poetics and ethical sensibilities that make them meaningful. It is as if people say: 'If we are not rich and powerful, we are at least decent and honourable.'

Furthermore, this rhetoric about 'eaters' and the like gives legitimacy to individual 'acts of resistance', such as illegal small-boat trawling (which is, of course, not only resistance). People often say things in the vein of, 'Why should we stick to the laws when we are "hungry", and the "eaters" do not comply with the laws?' However, such acts, as well as the resistance to the sonars, contribute to reinforce the educated ones' stereotypes of the 'common man' as being cahil and 'vulgar' (*kaba*). They thereby work to uphold the social barrier between different kinds of 'knowers'.

## Islam, Tradition and Modernity

The issues of corruption and ignorance are more fundamental in some respects than the Islam versus the West discourse. If I had started out with Islam-West as my primary analytical focus I may not have been able to recognize this. It is not Islam 'in itself' that comes to the fore or is the major concern for most people. But Islam constitutes a 'ready package' of embodied symbols and historical-moral legitimacy that can be mobilized to create a shared, objectified language out of 'individual' ethical sensibilities, to articulate concerns about morality in a situation of rapid social change. Interestingly, the main election slogan of the Islamist Welfare Party in 1996 was 'Just Order' (*Adil Düzen*), and not some more explicit Islamic rhetoric. The following case will bring out more nuances in the complex relations among state, modernity, Turkishness, Islam, the West, ignorance, custom and so forth.

Many places in the eastern Black Sea region, the beginning of summer has been marked by sea rituals that were sometimes codified as *hıdrellez* (a common spring ritual throughout Turkey), but more commonly as *Mayıs yedisi*.[89] It is claimed that the festival in Giresun builds on a 4000-year-long tradition (*Anadolu Ajansı* 20 May 1999: 'Karadeniz'de festival coşkusu'), and both Muslims and Christians probably participated side by side in these festivals. In 1998 I observed the ritual in Beşikdüzü together with fisher friends who went there to earn money by ferrying passengers in their boats. People were taken out to the sacred place where those wishing for fertility or health would throw some coins into the water. Notably, most of the participants were women and children from the inland. Almost no one from the coastal region attended it. Many claimed that it is improper to participate in the festival since it is a Rum affair, and attendance has decreased. For many this day had become just an occasion for joy and travel (*gezme*), and my fisher friends played down its symbolic importance. But I did note a certain tendency to join the celebration if one had constructed a new boat – to ensure its 'fertility'? Many believe in the health-giving power of the seawater collected here on this occasion and collect some to sprinkle on cattle, houses and so on.[90] The ritual is especially thought to be good for women who want to become pregnant. It is clearly a fertility ritual. Many of these people only get close to the seawater on this occasion each year. Unlike the Black Sea *yayla* (summer mountain pasture) festivities and the 'Istanbul' seaside, these sea festivals seem to have no association with alcohol, or the elite for that matter. The festivities were carried out without any kind of formal organization.

During the sea festival on 20 May 2000 two small fishing boats from Çarşıbaşı that carried people to the hollow stone (*delikli taş*) that gives luck and secures fertility, capsized. The boats were overloaded and thirty-eight people died. The Minister of Law, Hikmet Sami Türk, visited the Beşikdüzü Kaymakamlık (state office at district level) together with many other high-ranking state officials. The minister, who represented the Democratic Left Party, the party of Ecevit, stressed that 'one of the primary reasons for the tragedy was empty beliefs (*boş inançlar*) that stemmed from cehalet. We should not give permission to fishing boats carrying passengers. It is also necessary for us to enlighten the citizens' (Alhan 2000; *Cumhuriyet Gazetesi* 2000).

The ritual was banned for one year. Thereafter the state representatives took control of the festivities.[91] It was recast as the three-days-long Beşikdüzü Festival of Culture, Art and Sea (*Kültür Sanat ve Deniz Festivali*). It explicitly became a state-organized event: all members in the organizing committee, which was created for the new festival, are head of state institutions; there is a procession starting and ending at important state

**Figure 10.1. 'Seventh of May' sea festival.** Village women boarding small fishing boats from Çarşıbaşı during the 1998 sea festival in Beşikdüzü. For a negotiated small fee the women are taken out to the 'hollow stone' where many fetch water that they use to cure illnesses and secure fertility.

buildings; there is an official dinner given to state representatives and other important personae (*protokol yemeği*); the district governor stresses that people should comply with laws and regulations at sea; the authorities sponsor a large number of circumcisions; and, crucially, the whole festival is merged with the important 19 May national children's holiday to celebrate the arrival of Atatürk to Samsun which is held to signal the start of the War of Independence.

The new festival includes a range of activities, including handicraft exhibition, football matches, Jeep safari, regional food exhibition, traditional dances, boat trips, and – most high profiled - an evening concert with famous Turkish artists. Some activities explicitly negate the image of cehalet: female beach volleyball, the donation of a library, the panel of *hoca*s ('learned ones') that discuss the tradition. Above all, the expulsion of cehalet is expressed by the failure to explicitly mention the hollow stone. There is simultaneously a tendency to move the focus from the sea to the shore: many press reports stress that the tradition of washing the cows before taking them to the yayla is reinvigorated.

Thus, rather than being a secular and bureaucratic critique of 'traditional Islamic practices', the accusation of fishers' and sea festivals participants' ignorance is a shared secular-Islamic scholarly, textual, idealistic state-sponsored slap on 'backward rural practices and beliefs'. The cultivated critique of undesired practices in society is not necessarily directed towards 'Islamic practices', but rather addresses 'tradition' as the problem. The state enforced transformation of the Seventh of May festivity in Beşikdüzü into a tightly choreographed 'modern' festival demonstrates that science, Islam, Turkishness and state symbols are increasingly all articulated simultaneously in state efforts to transform local practices steeped in 'ignorance'.

In Parliament discussions a Nationalist Action Party MP from Trabzon answered to reactions to the tragedy which focused on the prevalence of 'empty beliefs' and cehalet among the Black Sea population (GNAT 2000):

> As much as the loss of lives, another thing has upset people in this region. To claim the cultural values of these people to be false belief, superstition (*batıl inanç, hurafe*) offends both people in the region as well the souls of the dead. Of these one-hundred per cent literate people no-one believes that one will have a child by passing below the hollow stone; these people give that much value to science that they know that the sick become healed by the help of medical science, not by seawater. Nevertheless, in a program televised yesterday evening, Black Sea people (*Karadenizli*) were accused for being unbelievers ('godless'), (*Allah'a şirk koşmakla suçlamak*). This is really the biggest injustice that can be done to the people in the region. ... As much as they know that the dead will be treated as martyrs before Allah, they know and live our glorious (*yüce*) religion.

This MP is very careful to distinguish superstition from Islam, cehalet from Islam. He also stresses the importance of education and science. There is, however, not agreement concerning what kind of education Turkey should have. It is a hotly contested cultural arena. Moreover, Islamist thinkers, and the Islamist discourse in general, have not given up on the concept of cahil. Some Muslim intellectuals write about the modern, secular way of life as a return to the cahiliyet (see Meeker 1994).

The MP's statement also indicates that the state is not alone in articulating a Turk-Islamic synthesis purified of superstition and 'Greekness' (Rum). In the Black Sea region Turkishness has, as I argued in the history of seafood consumption in Trabzon (Chapter 2), become closely associated with Islamic morals. And while the Trabzon fish food culture could be accused of being 'unmodern' and uncivilized, the new 'meat and fish' establishments are distinctly modern, Turkish, and accommodating to Islam

Istanbul Seafood culture is dirty because of its associations with Rum, alcohol and the corrupt elite. At the other end of the scale the 'traditional' Seventh of May ritual came to be seen as dirty since it was seen as based upon ignorance, superstition and Rum traditions. Interestingly, the new Beşikdüzü Festival of Culture, Art and Sea and the 'meat and fish' establishment articulate very similar symbols: modern Muslim Turkish middle-class leisure culture. Both are expressive of a new, increasingly standardized, seaside leisure culture which also finds expression in the new seaside parks created in front of many of the larger Black Sea cities since the mid 1990s. The new 'meat and fish' establishments are often located in such seaside-park environments.

The potency of the lifestyle symbolism becomes particularly important in Turkey since the state has had a very authoritarian approach to lifestyle articulations and attempted to develop a homogenous, 'modern' lifestyle with such zeal. The state may have become less authoritative in this respect during the last two decades, but the Beşikdüzü Sea Festival case demonstrates that state representatives still see it as their role to 'guide' people's lifestyle choices. And, although the development of 'meat and fish' may seem to be based solely upon 'popular' culture, there are indications that this is not that straightforward. At a time when the moderately islamist Justice and Development Party controlled central government, a leading figure in the party in Samsun contacted a fish dealer with a request for the establishment of a civilized, non-alcoholic family seafood restaurant.

In the Turkish version of modernism/nationalism little credit was given to 'living' traditions, practices, and codes. Official discourse and ideology did idealize tradition, but as a particular kind of imagined tradition, which has been articulated by many as a search for and desire to reinvent pre-Islamic traditions (cf. Gökalp). This ideology has not left much room for legitimizing current local practices by claiming them to be 'custom'. Islam was excluded because of its presumed lack of rationality, because it put

234 | *Fishers and Scientists in Modern Turkey*

'belief' above 'knowledge'. With the Turkish-Islamic Synthesis[92] the pre-Islamic tradition has to a large extent been replaced by 'universal' Sunni Islam, while the 'local' mahalle culture remains suspect. Local 'living' custom is, as is the 'Seventh of May' ritual in Beşikdüzü, seen either as backward tradition or as superstition (*batıl inançlar*).

The lack of room for local custom in the Turkish modernization project is one reason why there is no grounding for trying to legitimize local practices and custom as IK or TEK. The other reason is the sensitivity surrounding identity and minority issues in Turkey; there are no 'indigenous peoples' in Turkey. The First National Reports to The Convention on Biological Diversity were required to address the issue of traditional knowledge. Under the heading of 'Traditional Knowledge', all the First Turkish National Report (MARA and MOF 1997) has to say about this issue is: 'Strategic Action: Identify mechanisms to use traditional knowledge, innovations and practices with the involvement of the holders of such knowledge and practices, and encourage the equitable sharing of benefits.' This is an exact rephrasing of the Convention text and the report provides no further detail. Many other countries provide much more detail and demonstrate more dedication concerning support for 'traditional knowledge'.

The Republican State has not acknowledged the existence of local 'traditional' institutions, local culture and structures of cooperation, let alone fishers' knowledges or TEK. Yet, would a change in policy that identified fishers' knowledges as TEK or IK be epistemologically and politically sound? If I had chosen to limit my analytical framework to TEK/IK (in implicit or explicit opposition to science) I might very well not have been able to explore many important aspects of knowledge in Turkish fisheries. I therefore claim that in exploring the conditions under which management of natural resources takes place in a globalizing world it is insufficient to limit the framework for the study of resource users', managers' and other stakeholders' knowledge to the dichotomous design of science versus IK/TEK. Reliance on this simplified matrix (1) causes much knowledge to remain invisible; (2) constitutes scientific knowledge and technology as acultural and 'neutral'; (3) focuses attention on cultural aspects of local knowledge, IK, TEK and the like while ignoring history, context and power; and (4) obscures relations between science and other knowledge. This last issue includes the way knowledges interact and are intertwined, how science has depended upon and absorbed (other) local knowledges, and the way other (non-Western) scriptural traditions relate complexly with both science and local vernacular traditions (Tambiah 1990; Ellen and Harris 2000).

The research agenda of CPR has also been criticized for ignoring history, the social construction of ideas (such as 'property') and identities (Agrawal 2003; C. Johnson 2004). I have here sought to portray fishers', scientists' and other stakeholders' knowledge as complex, dynamic and open traditions that interact and overlap within a context characterized by different subject positions, power arrangements and historical trajectories. Thus, I argue, for example, that not only the local knowledge of fishers and institutions and rules in CPR management, but also the larger historical and ideological context of Turkish Black Sea fisheries - as manifest in, for example, state modernization policies, the practice of marine science, even styles of seafood consumption - should be accounted for to explain the current management regime.

## Knowledges as Moralities

In philosophical approaches to knowledge it is eminently possible to solve the dilemma of objectivist realism versus extreme relativism by positing the existence of alternative realities. Different systems, or cultures, may have different criteria for belief or truth, but we are as human beings bound to some basic reality. Thus, for example, the 'internal realism' view of Hilary Putnam (1981) 'permits the existence of alternative, incompatible conceptual schemes. It is not a total relativism because of the limits placed on it by experience of the real world' (Lakoff 1987: 264). This is all very well, but in the real social world, knowledges, different 'internal realisms', are not separate systems (e.g., science versus indigenous knowledge) or 'realities', but meet in conflict, ignorance, exploitation, cooperation and sometimes with curiosity. Differences between knowledges are not only, or even primarily, on the level of principles, abstract concepts, and the like. There can be no pure epistemological/theoretical fusing of traditions of knowledge because no traditions of knowledge are made up only of theory and epistemology. Differences cannot be settled simply by seeking a theoretical solution, trying to establish a congruence of epistemologies, bridging the traditions, or making the incommensurable commensurable. If knowledge is embedded in practice, in individuals, in nature, society, language and body, there can only be practical-cum-theoretical working settlements or solutions. Therefore, knowledge will always be an issue of power, temporary settlements, and moralities. Most, if not all, kinds of knowledge are in some way or other bound up with, or at least not isolated from, ethical or moral coping, often as parts of larger projects or discourses (be it 'modernization' or the maintenance of moral integrity in the local community).

A hundred years ago it would have been totally irrelevant, even impossible, to ask about the knowledge differences between fishers and marine scientists in Turkey. In Turkey the sciences, and the associated scripturalism and literalism, are closely connected to the moral thrust of the national modernization project. Fishing is intimately bound up with social pragmatics that are inherently 'moral'. We should not be paralyzed by this insight, nor should we discredit knowledge in general. However, it may imply that we enlarge the scope of who is entitled to speak. But in so doing, there is reason for caution. The moral foundation of a 'clearing of the horizon' of knowledges (Lambek 1993) should not be sought in 'epistemologized' and 'technologized' ethical know-that, in moral rules and laws. People situated within different traditions of knowledge, whether marine scientist, bureaucrat, fisher or anthropologist, should be guided rather by ethical sensibilities. I believe that such an approach would make it easier to transcend the boundaries of reified entities such as laws, cultures, disciplines, schools, classes, and so on. However, to bring this about, it may be imperative to share practice and interact face to face. This sharing is not only in order to have similar experiences of an environment and to 'know the ways of the others', but also to know others intersubjectively, to engage in each other. This of course all sounds very idealistic, and it is. Huge barriers of instituted practice, accumulated mistrust, and conflicting interests must be overcome. One of the largest challenges is to develop an understanding of science as socially embedded and constituted without removing totally the credibility of science, without perceiving all scientific knowledge as false.

Such a reconstitution of science must address the dangers that lie in science's constant drive to objectify and reify knowledge, to purge it of all 'disturbing' associations. To frame the conflicts that we have observed as controversies over knowledge may be to succumb to the hegemonic scientific discourse of knowledge, a discourse that has elevated knowledge, 'sterilized' it, made it transcendental and non-subjective. To raise the question of knowledge in the first place, and have it as the main topic of this book, is of course a reflection of this. Statements about knowledge are legitimate within the historical-social context in which we are living. But the concerns of the people whom I met with and have written about here were not primarily sterile knowledge or truth. Rather, they were concerned about power, moral standing, the name or taste of a fish, love, the value of the catch, intimacy, sharing, and a host of other things. The conflicts are just as much about power, dignity and sociality as about knowledge. Therefore, to regard for example the implementation of a potential quota system in the fisheries as only a question of knowledge would be inadequate.

In an introductory chapter to an edited volume on *The Ethnography of Moralities*, Signe Howell (1997: 8-9) claims that most humans, even in the West, generally do not separate fact and value. 'Moral principles ... express simultaneously an inherent dynamic relationship between the "ought" and the "is".' She cites 'sex' and 'politics' as prime examples of entangled fact and value within the 'modern' world. The separation of value and fact is specific to science and a cornerstone of its credibility and cultural authority in society (Nader 1996: 25). Kirsten Hastrup (1995: 173), drawing on Putnam (1981), makes a comparable claim and ventures that '[W]ithout values we would have no facts, not even a world. We would also have no science.' She calls for the 'disengaged scientists' to be replaced by the 'scholar who achieves understanding by way of involvement.' Although Lambek (1997) does not explicitly discuss science, the thrust of his approach goes in much the same direction, especially in his elaboration of dynamic 'ethical know-how' (*phronesis*), although he is careful to distinguish analytically, as I do, ethical know-how from *techne* (or technique).

I have claimed that morality not only impinges upon knowledge, or knowledge not only becomes simply a resource in ethical or moral discourses. Knowledge is already ethically impregnated by being socially constituted. We may say that in engaged practice, technical and ethical know-how is very much intertwined, but when the practice is objectified, fact and value are purified into two different systems: epistemology and moral rules or discourse. Latour (1999) is similarly concerned with deconstructing a comparable dichotomy, namely 'knowledge' versus 'belief'. I have demonstrated that an understanding of 'the sonar', as engaged by the fishers and scientists, require us to situate it somewhere between 'belief' and 'knowledge', as well as 'ethics'. Latour (1999: 275) has suggested that in place of the concepts 'fetish' (i.e., belief) and 'fact' (i.e., knowledge), we speak of 'factish' since 'it is because it is constructed that it is so very real'. The sonar as I have described it is a typical 'factish': a collage of fact and fetish. But where did the 'ethics' go?

I have observed here that the very definition of knowledge (becoming familiar with things, people and events, which are distant) that Latour (1987: 220) uses, privileges a view from a distance. I would add here that this approach to knowledge leads to a preoccupation with truth and belief. This comes to be because Latour tries almost exclusively to understand scientific practice. His strategy is to focus on the facts, collectives, factishes – or simply the things – instead of centring the analysis on humans. A study of scientific knowledge as engaged in the lives of scientists (experiences, lifestyles, moralities) within a wider sociocultural and historical framework – as I have tried to pursue here – is necessary for a fuller understanding of the role of knowledge in society. Most, if not all, kinds of knowledge are in some way connected to, or at least not isolated from, ethical or moral coping, often as part of larger projects or discourses – be it 'modernization' or the maintenance of moral integrity in the local community. In these discourses lifestyle and tastes, as articulated in Turkish society at large, are central. I have shown how important education, breeding and literalism are in the lifestyle formation of scientists and how scientific knowledge is instrument and ideal in the nation state's move towards governmentality.

One implication of this 'governmentalization' and 'scientification' of the state's approach to development and modernization, has been, on the level of ideology, a separation of 'fact' and 'value'. In an article on the involvement of local, national, and international environmental organizations in a international rainforest campaign focused on Sarawak, East Malaysia, Peter Brosius (1999: 51) argues that the 'indifferent bureaucratic and technoscientific forms' of intervention by these institutions resulted in the exclusion of moral and political issues. He fears that there may be a 'danger of displacing the moral/political ... to such an extent that it is regarded as disruptive or irrelevant, or can no longer be heard at all.'

If we accept that value and fact are inseparable and that knowledge is socially constituted, questions like 'Who is the knower?' and 'Who are you that can claim to know?' will always be legitimate. In practice both fishers and scientists do ask such questions and evaluate the other's knowledge in the (moral) frameworks of education/ignorance and 'hunger'/'eaters' respectively. Fishers tend to see only (bad) morals, and scientists see only (wrong) facts (i.e., belief) in the other part. How could fishers and scientists come to 'ask' in a more 'symmetrical' manner? Sharing more practice, through which they by necessity have to relate more with one another as both moral and knowledgeable persons, is obviously one important step. Although there is relatively little interaction, there is - often unacknowledged - a certain extent of sharing: in the pragmatics of state fishery policy; in the exchange of support between scientist and fishers; in the politics of the sonar; in the reliance of scientific projects upon fishers' input; in the fishers' reference to scientific knowledge; and not least in roughly common codes of friendship, sharing, politeness, hospitality, and so forth.

What this study shows, however, is that most people evaluate others' knowledge based largely on the identity of the holder. While concrete projects - such as the need for fishers to employ sophisticated technology or the involvement of fishers in scientific research - bring them together, identity politics in effect pulls knowledges apart, creating a greater distance between them and exacerbating the dichotomy between science and other knowledges. This propensity to categorize knowledge on the basis of the identity of its holder makes knowledge politics very exposed to global discourses of knowledge, reducing local complexities to crude stereotypes.

There are parallels in the master narratives about identity and knowledge. The categorizations as both indigenous populations/natives and as IK/TEK are tools to manage heterogeneity, plurality and ambivalences in order to create order and stability. They define the normal/common versus the marginal/peripheral. Underneath this ripples problematic assumptions about evolutionary development of human societies. This demonstrates that the prevalent association of knowledges with crude identity labels is problematic. I contend, therefore, that knowledge should be analytically decoupled from universal identity labels such as 'scientific' and 'indigenous'. We should be careful and perhaps not combine 'indigenous' and 'knowledge' into one expression. Identity refers to the meaningful identification of self within a specific social category. Knowledge refers to humans' capacities, abilities and competences. We should not assume that there is necessarily congruence between traditions of knowledge and 'cultural' groups.

# Notes

1. For history of ecological anthropology, see Ellen 1982 and Moran 2000. For a classic monograph inspired by system ecology, see Rappaport 1968.
2. Concerning sources on seafood consumption, popular and elitist approaches to seafood and restaurants are, contrary to the Trabzon fish culture, relatively well represented and thus accessible in the swelling Turkish literature on leisure and the like. I have also learned much of what I know from fish traders and others involved in the retail sector. For the Trabzon fish culture I rely more heavily on my own field experiences.
3. Çelikkale et al. 1999: 245; *Yeni Şafak*, 11 March 2003; Oral 2002; Köse and Oğut 2004; Elliott et al. 1996.
4. Çelikkale et al. 1999: 245; *Yeni Şafak*, 11 March 2003; Köse and Oğut 2004; Elliott et al. 1996; Elbek et al. 1997; Bobat and Delioğlan 2001.
5. Elbek et al. 1997; Köse and Oğut 2004; Sarı et al. 2000.
6. http://www.aktuel.medya.com accessed on 10 November 1998.
7. Nevertheless, shark, skate and eel are not commonly served in the restaurants, and dolphin and seal are regarded as inedible.
8. The monthly salary of teachers in the spring of 1998 was around U.S.$400. A newly employed industrial worker would have a salary just over U.S.$200.
9. In the winter of 2004 fishmongers in Beyoğlu, Istanbul, sold large red mullet for U.S.$40/kg.
10. Peyami Safa, 1951, 'Balıkların Şâhı' (The Shah of the fish), *Hamsi* 4: 4. Reprinted in Yüksel 1989: 25.
11. For a very typical example of the popular association of fishers with Rum/Greeks, drinking, sex and Beyoğlu, see the novel *Deniz Küstü* by Yaşar Kemal (1992: 234).
12. The Greeks of the Ottoman Empire, eastern Greek.
13. With regard to literature, see Stone 1973: 55.
14. Personal communication Anh Nga Longva; Tutunji 1996: 667.
15. Constantinople was the most commonly used name before the establishment of the Turkish Republic when Istanbul became the name of preference since it was not tainted by 'Ottoman and international associations' (Mansel 1995: 416).
16. This discussion is based on Mansel 1995: 25, 170, 173; Faroqhi 1994: 411–636; Sülker 1985: 151; Kömürciyan 1988: 35–36; Oğuz 1976: 851.
17. Modernizing reform program in the Ottoman Empire that granted civil rights, established secularized schooling and attempted to change systems of administration, taxation and conscription.
18. The seventeenth century traveller Evliya Çelebi stressed the importance of hamsi in Trabzon (İhsan 1972: 14–15). İhsan's book-length study and praise of

this fish is evidence of the importance of hamsi during the early Republican era.

19. '*Çok fakire kut-i can, çok hastaya derman olur'*. From the poem 'Muhammes' in Yüksel 1989: 43–46.
20. Abdullah Günel, 1945, 'Hamsi Bayramı', *İnan* 17: 25–27, reprinted in Yüksel 1989: 17.
21. From 1,649,879 in 1990 to 5,400,714 in 2004, a rise of 227% (SIS 2005a).
22. There were, in the seventeenth century, fisher's guilds specializing in fishing with fishing weirs (*dalyan*), seines (*ığrıp*), stake nets (*karatya* nets), common nets, cast nets (*saçma*), line, harpoons, pots (*çömlek*), baskets (*sepet*), as well as a guild specializing in oyster fishing (Efendi 1968: 158–161).
23. Charles White was in Constantinople for three years in the early 1840s as a correspondent for the Daily Telegraph; he mastered Ottoman Turkish and overall had a more intimate knowledge of various parts of Ottoman society than most other visitors and travellers of the time. The three volume work by Charles White is arguably 'the best and most complete account of the manners and customs of the various inhabitants of the Turkish capital' (Mansel 1995: 276).
24. Devedjian's very detailed work, which comprises more than six hundred pages in the 1926 French edition and includes many drawings, figures, maps and tables, as well as current laws, was the first study of fish and fisheries in Istanbul and the Ottoman Empire. A most welcome translation into modern Turkish was published in 2006 by Aras Yayıncılık (Deveciyan 2006). This edition benefits from the inclusion of a biographical introduction about the author.
25. Kanlica and Incirköy are two villages a little distance from each other on the shore opposite Stenia on the Bosporus. It is not clear from Devedjian's text whether these rules were inscribed (as text) or not.
26. Use of the small meshed hamsi nets was not accepted for other species since it would catch undersize and immature fish.
27. In all his descriptions of dalyans, Çelebi (or Evliya Efendi) made careful notes of the manner and amount of tax levied on their operators (Çelebi 1984: 185–187; Kahane et al. 1958: 478–80). Describing the Beykoz dalyan on the Bosporus, he writes that '[T]he rent for the lease of the dalyan amounts to seventy yük of aspers (i.e., seven million aspers)' (Pallis 1951: 97).
28. Koçu (1960: 2011) cites a 1577 *ferman* (Sultanic decree) that gives the impression that this sales tax was also farmed out, but the source is not detailed or clear enough to make any definite conclusions.
29. In modern Turkish *memoudes* is memur.
30. The annual taxes from the fisheries ranged from 22,635 to 87,803 Ottoman Lira in the period 1882 – 1914, making up 1 – 2.5% of total revenues of the Administration (Kazgan 1983: 691–716). In order to check illegal (i.e., non-taxed) fishing they set up their own office at the fish hall (Koçu 1960: 2011).
31. A law regulating the export of mussels and oysters was already in effect in 1867 (Çelikkale et al. 1999: 289).
32. Reprinted in the French edition 1926: VI.
33. Once the Public Debt Administration had laid hands on the profitable fish taxes, the privileges enjoyed by the tax farmers may have come to an end, as was apparently the case in many sectors (McCarty 1997: 310). Instead of the annual commission (*mukataa*) paid by more or less hereditary tax farmers, the administration initiated a system whereby right to fish was auctioned for a period of three years. According to Devedjian (1926: 389), the tax and share

regime for one kind of dalyan, the *şıra* dalyans in Istanbul, was approximately as follows:

Gross sales

– sales tax (*resmi-miri*) 20–24%
– commission (6-10%) to the patron of the voli (area) where the dalyan stood (alternatively, rent)
– expenses for food for the crew (*kumanya*)
– commission to the fish trader (*kabzımal*)
– transport to the fish market

---

= Net sales
– $\frac{3}{4}$ to proprietor of dalyan
– $\frac{1}{4}$ distributed as shares to the approximately twenty crew and woodworkers.
– However, the patron had the right to two shares.

That a commission was still paid to the owner of the voli may indicate that privileges were not entirely abolished. The same individuals may have retained the right to 'farm' the volis and dalyans.

34. The topics addressed in this section are discussed in more detail in Knudsen 2004.
35. The number of dalyans in operation in the Bosporus declined from thirty-eight in 1875 to twenty-seven in 1915. Also the large dalyan at the island of Cromyon, described by White, was abandoned in this period (Devedjian 1926: 396–403).
36. This intermingling is articulated in novels by writers such as Sait Faik (1944) and Halikarnas Balıkçısı (1969).
37. Russia invaded and occupied the Ottoman lands east of Tirebolu for two years between 1916 and 1918.
38. Calculated on the basis of figures given in İstanbul Belediyesi (1949).
39. Published 1941, quoted in Koçu (1960: 1992).
40. Although the sources are somewhat unclear on this point, the state probably transferred the right to tax fisheries to municipalities (Koçu 1960: 2011). This new tax was generally much lower (5–8%) than the state tax (20–22%) had been.
41 If not specified otherwise, the ensuing discussion is based upon the following sources: Yurt Ansiklopedisi 1981; Günlük 1983; Acara et al. 1989; Ergüven 1983; Özbey 1989; Tören 2007; and, the most comprehensive, Çelikkale et al. 1999. Note that there are often discrepancies between the sources, especially with regard to time frame.
42. I had problems making sense of this quotation, and therefore asked for the advice of Bernt Brendemoen, Professor in Turkish Language at the University of Oslo. I was reassured when he could tell me that the sentence 'is full of nonsense; it almost sounds like an election campaign speech with a lot of air and little concrete content. It is impossible to turn it into proper Norwegian (or English)'. Guided partly by his comments (in Norwegian), I have produced the present translation that hopefully conveys some of the convolutedness of the language.
43. By 2007 the Trabzon Fishery Research Institute had been responsible for a total of forty-five research projects (completed and in progress). Despite the

overwhelming importance of coastal and ocean fisheries in this region, only seventeen of these projects were related to fish stocks and fishing, while nineteen focused on aquaculture and the remaining addressed ocean pollution (Institute web site accessed on 09.07.2007).

44. One example is the VI Five Year Development Plan special issue on 'Water Produce and Water Produce Industry', which from the very beginning of the introduction and onward bases its discussion on the concern about nutrition and proteins (Acara et al. 1989: 1).

45. In the IV Five Year Development Plan it is stated that in Turkey 17.5% of the population consume too few calories, 10% consume too little protein, and 22.5% have an unbalanced intake of protein (cited in Tezcan 1982: 129).

46. Although the municipalities collect the fish tax, the revenue is transferred to the state treasury. Fishers have until recently paid no tax on income or profits. Now wealthy fishers pay some tax, but the amount is insignificant.

47. This measure would of course have no significant effect as the tax level is already quite low.

48. Professor Çelikkale of Sürmene Marine Research Faculty, addressing scientists, fishers and a general public at the opening of a panel discussion about the Black Sea during the FISHECO'98 international marine science symposium in Trabzon. I attended the meeting and taped the speech.

49. The dispersal of the water produce research and teaching sector was part of a general trend in higher education and research in Turkey following the 1980 military take-over (Öncü 1993; Szyliowicz 1994).

50. That means, for instance, that the unit responsible for 'Water Produce Control and Protection' is a 'Water Produce Section' (*şube*) which reports to 'Fisheries, Environment and Disasters Department' (*daire*) under the 'General Directorate (Genel Müdürlüğü) for Protection and Control', while statistics are handled by a 'Water Produce Department' in the 'General Directorate for Agricultural Production and Development', and research is administered by a 'Water Produce Section' within the 'General Directorate for Agricultural Research'.

51. See Acara et al. 2001, Chapter 5, for a full overview of the various institutions involved in fishery policy.

52. Today there are few dalyans left. It seems as if their use gradually decreased from around the turn of the century until the mid 1970s. In surveys and reports there is little mention of dalyans after 1970, and the few works (GDWP 1974: 21; Sarıkaya 1980: 105; Mert 1989) that do address dalyans clearly indicate that their number were small (twenty-five in 1972, twelve in 1989) and that most of them were small scale and rather dilapidated. The big dalyan at Beykoz (in the Bosporus) was, as the last dalyan in Istanbul, put up for the last time towards the end of the 1980s. Several factors have combined to relegate the dalyans to history: Competition from boat fishing; the disappearance of migratory fish such as swordfish and mackrel; the fact that fish do not approach the shore any longer because of all the human activities (Pasiner 1993/94: 545); and the restrictions caused by the increased traffic in the Bosporus (Sarıkaya 1980: 93).

53. All figures at current rates. Calculated on the basis of information in Acara et al. 1989; Çelikkale et al. 1999; SIS 2001.

54. Responding to pressure from the IMF, fishery credits were no longer subsidized from 1999. Moreover, the Agricultural Bank was privatized in 2001. In 2002 the volume of total accumulated fishery credits was only 2.75% of what it had been in 1999. See Knudsen and Zengin 2006 for details.

55. The official name for the township was changed to Çarşıbaşı in the 1960s, but in conversation the old name İskefiye is still preferred. To avoid confusion I have chosen to use İskefiye when referring to the township and Çarşıbaşı when referring to the district. See map, Figure 4.1.

56. Or, alternatively, IK and TEK may be given quasi-scientific legitimacy by elevating them to ethnoscience, thus construing such knowledge as a sub-category of science. In any case, definitions evoke science.

57. Prominent scholars within this discourse, such as D. Brokhensha, D. Warren and R. Chambers have all contributed to an incorporation of IK in the language of development. See Warren et al. 1995; F.Berkes 1999: 5; Ellen and Harris 2000: 13. For an example of how IK is now incorporated and implicated in the discourse concerning development and aid, see Brokensha 2001. For an assertion of the 'revolutionary' development afforded by this combination of IK studies and anthropology see Sillitoe 1998.

58. In 1982 the UN established the Working Group on Indigenous Populations which annually brings together representatives from indigenous organizations around the world.

59. See e.g. D'Andrade 1995; Lakoff and Johnson 1980; Bloch 1994; and Borofsky 1994.

60. Of course, the Foucaultian concept of 'discourse' transcends language. But even when scholars paradigmatically argue for a Foucultian approach to discourse, in analyses of ethnography one easily slips back into a more conventional operationalization of discourse as speech/language. Thus the edited collection *Language and the Politics of Emotion* (Lutz and Abu-Lughod 1990) primarily treats language about body and emotion and implicitly upholds the rigid distinction between language and body.

61. Examples include all the three names used for turbot: *mıhlı balığı* (naily fish), *kalkan* (shield) and *sofra balığı* (round table fish).

62. On each sea-snail boat there will usually be two or three persons working (2.5 on average) while the smaller boats on average employ 1.5 persons (one person when using hand-line, one or two persons when setting nets).

63. In 1997 the small boats in Keremköy had on average been constructed or purchased only 3.92 years earlier (Knudsen 1997).

64. To name but a few studies: Acheson 1988, 2003; Akimichi 1984; Hviding 1996. See also overviews and collections such as Acheson 1981; Cordell 1989; F.Berkes et al. 2001.

65. 'Firstcomer rights' have been documented in many fisheries around the world. See Akimichi 1984 for an example and McGoodwin 1990: 140 (on 'Etiquette') for a summary discussion.

66. This count probably includes only the *ığrıp/çevirme* (seine) teams and thereby excludes the teams primarily hunting for dolphins. There would have been some of these, hunting with shotguns from medium-sized or small boats, both in Sürmene and Çarşıbaşı in the 1950s.

67. 'Reis' was not his family name but is rather a label added to his first name to indicate that he was some kind of 'boss', here 'Ali the skipper'.

68. Hazelnuts are cultivated along most of the Turkish Black Sea coast. The household dynamics might have been different in tea (east of Trabzon) and tobacco (Bafra delta west of Samsun) growing regions since cultivation of these crops is much more labour intensive.

69. 1967: Investment in a boat and gear for a team: 500,000 lira, 0.25–0.5 lira/kg hamsi (Çakıroğlu 1969). 1990: Investment in a boat and gear for a team: 1,000 million lira, 200 lira/kg hamsi.

70. In 2004 four brothers from Fenerköy who had worked as hired captains on purse seiners, pooled resources, received credit and invested in a modern, but fairly small purse seiner. It remains to be seen whether they succeed. This case also illustrates the continued importance of family organization and previous experience in fishing.
71. I know of only one successful company that deviates from this pattern, namely Sürsan from Samsun.
72. Examples include religious institutions and the 'feudal' aga landowner-patrons that are important in the social matrix of south-eastern Turkey.
73. This scandal erupted in November 1996 when a car accident near the small town of Susurluk revealed close linkages between a network of leading politicians, high-ranking state security officials, probably some high-ranking military, and nationalist mafia killers (Kramer 2000: 258).
74. This is the official English name of the institution. A direct translation of the Turkish name is 'Trabzon Water Produce Research Institute'.
75. For an important deviation from this, see Bilecik 2003.
76. At the time this case was brought before the Military, Turkey was under military rule (1980 – 1983). The military was seen not only as the final arbiters in society, but also, by many, as the guardians of the scientific approach and objectivity. It is probable that the sonar case was decided by a military court.
77. A survey in the fishers village Keremköy showed that 81% of small boat fishers and big boat crew believed the sonar to be the main reason for the upset of the natural balance in the Black Sea (pollution ranking second, mentioned by 45%). 67% of non-fishers, and a surprising 50% of owners of big boats held the same opinion (Knudsen 1997, 2003).
78. For an elaboration of this, see Knudsen 2007.
79. The most important being the prohibition of all professional fishing during summer and the ban on trawling in the eastern Black Sea region.
80. While fishers now tend to express the idea that the sea is free, bureaucrats often stress that the state owns the sea.
81. International organizations such as the World Bank, NATO, and UN organizations, and, more recently, Turkish NGOs such as the Istanbul Chamber of Trade or TURMEPA. See Knudsen 1997, 1998, 2001.
82. Survey spring 1998 of 157 males in Keremköy, of which ninety-one are fishers (twenty-one big-boat owners, seventy small-boat fishers and crew). Most adult males in the village and a few men with origins in and continued strong links to Keremköy are included. For the purpose of this survey I have included only men between twenty and fifty-five years of age.
83. TEAE, 2006. 308 managers of fishing operations/boats (all sizes/kinds), mostly (more than 90%) boat owners. Boats owners and skippers, especially owners of and hired skippers on larger boats, are generally better educated than small-boat fishers and crew.
84. Results from Census of Population 2000. 672 employed persons above age 12 reported to have their main income from 'fishing and water produce'.
85. Survey of 345 fishers (including two women) in most fishing communities in the Province of Samsun, September 2005.
86. A survey of fishers in Keremköy revealed that more than 70% held 'too high fishing effort' to be one of the primary reasons for problems in the fisheries (Knudsen 1997: Table 8).
87. Postings on the subject of 'Eating, feeding, feedtrough' on H-Turk discussion list, http://www.h-net.org/~turk/, June 1-4 2001.

88. This is an ambivalence that is inherent in Gökalp's theory (see Chapter 6). The Turks were to look to Anatolia for their culture (*hars*), but to Europe for civilisation (*medeniyet*). It is interesting to note that the Turkish concept kültürlü has come to be used primarily for traits stemming from 'civilisation'.

89. 'Seventh of May', in accordance with old Julian calendar used by the Greeks, but celebrated on the twentieth of May according to the new Gregorian calendar.

90. This is clearly associated with Greek religious practice, but also with the *zamzam* water brought home from Mecca by Muslims.

91. The following is based upon news items and comments in the region newspaper *Karadeniz Gazetesi* (20 May 2002, 21 May 2002, 11 May 2003, 18 May 2003, 19 May 2004, 21 May 2004).

92. The Turkish-Islamic Synthesis developed from the mid 1970s and was to a certain extent sponsored by the military as a bulwark against communism during the 1980s (Magnarella 1998). It has since developed into a powerful cultural and political current, articulated in particular by the Nationalist Action Party.

# Bibliography

Acara, A. et al. 1989. Su *Ürünleri ve Su Ürünleri Sanayii Özel İhtisas Komisyonu Raporu*. Ankara: Turkish Republic State Planning Organisation.

———. 2001. *Su Ürünleri ve Su Ürünleri Sanayii Özel İhtisas Komisyonu Raporu*. Ankara: Turkish Republic State Planning Organization.

Acheson, J.M. 1981. 'Anthropology of Fishing', *Annual Review of Anthropology* 10: 275–316.

———. 1988. *The Lobster Gangs of Maine*. Hanover: University Press of New England.

———. 2003. *Capturing the Commons: Devising Institutions to Manage the Maine Lobster Industry*. Hanover: University Press of New England.

Aflalo, F.G. 1911. *Regilding the Crescent*. London: Martin Secker.

Agrawal, A. 2003. 'Sustainable Governance of Common-Pool Resources: Context, Method, and Politics', *Annual Review of Anthropology* 32: 243–262.

———. 2006. *Environmentality: Technologies of Government and the Making of Subjects*. Durham: Duke University Press.

Agricultural Bank. 1982. *Su Ürünleri Üretimi Artırma ve Kredi Yönledirme Sempozyumu*. Ankara: Turkish Republic Agricultural Bank. Fisheries Loan Department Publication 4.

———. 1984. *Su Ürünlerinin Planlı Üretimi, İşlenmesi, Soğuk Muhafaza ve Pazarlaması Paneli*. Izmir: Turkish Republic Agricultural Bank. Fisheries Loan Department Publication 6.

———. 1986. *Su Ürünleri Sektörünün Bugünkü Durumu ve Sorunları Sempozyumu*. Izmir: Turkish Republic Agricultural Bank. Fisheries Loan Department Publication 7.

Akimichi, T. 1984. 'Territorial Regulation in the Small-Scale Fisheries of Itoman, Okinawa', *Senri Ethnological Studies* 17: 89–120.

*Akşam Postası* 1938. 'Balık içhracatı için Banka Kuruluyor: Bu Husustaki Kanun Projesi Büyük Millet Meclisine Verildi,. 30 January: 3.

Alexander, C. 2002. *Personal States: Making Connections between People and Bureaucracy in Turkey*. Oxford: Oxford University Press.

Alhan, M. 2000. 'İbret Anıtı Dikilecek', *Akşam Gazetesi*, 23 May.

Anderson, B. 1991. *Imagined Communities: An Inquiry into the Origins and Spread of Nationalism*. London: Verso.

Andreadis, G. 1995. *The Cryptochristians*. Thessaloniki: Publishing House Kyrikidis Brothers.

Arkan, Ö.K. 1993/4. 'Lokantalar', in N. Akbayar et al. (eds), *Dünden Bugüne İstanbul Ansiklopedisi*. Istanbul: Türkiye Ekonomik ve Toplumsal Tarih Vakfı: 220–223.

Artan, T. 2000. 'Aspects of the Ottoman Elite's Food Consumption: Looking for "Staples", "Luxuries", and "Delicacies" in a Changing Century', in D. Quataert (ed.), *Consumption Studies and the History of the Ottoman Empire*. New York: State University of New York Press: 107–200.

Avşar, D. 1998. *Balıkçılık Biyolojisi ve Populasyon Dinamiği*. Ankara: Baki Kitabevi.

Aydın, R., A.A. Öğüt and T. Erengil (eds). 1995. *Kooperatifçilik, El Sanatları, Teşvik ve Destekleme*. Ankara: Turkish Republic Ministry for Agriculture and Rural Affairs, Teşkilatlanma ve Destekleme Genel Müdürlüğü.

Bailey, C. and C. Zerner 1992. 'Community-Based Fisheries Management Institutions in Indonesia', *MAST* 5(1): 1–17.

Balıkçısı, H. 1969. *Deniz Gurbetçileri*. Ankara: Bilgi Yayınevi.

Barnes, B. and D. Bloor. 1982. 'Relativism, Rationalism and the Sociology of Knowledge', in M. Hollies and S. Lukes (eds), *Rationality and Relativism*. Oxford: Basil Blackwell.

Barth, F. 1963. 'Introduction', in F. Barth (ed.), *The Role of the Entrepreneur in Social Change in Northern Norway*. Bergen: Norwegian University Press: 5–18.

———. 1967. 'Economic Spheres in Darfur', in R. Firth (ed.), *Themes in Economic Anthropology*. London: Tavistock.

Bates, D.G. and A. Rassam. 1983. *Peoples and Cultures of the Middle East*. Englewoods Cliffs, New Jersey: Prentice Hall.

Bateson, G. 1972. 'Style, Grace, and Information in Primitive Art', in Bateson, G. (ed.), *Steps to an Ecology of Mind*. New York: Ballantine Books: 128–153.

Baysal, K. 1969. 'Nüfusumuzun Beslenmesinde Balıkçılğn Önemi ve Balıkçılık Araştırmalarının Geliştirmesine ait bir Araştırma', *İstanbul Üniversitesi İktisat Fakültesi Mecmuası* 28(1–4): 71–78.

Belge, M. 2001. *Tarih Boyunca Yemek Kültürü*. Istanbul: İletişim Yayınları.

Benda-Beckmann, K.V. 2001. 'Folk, Indigenous, and Customary Law', in *International Encyclopedia of the Social and Behavioural Sciences*. Oxford: Pergamon.

Berkes, F. (ed.). 1989. *Common Property Resources, Ecology and Community-Based Sustainable Development*. London: Belhaven Press.

———. 1992. 'Success and Failure in Marine Coastal Fisheries of Turkey', in D.W. Bromley (ed.), *Making the Commons Work: Theory, Practice and Policy*. San Francisco: ICS Press: 161–182.

———. 1999. *Sacred Ecology: Traditional Ecological Knowledge and Resource Management*. London: Taylor and Francis.

Berkes, F. and C. Folke (eds). 1998. *Linking Social and Ecological Systems: Management Practices and Social Mechanisms for Building Resilience.* Cambridge: Cambridge University Press.

Berkes, F. et al. 2001. *Managing Small-Scale Fisheries. Alternative Directions and Methods.* Ottawa: International Development Research Centre.

Berkes, N. 1998 [1964]. *The Development of Secularism in Turkey.* London: Hurst.

Berlin, B. 1992. *Ethnobiology Classification: Principles of Categorization of Plants and Animals in Traditional Societies.* Princeton: Princeton University Press.

Biersack, A. 1999. 'Introduction: From the "New Ecology" to the New Ecologies', *American Anthropologist* 101(1): 1–18.

_____. 2006. 'Reimagining Political Ecology: Culture/Power/History/ Nature', in A. Biersack and J.B. Greenberg (eds), *Reimagining Political Ecology.* Durham: Duke University Press: 3–40.

Bilecik, N. 2003. *Herkes Yerine. Denizler Çölleşmeden, Balıklar yok Olmadan.* Izmir: Final Ofset.

Bingel, F. 2002. *Balık Populasyonların İncelemesi.* İçel: Baki Kitabevi.

Bloch, M. 1994. 'Language, Anthropology, and Cognitive Science', in R. Borofsky (ed.), *Assessing Cultural Anthropology.* New York: McGraw-Hill: 276–282.

Bloor, D. 1976. *Knowledge and Social Imagery.* London: Routledge and Kegan Paul.

Bobat, A. and A. Delioğlan. 2001. 'Balık Tüketiminde Tutum ve Davranışların Değerlendirilmesi', in *XI. Ulusal Su Ürünleri Sempozyumu*, 4–6 September 2001. Hatay: Mustafa Kemal Üniversitesi Su Ürünleri Fakültesi.

Boissevain, J. 1974. *Friends of Friends.* Oxford: Blackwell.

Bon, O. 1996. *The Sultan's Seraglio: An Intimate Portrait of Life at the Ottoman Court.* London: Saqi Books.

Bora, T. 1999. 'Istanbul and the Conqueror: The "Alternative Global City" Dreams of Political Islam', in Ç. Keyder (ed.), *Istanbul: Between the Global and the Local.* Lanham: Rowman and Littlefield Publishers: 47–58.

Borofsky, R. 1994. 'On the Knowledge and Knowing of Cultural Activities', in R. Borofsky (ed.), *Assessing Cultural Anthropology.* New York: McGraw-Hill: 320–328.

Bourdieu, P. 1977. *Outline of a Theory of Practice.* Cambridge: Cambridge University Press.

Bowen, J.R. 2003. *Islam, Law, and Equality in Indonesia: An Anthropology of Public Reasoning.* Cambridge: Cambridge University Press.

Bozdoğan, S. 2001. *Modernism and Nation-Building: Turkish Architectural Culture in the Early Republic.* Seattle: University of Washington Press.

Brokhensha, D. 2001. 'Development: Social-Anthropological Aspects', in *International Encyclopedia of the Social and Behavioural Sciences.* Oxford: Pergamon.

Bromberger, C. 1994. 'Eating Habits and Cultural Boundaries in Northern Iran', in S. Zubaida and R. Tapper (eds), *Culinary Cultures of the Middle East*. London: I.B. Tauris: 185–201.

Bromley, D. (ed.). 1992. *Making the Commons Work: Theory, Practice and Policy*. San Francisco: ICS Press.

Brosius, J.P. 1999. 'Green Dots, Pink Hearts: Displacing Politics from the Malaysian Rain Forest', *American Anthropologist* 101(1): 36–57.

Brox, O. 1990. 'Common Property Theory: Epistemological Status and Analytical Utility', *Human Organization* 49(3): 227–235.

Brush, S.B. 1993. 'Indigenous Knowledge of Biological Resources and Intellectual Property Rights: The Role of Anthropology', *American Anthropologist* 95(3): 653–686.

———. 1996. 'Whose Knowledge, Whose Genes, Whose Rights?', in S.B. Brush and D. Stabinsky (eds), *Valuing Local Knowledge. Indigenous People and Intellectual Property Rights*. Washington: Island Press: 1–24.

Bryer, A.A.M. 1980. *The Empire of Trebizond and the Pontos*. London: Variorum Reprints.

Buğra, A.E. 1994. *State and Business in Modern Turkey: A Comparative Study*. Albany: State University of New York.

Çakmak, E.H. 2004. *Structural Change and Market Opening in Agriculture: Turkey Towards EU Accession*. Ankara: Economic Research Center, Middle East Technical University. ERC Working Papers in Economics.

Çakıroğlu, S.B. (ed.) 1969. *Karadeniz Balıkçılık*. Ankara: Bilgi Basımevi.

Campbell, J.K. 1964. *Honour, Family, and Patronage: A Study of Institutions and Moral Values in a Greek Mountain Community*. Oxford: Clarendon.

Canalioğlu, M.V. 1997. *Trabzon Yöresel Yemekleri*. Trabzon: Trabzon Valiliği İl Turizm Müdürlüğü.

Çelebi, E. 1984. *Seyahatname (Rumeli – Solkol – Edirne)*. Ankara: Başbakanlık Basımevi.

———. 1991. *Evliya Çelebi Seyahatnamesinden Seçmeler*. Ankara: Kültür Bakanlığı.

Çeliker, S.A. 2003. 'Su Ürünleri', *TEAE Bakış* 2003(8): 1–4.

Çelikkale, M.S. 1988. 'Türkiye'de Hamsi Balığı Üretimi ve Avlanma Teknolojisinde Gelişmeler', in *Karadeniz'de Hamsi Balıkçılığı ve Sorunları iner (Tebliğler ve Panel), Ordu–Fatsa EBK Tesislerinde*. Seminar organized by İktisadi Araştırmalar Vakfı. Istanbul: Yaylacık.

Çelikkale, M.S., S. Ünsal, O. Demirel and A.F. Candeğer. 1988a. *Profesyonel Balıkçı Gemilerinde Kullanılan Sonar Cihazların Transmisyon Pulslarının Yerel Balıklar Üzerindeki Etkilerin Araştırılması (A Study of How the Transmission Pulses from Sonars in Use on Fishing Boats Influence Local Fish)*. Trabzon: Karadeniz Technical University.

Çelikkale, M.S., S. Ünsal, H.F. Durukanoğlu, H. Karaçam and E. Düzgüneş. 1988b. *Karadeniz'de Yaşayan Yunus Stoklarının Belirlenmesi ve Biyolojik Özelliklerinin Tesbiti*. Trabzon: Turkish Republic Ministry for Agriculture, Forestry and Rural Affairs, General Directorate for Projects and Implementation.

Çelikkale, M.S., E. Düzgüneş, İ. Okumuş and C. Mutlu. 1998. 'Problems and Future Prospects of the Black Sea Fisheries of Turkey', in *FISHECO'98: Proceedings of the First International Symposium on Fisheries and Ecology*. Trabzon: Karadeniz Technical University, Faculty of Marine Sciences: 11–17.

Çelikkale, M.S., E. Düzgüneş and İ. Okumuş. 1999. *Türkiye Su Ürünleri Sektörü. Potansiyeli, Mevcut Durumu, Sorunları ve Çözüm Önerileri*. Istanbul: Lebib Yalkın Yayımları.

Çıkın, A. and A.G. Elbek 1991. 'Marine Products Co-Operatives in the EU and Turkey', in *Symposium on Marine Products*. Izmir: Aegean University, Marine Products College: 166–179.

Çınar, A.İ. 1997. 'Refah Party and the City Administration of Istanbul: Liberal Islam, Localism and Hybridity', *New Perspectives on Turkey* (16): 23–40.

Cordell, J. (ed.). 1989. *A Sea of Small Boats*. Cambridge, Massachusetts: Cultural Survival.

Crofoot, J.M. 1993. 'The Economy of Gender and Knowledge in Ahmet Midhat's Felatun Bey Ile Rakım Efendi', *Turkish Studies Association Bulletin* 17(2): 44–57.

Csordas, T.J. 1990. 'Embodiment as a Paradigm for Anthropology', *Ethos* 18(1): 5–47.

———. 1999. 'The Body's Career in Anthropology', in H.L. Moore (ed.), *Anthropological Theory Today*. Cambridge: Polity Press: 175–205.

*Cumhuriyet Gazetesi* 2000. 'Deniz Faciası için Anıt Yapılacak', 23 May.

D'andrade, R. 1995. *The Development of Cognitive Anthropology*. Cambridge: Cambridge University Press.

Davies, J. 1977. *People of the Mediterranean: An Essay in Comparative Social Anthropology*. London: Routledge and Kegan Paul.

Demirci, R. 1986. 'Su Ürünleri Kooperatiflerinin Mevcut Durumu ve Sorunları (The Present Condition and Problems of Water Products Co-Operatives)', in *Su Ürünleri Sektörünün Bugünkü Durumu ve Sorunları Semposyumu*. Izmir: Turkish Republic Agricultural Bank, Fisheries Loan Department Publication 7: 167–178.

Deveciyan, K. 2006. *Türkiye'de Balık ve Balıkçılık*. Istanbul: Aras Yayıncılık.

Devedjian, K. 1926 [1915]. *Pêche et Pêcheries en Turquie*. Constantinople [Istanbul]: Imprimiere de l'Administration de la Dette Publique Ottomane.

Dikmen, M.O. 1988. 'Semposyumu Takdim Konuşması', in *Karadeniz'de Hamsi Balıkçılığı ve Sorunları : Seminer (Tebliğler ve Panel), Ordu-Fatsa EBK Tesislerinde*. Seminar organized by İktisadi Araştırmalar Vakfı. Istanbul: Yaylacık Matbaası.

DMP. 1982. *1980 Yılı Türkiye Su Ürünleri Kooperatif ve Birlikleri Araştırması*. Ankara: Turkish Republic Ministry for Agriculture and Forestry, Department for Marine Products.

Doğan, K. 1982. 'Balık Unu ve Yağı ile İlgili Sorunlar,' in *Su Ürünleri Üretimi Artırma ve Kredi Yönlendirme Sempozyumu*. Ankara: Turkish Republic Agricultural Bank. Fisheries Loan Department Publication 4: 278–298.

Dolşak, N. and E. Ostrom. 2003. 'The Challenge of the Commons', in N. Dolşak and E. Ostrom (eds), *The Commons in the New Millennium: Challenges and Adaptations*. Cambridge, Massachusetts: MIT Press: 3–34.

Dönmez, A. 2004. 'Boğaz manzaralı balık ekmek keyfi tarih oldu', *Zaman*, 7 September.

Douglas, M. 1966. *Purity and Danger: An Analysis of the Concepts of Pollution and Taboo*. London: Ark Paperbacks.

Duran, B. 1988. 'Karadeniz Bölgesinin 1870–1914 Arasında Tarımsal Gelişmesi', in M. Sağlam and et al. (eds), *İkinci Tarih Boyunca Karadeniz Bildirileri*. Samsun: Ondokuz Mayıs Üniversitesi Eğitim Fakültesi ve Fransız Anadolu Araştırmaları Enstitüsü: 58–67.

Durrenberger, E.P. and G. Pálsson. 1987. 'Ownership at Sea: Fishing Territories and Access to Sea Resources', *American Ethnologist* 14(3): 508–522.

Dursun, A.H. 1999. *İstanbul'da Yaşama Sanatı*. Istanbul: Ötüken Neşriyat.

Düzgüneş, E. and H. Karacam. 1991. 'A General Review of Institutional Factors and Marketing Channels in the Fishery of Turkey', in W.E. Schrank and N. Roy (eds), *Econometric Modelling of the World Trade in Groundfish*. London: Kluwer Academic Publishers: 329–345.

Düzgüneş, E., C. Mutlu and C. Şahin. 1995. 'Population Parameters of Anchovy in the Eastern Black Sea', in *MEDCOAST 95: The Second International Conference on the Mediterranean Coastal Environment*. Tarragona, Spain: MEDCOAST: 59–66.

Efendi, E. 1968 [1834]. *Narrative of Travels in Europe, Asia, and Africa, in the Seventeenth Century*. Tr. From Turkish by Ritter Joseph Von Hammer. London: Oriental Tr. Fund.

Elbek, A.G., D.İ.G. Emiroğlu and H. Saygı. 1997. 'Balık Tüketimi ve Tüketime Yönelik Survey', in B. Hoşsu (ed.), *Mediterranean Fisheries Congress*. Izmir: Ege University Faculty of Fisheries: 431–439.

Ellen, R. 1982. *Environment, Subsistence and System: The Ecology of Small–Scale Social Formations*. Cambridge: Cambridge University Press.

————. *The Cultural Relations of Classification: An Analysis of Nuaulu Animal Categories from Central Seram*. Cambridge: Cambridge University Press.

————. 2002. 'Environment and Anthropology', in *International Encyclopedia of the Social & Behavioural Sciences*. Oxford: Pergamon.

Ellen, R. and H. Harris. 2000. 'Introduction, in R. Ellen, P. Parkes and A. Bicker (eds), *Indigenous Environmental Knowledge and Its Transformations: Critical Anthropological Perspectives*. Amsterdam: Harwood Academic Publishers.

Elliott, M. and partners. 1996. *Türk Su Ürünlerinin Mevcut İç ve Dış Pazarları ile Gelecekteki Pazar Olanakları Üzerine bir Çalışma*. Volume 1. Ankara: Ministry for Agriculture and Rural Affairs.

Erginsoy, G. 1998. 'Global Encounters and Gender Hierarchies in the Community of Garipçe', *New Perspectives on Turkey* (18): 131–146.

Ergüven, H. 1983. 'Ülkemizde Balıkçılık Araştırma Çalışmaları ve Kurumları', in *Cumhuriyet Döneminde Türkiye Ansiklopedisi*. Istanbul: İletişim Yayınları: 2332–2333.

Escobar, A. 1999. 'After Nature. Steps to an Antiessentialist Political Ecology', *Current Anthropology* 40(1): 1–30.

Evkoyunca, İ. 1995. *Balıkçılık Biyolojisi ve Populasyon Dinamiği*. Sinop: Ondokuz Mayıs Universitesi.

Evran, E. 2004. 'Sahibinden, Doktor Kontrollü Balık', *Sabah*, 22 March.

Exertzoglu, H. 2003. 'The Cultural Uses of Consumption: Negotiating Class, Gender, and Nation in Ottoman Urban Centres During the 19th Century', *International Journal of Middle East Studies* 35(1): 77–101.

Fabian, J. 1983. *Time and the Other: How Anthropology Makes its Objects*. New York: Columbia University Press.

Faik, S. 1944. *Medarı Maişet Motoru*. Ankara: Bilgi yayınevi.

FAO. 1975. 'Report to the Government of Turkey on Fisheries Administration, Based on the Work of J.G. Simpson'. Rome: United Nations Development Programme.

———. 1980. *Echo Sounding and Sonar for Fishing*. Farnham: Fishing New Books.

Faroqhi, S. 1994. 'Part II: Crisis and Change, 1590–1699', in H. İnalcık and D. Quataert (eds), *An Economic and Social History of the Ottoman Empire*. Cambridge: Cambridge University Press: 411–636.

Feit, H. 1988. 'Self-Management and State-Management: Forms of Knowing and Managing Northern Wildlife', in I.M.M.R. Freeman, and L.N. Carbyn (eds), *Traditional Knowledge and Renewable Resource Management in Northern Region*. Edmont, Alberta: Boreal Institute for Northern Studies: 72–91.

Ferradás, C. 1998. 'Comment to Sillitoe: The Development of Indigenous Knowledge', *Current Anthropology* 39(2): 239–240.

Finlayson, A.C. 1994. *Fishing for Truth: A Sociological Analysis of Northern Cod Stock Assessments from 1977 to 1990*. St. John's, Newfoundland: Institute of Social and Economic Research, Memorial University of Newfoundland.

Fleck, L. 1979 [1935]. *Genesis and Development of a Scientific Fact*. Chicago: University of Chicago Press.

Foucault, M. 1977. *Discipline and Punish: The Birth of the Prison*. London: Penguin.

———. 1991. 'Governmentality', in E.A.G. Burchell (ed.), *The Foucault Effect: Studies in Governmentality*. London: Harvester: 87–101.

Franklin, S. 1995. 'Science as Culture, Cultures of Science', *Annual Review of Anthropology* 24: 163–84.

Freeman, M.M.R. and L.N. Carbyn (eds). 1988. *Traditional Knowledge and Renewable Resource Management in Northern Regions*. Edmont, Alberta: Boreal Institute for Northern Studies.

GDEP. n.d. 'Convention on Biological Diversity Thematic Report on Access and Benefit-Sharing – Turkey'. Ankara: Turkish Republic Ministry of Environment, General Directorate of Environmental Protection.

GDPC. 1997. *Denizlerde ve İçsularda Ticari Amaçlı Su Ürünleri Avcılığını Düzenleyen 31/1 Numara Sirküler*. Ankara: Turkish Republic Ministry for Agriculture and Rural Affairs, General Directorate for Protection and Control.

———. 1998. *Denizlerde ve İçsularda Ticari Amaçlı Su Ürünleri Avcılığını Düzenleyen 1998–1999 Av Döneminde Ait 32/1 Numaralı Sirküler*. Ankara: Turkish Republic Ministry for Agriculture and Rural Affairs, General Directorate for Protection and Control.

GDWP. 1974. *1972 Yılı Türkiye Su Ürünleri Ekonomik Araştırması*. Ankara: Turkish Republic Ministry for Food, Agriculture and Stockbreeding, General Directorate for Water Produce.

———. 1975. *1973 Yılı Su Ürünleri Kredileri ve Kooperatifleri Araştırması*. Ankara: Turkish Republic Ministry for Food, Agriculture and Stockbreeding, General Directorate for Water Produce.

Gedik, M.A. 1969. 'Karadeniz için Fabrika Gemiler de Düşünülmelidir', in S.B. Çakıroğlu (ed.), *Karadeniz Balıkçılık*. Ankara: Bilgi Basımevi: 128–130.

Geertz, C. 1983. *Local Knowledge: Further Essays in Interpretive Anthropology*. New York: Basic Books.

GEF-BSEP 1996. *Black Sea Transboundary Diagnostic Analysis*. Istanbul: Global Environment Facility - Black Sea Environmental Programme.

Gellner, E. 1983. *Nations and Nationalism*. Oxford: Basil Blackwell.

Gellner, E. and J. Waterbury (eds). 1977. *Patron and Clients in Mediterranean Societies*. London: Duckworth.

Giddens, A. 1979. *Central Problems in Social Theory: Action, Structure and Contradiction in Social Analysis*. Berkeley: University of California Press.

Gilles, P. 1988 [1561]. *The Antiques of Constantinople*. New York: Italica Press.

Gilsenan, M. 1996. *Lords of the Lebanese Marches: Violence and Narrative in an Arab Society*. London: I.B. Tauris.

GNAT. 2000. 'Grand National Assembly of Turkey Journal of Records (Tutanak Dergisi)', 97nci Birleşim, 23 May 2000. Ankara: Grand National Assembly of Turkey.

Gökbilgin, M.T. 1962. 'XVI. Yüzyıl Başlarında Trabzon Livası ve Doğu Karadeniz Bölgesi', *Belleten* XXVI(102): 243–337.

Göle, N. 1996. *The Forbidden Modern: Civilization and Veiling*. Ann Arbor: University of Michigan Press.

———. 1997. 'Secularism and Islamism in Turkey: The Making of Elites and Counter Elites', *Middle East Journal* 51(1): 46–58.

Gonzalez, R.J., L. Nader and C.J. Ou. 1995. 'Between Two Poles: Bronislaw Malinowski, Ludwig Fleck, and the Anthropology of Science', *Current Anthropology* 36(5): 866–869.

Goody, J. 1986. *The Logic of Writing and the Organisation of Society*. Cambridge: Cambridge University Press.

──── . 1987. *The Interface between the Written and the Oral.* Cambridge: Cambridge University Press.

──── . 1998. *Food and Love: A Cultural History of East and West.* London: Verso.

Grimen, H. 1997. 'The Strong Program'. Lecture at University of Bergen, 25 April.

Gülez, S. 1996. 'Relationship between Recreation Demand and Some Natural Landscape Elements in Turkey: A Case Study', *Environmental Management* 20(1): 113–122.

Güneş-Ayata, A. 1990. 'Class and Clientelism in the Republican Peoples Party', in A. Finkel and N. Sirman (eds), *Turkish State, Turkish Society.* London: Routledge: 159–184.

Güngör, H. 1998. 'The Production and Marketing of Fishery Products: A Case in the North-West Region of Turkey', in M.S. Çelikkale, et al. (eds.), in *FISHECO'98. The Proceedings of the First International Symposium on Fisheries and Ecology.* Trabzon: Karadeniz Technical University: 313–320.

Günlük, A. 1983. 'Su Ürünleri', in *Cumhuriyet Dönemi Türkiye Ansiklopedisi.* Istanbul: İletişim Yayınları: 2321–2336.

Gupta, A. 1992. 'The Song of the Nonaligned World: Transnational Identities and the Reinscription of Space in Late Capitalism', *Cultural Anthropology* 7(1): 63–79.

Hafez, S. 1994. 'Food as a Semiotic Code in Arabic Literature', in S. Zubaida and R. Tapper (eds), *Culinary Cultures of the Middle East.* London: I.B. Tauris: 257–280.

Hamilton, W.J. 1984 [1840]. *Researches in Asia Minor, Pontus and Armenia: With Some Account of Their Antiquities and Geology.* Hildesheim: Georg Olms Verlag.

Hann, C.M. 1990. *Tea and the Domestication of the Turkish State.* Huntingdon: Eothen Press.

──── . 1996. 'Introduction: Political Society and Civil Anthropology', in C.M. Hann and E. Dunn (eds), *Civil Society: Challenging Western Models.* London: Routledge: 1–26.

Hardin, G. 1968. 'The Tragedy of the Commons', *Science* 162(3859): 1243–1248.

──── . 1985. *Filters against Folly: How to Survive Despite Economists, Ecologists, and the Merely Eloquent.* New York: Viking Penguin.

Harris, M. 1977. *Cannibals and Kings.* New York: Random House.

Hastrup, K. 1995. *A Passage to Anthropology. Between Experience and Theory.* London: Routledge.

Hersoug, B. 2004. 'Exporting Fish, Importing Institutions – Fisheries Development in the Third World', in B. Hersoug, S. Jentoft and P. Degnbol (eds), *Fisheries Development: The Institutional Challenge.* Delft: Eburon Publishers: 21–92.

Herzfeld, M. 1985. *The Poetics of Manhood: Contest and Identity in a Cretan Mountain Village.* Princeton: Princeton University Press.

──── . 1987. *Anthropology through the Looking-Glass: Critical Ethnography in the Margins of Europe.* Cambridge: Cambridge University Press.

———. 1992. *The Social Production of Indifference: Exploring the Symbolic Roots of Western Bureaucracy*. Chicago: University of Chicago Press.

———. M. 2001. *Anthropology: Theoretical Practice in Culture and Society*. Oxford: Blackwell.

Heyman, J.M. 2005. 'The Political Ecology of Consumption: Beyond Greed and Guilt', in S. Paulson and L.L. Gezon (eds), *Political Ecology across Spaces, Scales and Social Groups*. New Brunswick: Rutgers University Press: 113–132.

Holm, P. 2003. 'Crossing the Border: On the Relationship between Science and Fishermen's Knowledge in a Resource Management Context', *MAST* 2(1): 5–49.

Howell, S. 1997. 'Introduction', in S. Howell (ed.), *The Ethnography of Moralities*. London: Routledge: 1–22.

Hviding, E. 1996. *Guardians of Marovo Lagoon: Practice, Place, and Politics in Maritime Melanesia*. Honolulu: University of Hawai'i Press.

Hviding, E. and E. Jul-Larsen. 1993. *Community-Based Resource Management in Tropical Fisheries*. Bergen: Centre for Development Studies, University of Bergen.

ICC 2006. *Ticaret ve Sanayi Odasında Müteşekkil İstanbul İktisat Komisyonu Tarafından Tanzim Edilen Rapor*. Istanbul: Istanbul Chamber of Commerce. Publication No. 2006–52. Translated from Ottoman Turkish by Aynur Karayılmazlar.

Iddison, P. 1997. 'A Fish Suq in the UAE Desert', Oxford University Symposium on Food and Cookery: Fish – Food from the Waters. Oxford.

İhsan, H. 1972 [1928]. *Hamsi-Name*. Istanbul: Yaylacık Matbaası.

İhsanoğlu, E. 1992. 'Ottoman Science in the Classical Period and Early Contacts with European Science and Technology', in E. İhsanoğlu (ed.), *Transfer of Modern Science and Technology to the Muslim World*. Istanbul: IRCICA – Research Centre for Islamic History, Art and Culture: 1–48.

Ingold, T. 1992. 'Culture and the Perception of the Environment', in E. Croll and D. Parkin (eds), *Bush Base - Forest Farm: Culture, Environment and Development*. London: Routledge: 39–56.

———. 1993a. 'Tool-Use, Sociality and Intelligence', in K.R. Gibson and T. Ingold (eds), *Tools, Language and Cognition in Human Evolution*. Cambridge: Cambridge University Press: 429–445.

———. 1993b. 'Epilogue. Technology, Language, Intelligence: A Reconsideration of Basic Concepts', in K.R. Gibson and T. Ingold (eds), *Tools, Language and Cognition in Human Evolution*. Cambridge: Cambridge University Press: 449–472.

———. 1995. 'Building, Dwelling, Living: How Animals and People Make Themselves at Home in the World', in M. Strathern (ed.), *Shifting Contexts: Transformations in Anthropological Knowledge*. London: Routledge: 57–80.

İstanbul Belediyesi 1949. 'İstanbul Şehri İstatistik Yıllığı 1944–48', *İstanbul Belediyesi Neşriyat ve İstatistik Müdürlüğü Yayını* 7: 83–84.

Ivanov, L. and T. Oğuz (eds). 1998. *NATO TU-Black Sea Project: Ecosystem Modelling as a Management Tool for the Black Sea.* Amsterdam: Kluwer Academic Publishers.

Johannes, R.E. (ed.). 1989. *Traditional Ecological Knowledge: A Collection of Essays.* Cambridge: IUCN - The World Conservation Union.

Johnson, C. 2004. 'Uncommon Ground: The "Poverty of History" in Common Property Discourse', *Development and Change* 35(3): 407–433.

Johnson, M. 1993. *Moral Imagination: Implications of Cognitive Science for Ethics.* Chicago: University of Chicago Press.

Kahane, H., R. Kahane and A. Tietze. 1958. *The Lingua Franca in the Levant: Turkish Nautical Terms of Italian and Greek Origin.* Urbana: University of Illinois Press.

Kalland, A. 1996. 'Marine Management in Coastal Japan', in K. Crean and D. Symes (eds), *Fisheries Management in Crisis.* Oxford: Fishing News Books: 71–83.

Karaömerlioğlu, M. A. 1998. 'The Village Institute Experience in Turkey', *British Journal of Middle Eastern Studies* 25(1): 57–73.

Karpat, K.H. 1992. 'The Ottoman Adoption of Statistics from the West in the 19th Century', in E. İhsanoğlu (ed.), *Transfer of Modern Science and Technology to the Muslim World.* Istanbul: Research Centre for Islamic History, Art and Culture: 283–295.

Kasaba, R.A. 1997. 'Kemalist Certainties and Modern Ambiguities', in S. Bozdoğan and R.A. Kasaba (eds), *Rethinking Modernity and National Identity in Turkey.* Seattle: University of Washington Press: 15–36.

Kazgan, H. 1983. 'Düyun-İ Umumiye', in *Türkiye Cumhuriyeti Tarihi Ansiklopedisi.* Istanbul: Toker Yayınları: 691–716.

Kazmaz, S. 1994. *Çayeli: Geçmiş Günleri ve Halk Kültürü.* Ankara: Türk Halk Kültürünü Araştırma ve Tanıtma Vakfı.

Keesing, R.M. 1989. 'Creating the Past: Custom and Identity in the Contemporary Pacific', *The Contemporary Pacific* 1(1): 19–42.

———. 1992. *Custom and Confrontation: The Kwaio Struggle for Cultural Autonomy.* Chicago: University of Chicago Press.

Kemal, Y.A. 1992 [1978]. *Deniz Küstü.* Istanbul: Toros Yayınları.

Keyder, Ç. 1999. 'The Setting', in Ç. Keyder (ed.), *Istanbul: Between the Global and Local.* Lanham: Rowman and Littlefield: 3–28.

Knauft, B.M. 2006. 'Anthropology in the Middle, *Anthropological Theory* 6(4): 407–430.

Knudsen, S. 1995. 'Fisheries Along the Eastern Back Sea Coast of Turkey: Informal Resource Management in Small-Scale Fishing in the Shadow of a Dominant Capitalist Fishery', *Human Organization* 54(4): 437–448.

———. 1997. *A Comparative Study of Fishing Communities and Public Awareness in Turkey and Ukraine.* Istanbul: Black Sea Environmental Programme.

———. 1998. 'What Role for the Turkish Fishery Co-Operatives? Organisational Preconditions for a New Management Regime in the

Black Sea'. in M.S. Celikkale et al. (eds.), in *FISHECO'98: The Proceedings of the First International Symposium on Fisheries and Ecology*. Trabzon: Karadeniz Technical University, Faculty of Marine Sciences: 100–107.

———. 2001. 'Entangled Knowledges of the Black Sea. Confrontation and Convergence between Turkish Fishermen and Marine Scientists'. Dr. Polit. dissertation. Bergen: University of Bergen.

———. 'Fishery Management in the Black Sea: From Ignorance to Politics?', *Journal of Southeast European and Black Sea Studies* 3(1): 46–62.

———. 2004. 'From Tax to Proteins. State Fishery Policy and the Disregard of Tradition in Turkey', *Middle Eastern Studies* 40(5): 109–157.

———. 2007. 'A Comparative Overview of Academic Discourse on Indigenous Knowledge in the Middle East and Africa', in E. Boon and L. Hens (eds), *Indigenous Knowledge Systems and Sustainable Development: Relevance for Africa*. Delhi: Kamla-Raj Enterprises.

Knudsen, S., W. Pelczarski and J. Brown 2007. *Joining the EU: The Impacts on Fisheries*. Bergen, Gdynia, London: European Lifestyles and Marine Ecosystems Project Deliverable 5.3.

Knudsen, S. and H. Toje. 2008. 'Post-Soviet Transformations in Russian and Ukrainian Black Sea Fisheries: Socio-Economic Dynamics and Property Relations', *South-east Europe and Black Sea Studies* 8(1): 17–32.

Knudsen, S. and M. Zengin 2006. *Case Study 2: Trawl and Sea Snail Fisheries in Samsun, Black Sea Coast of Turkey*. Bergen and Trabzon: European Lifestyles and Marine Ecosystems Project Deliverable 5.2.

Koçu, R.A.E. 1960. *İstanbul Ansiklopedisi*. Istanbul: Koçu Yayınları.

Kömürciyan, E.Ç. 1988. *İstanbul Tarihi. XVII Asırda İstanbul*. Istanbul: Eren Yayıncılık ve Kitapçılık.

Köse, S. and H. Oğut. 2004. 'A Survey on the Seafood Consumption and Marketing in Turkey', Pacific Fisheries Technologists' 55th Annual Meeting. Seattle, 29 February – 3 March 2004.

Kramer, H. 2000. *A Changing Turkey: The Challenge to Europe and the United States*. Washington: Brooking Institution Press.

Kuban, D. 1996. *Istanbul: An Urban History: Byzantinon, Constantinople, Istanbul*. Istanbul: The Economic and Social History Foundation of Turkey.

Kuhn, T.S. 1962. *The Structure of Scientific Revolutions*. Chicago: University of Chicago Press.

Kulingas, V. 1988. *Kios 1912–1922. Anamnisis Ewos Mikrasiat*. Athen: Dodoni.

Lakoff, G. 1987. *Women, Fire, and Dangerous Things: What Categories Reveal About the Mind*. Chicago: University of Chicago Press.

Lakoff, G. and M. Johnson 1980. *Metaphors We Live By*. Chicago: University of Chicago Press.

Lambek, M. 1993. *Knowledge and Practice in Mayotte: Local Discourses of Islam, Sorcery, and Spirit Possession*. Toronto: University of Toronto Press.

———. 1997. 'Knowledge and Practice in Mayotte. An Overview', *Cultural Dynamics* 9(2): 131–148.

Lansing, J.S. 1991. *Priests and Programmers: Technologies of Power in the Engineered Landscape of Bali.* Princeton: Princeton University Press.

Latour, B. 1987. *Science in Action.* Cambridge: Harvard University Press.

———. 1993. *We Have Never Been Modern.* New York: Harvester Wheatsheaf.

———. 1999. *Pandora's Hope: Essays on the Reality of Science Studies.* Cambridge: Harvard University Press.

Leach, M. and J. Fairhead. 2002. 'Manners of Contestation: "Citizen Science" and "Indigenous Knowledge" in West Africa and the Caribbean', *International Social Science Journal* 54 (Special issue on Indigenous Knowledge)(173): 299–311.

Lévi-Strauss, C. 1969. The Raw and the Cooked. New York: Harper and Row.

Little, M.A. and G.E.B. Morren. 1977. *Ecology, Energetics and Human Variability.* Duburque: William Brown.

Lowry, H.W. 1981. *Trabzon Şehirinin İslamlaşma ve Türkleşmesi (1461–1583).* Istanbul.

Lutz, C. and L. Abu-Lughod (eds). 1990. *Language and the Politics of Emotion.* Cambridge: Cambridge University Press.

Maclennan, D.N. and E.J. Simmonds 1992. *Fisheries Acoustics.* London: Chapman & Hall.

Magnarella, P.J. 1998. 'Desecularisation, State Corporatism, and Elite Behaviour in Turkey', in P.J. Magnarella (ed.), *Anatolia's Loom: Studies in Turkish Culture, Society, Politics and Law.* Istanbul: The ISIS Press: 233–256.

Malinowski, B. 1922. *Argonauts of the Western Pacific.* London: Routledge and Kegan Paul.

Mansel, P. 1995. *Constantinople: City of World's Desire, 1453 – 1924.* Cambridge: Cambridge University Press.

MARA and MOF. 1997. 'First National Report to the Convention on Biological Diversity'. Ankara: Turkish Republic Ministry for Agriculture and Rural Affairs, and Turkish Republic Ministry of Forestry.

Marciniak, B. and S. Jentoft. 1992. 'A Capitalist Fisheries Co-Operative: A Bulgarian Innovation', *MAST* 5(1): 53–66.

Marcus, G.E. and M.M.J. Fisher. 1986. *Anthropology as Cultural Critique: An Experimental Moment in the Human Sciences.* Chicago: University of Chicago Press.

Mardin, Ş. 1997a. 'Projects as Methodology. Some Thoughts on Modern Turkish Social Science', in S. Bozdoğan and R.A. Kasaba (eds), *Rethinking Modernity and National Identity in Turkey.* Seattle: University of Washington Press: 64–80.

———. 1997b. 'Religion and Secularism in Turkey', in A. Kazancığıl and E. Özbüdün (eds), *Atatürk: Founder of a Modern State.* London: Hurst and Company: 191–219.

McCarty, J. 1997. *The Ottoman Turks: An Introductory History to 1923.* London: Longman.

McCay, B.J. 2001. 'Environmental Anthropology at Sea', in C.L. Crumley (ed.), *New Directions in Anthropology and Environment.* Oxford: AltaMira Press: 254–272.

McCay, B.J. and J.M. Acheson (eds). 1987. *The Question of the Commons: The Culture and Ecology of Communal Resources.* Tuscon: University of Arizona Press.

McGoodwin, J.R. 1990. *Crisis in the World's Fisheries: People, Problems, and Policies.* Stanford: Stanford University Press.

Meeker, M.E. 1972. 'The Great Family Aghas of Turkey: A Study of a Changing Political Culture', in R. Antoun and I. Harik (eds), *Rural Politics and Social Change in the Middle East.* Bloomington: Indiana University Press: 237–266.

———. 1994. 'The Muslim Intellectual and His Audience: A New Configuration of Writer and Reader among Believers in the Republic of Turkey', in Ş. Mardin (ed.), *Cultural Transitions in the Middle East.* Leiden: E.J. Brill: 153–188.

———. 2002. *A Nation of Empire: The Ottoman Legacy of Turkish Modernity.* Berkeley: University of California Press.

Mercan, M.P. 2004. 'Başbakan Yemek Öncesi Künefe Yer', *Aktüel Pazar*, 23 May.

Merleau-Ponty, M. 1962. *Phenomenology of Perception.* London: Routledge.

Mert, İ. 1989. 'Ülkemizde Su Ürünlerinin Beş Önemli Problemi ve Çözüm', *Tarım Orman ve Köyişler* 38 (Nisan): 30–31.

———. 1996. 'Su Ürünlerinin Korumnası Ve Kontrolünde Oto-Kontrolün Sağlanabilmesi İçin Mevcut Yasada Düzenlemelere Gidilmesi Gerekmektedir (Interview)', *Su Ürünleri Vakfı Dergisi* 1(2): 9–12.

Millas, H. 1993/4. 'İstanbul'da Rum, in N. Akbayer et al. (eds), *Dünden Bugüne İstanbul Ansiklopedisi.* İstanbul: Türkiye Ekonomik ve Toplumsal Tarih Vakfı: 363–368.

Mintz, S.W. 1985. *Sweetness and Power: The Place of Sugar in Modern History.* Harmondsworth: Penguin Books.

Mintz, S.W. and C.M. Du Bois. 2002. 'The Anthropology of Food and Eating', *Annual Review of Anthropology* 31: 99–119.

Mitchell, T. 1988. *Colonising Egypt.* Berkeley: University of California Press.

Moran, E.F. 2000. *Human Adaptability: An Introduction to Ecological Anthropology.* Boulder: Westview Press.

Mülayim, Z.G. 1997. *The Fundamental Problems of Turkish Cooperatives and Proposal for Their Solution.* İstanbul: Friedrich Ebert Stiftung.

Murphey, R. 1990. 'Communal Living in Ottoman Istanbul: Searching for the Foundations of an Urban Tradition', *Journal of Urban History* 16(2): 115–131.

Nader, L. 1996. 'Introduction: Anthropological Inquiry into Boundaries, Power, and Knowledge', in L. Nader (ed.), *Naked Science: Anthropological Inquiry into Boundaries, Power, and Knowledge.* New York: Routledge: 1–25.

Nalbatanoğlu, H.Ü. 1994. 'Modernity, State, and Religion: Theoretical Notes Towards a Comparative Study', *Sojourn* 8(2): 345–360.

Naval Intelligence Division. 1944. *Greece: Economic Geography, Ports and Communications.* Naval Intelligence Division, UK.

Navaro-Yashin, Y. 2002. *Faces of the State: Secularism and the Public Life in Turkey.* Princeton: Princeton University Press.

Neave, D.L. 1933. *Twenty -Six Years on the Bosphorus.* London: Grayson and Grayson.

Nicely, R. 2000. *Turkey Retail Foods Sector 1999.* Ankara: USDA Foreign Agricultural Service. Foreign Agricultural Service GAIN Report.

Odabaşıoğlu, C. n.d. *Trabzon 1869–1933 Yılları Yaşantısı.* Ankara: İlk-San Matbaası.

Oğuz, B. 1976. *Türkiye Halkının Kültür Kökenleri. Teknikleri, Müesseseleri, İnanç ve Âdetleri.* Istanbul: Doğu-Batı.

Öncü, A.E. 1993. 'Academics: The West in the Discourse of University Reform', in M. Heper, A.E. Öncü and H. Kramer (eds), *Turkey and the West: Changing Political and Cultural Identities.* London: I.B. Tauris: 142–176.

Ong, W.J. 1982. *Orality and Literacy: The Technologising of the Word.* London: Routledge.

Oral, N. 2002. 'Tarımı, Uyumlandırma Programı Hayvancılığı Çökertti', *Evrensel,* 5 December.

Orga, I. 1958. *The Caravan Moves On.* London: Secker and Warburg.

Orhon, H. 1969. 'Balıkçılığımız', in S.B. Çakıroğlu (ed.), *Karadeniz Balıkçılık.* Ankara: Bilgi Basımevi: 115–117.

Østerberg, D. 1994. 'Innledning', in M. Merleau-Ponty, *Kroppens Fenomenologi.* Oslo: Pax Forlag.

Ostrom, E. 1990. *Governing the Commons: The Evolution of Institutions for Collective Action.* Cambridge: Cambridge University Press.

Otyam, F. 1982. *Ha Bu Diyar: Doğudan Gezi Notları/Harran/Hoyrat/Mayın ve Irıp: Gide Gide 1/2/3.* Istanbul: Adam Yayıncılık.

Özbey, E. 1989. 'Ülkemizdeki Su Ürünleri Çalışmaların Tarihçesi', *Tarım, Orman ve Köyişler,* 2 April: 38.

Özdalga, E. 1998. *The Veiling Issue, Official Secularism and Popular Islam in Modern Turkey.* Richmond, Surrey: Curzon Press.

Özdemir, H. 1983. 'Cumhuriyet Döneminde Bilimsel ve Teknolojik Araştırma', in *Cumhuriyet Dönemi Türkiye Ansiklopedisi.* Istanbul: İletişim Yayınları: 266–276.

Özer, A. (ed.). 1990. *1940'lı Yılların Çağdaş Eğitim Kurumlarına Yöremizden bir Örnek: Beşikdüzü Köy Enstitüsü.* Trabzon: Trabzon İli ve İlçeleri Eğitim, Kültür ve Sosyal Yardımlaşma Vakfı.

Öztürk, B. (ed.) 1998. *Turkish Black Sea Bibliography.* Istanbul: Türk Deniz Araştırmaları Vakfı.

———. 2000. 'Boğaz'da Biten Balıkçılık ve Çöküşün Hikayesi', *İstanbul* (32): 81–85.

Pallis, A. 1951. *In the Days of the Janissaries: Old Turkish Life as Depicted in The 'Travel Book' of Evliyá Chelebí.* London: Hutchinson.

Pálsson, G. 1991. *Coastal Economies, Cultural Accounts: Human Ecology and Icelandic Discourse.* Manchester: Manchester University Press.

———. 1998a. 'The Birth of the Aquarium: The Political Ecology of Icelandic Fishing', in T.S. Gray (ed.), *The Politics of Fishing.* London: Macmillan: 209–227.

_____. 1998b. 'Learning by Fishing: Practical Engagement and Environmental Concerns', in F. Berkes and C. Folke (eds), *Linking Social and Ecological Systems: Management Practices and Social Mechanisms for Building Resilience.* Cambridge: Cambridge University Press: 48–66.

Pamukciyan, K. 1988. 'Notes', in E.Ç. *Kömürciyan: İstanbul Tarihi: XVII Asırda İstanbul.* Istanbul: Eren Yayıncılık ve Kitapçılık: 61–299.

Pardoe, J. 1837. *The City of the Sultan and Domestic Manners of the Turks in 1836.* London: Henry Colburn.

Pasiner, A. 1993/4. 'Dalyan', in N. Akbayer et al. (eds), *Dünden Bugüne İstanbul Ansiklopedisi.* Istanbul: Türkiye Ekonomik ve Toplumsal Tarih Vakfı: 544–545.

Pauly, D. and J. Maclean. 2002. *In a Perfect Ocean: The State of Fisheries and Ecosystems in the North Atlantic Ocean.* Washington: Island Press.

Pellat, C. et al. 1995. 'Hayawan', in *The Encyclopedia of Islam.* Leiden: E.J. Brill.

Pfaffenberger, B. 1988. 'Fetishised Objects and Humanised Nature: Towards an Anthropology of Technology', *Man* 23(2): 236–252.

_____. 1992. Social Anthropology of Technology', *Annual Review of Anthropology* 21: 491–516.

Philip, K.S. 2002. 'Indigenous Knowledge: Science and Technology Studies', *International Encyclopedia of the Social and Behavioural Sciences.* Oxford: Pergamon.

Putnam, H. 1981. *Reason, Truth and History.* Cambridge: Cambridge University Press.

Quataert, D. 1994. 'Part IV the Age of Reforms, 1812–1914', in H. İnalcık and D. Quataert (eds), *An Economic and Social History of the Ottoman Empire, 1300–1914.* Cambridge: Cambridge University Press: 759–943.

_____. 2000. *The Ottoman Empire, 1700–1922.* Cambridge: Cambridge University Press.

Rappaport, R.A. 1968. *Pigs for the Ancestors: Ritual in the Ecology of a New Guinea People.* New Haven: Yale University Press.

Reyhanlı, T. 1983. *İngiliz Gezginlerine Göre XVI Yüzyılda İstanbul'da Hayat (1582–1599).* Ankara: Kültür ve Türizm Bakanlığı.

Ritter Von Kral, A. 1938. *Kamâl Atatürk's Land: The Evolution of Modern Turkey.* London: P.S. King and Son.

Rosen, L. 1984. *Bargaining for Reality: The Construction of Social Relations in a Muslim Community.* Chicago: University of Chicago Press.

Rouse, C. and J. Hoskins. 2004. 'Purity, Soul Food, and Sunni Islam: Explorations at the Intersection of Consumption and Resistance', *Cultural Anthropology* 19(2): 226–249.

Ruddle, K. 1985. 'The Continuity of Traditional Management Practices: The Case of Japanese Coastal Fisheries', in K. Ruddle and R.E. Johannes (eds), *The Traditional Knowledge and Management of Coastal Systems in Asia and the Pacific.* Jakarta: UNESCO-ROSTSEA:157–179.

_____. 1987. *Administration and Conflict Management in Japanese Coastal Fisheries.* Rome: FAO Fisheries Technical Paper 273.

Sahlins, M. 1976. *Culture and Practical Reason*. Chicago: Chicago University Press.

Said, E. 1978. *Orientalism*. New York: Vintage.

Saktanber, A.E. 2002. *Living Islam: Women, Religion and the Politicization of Culture in Turkey*. London: I.B. Tauris.

Salomone, S.D. 1987. *In the Shadow of the Holy Mountain: The Genesis of a Rural Greek Community and Its Refugee Heritage*. New York: Columbia University Press.

Salzman, A. 2000. 'The Age of Tulips: Confluence and Conflict in Early Modern Consumer Culture (1550–1730)', in D. Quataert (ed.), *Consumption Studies and the History of the Ottoman Empire, 1550–1922: An Introduction*. New York: State University of New York Press: 45–82.

Sarı, M., H. Demirulus and B. Söğüt. 2000. 'Van İli'nde Öğrencilerin Balık Eti Tüketimi Alışkanlığının Belirlenmesi Üzerine Bir Araştırma', in *Doğu Anadolu Bölgesi IV. Su Ürünleri Sempozyumu*. Erzurum: Atatürk Üniversitesi, Ziraat Fakültesi Su Ürünleri Bölümü: 627–637.

Sarıkaya, S. 1980. *Su Ürünleri Avcılığı ve Av Teknolojisi*. Ankara: Turkish Republic Ministry for Food, Agriculture and Stockbreeding, General Directorate for Water Produce.

Scott, J.C. 1986. 'Everyday Forms of Peasant Resistance', *The Journal of Peasant Studies* 13(2): 5–35.

———. 1998. *Seeing Like a State: How Certain Schemes to Improve the Human Condition Have Failed*. New Haven: Yale University Press.

Şen, Ö. 1998. *Trabzon Tarihi*. Trabzon: Derya.

Şener, İ.H. 1987. *Su Ürünleri Pazarlaması*. Trabzon: Karadeniz Technical University, Deniz Bilimleri ve Teknolojisi Yüksekokulu.

Şenol, L.F. 1998. 'İktidar Mücadelesinin Savaş Meydanı: Mekan. Cumhuriyet'in İlk Yıllarında Ankara'da Eğlence Mekanları', *Toplum ve Bilim* (76): 86–103.

Serjeant, R.B. 1966. 'Maritime Customary Law Off the Arabian Coasts', in M. Mollat (ed.), *Sociétés et compagnies de commerce en Orient et dans l'Océan Indien. VIIIiéme Colloque International Maritime*. Beyrouth: S.E.V.P.E.N.

———. 1968. 'Fisher-Folk and Fish-Traps in Al-Bahrain', *Bulletin of the School of Oriental and African Studies* 31(3): 486–514.

Serjeant, R.B. and T. Adams. 1980. 'Customary Law among the Fishermen of Al-Shihr', in B.C. Bloomfield (ed.), *Middle East Studies and Libraries: A Felicitation Volume for Professor J.D. Pearson*. London: Mansell: 193–204.

Shore, B. 1996. *Culture in Mind: Cognition, Culture and the Problem of Meaning*. Oxford: Oxford University Press.

Sillitoe, P. 1998. 'The Development of Indigenous Knowledge: A New Applied Anthropology', *Current Anthropology* 39(2): 223–252.

Sirtioğlu, İ. 2004. 'Branded Products Best Bets in Turkey's Retail Market', *AgExporter* (July): 14–16.

SIS. 2001. 'Agricultural Credits by Type'. Ankara: State Institute of Statistics Prime Ministry, Republic of Turkey.

———. 1997. 'Distribution of Household and Household's Disposable Income by Quintiles, 1994', *Statistical Yearbook of Turkey 1997*. Ankara: State Institute of Statistics Prime Ministry, Republic of Turkey.

———. 2002. *Fishery Statistics 2001*. Ankara: State Institute of Statistics Prime Ministry, Republic of Turkey.

———. 2005a. 'Motorlu Kara Taşıtları, Table 3. Yıllara Göre Motorlu Kara Taşıtı Sayısı, 1992–2005'. Ankara: State Institute of Statistics Prime Ministry, Republic of Turkey.

———. 2005b. 'Motorlu Kara Taşıtları, Table 2. İllere Göre Motorlu Kara Taşıtı Sayısı, 2005'. Ankara: State Institute of Statistics Prime Ministry, Republic of Turkey.

Somçağ, S. 1993/4. 'Balıkçılık, in N. Aksayer et al. (eds), *Dünden Bugüne İstanbul Ansiklopedisi*. Istanbul: Türkiye Ekonomik ve Toplumsal Tarih Vakfı: 17–21.

Stirling, P. 1993. 'Introduction: Growth and Changes. Speed, Scale, Complexity', in P. Stirling (ed.), *Culture and Economy: Changes in Turkish Villages*. Huntingdon: The Eothen Press: 1–16.

Stone, F.A. 1973. *The Rub of Cultures in Modern Turkey: Literary Views of Education*. Bloomington: Indiana University Press.

Sülker, K. 1985. *Osmanlı'dan Günümüze İçki ve Toplum*. Istanbul: Süreç.

Symes, D. 2007. 'Fisheries Management and Institutional Reform: A European Perspective', *ICES Journal of Marine Science* 64(4): 779–785.

Szyliowicz, J.S. 1994. 'Education and Political Development', in M. Heper and A. Evin (eds), *Politics in the Third Turkish Republic*. Boulder: Westview Press: 147–159.

Tambiah, S.J. 1990. *Magic, Science, Religion, and the Scope of Rationality*. Cambridge: Cambridge University Press.

Taner, L. 1991. 'The Fishermans Problem in the Marmara Sea'. Ph.D. dissertation. Istanbul: Bosporus University.

*Tan Gazetesi* 1936. 'Ankarada yakında balıkçılık için bir kongre toplanıyor: Yeni kanun projesine göre balıkçılık bankası kurulacak'. 17 November: 2.

Tansaş. 2003. Tansaş – Presentation on Food Retail Sector, www.Tansas.Com.Tr/Docs/Sunum_Sonuclar/Sunumlar/Foodretailmarketandposition oftansas.Pdf. Access date: 24 September 2004.

Tapper, R. and N. Tapper. 1991. 'Religion, Education and Continuity in a Provincial Town', in R. Tapper (ed.), *Islam in Modern Turkey: Religion, Politics and Literature in a Secular State*. London: I.B. Tauris: 56–83.

Tapper, R. and S. Zubaida. 1994. 'Introduction', in S. Zubaida and R. Tapper (eds), *Culinary Cultures of the Middle East*. London: I.B. Tauris: 1–17.

Terzis, A. 1997. *Aliste Mnimes. Hilites*. Alexandrupoli.

Tezcan, M. 1982. 'Türklerde Yemek Yeme Alışkanlıkları ve buna İlişkin Davranış Kalıpları', in *Türk Mutfağı Sempozyumu Bildirileri*. Ankara: Ankara Üniversitesi Basımevi: 113–132.

TFRI. 1992. *Karadeniz'de Av Araç ve Gereçleri ile Avlanma Teknolojisinin Belirlemesi Projesi*. Trabzon: Trabzon Fisheries Research Institute.

TKK. 1997. *Türkiye'de Kooperatifçilik*. Ankara: Türk Kooperatifçilik Kurumu.

Tören, T. 2007. *Yeniden Yapılan Dünya Ekonomisine Marshall Planı ve Türkiye Uygulamasi.* Istanbul: Sosyal Araştırmalar Vakfı.

*Trabzon Vilayeti Kalkınma Kongresi 1952.* Ankara: Trabzon İlini Kalkındırma Cemiyeti Neşriyati.

*Trabzon Vilayeti Salnamesi 1871.* 1993. Ankara: Trabzon İli ve İlçeleri Eğitim, Kültür ve Sosyal Yardımlaşma Vakfı Yayınları, Volume 3.

*Trabzon Vilayeti Salnamesi 1876.* 1995. Ankara: Trabzon İli ve İlçeleri Eğitim, Kültür ve Sosyal Yardımlaşma Vakfı Yayınları, Volume 8.

Tsing, A.L. 2001. 'Nature in the Making', in C.L. Crumley (ed.), *New Directions in Anthropology and Environment.* Oxford: AltaMira Press: 3–23.

Turabi 1987 [1864]. *Turkish Cookery Book: A Collection of Receipts.* Rottingdean, Sussex: Cooks Books.

Turgay, A.Ü. 1982. 'Trade and Merchants in Nineteenth-Century Trabzon: Elements of Ethnic Conflict', in B. Braude and B. Lewis (eds), *Christians and Jews in the Ottoman Empire.* New York: Holmes and Meier: 287–318.

Tutel, E. 1998. 'Altmış Yıl Önce Çarşı-Pazarda Fiyatlar', *Tarih ve Toplum* (176): 46–48.

Tutunji, J. 1996. 'Fish and Fishing', in *Encyclopedia of the Modern Middle East.* London: Simon and Schuster and Prentice Hall: 667.

Ünal, M.A. 1988. 'Tahbir Defterlerine Göre Sinop Şehri', in M. Sağlamand et al. (eds) *İkinci Tarih Boyunca Karadeniz Kongresi Bildirileri.* Samsun: T.C. Ondokuz Mayıs Üniversitesi Eğitim Fakültesi ve Fransiz Anadolu Araştırmaları Enstitüsü: 185–192.

Ünsal, A. 1998. 'Ah Şu Balıkçı Barınağı!', *Radikal,* 19 May.

Varela, F.J. 1999. *Ethical Know-How.* Stanford: Stanford University Press.

Viré, F. 1995. 'Samak', in *The Encyclopaedia of Islam.* New Edition, Volume 8. Leiden: E.J.Brill: 1020–1023.

Von Brandt, A. 1984. *Fish Catching Methods of the World.* Farnham, Surrey: Fishing News Books.

Warren, C. 1993. *Adat and Dinas: Balinese Communities in the Indonesian State.* Kuala Lumpur: Oxford University Press.

Warren, M.D., L.J. Slikkerveer and D. Brokensha (eds). 1995. *The Cultural Dimension of Development: Indigenous Knowledge Systems.* London: Intermediate Technology.

Weber, M. 1930. *The Protestant Ethic and the Spirit of Capitalism.* London: George Allen and Unwin.

White, C. 1845. *Three Years in Constantinople; or Domestic Manners of the Turks in 1844.* London: Henry Colburn.

White, J.B. 1994. *Money Makes Us Relatives. Woman's Labor in Urban Turkey.* Austin: University of Texas Press.

———. 1996. 'Civic Culture and Islam in Urban Turkey', in C.M. Hann and E. Dunn (eds), *Civil Society: Challenging Western Models.* London: Routledge: 143–154.

———. 1999. 'Islamic Chic', in Ç. Keyder (ed.), *Istanbul: Between the Global and the Local.* Lanham: Rowman and Littlefield: 77–91.

————. 2002. *Islamist Mobilization in Turkey: A Study in Vernacular Politics*. Seattle: University of Washington Press.

White, L.A. 1943. 'Energy and the Evolution of Culture', *American Anthropologist* 45(3): 335–356.

Wilk, R. 2006. '"But the Young Men Don't Want to Farm Any More": Political Ecology and Consumer Culture in Belize', in A. Biersack and J.B. Greenberg (eds), *Reimagining Political Ecology*. Durham: Duke University Press: 149–170.

World Bank 2000. *Turkey: Country Economic Memorandum: Structural Reforms for Sustainable Growth*. Washington: World Bank, Poverty Reduction and Economic Management Unit, Europe and Central Asia Region. Report No. 33549–TR.

Worsley, P. 1997. *Knowledges: What Different Peoples Make of the World*. London: Profile Books.

Yıldırım, Ö. 1990. 'III Bölüm: Ekonomi', in M. Bilgin and Ö. Yıldırım (eds), *Sürmene*. Sürmene: Sürmene Belediyesi: 493–520.

Yordanidu, M. 1990 [1963]. *Loksandra. İstanbul Düşü*. Istanbul: Belge/Uluslararası Yayıncılık.

Yüksel, M. 1989. *Türk Edebiyatında Hamsi*. Trabzon: Trabzon Kültür ve Turizm Müdürlüğü.

*Yurt Ansiklopedisi* 1981. 'Su Ürünleri'. Istanbul: Anadolu Yayıncılık: 3917–3919.

Zat, V. 1993/4. 'Meyhaneler', in N. Akbayer et al. (eds), *Dünden Bugüne İstanbul Ansiklopedisi*. Istanbul: Türkiye Ekonomik ve Toplumsal Tarih Vakfı: 434–438.

Zengin, M. 2000. 'Hamsiye Dayali Olarak Üretim Faaliyetinde Bulunan Balık Unu-Yağı Fabrıkalarının Bugünkü Durumu ve bu Fabrıkaların için Alternatif Hammadde Oluşturabilecek Balıkçılık Kaynakları', in *2000 Su Ürünleri Sempozyumu*. Sinop: Ondokuz Mayıs Üniversitesi Sinop Su Ürünleri Fakültesi: 327–341.

Zengin, M., Y. Genç and İ. Tabak. 1998. *Karadeniz'de 1990–1995 Yılları Arasında Avlanan Önemli Ticari Balık Türlerinin Av Verileri Üzerine Araştırmalar*. Trabzon: Trabzon Fisheries Research Institute.

Zubaida, S. 1994. 'National, Communal and Global Dimensions in Middle Eastern Food Cultures', in S. Zubaida and R. Tapper (eds), *Culinary Cultures of the Middle East*. London: I.B. Tauris: 33–45.

Zürcher, E.J. 1993. *Turkey: A Modern History*. London: I.B Tauris.

# Glossary of Turkish Words Frequently Used

| | |
|---|---|
| aç | – hungry, hunger, 'poverty'. |
| açık | – open, 'uncovered'. |
| ada | – island, here used for shallow waters, fishing banks. |
| adet | – custom, usage, practice. |
| aile | – family. |
| aga | – (local) lord. |
| alametre | – boat design, here usually 7–12 m. decked boat with small cabin. |
| algarna | – dredge. |
| alim | – learned, wise, scholar. |
| ayıp | – shame, disgrace, fault, shameful. |
| bilgi | – knowledge, learning, information. |
| bilinçli | – conscious, aware, have foresight. |
| bilinçsiz | – unconscious, unaware. |
| bot | – little boat, here used to pull out the purse seine. |
| cahil | – ignorant. |
| cehalet | – ignorance. |
| çevre | – environment, circle, one's friends and associates. |
| Cumhuriyet | – Republic. |
| dalyan | – fishing weir, fishing trap. |
| dayı | – maternal uncle, 'influential friend'. |

| | |
|---|---|
| dershane | – private teaching institution. |
| doçent | – associate professor. |
| doktora | – PhD, doctoral degree. |
| eğitim | – education. |
| Evkaf | – the government department in control of estates in mortmain. |
| gazino | – outdoor café, nightclub. |
| gırgır | – purse seine. |
| günah | – sin. |
| halk | – people, the common people. |
| hamsi | – anchovy. |
| haram | – forbidden by religion, wrong. |
| kaba | – coarse, vulgar, rude. |
| kabzımal | – fish trader. |
| Kadro | – nationalist-communist movement in the early 1930s. |
| kahve | – coffeehouse. |
| kapalı | – closed, 'being covered'. |
| koltuk | – armpit, curved ends of fishing nets. |
| komisyoncu | – 'one who takes a commission', fish trader. |
| kosmopolit | – cosmopolite. |
| köy | – village. |
| kültürlü | – cultured, cultivated, sophisticated. |
| kuyu | – well, used for deep waters surrounded by shallower waters. |
| lise | – high school. |
| lokanta | – restaurant. |
| lüfer | – bluefish. |
| mahalle | – quarter. |
| mayo | – bathing suit. |
| memur | – civil servant, bureaucrat. |

| | |
|---|---|
| meyhane | – traditional style drinking establishment, bar, pub. |
| meze | – spread of appetizers. |
| molozma | – 'take all' bottom trammel-net. |
| muhabbet | – 'sweet' conversation. |
| namaz | – ritual of worship centred in prayer (Islam). |
| namus | – honour, (a woman's) virtue, chastity. |
| politika | – politics. |
| poyraz | – northeast wind. |
| rahat | – relaxed, easy–going, comfortable. |
| rakı | – raki, anise-flavoured strong alcoholic drink. |
| reis | – skipper. |
| reislik | – skipperhood. |
| Rum | – Greeks, eastern Greeks. |
| sahil | – seaside. |
| şeref | – honour. |
| sosyal | – social. |
| Tanzimat | – political reforms in the Ottoman State 1839–1876. |
| tecrübe | – experience, practical experience. |
| tekir | – a red mullet species. |
| torpil | – 'torpedo', influential person, middleman broker. |
| voli | – casting of a large fishing net. |
| yayla | – summer mountain pasture. |
| yazıhane | – office. |
| yiyici | – one who takes bribes, corrupt. |
| yiyicilik | – corruption, taking of bribes. |

# Index

www.ingramcontent.com/pod-product-compliance
Lightning Source LLC
Chambersburg PA
CBHW072054020426
42334CB00017B/1510